LC0002309.
HRH016601
24/7/91.

D0001279

HIGH ROYDS HOSPITAL
MEDICAL

NONPARAMETRIC STATISTICS FOR THE BEHAVIORAL SCIENCES

NONPARAMETRIC STATISTICS FOR THE BEHAVIORAL SCIENCES

Second Edition

Sidney Siegel

Late Professor of the Pennsylvania State University

N. John Castellan, Jr.

Indiana University

McGRAW-HILL BOOK COMPANY

New York St. Louis San Francisco Auckland Bogotá Caracas Colorado Springs Hamburg Lisbon London Madrid Mexico Milan Montreal New Delhi Oklahoma City Panama Paris San Juan São Paulo Singapore Sydney Tokyo Toronto

NONPARAMETRIC SYSTEMS FOR THE BEHAVIORAL SCIENCES
INTERNATIONAL EDITION

Copyright © 1988
Exclusive rights by McGraw-Hill Book Co. — Singapore for manufacture and export. This book cannot be re-exported from the country to which it is consigned by McGraw-Hill.

4 5 6 7 8 9 0 FSP 9 4 3 2 1 0

Copyright © 1988, 1956 by McGraw-Hill, Inc. All rights reserved. Except as permitted under the United States Copyright Act of 1976, no part of this publication may be reproduced or distributed in any form or by any means, or stored in a data base or retrieval system, without the prior written permission of the publisher.

This book was set in Times Roman by Syntax International.
The editor was James D. Anker.
The production supervisor was Denise L. Puryear.

Library of Congress Cataloging-in-Publication Data

Siegel, Sidney
Nonparametric statistics for the behavioral sciences.

Bibliography: p.
Includes index.
1. Psychometrics. 2. Nonparametric statistics.
3. Social sciences—Statistical methods. I. Castellan, N. John II. Title.
BF39.S464 1988 519.5 87-16923
ISBN 0-07-057357-3

When ordering this title use ISBN 0-07-100326-6

Printed in Singapore

ABOUT THE AUTHORS

Sidney Siegel was Research Professor of Psychology at the Pennsylvania State University at the time of his death in 1961 at age forty-five. A native of New York City, he was educated in California and received his Ph.D. in psychology from Stanford University in 1953. From then until his death he served on the Penn State faculty, except for a year as a Fellow at the Center for Advanced Study in the Behavioral Sciences, at Stanford.

He was the author or coauthor of four books published by McGraw-Hill. *Bargaining and Group Decision Making* (1960), with Lawrence E. Fouraker, was the recipient of the Monograph Prize of the American Academy of Arts and Sciences in 1959. Its sequel was *Bargaining Behavior* (1963), also with Fouraker. *Choice, Strategy, and Utility* was published by McGraw-Hill in 1964 after it was completed posthumously by Alberta E. Siegel and Julia McMichael Andrews. As well, McGraw-Hill published his collected writings in 1964, under the title *Decision and Choice*, edited by Samuel Messick and Arthur H. Brayfield. Included is a memoir by Ms. Siegel. The earliest of his books was *Nonparametric Statistics for the Behavioral Sciences* (1956), which has appeared in Japanese, Italian, German, and Spanish, as well as English.

N. John Castellan, Jr. is professor of psychology at Indiana University at Bloomington. He received his A.B. from Stanford University and his Ph.D. from the University of Colorado. He has served as visiting research associate at the Oregon Research Institute and visiting professor of computer science at the University of Colorado.

Professor Castellan has served as a consultant on statistics and computing to business and industry, and served as associate dean for research and graduate development at Indiana University. He has served on the editorial boards of several professional journals, is past president of the Society for Computers in Psychology, and is editor of the *Judgment/Decision Making Newsletter*. He is a Fellow of the American Psychological Association and the American Association for the Advancement of Science.

He is coauthor of *Introduction to the Statistical Method*, (2d Ed.), and was coeditor of the three-volume monograph series *Cognitive Theory*. He has published over 50 papers on statistics, decision making, and the applications of computers to research and instruction.

To JAY
Sidney Siegel
(first edition)

To CARYN, NORMAN, & TANYA
John Castellan
(second edition)

CONTENTS

ACKNOWLEDGMENTS

I am indebted to the following publishers and authors who kindly granted permission to reproduce one or more of the Appendix tables.

I am grateful to the Literary Executor of the late Sir Ronald A. Fisher, F.R.S. to Frank Yates, F.R.S. and the Longman Group Ltd, London for permission to reprint tables III and IV from their book *Statistical Tables for Biological, Agricultural and Medical Research* (6th Edition 1974).

The Biometrika trustees, publisher of *Biometrika* and *Biometrika Tables for Statisticians, Volume I*, (3d Edition 1966).

Charles Griffin & Co. Ltd for materials from Kendall's *Rank Correlation Methods* (4th Edition 1970).

The American Statistical Association, publisher of the *Journal of the American Statistical Association* and *Technometrics*; the Biometric Society, publisher of *Biometrics*; the Institute of Mathematical Statistics, publisher of the *Annals of Mathematical Statistics*; Gordon and Breach Science Publishers, Inc., publisher of the *Journal of Statistical Computation and Simulation*; Alfred A. Knopf; John Wiley; Macmillan; and McGraw-Hill.

W. J. Dixon, C. W. Dunnett, M. A. Fligner, M. H. Gail, S. S. Gupta, K. R. Hammond, M. Hollander, J. E. Householder, F. J. Massey, Jr., C. Eisenhart, S. Maghsoodloo, M. R. Mickey, Jr., R. E. Odeh, E. B. Page, D. W. Stilson, and J. H. Zar gave me permission to reproduce statistical tables from their published work.

PREFACE TO THE SECOND EDITION

In revising *Nonparametric Statistics for the Behavioral Sciences*, I have included techniques which I believe are of special value to behavioral scientists. Because of developments in nonparametric and distribution-free statistics since the first edition, some procedures have been replaced by newer techniques and the coverage of topics has been greatly expanded. In particular, the coverage of k-sample techniques (Chapters 7 and 8) has been expanded and there is a presentation of comparison procedures. Chapter 9 on measures of association has been expanded significantly.

A distinctive feature of the first edition was the step-by-step outline of application of each procedure to actual data. In preparing this revision, I have tried to preserve this aspect of the text. Although some of the examples used in the first edition have been replaced, others remain. The goal has been to provide a clear illustration of the rationale, use, calculation, and interpretation of each statistic.

Because of the large variety of nonparametric procedures and the limited space available, it has been difficult to choose among methods. My choice has been based in part upon the judged usefulness of each procedure and upon an effort to minimize inclusion of tests which are similar.

Some choices bear some specific mention: I have opted to include the Pearson chi-square tests for contingency tables rather than log-linear models. The reason is twofold: I have found that students are often able to grasp the concepts of the Pearson tests more quickly, and there is some evidence that suggests that the Pearson tests have better small sample properties.

I have also omitted multivariate tests and, except for a couple of instances, tests on sequences of behaviors. Although these are important topics for the behavioral scientist, each requires extensive discussion to provide adequate coverage.

Readers with minimal background in statistics can use the book; however, those readers will find Chapters 2 and 3 rather terse but complete. Readers who have had one or more courses in statistics can skim Chapters 2 and 3.

One aspect of the book is bound to be controversial. In the first edition, scales of measurement were stressed throughout the book. In the revision, I have included an extensive discussion of measurement scales in Chapter 3, but have "softened" most of the language concerning the importance of scales in the discussion of particular techniques. The role of measurement scales in *research* is a complicated one, and this role is often considered to be independent of *statistics*. My experience in teaching and consulting has led me to believe that measurement is all too often given short shrift with unfortunate results. Measurement does affect the *interpretation* of the data one obtains in research, and I have found that emphasis on scales helps researchers to make appropriate interpretations of their data. Although advocates of the various views concerning the role of scales of measurement in statistics may be dissatisfied with the emphasis which I have chosen, I believe that a balance has been struck which will help researchers to do better research.

An added feature of this edition is the inclusion of computer program listings for some of the procedures. Computations for many of the techniques presented in the text can be accomplished easily by hand or with an inexpensive electronic calculator. However, other techniques are computationally more difficult or tedious. For these, program listings are included in Appendix II. These listings are in BASIC because that language is accessible to virtually every user of microcomputers (and larger systems). An effort has been made to make the listings easy to interpret so that one can understand the logic of the program, and each is self-contained and does not involve any other programs. As a result, the programs are not as efficient or elegant as they might otherwise be. Again, the goal was clarity and ease of use. It should be noted that, at the present time there is no single package of computer programs which can do all of the analyses described in the book.[1]

In preparing this edition, I want to acknowledge the encouragement and support I received from Alberta Siegel in initiating and continuing the project. In addition, I would like to express my gratitude to the many students who labored over the early drafts of the revision and offered much critical assistance. I am particularly indebted to my colleagues who read and commented on one or more drafts of the manuscript: Helena Chmura Kraemer, Richard Lehman, Thomas Nygren, James L. Phillips, J. B. Spalding, and B. James Starr. Finally, the greatest support came from my wife and children, who, if they did not always understand what I was doing, did give me the encouragement and incentive to complete the task.

N. John Castellan, Jr.

---

[1] A complete set of all of the statistical procedures discussed in this book is available as an integrated nonparametric statistical package for microcomputers. For further information concerning the package, contact N. John Castellan, Jr., Department of Psychology, Indiana University, Bloomington, In. 47405.

PREFACE TO THE FIRST EDITION

I believe that the nonparametric techniques of hypothesis testing are uniquely suited to the data of the behavioral sciences. The two alternative names which are frequently given to these tests suggest two reasons for their suitability. The tests are often called "distribution-free," one of their primary merits being that they do not assume that the scores under analysis were drawn from a population distributed in a certain way, e.g., from a normally distributed population. Alternatively, many of these tests are identified as "ranking tests," and this title suggests their other principal merit: nonparametric techniques may be used with scores which are not exact in any numerical sense, but which in effect are simply ranks. A third advantage of these techniques, of course, is their computational simplicity. Many believe that researchers and students in the behavioral sciences need to spend more time and reflection in the careful formulation of their research problems and in collecting precise and relevant data. Perhaps they will turn more attention to these pursuits if they are relieved of the necessity of computing statistics which are complicated and time-consuming. A final advantage of the nonparametric tests is their usefulness with small samples, a feature which should be helpful to the researcher collecting pilot study data and to the researcher whose samples must be small because of their very nature (e.g., samples of persons with a rare form of mental illness, or samples of cultures).

To date, no source is available which presents the nonparametric techniques in usable form and in terms which are familiar to the behavioral scientist. The techniques are presented in various mathematics and statistics publications. Most behavioral scientists do not have the mathematical sophistication required for consulting these sources. In addition, certain writers have presented summaries of these techniques in articles addressed to social scientists. Notables among these are Blum and Fattu (1954), Moses (1952a), Mosteller and Bush (1954), and Smith (1953). Moreover, some of the newer texts on statistics for social scientists have contained chapters on nonparametric methods. These include the texts by Edwards (1954), McNemar (1955), and Walker and Lev (1953). Valuable as these sources are, they have typically either been highly selective in the techniques presented or have not included the tables of significance values which are used in the application of the various tests. Therefore I have felt that a text on the nonparametric methods would be a desirable addition to the literature formed by the sources mentioned.

In this book I have presented the tests according to the research design for which each is suited. In discussing each test, I have attempted to indicate its "function," i.e., to indicate the sort of data to which it is applicable, to convey some notion of the rationale or proof underlying the test, to explain its computation, to give examples of its application in behavioral scientific research, and to compare the test to its parametric equivalent, if any, and to any nonparametric tests of similar function.

The reader may be surprised at the amount of space given to examples of the use of these tests, and even astonished at the repetitiousness which these examples introduce. I may justify this allocation of space by pointing out that (*a*) the examples help to teach the computation of the test, (*b*) the examples illustrate the application of the test to research problems in the behavioral sciences, and (*c*) the use of the same six steps in every hypothesis test demonstrates that identical logic underlies each of the many statistical techniques, a fact which is not well understood by many researchers.

Since I have tried to present all the raw data for each of the examples, I was not able to draw these from a catholic group of sources. Research publications typically do not present raw data, and therefore I was compelled to draw upon a rather parochial group of sources for most examples—those sources from which raw data were readily available. The reader will understand that this is an apology for the frequency with which I have presented in the examples my own research and that of my immediate colleagues. Sometimes I have not found appropriate data to illustrate the use of a test and therefore have "concocted" data for the purpose.

In writing this book, I have become acutely aware of the important influence which various teachers and colleagues have exercised upon my thinking. Professor Quinn McNemar gave me fundamental training in statistical inference and first introduced me to the importance of the assumptions underlying various statistical tests. Professor Lincoln Moses has enriched my understanding of statistics, and it was he who first interested me in the literature of nonparametric statistics. My study with Professor George Polya yielded exciting insights in probability theory. Professors Kenneth J. Arrow, Albert H. Bowker, Douglas H. Lawrence, and the late J. C. C. McKinsey have each contributed significantly to my understanding of statistics and experimental design. My comprehension of measurement theory was deepened by my research collaboration with Professors Donald Davidson and Patrick Suppes.

This book has benefited enormously from the stimulating and detailed suggestions and criticisms which Professors James B. Bartoo, Quinn McNemar, and Lincoln Moses gave me after each had read the manuscript. I am greatly indebted to each of them for their valuable gifts of time and knowledge. I am also grateful to Professors John F. Hall and Robert E. Stover, who encouraged my undertaking to write this book and who contributed helpful critical comments on some of the chapters. Of course, none of these persons is in any way responsible for the faults which remain; these are entirely my responsibility, and I should be grateful if any readers who detect errors and obscurities would call my attention to them.

Much of the usefulness of this book is due to the generosity of the many authors and publishers who have kindly permitted me to adapt or reproduce tables and other material originally presented by them. I have mentioned each source where the materials appear, and I also wish to mention here my gratitude to Donovan Auble, Irvin L. Child, Frieda Swed Cohn, Churchill Eisenhart, D. J. Finney, Milton Friedman, Leo A. Goodman, M. G. Kendall, William Kruskal, Joseph Lev, Henry B. Mann, Frank J. Massey, Jr., Edwin G. Olds, George W. Snedecor, Helen M. Walker, W. Allen Wallis, John E. Walsh, John W. M. Whiting, D. R. Whitney, and Frank Wilcoxon, and to the Institute of Mathematical Statistics, the American Statistical Association, *Biometrika*, the American Psychological Association, Iowa State College Press, Yale University Press, the Institute of Educational Research at Indiana University, the American Cyanamid Company, Charles Griffin & Co., Ltd., John Wiley & Sons, Inc., and Henry Holt and Company, Inc. I am indebted to Professor Sir Ronald A. Fisher, Cambridge, to Dr. Frank Yates, Rothamsted, and to Messrs. Oliver and Boyd, Ltd., Edinburgh, for permission to reprint Tables No. III and IV from their book *Statistical Tables for Biological, Agricultural, and Medical Research.*

My greatest personal indebtedness is to my wife, Dr. Alberta Engvall Siegel, without whose help this book could not have been written. She has worked closely with me in every phase of its planning and writing. I know it has benefited not only from her knowledge of the behavioral sciences but also from her careful editing, which has greatly enhanced any expository merits the book may have.

Sidney Siegel

GLOSSARY OF SYMBOLS

Note: Entries in parentheses refer to sections of the book in which the symbols are defined or initially used.

a_{ij}	Preference count used in the calculation of the Kendall coefficient of agreement (9.7).
$A(x_i)$	Denotes the attribute of an object x_i (3.3).
α	Alpha. The probability of a Type I error—the probability of rejecting H_0 when H_0 is in fact true.
β	Beta. The probability of a Type II error—the probability of rejecting H_1 when H_1 is in fact true.
C	The Cramér coefficient (9.1).
C_j	Denotes the sum of the frequencies in the jth column in a contingency table (8.1.3), (9.1).
γ	Gamma. The population gamma index of association between ordered variables (9.9).
d_{BA}	Somers' d, an index of asymmetric association for ordered variables (9.11).
d_i	Difference between matched scores: $X_i - Y_i$. Used in the Wilcoxon signed ranks test (5.3), the permutation test for paired replicates (5.4), and the Spearman rank-order correlation (9.3).
d_{ij}	Adjusted or standardized residual used in testing individual cell deviations in the chi-square test (8.1.3).
$D_{m,n}$	Statistic associated with Kolmogorov-Smirnov tests (4.6), (6.6).
$D(X_j)$	Dispersion index used in the Moses rank-like test for scale differences (6.9).
df	Degrees of freedom associated with various statistical tests, usually chi-square tests and t tests.

Δ_{BA}	Delta. The population parameter corresponding to Somers' d, an index of asymmetrical association for ordered variables (9.11).
E_i	Expected value used in chi-square tests (4.2), (5.1).
E_{ij}	Expected value used in chi-square tests (6.2), (8.1), (8.2).
$F_0(X)$	Cumulative frequency distribution specified by the null hypothesis in the Kolmogorov-Smirnov test (4.3).
F_r	The Friedman two-way analysis of variance by ranks statistic (7.2).
G	The gamma statistic for measuring the association among ordered variables (9.9).
H_0	Denotes the null hypothesis.
H_1	Denotes the alternative hypothesis.
θ_x	Theta. The population median of the variable X.
J	The Jonckheere test for ordered alternatives statistic (8.4).
J^*	The large-sample approximation test for the Jonckheere statistic (8.4.2).
K	The kappa statistic, an index of agreement for nominally scaled data (9.8).
$K_{m,n}$	Statistic associated with the large-sample form of the change-point test (4.6).
KW	The Kruskal-Wallis one-way analysis of variance by ranks statistic (8.3).
κ	Kappa. The population kappa index of agreement for nominally scaled data (9.8).
L	The Page test statistic for ordered alternatives (7.3).
$L(x_i)$	Denotes the labeling function for an object x_i (3.3).
L_B, L_A	The lambda statistic for measuring asymmetrical association between nominally scaled variables (9.10).
λ_B, λ_A	Lambda. The population lambda index of asymmetrical association between nominally scaled variables (9.10).
$\mathbf{M}_{ij}^+$, $\mathbf{N}_{ij}^+$	Frequency counts for contingency tables. Used in the computation of the Gamma statistic (9.9).
m	Larger sample size in two-sample tests.
m', n'	Adjusted sample sizes in the Moses rank-like test for scale differences (6.9).
$\max(X)$	The maximum value of the variable X.
$\text{med}(X)$	The median of the variable X.
$\text{med}(X_i, X_j, X_k)$	The median of the variables X_i, X_j, and X_k.
$\min(X)$	The minimum value of the variable X.
μ	Mu. The population mean.
μ_x	The population mean of the variable X.

n	Smaller sample size in two-sample tests.
n_{ij}	Observed value, used in chi-square tests (6.2), (8.1), (8.2).
N	Sample size.
$\binom{N}{k} = \frac{N!}{k!(N-k)!}$	Binomial coefficient. Expresses the number of combinations of N objects taken k at a time (4.1.1).
$N!$	Factorial. $N! = N(N-1)(N-2)(N-3)\cdots(2)(1)$, e.g., $5! = (5)(4)(3)(2)(1) = 120$. *Note:* By definition, $0! = 1$ (4.1.1).
O_i	Observed value, used in chi-square tests (4.2), (5.1).
p	Probability. Used in place of $P[X]$ when the context is clear.
$P[H]$	The probability of the random variable H.
q	Probability. Usually used to denote the probability associated with a binary outcome, $q = 1 - p$ (4.1.1).
$q(\alpha, \#c)$	Statistic used in comparing related groups or conditions with a control (7.2.4).
Q	The Cochran Q-test statistic for comparing correlated proportions (7.1).
r	Number of runs in the one-sample runs test (4.5).
r_ϕ	The phi coefficient for 2×2 contingency tables (9.2).
r_s	The Spearman rank-order correlation coefficient (9.3).
R_i	Denotes the sum of the frequencies in the ith row in a contingency table (8.1.3), (9.1).
R_j	The sum of the ranks in the jth group (7.2), (8.3), (9.6).
$\bar{R}_j$	The average of the ranks in the jth group (7.2), (8.3), (9.6).
ρ_s	Rho. The population Spearman rank-order correlation coefficient (9.3.5).
S	The number of agreements less the number of disagreements in rank orderings in two sets of data. Used to compute the Kendall rank-order correlation coefficient (9.4.3).
$S_N(X)$	Cumulative frequency distribution for sample of size N. Used in the Kolmogorov-Smirnov test (4.3), (6.6).
σ	Sigma. The population standard deviation.
σ_x	The population standard deviation of the variable X.
$\sigma_{\bar{X}}$	The population standard error of the mean.
σ^2	The population variance.
t	The statistic for Student's t test.
t_j	The number of tied ranks in the jth grouping of ties. Used in tests in which the data are rankings (6.4).
T, T_{xy}	The Kendall rank-order correlation coefficient (9.4).
$T_{xy.z}$	The Kendall partial rank-order correlation coefficient (9.5).
T_C	The correlation between several judges and a criterion ranking (9.7.4).

T^+	Sum of positive differences in the Wilcoxon signed ranks test (5.3).
T^-	Sum of negative differences in the Wilcoxon signed ranks test (5.3).
T_x, T_y	Correction factor for tied ranks in the Spearman rank-order correlation coefficient (9.3.4).
T_x, T_y	Correction factor for tied ranks in the Kendall rank-order correlation coefficient (9.4.4). (The values of T_x and T_y will differ when applied to the Spearman and Kendall rank-order correlation coefficients.)
τ	Tau. The population Kendall rank-order correlation coefficient (9.4).
$\tau_{xy.z}$	The population Kendall partial rank-order correlation coefficient (9.5).
$\bar{\tau}$	Population average tau for testing significance of the Kendall coefficient of agreement when data are rankings (9.7.2).
u	The Kendall coefficient of agreement (9.7).
U_{ij}	Mann-Whitney U-count statistic. Used in computing the Jonckheere statistic (8.4.2).
$U(YX)$	The average placement of a set of X scores with respect to a set of Y scores. Used in the robust rank-order test (6.5).
$U(YX_i)$	The *placement* of the score X_i with respect to the Y scores. Used in the robust rank-order test (6.5).
$\grave{U}$	Test statistic for the robust rank-order test (6.5).
υ	Upsilon. The population parameter for the Kendall coefficient of agreement when the data are paired comparisons (9.7.2).
ϕ	Phi. Subscript used for r_ϕ, the phi coefficient (9.2).
V_x, V_y	Variancelike statistic for the robust rank-order test (6.5).
W	The Kendall coefficient of concordance between multiple rankings (9.6).
W_T	An index of agreement among judges. Similar to the Kendall coefficient of concordance (9.7.1).
W_x	The sum of ranks for the group X in the Wilcoxon-Mann-Whitney test (6.4). Also used in the Siegel-Tukey test for scale differences (6.8).
X, X_i	An observed score or datum.
$\bar{X}$	The sample mean of the variable X.
X^2	The chi-squared statistic (4.2), (5.1), (6.2), (6.3), (8.1).
X_i^2	The chi-squared statistic for partitions of a contingency table (6.2), (8.1.3).
χ^2	Chi-squared. The chi-square distribution (4.2), (5.1), (6.2), (8.1).

z	z score. Usually used to denote a variable transformed to *standard form*, i.e., with mean zero and standard deviation one.
#	Counting function. For example:
#H	The number of heads (2.7).
#(+)	The number of agreements in orderings of objects in two groups (9.9.3).
#(−)	The number of disagreements in orderings of objects in two groups (9.9.3).

NONPARAMETRIC STATISTICS FOR THE BEHAVIORAL SCIENCES

CHAPTER 1

INTRODUCTION

Students in the behavioral and social sciences soon grow accustomed to using familiar words in initially unfamiliar ways. Early in their studies they learn that a behavioral scientist speaking of *society* is not referring to that leisured group of people whose names appear in the society pages of our newspapers. They know that the scientific denotation of the term *personality* has little or nothing in common with the teenager's meaning. Although a high school student may contemptuously dismiss one of his or her peers for having "no personality," the behavioral scientist scarcely can conceive such a condition. The students learn that *culture*, when used technically, encompasses far more than aesthetic refinement. And they would not now be caught in the blunder of saying that a salesperson "uses" *psychology* in persuading a customer to purchase a particular product.

Similarly, the students discover that the field of *statistics* is quite different from the common conception of it. In newspapers and on radio and television the statistician is represented as one who collects large amounts of quantitative information and then summarizes it, manipulates it, and disseminates it. We are all familiar with the notion that the determination of the average hourly wage in an industry or of the average number of children in urban American families is the statistician's job. More familiar to some is the role of the statistician in sporting events. But students who have taken even one introductory course in statistics know that description is only one function of statistics.

A central function of modern statistics is *statistical inference*. Statistical inference is concerned with two types of problems: estimation of population parameters and tests of hypotheses. It is the latter, tests of hypotheses, that will be our primary concern in this book.

Webster tells us that the verb "to infer" means "to derive as a consequence, conclusion, or probability." When we see a woman who wears no ring on the third finger of her left hand, we may *infer* that she is unmarried. However, this inference could be incorrect. For example, the woman may be from Europe where the wedding ring is frequently worn on the right hand. Or she simply may have chosen not to wear a ring.

In statistical inference we are concerned with how to draw conclusions about large groups of subjects, or about events yet to occur on the basis of observation of a few subjects, or what has occurred in the past. Statistics provides tools which formalize and standardize our procedures for drawing such conclusions. For example, we might wish to determine which of three varieties of tomato sauce is most popular with American cooks. Informally, we might gather information on this question by stationing ourselves near the tomato sauce section of a grocery store and counting the number of cans of each variety which are purchased in the course of a day. Almost certainly the number of purchases of the three varieties will be unequal. But can we *infer* that the one most frequently chosen on *that* day in *that* store by *that* day's customers is really the most popular among American cooks? Whether we can make such an inference must depend on the margin of popularity held by the most frequently chosen brand, on the representativeness of the grocery store, and also on the representativeness of the group of purchasers whom we observed.

The procedures of statistical inference introduce order into any attempt to draw conclusions from the evidence provided by samples. The logic of the procedures dictates some of the conditions under which the evidence must be collected, and statistical tests determine whether, from the evidence we collect, we can have confidence in what we conclude about the larger group from which only a few subjects were sampled.

A common problem for statistical inference is to determine, in terms of a probability, whether observed differences between two samples signify that the populations sampled are themselves really different. Now, even if we collect two groups of scores by taking random samples from the same population, we are likely to find that the scores differ to some extent. Differences may occur simply because of the operation of chance. How can we determine in any given case whether the observed differences between two samples are due merely to chance or are caused by other factors? The procedures of statistical inference enable us to determine whether the observed differences are within the range which easily could have occurred by chance or not. Another common problem is to determine whether a sample of scores is from some specified population. Still another problem is to decide whether we may legitimately infer that several groups differ among themselves. In this book we shall be concerned with each of these problems in statistical inference.

In the development of modern statistical methods, the first techniques of inference which appeared were those that made a good many assumptions about the nature of the populations from which the observations or data were drawn. These statistical techniques are called *parametric*. For example, a technique of inference may be based on the assumption that the data were drawn from what is termed a *normally distributed population.* Or a technique of inference may be based on the assumption that two sets of data were drawn from populations having the same variance (σ^2) or spread of scores. Such techniques produce conclusions which contain qualifiers, e.g., "If the assumptions regarding the shape of the population distribution(s) are valid, then we may conclude that. . . ." Because of common assumptions, such tests are easily systematized and thought to be easier to teach and to apply.

Somewhat more recently we have seen the development of a large number of techniques of inference which do not make numerous or stringent assumptions about the population from which we have sampled the data. These *distribution-free* or *nonparametric* techniques result in conclusions which require fewer qualifications. Having used one of them, we might be able to say that, "Regardless of the shape of the population(s), we may conclude that. . . ." It is with these techniques that we shall be concerned in this book.

Some nonparametric techniques are *ranking tests* or *order tests*, and these labels suggest another way in which nonparametric tests differ from parametric tests. When we use any statistical test, we implicitly make certain assumptions about the numerical assignments made to the objects observed. As we shall see in Chap. 3, the rules for numerical assignment constitute a measurement scale. The assignment rule we use (i.e., the scale) puts constraints on the kinds of interpretations and operations which are appropriate to those assignments. When the application of a statistical test transforms scale values in inappropriate ways, it becomes difficult to interpret the result. Although we may compute a parametric statistical test for data of any type, the ease of interpretation of the test depends upon the manner in which the observations are transformed into numbers for analysis. Many nonparametric tests, on the other hand, focus on the order or ranking of the scores, not on their "numerical" values, and other nonparametric techniques are useful with data for which even ordering is impossible (i.e., with classificatory data). Whereas a parametric test may focus on the difference between the means of two populations, the analogous nonparametric test may focus on the difference between the medians. The advantages of statistics based upon orderings for data in the behavioral sciences (in which "numerical" scores may be precisely numerical in appearance only!) should be apparent. We shall discuss this point at greater length in Chap. 3, in which parametric and nonparametric tests are contrasted.

Of the nine chapters in this book, six are devoted to the presentation of the various nonparametric statistical tests. The tests are assigned to chapters according to the research design for which they are appropriate. Chapter 4 contains tests which may be used when one wishes to determine whether a single sample is from a specified population. Two chapters contain tests which may be used when one wishes to compare the scores yielded by two samples; Chap. 5 considers tests for two related samples, while Chap. 6 considers tests for two independent samples. Similarly, two chapters are devoted to significance tests for three or more samples; Chap. 7 presents tests for three or more related samples and Chap. 8 presents tests for three or more independent samples. Chapter 9 describes nonparametric measures of association and tests of significance for them.

Moreover, we have tried to make the book intelligible to the reader whose mathematical training is limited to elementary algebra. This orientation has precluded the presentation of many derivations. Where possible we have tried to convey an "intuitive" understanding of the rationale underlying a test since we believe that this understanding will be more useful than an attempt to follow the derivation. The more mathematically sophisticated reader will want to pursue the topics covered in this book by turning to the sources to which we have made reference.

Readers whose mathematical training is limited, and especially readers whose educational experience has been such that they have developed negative emotional responses to symbols, often find statistics books difficult because of the extensive use of symbols. Such readers may find that much of this difficulty will disappear if they read more slowly than is their custom and relate the textual presentation to the tabular data presentations. Also, the reader is encouraged to learn to read equations and formulas as if they were sentences, substituting the names of the variables for the names of the symbols. It is not to be expected that a reader schooled in the behavioral or social sciences can maintain the same fast clip in reading a statistics book that he or she maintains in reading a book on, say, personality, or on intergroup hostility, or on the role of geography in cultural differences. Statistical writing is more condensed than most social scientific writing—we use symbols for brevity as well as preciseness—and, therefore, it requires slower reading. The reader who finds symbols difficult may also be aided by the glossary which is included. That glossary summarizes the meanings of the various symbols used in the book. One reason that extensive use of symbols makes material more difficult may be that symbols are general or abstract terms, which acquire a variety of specific meanings in a variety of specific cases. Thus when we speak of k samples we mean any number of samples, 3 or 4 or 8 or 5, or any other number. In the examples, of course, the symbols each acquire a specific numerical value, and thus the examples may serve to "concretize" the discussion for the reader.

Most readers have electronic calculators on which they may compute most of the statistics described in this book. Other readers have ready access to statistical "packages" for use on computers. Although computers may make the drudgery of data analysis minimal, it is important that the user understands the statistic—its assumptions *and* what it does with the data. One way better to understand the statistical techniques is to actually compute them on one's own data. In our presentation of techniques, we have chosen to describe procedures in a manner amenable to quick analysis at one's desk. Although computer packages certainly could be used (and should be used in many cases), it is often faster to analyze small sets of data "by hand" with a calculator. For some of the more complicated statistics, we have included listings of simple computer programs which will help to analyze the data if the procedure is not readily available in other packages.

Finally, the reader with limited mathematical training also may find the examples especially helpful. An example is given of the use in research of every statistical test presented in this book. The examples also serve to illustrate the role and importance of statistics in the research of the behavioral scientist. This may be their most useful function, because we have addressed this book to the researcher whose primary interest is in the substance or topical fields of the behavioral and social sciences rather than in their methodology. The examples demonstrate the intimate interrelation of substance and method in these sciences.

CHAPTER 2

THE USE OF STATISTICAL TESTS IN RESEARCH

In the behavioral sciences we conduct research in order to test hypotheses which we derive from our theories of behavior. Having stated a specific hypothesis which seems important to a certain theory, we collect data which should enable us to make a decision concerning the hypothesis. Our decision may lead us to retain, revise, or reject the hypothesis and the theory which was its source.

To reach an objective decision as to whether a particular hypothesis is confirmed by a set of data, we must have an objective procedure for either rejecting or accepting that hypothesis. Objectivity is emphasized because one important aspect of the scientific method is that one should arrive at conclusions by methods that are public and which may be repeated by other competent investigators.

This objective procedure should be based on the information or data we obtain in our research and on the risk we are willing to take that our decision concerning the hypothesis may be incorrect.

The procedure usually followed involves several steps. We list these steps in order of performance; this and the next chapter are devoted to discussing each in some detail. They are stated here first in order for the reader to get an overview of the overall procedure.

i. State the null hypothesis (H_0) and its alternative (H_1). Decide what data to collect and under what conditions.

Choose a statistical test (with its associated statistical model) for testing H_0.

ii. From among the several tests which might be used with a given research design, choose that test the model of which most closely approximates the conditions of the research in terms of the assumptions on which the test is based.

iii. Specify a significance level (α) and a sample size (N).

iv. Find the sampling distribution of the statistical test under the assumption that H_0 is true.

v. On the basis of (ii), (iii), and (iv) above, define the region of rejection for the statistical test.

vi. Collect the data. Using the data obtained from the sample(s), compute the value of the test statistic. If that value is in the region of rejection, the decision is to reject H_0; if that value is outside the region of rejection, the decision is that H_0 cannot be rejected at the chosen level of significance.

A number of statistical tests are presented in this book. In most of the presentations, one or more examples are given to illustrate the use of the test. Each example follows the six steps given above. A basic understanding of the reason for each of these steps is essential to understanding the role of statistics in testing hypotheses.

2.1 THE NULL HYPOTHESIS

The first step in the decision-making procedure is to state the null hypothesis (H_0). The *null hypothesis* is an hypothesis of "no effect" and is usually formulated for the express purpose of being rejected; that is, it is the negation of the point one is trying to make. If it is rejected, the alternative hypothesis (H_1) is supported. The *alternative hypothesis* is the operational statement of the experimenter's research hypothesis. The *research hypothesis* is the prediction derived from the theory under test.

When we want to make a decision about differences, we test H_0 against H_1. H_1 constitutes the assertion or hypothesis that is accepted if H_0 is rejected.

Suppose a certain social-psychological theory would lead us to predict that two specified groups of people differ in the amount of time they spend reading newspapers. This prediction would be our research hypothesis. Generally speaking, our research hypothesis is that the groups differ. Confirmation of that prediction would lend support to the theory from which it was derived. To test this research hypothesis, we state it in operational form as the alternative hypothesis H_1. But how? One measure would be to use the mean amount of time each group spent reading newspapers. Then H_1 would be that $\mu_1 \neq \mu_2$, that is, the mean amount of time spent reading newspapers by the members of the two populations is unequal. H_0 would be that $\mu_1 = \mu_2$, that is, the mean amount of time spent reading newspapers by the members of the two populations is the same. If the data permit us to reject H_0, then we would accept H_1, since the data support the research hypothesis and its underlying theory.

The nature of the research hypothesis determines how H_1 should be stated. If the research hypothesis simply states that two groups will differ with respect to means, then H_1 is that $\mu_1 \neq \mu_2$. But if the theory predicts the *direction* of the difference, that is, one specified group will have a larger mean than the other, then H_1 may be either that $\mu_1 > \mu_2$ or that $\mu_1 < \mu_2$, that is, the mean for group 1 is greater than or less than the mean for group 2, respectively.

It should be noted that, although we may say that the data support H_1 and we would like to accept that hypothesis, we cannot say that H_1 is true. As we shall see in Sec. 2.3, our data only permit us to make probabilistic statements concerning the hypotheses. Although we may *say* that we are rejecting one hypothesis and accepting its alternative, we cannot say that the alternative hypothesis is true.

2.2 THE CHOICE OF STATISTICAL TEST

The field of statistics has developed to the extent that we now have, for almost all research designs, alternative valid statistical tests which might be used to reach a decision about an hypothesis. Having alternative valid tests, we need some rational basis for choosing among them. Since this book is concerned with nonparametric statistics, the choice between parametric and nonparametric statistical procedures is one of its central topics. Discussion of this point is reserved for a separate chapter. Chapter 3 gives an extended discussion of the bases for choosing among the various tests applicable to a given research design. Although we do not have a complete discussion here, it is important to remember that choosing the statistical tests is the second step of the procedure.

2.3 THE LEVEL OF SIGNIFICANCE AND THE SAMPLE SIZE

When the null hypothesis and the alternative hypothesis have been stated, and when the appropriate statistical test has been selected, the next step is to specify a level of significance (α) and to select a sample size (N).

In brief, this is our decision-making procedure: In advance of the data collection, we specify a set of all possible samples that could occur when H_0 is true. From these, we specify a subset of possible samples which are so inconsistent with H_0 (or so extreme) that the probability is very small, when H_0 is true, that the sample we actually observe will be among them. Then, if in our research we actually observe a sample which is included in that subset, we reject H_0.

Stated differently, our procedure is to reject H_0 in favor of H_1 if a statistical test yields a value whose associated probability of occurrence under H_0 is equal to or less than some small probability, usually denoted α. That probability is called the *level of significance*. Common values of α are .05 and .01.[1] To repeat: If the probability associated with the occurrence under H_0, (i.e., when the null hypothesis is true) of the particular value yielded by a statistical test (and more extreme values) is equal to or less than α, we reject H_0 in favor of H_1, the operational statement of the research hypothesis. The purpose of setting a significance level is to define a rare event under H_0 when the null hypothesis is true. Thus, if H_0 were, in fact, true, and if the result of a statistical test on a set of observed data has a probability less than or equal to α, it is the occurrence of a rare event that would lead us, on a probabilistic basis, to reject H_0.

It can be seen, then, that α gives the probability of mistakenly or falsely rejecting H_0. Falsely rejecting H_0 is called a Type I error and will be discussed later in this chapter.

Since the probability α enters into the determination of whether H_0 is or is not rejected, the requirement of objectivity demands that α be specified before the data are collected. The level at which the researcher chooses to set α should be determined by an estimate of the importance or possible practical significance of the result which will be obtained. In a study of the possible therapeutic effect of brain surgery, for example, the researcher may well choose to set a rather stringent level of significance, because the consequences of rejecting the null hypothesis improperly (and, therefore, unjustifiably advocating or recommending a drastic clinical technique) is great indeed. In reporting results, the researcher should indicate the actual probability level associated with the obtained results so that readers may use their own judgment in deciding whether or not the null hypothesis should be rejected. A researcher may decide to work at the .05 level, but a reader may refuse to accept any result not significant at the .01, .005, or .001 level, whereas another reader may be interested in any result which reaches, say, the .08 or .10 level. These differences often reflect different subjective or perceived consequences of the application of the results by different individuals. Whenever possible, the researcher should give readers the information they may require by reporting the probability level actually associated with the data.

There are two types of errors which may be made in arriving at a decision about H_0. The first, *Type I error*, involves rejecting the hypothesis H_0 when it is, in fact, true. The second, *Type II error*, involves failing to reject the null hypothesis H_0 when, in fact, it is false.

The probability of committing a Type I error is denoted α. The larger the probability α, the more likely it is that H_0 will be rejected falsely, i.e., the more likely it is that a Type I error will be committed. The Type II error is usually

---

[1] From the discussion of significance levels given in this book, the reader should not infer that we believe in a rigid or hard-and-fast approach to the setting of significance levels. Rather, it is for heuristic reasons that significance levels are emphasized; such an exposition seems the best method of clarifying the role which the information contained in the sampling distribution plays in the decision-making process.

denoted β. α and β will be used to indicate both the type of error and the probability of making that error. That is,

$$P[\text{Type I error}] = \alpha$$

$$P[\text{Type II error}] = \beta$$

Ideally, the particular values of both α and β should be chosen by the experimenter before beginning research. These values would determine the size of the sample N that would need to be drawn in using the statistical test which was chosen.

In practice, however, it is more common for α and N to be specified in advance. Once α and N have been specified, β is determined. Inasmuch as there is an inverse relation between the likelihood of making the two types of errors, a decrease in α will increase β for any given N. If we wish to reduce the possibility of both types of errors, we must increase the sample size N.

It should be clear that in any statistical inference a danger exists of committing one of the two alternative types of errors, and, therefore, the researcher should reach some compromise which optimizes the balance between the probabilities of making the two errors. The various statistical tests offer the possibility of different balances among these factors. It is in achieving this balance that the notion of the power of a statistical test is relevant.

The *power of a test* is defined as the probability of rejecting H_0 when it is in fact *false*. That is,

$$\text{Power} = 1 - P[\text{Type II error}] = 1 - \beta$$

The curves in Fig. 2.1 show that, for a particular test, the probability of committing a Type II error β decreases as the sample size N increases, and thus that the power increases with the size of N. One might consider $1 - \beta$ to be the "strength of the evidence." Also, the power of a parametric test increases with the difference between the "true" population parameter, say μ, and the value specified by H_0,

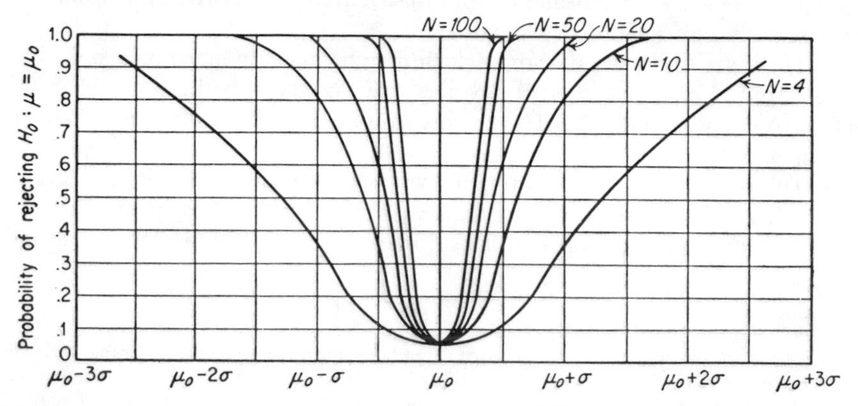

FIGURE 2.1
Power curves of the two-tailed test at $\alpha = .05$ with varying sample sizes.

say μ_0. Figure 2.1 illustrates the increase in power of the two-tailed test of the mean which comes with increasing samples sizes: $N = 4, 10, 20, 50, 100$. These samples are drawn from populations having normal distributions with variance σ^2.[2] When the null hypothesis is true, the mean is μ_0, that is, $\mu = \mu_0$.

Figure 2.1 depicts the power curves for tests where $\alpha = .05$. That is, the curves were drawn assuming that when H_0 is true—when the true mean is μ_0—the probability of rejecting H_0 is equal to .05.

From this discussion it is important for the reader to understand the following five points, which summarize what we have said about the selection of the level of significance and the sample size:

1. The significance level α of a test is the probability that, when the hypothesis H_0 is true, a statistical test will yield a value of the test statistic that will lead to rejection of H_0; that is, the significance level indicates the probability of committing a Type I error.
2. β is the probability that a statistical test will yield a value of the test statistic under which the null hypothesis would not be rejected when in fact it is false; that is, β is the probability of committing a Type II error.
3. The power of a test, $1 - \beta$, is the probability of rejecting the null hypothesis when it is false (and thus should be rejected).
4. Power is a function of the statistical test chosen.[3]
5. Generally, the power of a statistical test increases as the sample size increases.

2.4 THE SAMPLING DISTRIBUTION

After an experimenter has chosen a certain statistical test to use with a set of data, the sampling distribution of the test statistic must be determined.

The sampling distribution is a theoretical distribution. It is that distribution we would have if we took *all possible* samples of the same size from the same population, drawing each randomly. Another way of saying this is that the sampling distribution is the distribution, when H_0 is true, of all possible values that some statistic (say, the sample mean $\bar{X}$) can take when that statistic is computed from many equally sized samples drawn from the same population.

---

[2] The normal distribution is the distribution of a random variable x having the following form:

$$f(x) = \frac{1}{\sqrt{2\pi}\sigma} e^{-1/2[(x-\mu)/\sigma]^2}$$

where μ is the mean, and σ is the standard deviation of the distribution. It is the familiar "bell-shaped" distribution.

[3] Power also is related to the nature of H_1. If H_1 has direction, a one-tailed test is used. A one-tailed test is more powerful than a two-tailed test. This should be clear from the definition of power. One- and two-tailed tests are described in Sec. 2.5. Power also is related to the sample size N, variance σ^2, the significance level α, and other variables, depending upon the test being done.

The null sampling distribution of a statistic consists of the probabilities under H_0 associated with various possible numerical values of the statistic. The probability "associated with" the occurrence of a particular value of the statistic when H_0 is true is *not* the exact probability of just that value. Rather, "the probability associated with the occurrence under H_0" is used here to refer to the probability of a particular value *plus* the probabilities of all possible values which are more extreme or more inconsistent with H_0. That is, the "associated probability" or "the probability associated with the occurrence under H_0" is the probability of the occurrence under H_0 of a value "as extreme as or more extreme than" the particular value of the test statistic. In this book we shall have frequent occasion to use the above phrases, and in every case each carries the meaning given above.

Suppose we were interested in the probability that three heads would show when three "fair" coins were tossed simultaneously. The sampling distribution of the number of heads could be drawn from the list of all possible results of tossing three fair coins, which is given in Table 2.1. The total number of possible events (possible combinations of H's and T's—heads and tails) is eight, only one of which is the event in which we are interested: the simultaneous occurrence of three H's. Thus the probability of the occurrence under H_0 of three heads on the toss of three coins is $\frac{1}{8}$. Here H_0 is the assertion that the coins are "fair," which means that for each coin the probability of a head occurring is equal to the probability of a tail occurring.

The sampling distribution of all possible events yields the probability of the occurrence when H_0 is true of the event with which we are concerned.

It is obvious that it would be essentially impossible for us to use this method of imagining all possible results in order to write down the sampling distribution for even moderately large samples from large populations. This being the case, we rely on the authority of statements of mathematical theorems. These theorems invariably involve assumptions, and in applying the theorems we must keep those assumptions in mind. Usually these assumptions concern the distribution of the

TABLE 2.1
Possible outcomes of the toss of three coins

	Coins		
Outcome	**1**	**2**	**3**
1	H	H	H
2	H	H	T
3	H	T	H
4	H	T	T
5	T	H	H
6	T	H	T
7	T	T	H
8	T	T	T

population and/or the size of the sample. An example of such a theorem is the *central limit theorem.*

When a variable is normally distributed, its distribution is completely characterized by its mean and standard deviation. This being the case, we know, from the analysis of the distribution, that the probability that an observed value of the variable will differ from the population mean by more than 1.96 standard deviations is less than .05. (The probabilities associated with any difference in standard deviations from the mean of a normally distributed variable are given in Appendix Table A.)

Suppose we want to know, before the sample is drawn, the probability associated with the occurrence of a particular value of $\bar{X}$ (the mean of the sample), i.e., the probability under H_0 of the occurrence of a value at least as large as a particular value of $\bar{X}$ when the sample is randomly drawn from some population, the mean μ and standard deviation σ of which we know. One version of the central limit theorem states that:

> If a variable is distributed with mean $= \mu$ and standard deviation $= \sigma$, and if random samples of size N are drawn, then the means of these samples, the $\bar{X}$'s, will be approximately normally distributed with mean μ and standard deviation $\sigma/\sqrt{N}$ when N is large.[4]

In other words, we know that the sampling distribution of $\bar{X}$ has a mean equal to the population mean μ, a standard deviation equal to the population standard deviation divided by the square root of the sample size, that is, $\sigma_{\bar{X}} = \sigma/\sqrt{N}$, and if N is sufficiently large, it is approximately normal.

For example, suppose we know that in the population of American college students, some psychological attribute, as measured by some test, is distributed with $\mu = 100$ and $\sigma = 16$. Now we want to know the probability of drawing a random sample of $N = 64$ cases from this population and finding that the mean score in that sample, $\bar{X}$, is as large as 104. The sampling distribution of $\bar{X}$'s of all possible samples of size 64 will have a mean equal to 100 ($\mu = 100$) and a standard deviation equal to $\sigma/\sqrt{N} = 16/\sqrt{64} = 2$, and the central limit theorem tells us that the distribution of $\bar{X}$ will be approximately normal as N gets large. (If the variable X had a normal distribution to begin, $\bar{X}$ would have a normal distribution regardless of sample size.) We can see that 104 differs from 100 by two standard errors.[5] Reference to Appendix Table A reveals that the probability associated with the occurrence under H_0 of a value as large as the observed value of $\bar{X}$, that is, of an

---

[4] Although we say that the distribution becomes *approximately* normal as N gets large, the central limit theorem states that as $N \to \infty$, the distribution becomes normal. However, since all samples are finite, the terminology "approximate" is appropriate.

[5] The standard deviation of a sampling distribution of the sample mean is often denoted as the *standard error* of the distribution.

$\bar{X}$ which is at least two standard errors above the mean ($z \geq 2.0$), is $p < .023$. This computation may be represented in following form:

$$z = \frac{\bar{X} - \mu}{\sigma/\sqrt{N}}$$

$$= \frac{104 - 100}{16/\sqrt{64}}$$

$$= 2$$

It should be clear from this discussion and this example that, by knowing the sampling distribution of some statistic, we can make statements about the probability of occurrence of certain numerical values of a statistic. The following sections will show how we use such probability statements in making a decision about H_0.

2.5 THE REGION OF REJECTION

The region of rejection is a region of the null sampling distribution. The sampling distribution includes *all* possible values that a test statistic can take on. The region of rejection consists of a subset of these possible values, and is chosen so that the probability under H_0 of the occurrence of a test statistic having a value which is in that subset is α. In other words, the region of rejection consists of a set of possible values which are so extreme that when H_0 is true the probability is very small (i.e., equal to α) that the sample we actually observe will yield a value which is among them. The probability *associated* with any value in the region of rejection is equal to or less than α.

The nature of the region of rejection is affected by the form of the alternative hypothesis H_1. If H_1 also indicates the predicted direction of the difference, then a one-tailed test is used. If H_1 does not indicate the direction of the predicted difference, then a two-tailed test is used. One-tailed and two-tailed tests differ in the location (but not the size) of the region of rejection. That is, in a one-tailed test the region of rejection is entirely at one end (or tail) of the sampling distribution. In a two-tailed test, the region of rejection is located at both ends (or tails) of the sampling distribution.

As an example, suppose a researcher wanted to determine whether a particular training regimen had an effect on the ability to recall geographic place names. The null hypothesis would be that the performance of a control group that received no special training would not differ from that of the training group. If the researcher merely wanted to know if there were a difference, then either large increases or large decrements in performance would lead to rejection of H_0. Since a difference in either direction would lead to rejection of H_0, a two-tailed test would be used. However, if the researcher were only interested in determining whether the training regimen would lead to increased performance, only large increases in performance would lead to rejection of H_0 and a one-tailed test would be used.

The size of the region of rejection is expressed by α, the level of significance. If $\alpha = .05$, then the size of the region of rejection comprises 5 percent of the entire

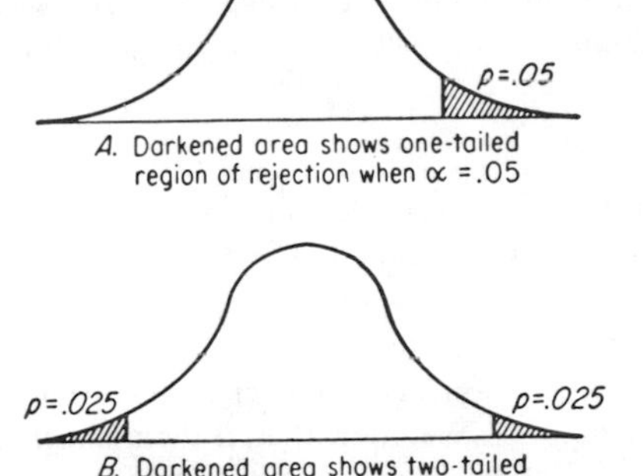
p=.05
A. Darkened area shows one-tailed region of rejection when α =.05
p=.025
p=.025
B. Darkened area shows two-tailed region of rejection when α =.05

FIGURE 2.2
Regions of rejection for one-tailed and two-tailed tests.

area included under the "curve" of the sampling distribution. One-tailed and two-tailed regions of rejection for $\alpha = .05$ are illustrated in Fig. 2.2. Note that these two regions differ in location but not in total size.

2.6 THE DECISION

If the statistical test yields a value which is in the region of rejection, we reject H_0.

The reasoning behind this decision process is very simple. If the probability associated with the occurrence under the null hypothesis of a particular value in the sampling distribution is very small, we may explain the actual occurrence of that value in one of two ways; first, we may explain it by deciding that the null hypothesis is false or, second, we may explain it by deciding that a rare and unlikely event has occurred. In the decision process we choose the first of these explanations. Occasionally, of course, the second may be the correct explanation. In fact, the probability associated with the second explanation is given by α, since rejecting H_0 when it is, in fact, true is the Type I error.

When the probability associated with an observed value of a statistical test is equal to or less than the previously determined value of α, we conclude that H_0 is false. Such an observed value is called "significant." H_0, the hypothesis under test, is rejected whenever a significant result occurs. A significant value is one that is found in the region of rejection and whose associated probability of occurrence under H_0 (as shown by the sampling distribution) is equal to or less than α.

2.7 ILLUSTRATIVE EXAMPLE

In the discussion of the various nonparametric statistical tests many examples of statistical decisions will be given in this book. Here we shall give just one example of how a statistical decision is reached in order to illustrate the points made in this chapter.

Example 2.7 Suppose we suspect that a particular coin is biased. One suspicion is that the coin is biased to land with head up. To test this suspicion (which we shall call our "research hypothesis"), we decide to toss the coin 12 times and to observe the frequency with which the outcome head occurs.

i. Null hypothesis. H_0: $P[\mathrm{H}] = P[\mathrm{T}] = \frac{1}{2}$. For this coin there is no difference between the probability of the occurrence of a head, i.e., $P[\mathrm{H}]$, and the probability of a tail, i.e., $P[\mathrm{T}]$. Put yet another way, the coin is "fair." The alternative hypothesis H_1: $P[\mathrm{H}] > \frac{1}{2}$ is a representation of the research hypothesis.

ii. Statistical test. The statistical test which is appropriate to test our hypothesis is the binomial test, which is based on the binomial distribution. (The number of heads observed when tossing a coin has a binomial distribution. We know that, if the number of heads observed is too large, we will want to reject H_0. However, we need to know the probabilities of different possible outcomes for the experiment. The binomial distribution gives us these probabilities. This distribution and the associated test is discussed fully in Chap. 4.)

iii. Significance level. In advance we decide to use $\alpha = .01$ as our level of significance. $N = 12$ equals the number of independent tosses of the coin.

iv. Sampling distribution. The sampling distribution which gives the probability of obtaining #H heads and $N - \#\mathrm{H}$ tails under the null hypothesis (the hypothesis that the coin is, in fact, fair) is the binomial distribution function:

$$P[\#\mathrm{H}] = \frac{N!}{(\#\mathrm{H})!(N - \#\mathrm{H})!}\left(\frac{1}{2}\right)^N \qquad \#\mathrm{H} = 0, 1, 2, \ldots, N$$

Table 2.2 shows the sampling distribution of #H, the number of heads when a fair coin is tossed 12 times.[6] This sampling distribution shows that the most likely outcome when tossing a coin 12 times is 6 heads and 6 tails. Obtaining 7 heads and 5 tails is somewhat less likely but still quite probable. But the occurrence of 12 heads on 12 tosses is very unlikely indeed. The occurrence of 0 heads (12 tails) is equally unlikely.

v. Rejection region. Since H_1: $p > \frac{1}{2}$ specifies a direction of difference, a one-tailed test will be used, and the region of rejection is entirely at one end of the sampling distribution, i.e., when the number of heads is large. The region of rejection consists of all values of #H which are so large that the probability associated with their occurrence under H_0 is equal to or less than $\alpha = .01$.

The probability of obtaining 12 heads is $1/4096 = .00024$. Since $p = .00024$ is smaller than $\alpha = .01$, clearly the occurrence of 12 heads would be in the region of rejection.

The probability of obtaining either 12 *or* 11 heads is

$$\frac{1}{4096} + \frac{12}{4096} = \frac{13}{4096} = .003$$

Since $p = .003$ is smaller than $\alpha = .01$, the occurrence of 11 heads would also be in the region of rejection.

---

[6] The details and rationale for the binomial distribution are discussed fully in Sec. 4.1. For the example given here, it is necessary only to understand that the sampling distribution of #H can be determined analytically.

TABLE 2.2
Sampling distribution of #H (number of heads) for 2^{12} samples of size $N = 12$

Number of heads	Sampling distribution*	Probability
12	1	.00024
11	12	.0029
10	66	.0161
9	220	.0537
8	495	.1208
7	792	.1936
6	924	.2256
5	792	.1936
4	495	.1208
3	220	.0537
2	66	.0161
1	12	.0029
0	1	.00024
	4096	1.000

* Expected frequency of occurrence if 2^{12} samples of 12 tosses were taken.

The probability of obtaining 10 heads (or a value more extreme) is

$$\frac{1}{4096} + \frac{12}{4096} + \frac{66}{4096} = \frac{79}{4096} = .019$$

Since $p = .019$ is larger than $\alpha = .01$, the occurrence of 10 heads would not be in the region of rejection.[7] That is, if 10 or fewer heads turn up in our sample of 12 tosses, we cannot reject H_0 at the $\alpha = .01$ level of significance.

vi. *Decision.* Suppose in our sample of 12 tosses we obtained 11 heads. The probability associated with an occurrence as extreme as this is $p = .003$. Inasmuch as this probability is smaller than our previously set level of significance ($\alpha = .01$), our decision would be to reject H_0 in favor of H_1. We would conclude that the coin is biased to land head up.

In this chapter we discussed the procedure for making a decision about whether a particular hypothesis, as operationally defined, should be accepted or rejected in terms of the information yielded by the data obtained in the research. Chapter 3 completes the general discussion by going into the question of how one may choose the most appropriate statistical test for use with one's research data. (This choice is step 2 in the procedure that is outlined above.) The discussion in

[7] Because the sampling distributions for many nonparametric statistics are discrete, it may not be possible to select the region of rejection so that α is exactly equal to the predetermined value. Therefore, the cut point which divides the distribution should be chosen so that the probability associated with the region of rejection is as large as possible *but less than* the chosen significance level α. While this results in a conservative test, it provides a simple rule for use in hypothesis testing.

Chap. 3 clarifies the conditions under which parametric tests are optimum and indicates the conditions under which nonparametric tests are more appropriate.

2.8 REFERENCES

The reader who wishes to gain a more comprehensive or fundamental understanding of the topics summarized in the bare outline of the present chapter may refer to textbooks on statistics in the behavioral and social sciences. Especially worthwhile are Bailey (1971) and Hays (1982).

CHAPTER 3

CHOOSING AN APPROPRIATE STATISTICAL TEST

When alternative and valid statistical tests are available for a particular research hypothesis, as is very often the case, it is necessary to employ some rationale for choosing among them. In Chap. 2 we presented one criterion to use for choosing among alternative valid statistical tests—the criterion of power. In this chapter other criteria will be presented.

The reader will remember that the *power* of a statistical analysis is partly a function of which statistical test is employed in the analysis. A statistical test is a good one if the probability of rejecting H_0, when H_0 is true, is equal to whatever was chosen as α. It is a powerful test if it has a large probability of rejecting H_0 when H_0 is false. Suppose we find two statistical tests, A and B, both of which have the same probability of rejecting H_0 when it is true. That means that both tests are equally valid. It might seem that we should simply select the one that has the larger probability of rejecting H_0 when it is false.

However, there are considerations other than power which enter into the choice of a statistical test. In this choice we must consider the manner in which the sample of scores or data was drawn, the nature of the population from which the sample was drawn, the particular hypotheses we wish to test, and the kind of measurement or scaling which was employed in the operational definitions of the variables involved, i.e., in the scores. All these matters enter into determining which statistical test is optimum or most appropriate for analyzing a particular set of research data.

3.1 THE STATISTICAL MODEL

When we have asserted the nature of the population and the manner of sampling, we have established a statistical model. Associated with every statistical test is a model and a measurement requirement. The test is valid under certain conditions, and the model and the measurement requirement specify those conditions. Sometimes we are able to test whether the conditions of a particular statistical model are met, but more often we have to *assume* that they are met. We must examine the situation and determine whether or not it is reasonable to assume that the model is correct. Thus the conditions of the statistical model of a test are often called the "assumptions" of the test. All decisions arrived at by the use of any statistical test must carry with them this qualification: "If the model used was correct, and if the measurement requirement was satisfied, then. . . ."

It is obvious that the fewer or weaker the assumptions that define a particular model, the less we need to qualify the decision reached by the statistical test associated with that model; that is, the fewer or weaker are the assumptions, the more general are the conclusions.

However, the most powerful tests are those that have the strongest or most extensive assumptions. Parametric tests, for example, the t test or F test, have a variety of strong assumptions underlying their use. If those assumptions are valid, tests based on these assumptions are the most likely of all tests to reject H_0 when H_0 is false; that is, when research data may be analyzed appropriately by a parametric test, that test will be more powerful than any other. Notice, however, the requirement that the research data must be appropriate for the test. What constitutes appropriateness? What are the conditions associated with the statistical model and the measurement requirement underlying, say, the t test? The conditions which must be satisfied to make the t test the most powerful one, and before any confidence can be placed in any probability statement obtained by the use of the t test, are at least these:

1. The observations must be independent, i.e., the selection of any one case from the population for inclusion in the sample must not bias the chances of any other case for inclusion, and the score which is assigned to any case must not bias the score which is assigned to any other case.
2. The observations must be drawn from normally distributed populations.
3. In the case of analyses concerning two groups, the populations must have the same variance (or, in special cases, they must have a known ratio of variances).
4. The variables must have been measured in *at least* an interval scale, so that it is possible to *interpret* the results.

All the above conditions (including condition 4, which states the measurement requirement) are elements of the *parametric statistical model* associated with the normal distribution. With the possible exception of the assumption of equal variances, these conditions are ordinarily not tested in the course of the performance of a statistical analysis. Rather, they are presumptions which are accepted, and their truth or falsity determines the accuracy and meaningfulness of the probability statement arrived at by the parametric test. It should be noted that parametric tests test hypotheses about specific *parameters*, such as the mean. It is assumed that hypotheses about such parameters are central to our research hypotheses.

When we have reason to believe that these conditions are met in the data being analyzed, then we should certainly choose a parametric statistical test, such as t or F, for analyzing those data. Such a choice is optimum because the parametric test will be a valid and most powerful test.

But what if these conditions are not met? What happens when the population is *not* normally distributed? What happens when the measurement is *not* as strong as an interval scale? If there are multiple measures or groups, what happens when the populations are *not* equal in variance?

When the assumptions constituting the statistical model for a test are, in fact, not met, then the test may not be valid, i.e., a test statistic may fall in the rejection region with a probability greater than α. It is even difficult to estimate the extent to which a probability statement varies because of the inappropriate application of the test. Although some empirical evidence has been gathered to show that slight deviations in meeting the assumptions underlying parametric tests may not have radical effects on the obtained probability levels, there is no general agreement as to what constitutes a "slight" deviation. Moreover, slight deviations in more than one factor or assumption may have major consequences.

3.2 EFFICIENCY

We have already pointed out that the fewer or weaker the assumptions that constitute a particular model, the less powerful are the available valid tests. This assertion is generally true for any given sample size. But it may not be true when comparing two statistical tests which are applied to two samples of unequal size; that is, if $N = 30$ in both instances, test A may be more powerful than test B. But the same test B may be more powerful with $N = 30$ than is test A with $N = 20$. Remember that the power of any test increases as N increases. So we could use a less powerful test with a larger sample size. In other words, we can avoid the dilemma of having to choose between power and generality by selecting a statistical test which has broad generality and then increasing its power to that of the most powerful test available by enlarging the size of the sample.

The concept of *power-efficiency* is concerned with the increase in sample size which is necessary to make test B as powerful as test A when the significance level is held constant and the sample size of test A is held constant. If test A is the most powerful known test of its type (when used with data which meet its conditions), and if test B is another test for the same research design which is just as powerful with N_B cases as is test A with N_A cases, then

$$\text{Power-efficiency of test } B = \frac{100N_A}{N_B} \text{ percent}$$

For example, if test B requires a sample of $N = 25$ cases to have the same power as test A has with $N = 20$ cases when the significance level is α, then test B has power-efficiency of $(100)(\frac{20}{25}) = 80$ percent. A power-efficiency of 80 percent means that in order to equate the power of test A and test B (when all the conditions of both tests are met, and when test A is the more powerful), we need to draw 10 cases for test B for every 8 cases drawn for test A.

Statisticians also compare models by calculating the *asymptotic relative efficiency* of a statistic. Like power-efficiency, asymptotic relative efficiency is a way of determining the sample size needed for test B to have the same power as test A. However, unlike power-efficiency, this ratio is expressed independently of the sample size of test A. The ratio is asymptotic in that it is the ratio of sample sizes required for fixed α as the sample size of test A increases without limit ($N_A \rightarrow \infty$). It can be expressed as the following:

$$\text{Asymptotic relative efficiency of test } B = 100 \lim_{N_A \rightarrow \infty} \frac{N_A}{N_B} \text{ percent}$$

Asymptotic relative efficiency has some advantages over power-efficiency. One is that the limit usually turns out to be independent of α. On the other hand, a disadvantage of asymptotic relative efficiency is that it is a limit based upon large samples whereas many of the tests of interest in this book are applied to small samples. Fortunately for some of the tests, the asymptotic relative efficiency is reached with fairly small samples. Power-efficiency and asymptotic relative efficiency are important characteristics of statistical tests. In a sense, they are complementary concepts because they give us information about how well a valid test performs relative to another.

In summary, we can avoid losing power by simply choosing a different test and drawing a larger sample. In other words, by choosing another statistical test with fewer assumptions in its model and, thus, with greater generality than the t and F tests, and by increasing N, we can avoid having to satisfy conditions 2 and 3 given in Sec. 3.1, and still retain equivalent power to reject H_0. This is especially important when we believe that the assumptions of the statistical model are inappropriate. The researcher has the responsibility of appropriately studying the situation and making only reasonable assumptions.

Two other conditions, 1 and 4 of Sec. 3.1, underlie the use and interpretation of parametric statistical tests based upon the normal distribution. Condition 1, that the scores be independently drawn from the population, is an assumption which underlies all statistical tests. But condition 4, which concerns the strength of measurement required for proper *interpretation* of parametric tests based on the normal distribution is not shared by all statistical tests. Different tests assume measurement of different strengths. To understand the measurement requirement necessary for the meaningful interpretation of various statistical tests, the reader should be conversant with some of the basic notions in the theory of measurement. The discussion of measurement in the next section gives an overview of important aspects of measurement.

3.3 MEASUREMENT

When a physical scientist talks about measurement, he or she usually means the assigning of numbers to observations in such a way that the numbers are amenable to analysis by manipulation or operations according to certain rules. The purpose of this analysis by manipulation is to reveal new information about the objects being measured. In other words, the relation between the things being observed and the numbers assigned to the observations is so direct that by manipulating the numbers the physical scientist obtains new information about the objects. For example, the scientist may determine how much a homogeneous mass of material would weigh if cut in half by simply dividing its weight by 2.

The social or behavioral scientist, taking physics as a model, usually attempts to do likewise in the scoring or measurement of social or behavioral variables. But in scaling such data, the scientist often overlooks a fundamental fact in measurement theory. Overlooked is the fact that, in order to perform certain operations on numbers that have been assigned to observations, the structure of the method of mapping numbers (assigning scores) to observations must be *isomorphic* to some numerical structure which includes these operations. If two systems are isomorphic, their structures are the same in the relations and operations they allow.

For example, if a researcher collects data made up of numerical scores and then manipulates these scores by, say, adding and squaring (which are necessary operations in finding means and standard deviations), he or she assumes that the structure of the measurement is isomorphic to the numerical structure known as arithmetic; that is, it is assumed that a high level of measurement has been attained.

The theory of measurement consists of a set of separate or distinct theories, each concerning a distinct *level* of measurement. The interpretable operations on a given set of scores are dependent on the level of measurement achieved. Here we shall discuss four levels or types of measurement—nominal, ordinal, interval, and ratio—and the implications of each for the interpretation of statistical tests.[1]

3.3.1 The Nominal or Categorical Scale

DEFINITION. Measurement at its weakest level exists when numbers or other symbols are used simply to classify an object, person, or characteristic. When numbers or other symbols are used to identify the groups to which various objects belong, these numbers or symbols constitute a nominal or categorical scale. This scale also is known as a *classificatory scale*.

EXAMPLES. The psychiatric system of diagnostic groups constitutes a nominal scale. When a diagnostician identifies a person as "schizophrenic," "paranoid,"

---

[1] There are many ways to describe and categorize measurement. Many scales, subscales, and generalizations of scales have been proposed. The measurement levels described here are those which have the most practical implications for most researchers.

"manic-depressive," or "neurotic," he or she is using a symbol to represent the class of people to which the person belongs, and thus a nominal or categorical scale is being used.

The numbers on automobile license plates constitute a nominal scale. If the assignment of plate numbers is purely arbitrary, then each plated car is a member of a unique subclass. But if, as is common in some states, a certain number or set of letters on the license plate indicates the county in which the car is registered, then each subclass in the nominal scale consists of several entities—cars registered in a particular county. Here the assignment of numbers must be such that the same code number (or code letters) is given to all automobiles registered in the same county and different numbers (or letters) are assigned to automobiles registered in different counties. That is, the number or letter code on the license plate must clearly indicate to which set of mutually exclusive subclasses the auto belongs.

Numbers on football jerseys and social-security numbers are other examples of the use of numbers in nominal or categorical scaling.

FORMAL PROPERTIES. All scales have certain formal properties. These properties provide fairly exact definitions of the scale's characteristics, more exact definitions than may be given in verbal terms. These properties may be formulated more abstractly than we have done here by a set of axioms specifying the operations of scaling and the relations among the objects that have been scaled.

In a nominal scale, the scaling operations partition a given class into a set of mutually exclusive subclasses. The only relation involved is that of *equivalence*; that is, the members of any one subclass must be equivalent in the property being scaled. This relation is symbolized by the familiar equal sign (=). The equivalence relation is reflexive, symmetrical, and transitive.[2]

Consider a set of objects, $x_1, x_2, \ldots, x_N$. Suppose object x_i has some *true* attribute, $A(x_i)$. Then for any pair of attributes in the set,

$$A(x_i) = A(x_j) \qquad \text{if } x_i \text{ and } x_j \text{ are in the same class}$$

and

$$A(x_i) \neq A(x_j) \qquad \text{if } x_i \text{ and } x_j \text{ are in different classes}$$

A *nominal scale* is a *labeling* system, $L(x)$, of the objects such that

$$L(x_i) = L(x_j) \qquad \text{if and only if } A(x_i) = A(x_j)$$

and

$$L(x_i) \neq L(x_j) \qquad \text{if and only if } A(x_i) \neq A(x_j)$$

ADMISSIBLE OPERATIONS. Since in any nominal scale the classification may be equally well represented by any set of symbols, the nominal scale is said to be "unique up to a one-to-one transformation." The symbols designating the various subclasses in the scale may be interchanged if this is done consistently and completely. For example, when new license plates are issued, the license code which

---

[2] *Reflexive*: $x = x$ for all values of x. *Symmetrical*: if $x = y$, then $y = x$. *Transitive*: if $x = y$ and $y = z$, then $x = z$.

previously stood for one county can be interchanged with that which stood for another county. Nominal scaling would be preserved if this changeover were performed consistently and thoroughly in the issuing of all license plates.

Since the symbols which designate the various groups on a nominal scale may be interchanged without altering the essential information in the scale, the only kinds of admissible descriptive statistics are those which would be unchanged by such a transformation—the mode, frequency counts, etc. Under certain conditions, we can test hypotheses regarding the distribution of cases among categories by using nonparametric tests such as the chi-square test or by using a test based upon the binomial distribution. These tests are appropriate for nominally scaled data because they focus on frequencies in categories, i.e., on enumerative data. In summary, when data lie on a nominal scale, we can label the categories "1", "2", "3", . . . , *in any order we choose*. In a sample we can count the number of "1"s, the number of "2"s, etc. (These are frequency counts.) We could calculate the percentage of "1"s in the sample, the percentage of "2"s, etc. (This is the relative frequency distribution.) And we could report which category had the largest frequency. (This is the mode.) But in general, we could not "add" category "1" and "2" to form category "3" since it would violate the assumptions of the nominal labeling system. In subsequent chapters we shall discuss a number of different statistical techniques appropriate to nominally scaled or categorical data.

3.3.2 The Ordinal or Ranking Scale

DEFINITION. It may happen that the objects in one category of a scale are not only different from the objects in other categories of that scale but also stand in some kind of *relation* to them. Typical relations among classes are: higher, more preferred, more difficult, more disturbed, more mature, etc. Such relations may be designated by means of the symbol > which, in general, means "greater than." In reference to particular scales, > may be used to designate *is preferred to, is higher than, is more difficult than,* etc. Its specific meaning depends on the nature of the relation that defines the scale.

Given a group of equivalence classes (i.e., given a nominal scale), if the relation > holds between some but not all pairs of classes, we have a *partially ordered scale*. If the relation > holds for all pairs of classes so that a complete rank ordering of classes is possible, we have an *ordinal scale*.

EXAMPLES. Socioeconomic status, as commonly conceived, constitutes an ordinal scale. In prestige or social acceptability, all members of the upper middle class are higher than (>) all members of the lower middle class. The lower middles, in turn, are higher than the upper lowers. The = relation holds among members of the same class, and the > relation holds between any pair of classes.

The system of grades in the military services is another example of an ordinal scale—sergeant > corporal > private.

Many personality inventories and tests of ability or aptitude result in scores that have the strength of ranks. Although the scores may appear to be more precise than ranks, generally these scales do not meet the requirements of any higher level of measurement and should properly be viewed as ordinal.

A final example of an ordinal scale would be the grades assigned in a course. Letter grades assigned are usually *A*, *B*, *C*, *D*, and *F*. These constitute an ordering of performance: $A > B > C > D > F$. For various reasons, numbers may be assigned to these letter grades; usually, $A = 4$, $B = 3$, $C = 2$, $D = 1$, $F = 0$. These numerical assignments are arbitrary—any other numerical assignment could be made which preserves the intended order (e.g., $A = 10$, $B = 7$, $C = 5$, $D = 3$, $F = 0$).

FORMAL PROPERTIES. Axiomatically, the fundamental difference between a nominal and an ordinal scale is that the ordinal scale incorporates not only the relation of equivalence (=) but also the relation "greater than" (>). The latter relation is irreflexive, asymmetrical, and transitive.[3]

Consider a set of objects, $x_1, x_2, \ldots, x_N$. Suppose the *true* attributes of the objects exist in some relation to each other in addition to their equivalence within categories. That is,

$$A(x_i) = A(x_j) \qquad \text{if } x_i \text{ and } x_j \text{ are in the same class}$$

$$A(x_i) \neq A(x_j) \qquad \text{if } x_i \text{ and } x_j \text{ are in different classes}$$

and $$A(x_i) > A(x_j) \qquad \text{if } x_i \text{ exceeds } x_j \text{ in the "amount" of the attribute it has}$$

Then an *ordinal* scale is a *labeling* system, $L(x)$, of the objects such that

$$L(x_i) = L(x_j) \qquad \text{if and only if } A(x_i) = A(x_j)$$

and $$L(x_i) \neq L(x_j) \qquad \text{if and only if } A(x_i) \neq A(x_j)$$

In addition,

$$L(x_i) > L(x_j) \qquad \text{if and only if } A(x_i) > A(x_j)$$

That is, the labeling function orders the objects in the same way that the attributes are in fact ordered.

ADMISSIBLE OPERATIONS. Since any order-preserving transformation does not change the information contained in an ordinal scale, the scale is said to be "unique up to a monotonic transformation." A monotonic transformation is one which preserves the ordering of objects. That is, it does not matter what numbers we give to a pair of classes or to members of those classes, just as long as we assign a higher number to the members of the class which is "greater" or "more preferred." (Of course, one may use the lower numbers for the "more preferred" classes. Thus we usually refer to excellent performance as "first class," and to progressively in-

---

[3] *Irreflexive*: it is not true for any x that $x > x$. *Asymmetrical*: if $x > y$, then $y \ngtr x$. *Transitive*: if $x > y$ and $y > z$, then $x > z$.

ferior performances as "second class" and "third class." As long as we are consistent, it does not matter whether higher or lower numbers are used to denote "greater" or "more preferred.")

For example, a corporal in the army wears two stripes on his sleeve and a sergeant wears three. These insignia denote that sergeant > corporal, and the > symbol denotes "ranks higher than." This relation would be equally well expressed if the corporal wore four stripes and the sergeant wore seven. That is, a transformation which does not change the order of the classes is completely admissible because *it does not involve any loss of information.* Any or all numbers applied to classes in an ordinal scale may be changed in any fashion which does not alter the ordering (ranking) of the objects. *Any* monotonic transformation may be applied and still preserve the properties of the scale, i.e., preserve the relations among the objects.

The statistic most appropriate for describing the central tendency of scores in an ordinal scale is the median, since, relative to the distribution of scores, the median is not affected by changes of any scores which are above or below it as long as the number of scores above and below remains the same.[4] With ordinal scaling, hypotheses can be tested by using that large group of nonparametric statistical tests which are sometimes called *ranking statistics* or *order statistics.*

In addition to the assumption of independence, the only assumption made by some ranking tests is that the scores we observe are drawn from an underlying continuous distribution. Parametric tests also make this assumption, but, in addition, make specific assumptions about the *form* of the continuous distribution, e.g., that it is normal. An underlying continuous variable is one that may have any value in a certain interval, e.g., any value between 0 and 100. A discrete variable, on the other hand, is one which can take on only a finite (countable) number of values, e.g., 0, 10, 20, . . . , 100. In addition, a continuous variable is one which may take on an infinite (uncountable) number of different values as well as values *between* any two values.

For some statistical techniques which require ordinal measurement, the requirement is that there be a continuum *underlying* the observed scores, while the actual scores we observe may fall into discrete categories. For example, in a classroom test, the actual recorded scores may be either "pass" or "fail" on a particular item. We may well assume that underlying such a dichotomy there is a continuum of possible results. That is, some individuals who were categorized as failing may have been closer to passing than were others who were categorized as failing. Similarly, some passed only minimally, whereas others passed with ease and dispatch. The assumption is that "pass" and "fail" represent a continuum dichotomized into two intervals. For example, actual scores might have been 0, 1, 2, . . . , 100, and what underlies "pass" is any score ≥ 70, and "fail" includes any score < 70.

---

[4] It should be remarked that, if the numerical assignments to the scores are changed, the median will change relative to the change in assignments but will still lay in the middle of the distribution. A similar general statement cannot be made about the mean.

Similarly, in matters of opinion those who are classified as "agree," "ambivalent," and "disagree" may be thought to fall on a continuum reflecting strength of agreement/disagreement. Some who are scored as "agree" actually may not be very concerned with the issue, whereas others may be strongly convinced of their position. Those who "disagree" include those who are only mildly in disagreement as well as die-hard opponents.

Frequently the crudeness of our measuring devices obscures the underlying continuity that may exist. If a variable is truly continuously distributed, then the probability of a tie is zero. However, tied scores frequently occur. Tied scores almost invariably are a reflection of the lack of sensitivity of our measuring instruments, i.e., our instruments' inability to distinguish the small differences which really exist between the observations that consequently are recorded as ties. Therefore, even when ties are observed it is possible that a continuous distribution underlies our gross measures.

3.3.3 The Interval Scale

DEFINITION. When a scale has all the characteristics of an ordinal scale, and when in addition the *distances* or *differences* between any two numbers on the scale have meaning, then measurement considerably stronger than ordinal has been achieved. In such a case measurement has been achieved in the sense of an interval scale. That is, if our mapping of several classes of objects is so precise that we know just how large the intervals (distances) are between all objects on the scale, and these intervals have substantive meaning, then we have achieved interval measurement. An interval scale is characterized by a common and constant unit of measurement which assigns a number to all pairs of objects in the ordered set. In this sort of measurement, the ratio of any two intervals is independent of the unit of measurement and of the zero point. In an interval scale, the zero point and the unit of measurement are arbitrary.

EXAMPLES. We measure temperature on an interval scale. In fact, two different scales—Celsius and Fahrenheit—are commonly used. The unit of measurement and the zero point in measuring temperature are arbitrary; they are different for the two scales. However, both scales contain the same amount and the same kind of information. This is the case because they are linearly related. That is, a reading on one scale can be transformed to the equivalent reading on the other by the linear transformation[5]

$$^\circ F = \tfrac{9}{5}{}^\circ C + 32$$

where $^\circ F$ = number of degrees on Fahrenheit scale
$^\circ C$ = number of degrees on Celsius scale

[5] Mathematically, such transformations are referred to as *affine*; however, in the applied statistical literature linear transformation is the more common referrent.

It can be shown that the ratios of temperature differences (intervals) are independent of the unit of measurement and of the zero point. For instance, "freezing" occurs at 0° on the Celsius scale, and "boiling" occurs at 100°. On the Fahrenheit scale, "freezing" occurs at 32° and "boiling" at 212°. Some other readings of the same temperature on the two scales are:

Celsius	−18	0	10	30	100
Fahrenheit	0	32	50	86	212

Notice that the ratio of the *differences* between temperature readings on one scale is equal to the ratio between the equivalent differences on the other scale. For example, on the Celsius scale the ratio of the differences between 30 and 10, and 10 and 0, is $(30 - 10)/(10 - 0) = 2$. For the comparable readings on the Fahrenheit scale, the ratio is $(86 - 50)/(50 - 32) = 2$. The ratios in both cases happen to be the same, namely 2. In other words, in an interval scale, the ratio of any two intervals is independent of the unit used and the zero point, both of which are arbitrary.

Many behavioral scientists aspire to create interval scales, and on infrequent occasions they succeed. Usually, however, what is taken for success comes because of the untested assumptions the scale maker is willing to make. One frequent assumption is that the variable being scaled is normally distributed in the individuals being tested. Having made this assumption, the scale maker manipulates the units of the scale until the *assumed* normal distribution is recovered from the individuals' scores. This procedure, of course, is only as good as the intuition of the investigator in choosing the distribution to assume.

Another assumption which is often made to create an apparent interval scale is the assumption that the person's answer of "yes" on any one item is exactly equivalent to answering affirmatively on any other item. This assumption is made to satisfy the requirement that an interval scale must have a common and constant unit of measurement. In ability or aptitude scales, the equivalent assumption is that giving the correct answer to any one item is exactly equivalent (in amount of ability shown) to giving the correct answer to any other item.

FORMAL PROPERTIES. Axiomatically, it can be shown that the operations and relations which give rise to the structure of an interval scale are such that the *differences* in the scale are isomorphic to the structure of arithmetic. Numbers may be associated with the positions of the objects on an interval scale such that the operations of arithmetic may be meaningfully performed on the *differences* between these numbers.

In constructing an interval scale, one must not only be able to specify equivalences, as in a nominal scale, and greater-than relations, as in an ordinal scale, but one must also be able to specify the ratio of any two intervals.

Consider a set of objects, $x_1, x_2, \ldots, x_N$. Suppose the *true* attributes of the objects exist in some relation to each other, in addition to their equivalence within categories. That is,

$$A(x_i) = A(x_j) \qquad \text{if } x_i \text{ and } x_j \text{ are in the same class}$$

$$A(x_i) \neq A(x_j) \qquad \text{if } x_i \text{ and } x_j \text{ are in different classes}$$

$$\text{and} \quad A(x_i) > A(x_j) \qquad \text{if } x_i \text{ exceeds } x_j \text{ in the "amount" of the attribute it has}$$

Then an *interval* scale is a *labeling* system $L(x)$ of the objects having the properties of an ordinal scale and, in addition,

$$L(x) = cA(x) + b \qquad c > 0$$

Note that in this case, the difference between the attributes of two objects is proportional to the difference between the labeling assignments:

$$L(x_i) - L(x_j) = c[A(x_i) - A(x_j)]$$

The reader should be able to verify that the ratio of the differences between the true attributes will be equal to the ratio of the differences between the labeling assignments made to the objects.

ADMISSIBLE OPERATIONS. Any change in the numbers associated with the positions of the objects measured in an interval scale must preserve not only the ordering of the objects but also the relative differences between the objects. That is, the interval scale is "unique up to a linear transformation." Thus, as noted above, the information yielded by the scale is not affected if each number is multiplied by a positive constant and then a constant is added to this product, that is, $f(x) = cx + b$. (In the temperature example, $c = \frac{9}{5}$ and $b = 32$.)

We have already noticed that the zero point in an interval scale is arbitrary. This is inherent in the fact that the scale is subject to transformations which consist of adding a constant to the numbers making up the scale.

The interval scale is the first truly "*quantitative*" scale that we have encountered. All of the common parametric statistics (means, standard deviations, product-moment correlations, etc.) are applicable to data in an interval scale. If measurement in the sense of an interval scale has, in fact, been achieved, *and* if all of the assumptions of the parametric statistical model (given in Sec. 3.1) are appropriately met, then the researcher should utilize parametric statistical tests such as the t test or F test. In such a case, nonparametric methods usually would not take advantage of all of the information contained in the research data. It should be noted that an interval scale is necessary but not sufficient for use of a parametric test involving the normal distribution.

3.3.4 The Ratio Scale

DEFINITION. When a scale has all the characteristics of an interval scale and, in addition, has a true zero point as its origin, it is called a *ratio scale*. In a ratio scale, the ratio of any two scale points is independent of the unit of measurement.

EXAMPLE. We measure mass or weight in a ratio scale. The scale of ounces and pounds has a true zero point; so does the scale of grams. The ratio between any two weights is independent of the unit of measurement. For example, if we determine the weights of two different objects not only in pounds but also in grams, we should find that the ratio of the two weights in pounds is identical to the ratio of the two weights in grams.

Although meaningful examples from the social and behavioral sciences are difficult to identify, counterexamples abound. We shall consider two. We noted earlier that grades are measured in an ordinal scale. Consider two students, one of whom receives an A and the other of whom receives a C, and suppose the numerical assignments were 4 and 2, respectively. While the ratio of the two grades is two ($\frac{4}{2} = 2$), it may not make sense to say that the student with the A has twice as much of "something" as the student who received the C. (The student does have twice as many points, but it is not clear whether this has any substantive meaning in knowledge, ability, or perseverance.) Finally, in the case of temperature, consider a change in temperature from 10° to 30°C. We cannot say that the increase represents a threefold increase in heat. To see this, note that the change in temperature is equivalent to a change from 50° to 86°F. Because the ratios of the temperatures on the two scales are clearly different, the ratio does not make interpretable sense.

FORMAL PROPERTIES. The operations and relations which give rise to the numerical values in a ratio scale are such that the scale is isomorphic to the structure of arithmetic. Therefore, the operations of arithmetic are permissible on the numerical values assigned to the objects themselves as well as on the intervals between numbers, as is the case in the interval scale.

Ratio scales, most commonly encountered in the physical sciences, are achieved only when all four of these relations are operationally possible to attain: (1) equivalence, (2) greater than, (3) known ratio between any two intervals, and (4) known ratio of any two scale values.

Consider a set of objects, $x_1, x_2, \ldots, x_N$. Suppose the *true* attributes of the objects exist in some relation to each other, in addition to their equivalence within categories. That is,

$$A(x_i) = A(x_j) \qquad \text{if } x_i \text{ and } x_j \text{ are in the same class}$$

$$A(x_i) \neq A(x_j) \qquad \text{if } x_i \text{ and } x_j \text{ are in different classes}$$

and $$A(x_i) > A(x_j) \qquad \text{if } x_i \text{ exceeds } x_j \text{ in the "amount" of the attribute it has}$$

Then a *ratio* scale is a *labeling* system $L(x)$ of the objects if

$$L(x_i) = cA(x_i) \qquad c > 0$$

Thus,

$$\frac{L(x_i)}{L(x_j)} = \frac{A(x_i)}{A(x_j)}$$

and the ratio of the assigned labels is equal to the ratio of the true attributes.

ADMISSIBLE OPERATIONS. The numbers associated with the ratio scale values are "true" numbers with a true zero; only the unit of measurement is arbitrary. Thus, the ratio scale is unique up to multiplication by a positive constant. That is, the ratios between any two numbers are preserved when the scale values are all multiplied by a positive constant, and, thus, such a transformation does not alter the information contained in the scale.

Any parametric statistical test is usable when ratio measurement has been achieved and the additional assumptions concerning the distribution are met. Moreover, there are some statistics which apply only to data which lie in a ratio scale. Because of the strong assumptions which underlie the scale, most of these are parametric tests.

3.3.5 Summary

Measurement is the process of mapping or assigning numbers to objects or observations. The kind of measurement achieved is a function of the rules under which the numbers are assigned to objects. The operations and relations employed in obtaining the scores define and limit the manipulations and operations which are permissible in handling the scores; the manipulations and operations must be those of the numerical structure to which the particular measurement is isomorphic.

Four of the most general scales were discussed: nominal, ordinal, interval, and ratios scales; Table 3.1 summarizes these scales of measurement. Nominal and ordinal measurement are the most common types achieved in the social and behavioral sciences. Data measured by either nominal or ordinal scales must be analyzed by nonparametric methods. Data measured in interval or ratio scales may be analyzed by parametric methods if the statistical model is valid for the data. Whether parametric tests can be used depends on whether the assumptions of the particular parametric statistical model are tenable. As noted earlier, these assumptions are never met unless we have interval or ratio scale data.

TABLE 3.1
Four levels of measurement

Scale	Defining relations
Nominal	1. Equivalence
Ordinal	1. Equivalence 2. Greater than
Interval	1. Equivalence 2. Greater than 3. Known ratio of any two intervals
Ratio	1. Equivalence 2. Greater than 3. Known ratio of any two intervals 4. Known ratio of any two scale values

At the risk of being excessively repetitious, we wish to emphasize here that some parametric statistical tests which assume the scores have an underlying normal distribution, and which use means and standard deviations (i.e., which require the operations of arithmetic on the original scores), ought not to be used with data that are not in an interval scale. The properties of an ordinal scale are *not* isomorphic to the numerical system known as arithmetic. When only the rank order of scores is known, means and standard deviations found on the scores themselves are *in error* or *misleading* to the extent that the successive intervals (distances between classes) on the scale are not equal and *do not have substantive meaning*. When parametric techniques of statistical inference are used with such data, any decisions about hypotheses are problematic. Probability statements derived from the applications of parametric statistical tests to ordinal data may be in error when the variables do not satisfy the parametric assumptions. Inasmuch as most of the measurements made by behavioral scientists culminate in nominal or ordinal scales, this point deserves strong emphasis.

It should be emphasized that we are talking about the numerical assignments used in our research. It should be obvious that a mean and standard deviation may be computed for any set of numbers. However, statistics computed from these numbers only "make sense" if the original assignment procedure imparted "arithmetical" interpretations to the assignments. This is a subtle and critical point to which we shall return later.

Since this book is addressed to behavioral and social scientists, and since the scales used by them typically are at best no stronger than ordinal, the major portion of this book is devoted to methods which are appropriate for testing hypotheses with data measured in an ordinal scale. These methods, which are based on less circumscribing or restrictive assumptions in their statistical models than parametric tests, make up the bulk of the nonparametric tests.

3.3.6 References

The reader may find other discussions of measurement in Bailey (1971), Hays (1983), Davidson, Siegel, and Suppes (1955), and an especially readable account by Townsend and Ashby (1984).

3.4 PARAMETRIC AND NONPARAMETRIC STATISTICAL TESTS

A parametric statistical test specifies certain conditions about the distribution of responses in the population from which the research sample was drawn. Since these conditions are not ordinarily tested, they are assumed to hold. The meaningfulness of the results of a parametric test depends on the validity of these assumptions. Proper interpretation of parametric tests based on the normal distribution also assumes that the scores being analyzed result from measurement in at least an interval scale.

A nonparametric statistical test is based on a model that specifies only very general conditions and none regarding the specific form of the distribution from which the sample was drawn. Certain assumptions are associated with most nonparametric statistical tests, namely, that the observations are independent, perhaps that the variable under study has underlying continuity, but these assumptions are fewer and weaker than those associated with parametric tests. Moreover, as we shall see, nonparametric procedures often test different hypotheses about the population than do parametric procedures. Finally, unlike parametric tests, there are nonparametric tests that may be applied appropriately to data measured in an ordinal scale, and others to data in a nominal or categorical scale.

In this chapter we have discussed the various criteria which should be considered in the choice of a statistical test for use in making a decision about a research hypothesis. These criteria are (1) the applicability or validity of the test (which includes the level of measurement and the other assumptions of the test) and (2) the power and efficiency of the test. It has been stated that a parametric statistical test is most powerful when all the assumptions of its statistical model are met. However, even when all of the parametric test's assumptions about the population and requirements about strength of measurement are satisfied, we know from the concept of efficiency (either power-efficiency or asymptotic relative efficiency) that we can increase the sample size by an appropriate amount, use a nonparametric test, and yet retain the same power to reject H_0.

Because the power of any test may be increased by simply increasing N, and because behavioral scientists rarely have data satisfying the assumptions of the parametric test which includes achieving the sort of measurement permitting the meaningful interpretation of parametric tests, nonparametric statistical tests play a prominent role in research in the behavioral and social sciences. This book presents a variety of nonparametric tests. The use of parametric tests based upon the normal distribution in research has been presented in a variety of sources[6] and therefore we will not review those tests.

In many of the nonparametric statistical tests to be presented in this book, the data are changed from scores to ranks or even to signs. Such methods may arouse the criticism that they "do not use all of the information in the sample" or that they "throw away information." The answer to this objection is in the answers to these questions:

1. Of the methods available, parametric and nonparametric, which uses the information in the sample appropriately? That is, which test is valid?
2. Have the assumptions underlying a particular statistical model or test been satisfied?
3. Are the hypotheses tested by the statistical model appropriate for the situation?

[6] Among the many sources on parametric statistical tests, these are especially useful: Hays (1983), Bailey (1971), Edwards (1967).

The answer to the first question depends upon the level of measurement achieved in the research and on the researcher's knowledge of the population. If the measurement is weaker than that of an interval scale, by using a parametric test, the researcher would "add information" and, thereby, create distortions which may be as great and as damaging as those introduced by the "throwing away of information" which occurs when scores are converted to ranks. Moreover, assumptions which must be made to justify the use of parametric tests usually rest on conjecture and hope, for knowledge about the population parameters almost invariably is lacking. Finally, for some population distributions a nonparametric statistical test is clearly superior in power to a parametric one.

The answer to the second and third questions can be given only by the investigator as he or she considers the substantive aspects of the research problem and examines the data.

The relevance of the discussion of this chapter to the choice between parametric and nonparametric statistical tests may be sharpened by the summaries in Secs. 3.4.1 and 3.4.2, which list the advantages and disadvantages of nonparametric statistical tests.

3.4.1 Advantages of Nonparametric Statistical Tests

1. If the sample size is very small, there may be no alternative to using a nonparametric statistical test unless the nature of the population distribution is *known exactly.*
2. Nonparametric tests typically make fewer assumptions about the data and may be more relevant to a particular situation. In addition, the hypothesis tested by the nonparametric test may be more appropriate for the research investigation.
3. Nonparametric statistical tests are available to analyze data which are inherently in ranks as well as data whose seemingly numerical scores have the strength of ranks. That is, the researcher may only be able to say of his or her subjects that one has more or less of the characteristic than another, without being able to say *how much* more or less. For example, in studying such a variable such as anxiety, we may be able to state that subject *A* is more anxious than subject *B* without knowing at all exactly how much more anxious *A* is. If data are inherently in ranks, or even if they can be categorized only as plus or minus (more or less, better or worse), they can be treated by nonparametric methods, whereas they cannot be treated by parametric methods unless precarious and, perhaps, unrealistic assumptions are made about the underlying distributions.
4. Nonparametric methods are available to treat data which are simply classificatory or categorical, i.e., are measured in a nominal scale. No parametric technique applies to such data.
5. There are suitable nonparametric statistical tests for treating samples made up of observations from several *different* populations. Parametric tests often can-

not handle such data without requiring us to make seemingly unrealistic assumptions or requiring cumbersome computations.

6. Nonparametric statistical tests typically are much easier to learn and to apply than are parametric tests. In addition, their interpretation often is more direct than the interpretation of parametric tests.

3.4.2 Presumed Disadvantages of Nonparametric Statistical Tests

If all of the assumptions of a parametric statistical model are, in fact, met in the data and the research hypothesis could be tested with a parametric test, then nonparametric statistical tests are wasteful. The degree of wastefulness is expressed by the power-efficiency of the nonparametric test. (It will be remembered that, if a nonparametric statistical test has power-efficiency of, say, 90 percent, this means that *when all the conditions of the parametric statistical test are satisfied* the appropriate parametric test would be just as effective with a sample which is 10 percent smaller than that used in the nonparametric analysis.)

Another objection to nonparametric statistical tests is that they are not *systematic*, whereas parametric statistical tests have been systematized, and different tests are simply variations on a central theme. Although this is partly true, it does not seem to us that the value of systematic approaches justifies the cost. Moreover, careful examination of nonparametric tests does reveal common themes—the tests for categorical data *are* systematic, as are many of the tests applied to ordered data. The differences are on the surface, i.e., the computational formulas sometimes obscure the underlying relations between tests.

Another objection to nonparametric statistical tests has to do with convenience. Tables necessary to implement nonparametric tests are scattered widely and appear in different formats. (The same is true of many parametric tests.) In this book we have tried to draw together many of the tables needed to test conveniently hypotheses by using nonparametric statistical tests and to present them in a systematic format.

In this book we have attempted to present most of the nonparametric techniques of statistical inference and measures of association that the behavioral and social scientist is likely to need, and provide the tables necessary to apply these techniques. Although this text is not exhaustive in its coverage of nonparametric tests—it could not be without being excessively redundant and extremely bulky—enough tests are included in the following chapters to give behavioral scientists wide latitude in choosing a nonparametric technique appropriate to their research designs and useful for testing their research hypotheses.

CHAPTER 4

THE SINGLE-SAMPLE CASE

In this chapter we present several nonparametric statistical tests which may be used to test a hypothesis which calls for drawing just one sample. The tests tell us whether the particular sample could have come from some specified population. These tests are in contrast to two-sample tests, which compare two samples and test whether it is likely that the two came from the same population. The two-sample test may be more familiar to some readers.

The one-sample test is often a goodness-of-fit test. In the typical case, we draw a random sample from some population and then test the hypothesis that the sample was drawn from a population with a specified distribution or specified characteristics. The one-sample tests can answer questions like these:

1. Is there a significant difference in location (central tendency) between the sample and the population?
2. Is there a significant difference between the observed frequencies and the frequencies we would expect on the basis of some theory?
3. Is there a significant difference between observed and expected proportions in a series of dichotomous observations?
4. Is it reasonable to believe that the sample was drawn from a population with a specified shape or form (e.g., normal or uniform)?

5. Is it reasonable to believe that the sample was a random sample from some known population?
6. In a series of observations, is there a change in the underlying theoretical model which is assumed to generate the data?

In the one-sample case a common parametric technique is to apply a *t* test to the difference between the observed (sample) mean and the expected (population) mean. The *t* test, strictly speaking, assumes that the observations or scores in the sample have come from a normally distributed population. Proper interpretation of the *t* test assumes that the variables are measured on at least an interval scale.

There are many sorts of data for which the *t* test may be inappropriate. The experimenter may find that:

1. The assumptions and requirements for proper interpretation of the *t* test are unrealistic for the data.
2. It is preferable to avoid making the assumptions of the *t* test and thus gain greater generality for the conclusions.
3. The data are inherently in ranks (i.e., ordinal) and, therefore, standard parametric tests may be inappropriate.
4. The data may be categorical or classificatory.
5. There is no useful parametric test for the particular hypothesis to be tested.

In such instances the experimenter may choose one of the one-sample nonparametric statistical tests presented in this chapter.

Several tests for the one-sample case will be presented in this chapter. The next chapter contains additional one-sample tests based upon multiple or repeated observations. The chapter concludes with a comparison and contrast of the tests, which should aid the researcher in selecting the test best suited to a particular hypothesis.

4.1 THE BINOMIAL TEST

4.1.1 Function and Rationale

There are many populations which are conceived as consisting of only two classes. Examples of such classes are: male and female, literate and illiterate, member and nonmember, married and single, institutionalized and ambulatory. For such cases, all of the possible observations from the population will fall into one of two discrete categories. Such a population is usually called a *binary population* or a dichotomous population.

Suppose a population consists of only two categories or classes. Then each observation (X) sampled from the population may take on one of two values, depending on the category sampled. We could denote the possible values of the random variable by using any pair of values, but it is most convenient to denote each outcome as either 1 or 0. We shall assume further that the probability of sampling an object from the first category is p, and the probability of sampling an object from the other category is $q = 1 - p$. That is,

$$P[X = 1] = p \qquad \text{and} \qquad P[X = 0] = 1 - p = q$$

It is also assumed that each probability is constant regardless of the number of objects sampled or observed.

Although the value of p may vary from population to population, it is fixed for any one population. However, even if we know (or assume) the value of p for some population, we cannot expect that a random sample of observations from the population will contain exactly the proportions p and $1 - p$ for each of the two categories. Random sampling will usually prevent the sample from duplicating precisely the population values of p and q. For example, we may know from the official records that the voters in a certain county are evenly split between the Republican and Democratic parties in registration. But a random sample of the registered voters in that county might contain 47 percent Democrats and 53 percent Republicans, or even 56 percent Democrats and 44 percent Republicans. Such differences between the observed and the population values arise because of "chance" or random fluctuations in the observations. We should not be surprised by small deviations from the population values; however, large deviations—although possible—are unlikely.

The *binomial distribution* is used to determine the probabilities of the possible outcomes we might observe if we sampled from a binomial population. If our hypothesis is H_0: $p = p_0$, we can calculate the probabilities of the various outcomes when we assume that H_0 is true. The test will tell us whether it is reasonable to believe that the proportions (or frequencies) of the two categories in our sample could have been drawn from a population with the hypothesized values of p_0 and $1 - p_0$. For convenience in discussing the binomial distribution, we shall denote the outcome $X = 1$ as "success" and the outcome $X = 0$ as "failure." In addition, in a series of N observations,

$$Y = \sum_{i=1}^{N} X_i$$

is the number of "successes" or the number of outcomes of the type $X = 1$.

4.1.2 Method

In a sample of size N, the probability of obtaining k objects in one category and $N - k$ objects in the other category is given by

$$P[Y = k] = \binom{N}{k} p^k q^{N-k} \qquad k = 0, 1, \ldots, N \tag{4.1}$$

where p = the proportion of observations expected where $X = 1$
q = the proportion of observations expected where $X = 0$

and $$\binom{N}{k} = \frac{N!}{k!(N-k)!}$$ (see Footnote 1)

Appendix Table E has values of $P[Y = k]$ for various values of N and p.

A simple illustration will clarify Eq. (4.1). Suppose a fair die is rolled five times. What is the probability that exactly two of the rolls will show "six"? In this case, Y is the random variable (the outcome of five tosses of the die), $N =$ the number of rolls (5), $k =$ the observed number of sixes (2), $p =$ the expected proportion of sixes ($\frac{1}{6}$), and $q = \frac{5}{6}$. The probability that exactly two of the five rolls will show six is given by Eq. (4.1):

$$P[Y = k] = \binom{N}{k} p^k (1-p)^{N-k}$$

$$P[Y = 2] = \frac{5!}{2!3!}\left(\frac{1}{6}\right)^2\left(\frac{5}{6}\right)^3 = .16$$

The application of the formula to the problem shows us that the probability of obtaining exactly two "sixes" when rolling a fair die five times is $p = .16$.

Now when we test hypotheses, the question is usually *not*, "What is the probability of obtaining *exactly* the values which were observed?" Rather, we usually ask, "What is the probability of obtaining values *as extreme or more extreme than* the observed value when we assume the data are generated by a particular process?" To answer questions of this type, the probability desired is

$$P[Y \geq k] = \sum_{i=k}^{N} \binom{N}{i} p^i q^{N-i} \tag{4.2}$$

In other words, we sum the probability of the observed outcome with the probabilities of outcomes which are even more extreme.

Suppose now that we want to know the probability of obtaining two *or fewer* sixes when a fair die is rolled five times. Here again $N = 5$, $k = 2$, $p = \frac{1}{6}$, and $q = \frac{5}{6}$. Now the probability of obtaining 2 or fewer sixes is denoted $P[Y \leq 2]$. From Eq. (4.1) the probability of obtaining 0 sixes is $P[Y = 0]$, the probability of obtaining one six is $P[Y = 1]$, etc. Using Eq. (4.2) we have

$$P[Y \leq 2] = P[Y = 0] + P[Y = 1] + P[Y = 2]$$

---

[1] $N!$ is "N *factorial*," which is defined as

$$N! = N(N-1)(N-2)\cdots(2)(1).$$

For example, $4! = (4)(3)(2)(1) = 24$ and $5! = 120$. By definition, $0! = 1$. Appendix Table W gives factorials for values of N through 20. Appendix Table X gives binomial coefficients

$$\binom{N}{x} = \frac{N!}{x!(N-x)!}$$

for values of N through 20.

That is, the probability of obtaining two or fewer sixes is the sum of three probabilities. If we use Eq. (4.1) to determine the three probabilities, we have

$$P[Y = 0] = \frac{5!}{0!5!}\left(\frac{1}{6}\right)^0\left(\frac{5}{6}\right)^5 = .40$$

$$P[Y = 1] = \frac{5!}{1!4!}\left(\frac{1}{6}\right)^1\left(\frac{5}{6}\right)^4 = .40$$

$$P[Y = 2] = \frac{5!}{2!3!}\left(\frac{1}{6}\right)^2\left(\frac{5}{6}\right)^3 = .16$$

and thus

$$\begin{aligned} P[Y \leq 2] &= P[Y = 0] + P[Y = 1] + P[Y = 2] \\ &= .40 + .40 + .16 \\ &= .96 \end{aligned}$$

We have determined that the probability under H_0 (the assumption of a fair die) of obtaining two or fewer sixes when a die is rolled five times is $p = .96$.

SMALL SAMPLES. In the one-sample case, when binary categories are used, a common hypothesis is H_0: $p = \frac{1}{2}$. Table D of the Appendix gives the one-tailed probabilities associated with the occurrence of various values as extreme as k under the null hypothesis H_0: $p = \frac{1}{2}$. When referring to Appendix Table D, let k equal the smaller of the observed frequencies. This table is useful when $N \leq 35$. Although Eq. (4.2) could be used, the table is more convenient. Table D gives the probabilities associated with the occurrence of various values as small as k for various N's. For example, suppose we observe seven successes and three failures. Here $N = 10$ and $k = 7$. Table D shows that the one-tailed probability of occurrence under H_0: $p = \frac{1}{2}$ for $Y \leq 3$ when $N = 10$ to be .172. Because of the symmetry of the binomial distribution when $p = \frac{1}{2}$, $P[Y \geq k] = P[Y \leq N - k]$. Thus, in this example, $P[Y \leq 3] = P[Y \geq 7] = .172$.

The probabilities given in Table D are one-tailed. A one-tailed test is used when we have predicted in advance which of the two categories should contain the smaller number of cases. When the prediction is simply that the two frequencies will differ, a two-tailed test would be used. For a two-tailed test, the probability values in Appendix Table D would be doubled. Thus for $N = 10$ and $k = 7$, the two-tailed probability associated with the occurrence under H_0 is .344.

The following example illustrates the use of the binomial test in a study in which H_0: $p = \frac{1}{2}$.

Example 4.1. In a study of the effects of stress,[2] an experimenter taught 18 college students 2 different methods of tying the same knot. Half of the subjects (randomly selected from

[2] Barthol, R. P., and Ku, N. D. (1953). Specific regression under a non-related stress situation. *American Psychologist*, **10**, 482.

TABLE 4.1
Knot-tying method chosen under stress

	Method chosen		
	First-learned	**Second-learned**	**Total**
Frequency	16	2	18

the group of 18) learned method A first, and half learned method B first. Later—at midnight, after a 4-hour final examination—each subject was asked to tie the knot. The prediction was that stress would induce regression, i.e., that the subjects would revert to the first-learned method of tying the knot. Each subject was categorized according to whether the subject used the knot-tying method learned first or the one learned second when asked to tie the knot under stress.

i. Null hypothesis. H_0: $p = q = \frac{1}{2}$, that is, there is no difference between the probability of using the first-learned method under stress (p) and the probability of using the second-learned method under stress (q). Any difference between the frequencies which may be observed is of such magnitude that it might be expected in a sample from the population of possible results under H_0. H_1: $p > q$, that is, when under stress, the probability of using the first-learned method is greater than the probability of using the second-learned method.

ii. Statistical test. The binomial test is chosen because the data are in two discrete categories and the design is of the one-sample type. Since methods A and B were randomly assigned to being first-learned and second-learned, there is no reason to think that the first-learned method would be preferred to the second-learned under H_0, and thus $p = q = \frac{1}{2}$.

iii. Significance level. Let $\alpha = .01$ and N is the number of cases $= 18$.

iv. Sampling distribution. The sampling distribution is given in Eq. (4.2) above. However, when $N \leq 35$, and when $p = q = \frac{1}{2}$, Table D gives the probabilities associated with the occurrence under H_0 of observed value as small as k, and thus it is not necessary to calculate the sampling distribution directly in this example.

v. Rejection region. The region of rejection consists of all values of Y (where Y is the number of subjects who used the second-learned method under stress), which are so small that the probability associated with their occurrence under H_0 is equal to or less than $\alpha = .01$. Since the direction of the difference was predicted in advance, the region of rejection is one-tailed.

vi. Decision. In the experiment, all but two of the subjects used the first-learned method when asked to tie the knot under stress (late at night after a long, final examination). These data are shown in Table 4.1. In this case, N is the number of independent observations $= 18$. k is the smaller frequency $= 2$. Appendix Table D shows that for $N = 18$, the probability associated with $k \leq 2$ is .001. Inasmuch as this probability is smaller than $\alpha = .01$, the decision is to reject H_0 in favor of H_1. Thus we conclude that $p > q$, that is, that people under stress revert to the first-learned of two methods.

LARGE SAMPLES. Appendix Table D cannot be used when N is larger than 35. However, it can be shown that, as N increases, the binomial distribution tends toward the normal distribution. More precisely, as N increases, the distribution of the variable Y approaches a normal distribution. The tendency is rapid when p is close to $\frac{1}{2}$, but is slower when p is close to 0 or 1. That is, the greater the disparity between p and q, the larger must be N before the approximation is usefully close to the normal distribution. When p is near $\frac{1}{2}$, the approximation may be used for a statistical test when $N > 25$. When p is near 0 or 1, a rule of thumb is that Npq should be greater than 9 before the statistical test based on the normal approximation is sufficiently accurate to use. Within these limitations, the sampling distribution of Y is approximately normal, with mean Np and variance Npq, and, therefore, H_0 may be tested by

$$z = \frac{x - \mu_x}{\sigma_x} = \frac{Y - Np}{\sqrt{Npq}} \tag{4.3}$$

where z is approximately normally distributed with mean 0 and standard deviation 1.

The approximation to the normal distribution becomes better if a correction for "continuity" is used. The correction is necessary because the normal distribution is continuous while the binomial distribution involves discrete variables. To correct for continuity, we regard the observed frequency Y of Eq. (4.3) as occupying an interval, the lower limit of which is one-half unit below the observed frequency while the upper limit is one-half unit above the observed frequency. The correction for continuity consists of reducing, by .5, the difference between the observed value of Y and its expected value $\mu_Y = Np$. Therefore, when $Y < \mu_Y$ we add .5 to Y, and when $Y > \mu_Y$ we subtract .5 from Y. That is, the observed difference is reduced by .5. Thus z becomes

$$z = \frac{(Y \pm .5) - Np}{\sqrt{Npq}} \tag{4.4}$$

where $Y + .5$ is used when $Y < Np$, and $Y - .5$ is used when $Y > Np$. The value of z obtained by the application of Eq. (4.4) is asymptotically normally distributed with mean 0 and variance 1. Therefore, the significance of an obtained z may be determined by reference to Table A of the Appendix. Table A gives the one-tailed probability associated with the occurrence under H_0 of values as extreme as an observed z. (If a two-tailed test is required, the probability yielded by Appendix Table A must be doubled.)

To show how good this approximation is when $p = \frac{1}{2}$ even for $N < 25$, we can apply it to the knot-tying data discussed earlier. In that case, $N = 18$, $Y = 2$, and $p = q = \frac{1}{2}$. For these data, $Y < Np$, that is, $2 < 9$, and by Eq. (4.4),

$$\begin{aligned} z &= \frac{(2 + .5) - (18)(1/2)}{\sqrt{(18)(1/2)(1/2)}} \\ &= -3.06 \end{aligned}$$

Appendix Table A shows that a value of z as extreme as -3.06 has a one-tailed probability associated with its occurrence under H_0 of .0011. This is essentially the same probability we found by the other analysis, which used a table of exact probabilities. However, remember that in this example $p = \frac{1}{2}$, so the approximation should do well.

4.1.3 Summary of Procedure

In brief, these are the steps in the use of the binomial test of H_0: $p = \frac{1}{2}$:

1. Determine N = the total number of cases observed.
2. Determine the frequencies of the observed occurrences in each of the two categories.
3. The method of finding the probability of occurrence under H_0 of the observed values, or values even more extreme, depends upon the sample size:
   (*a*) If $N \leq 35$, Appendix Table D gives the one-tailed probabilities under H_0 of various values as small as an observed Y. Specify H_1, and determine whether the test should be one-tailed or two-tailed.
   (*b*) If $N > 35$, test H_0 by using Eq. (4.4). Appendix Table A gives the probability associated with the occurrence under H_0 of values as large as an observed z. Table A gives one-tailed probabilities; for a two-tailed test, double the obtained probability.
4. If the probability associated with the observed value of Y or an even more extreme value is equal to or less than α, reject H_0. Otherwise, do not reject H_0.

4.1.4 Power-Efficiency

Since there is no parametric technique applicable to data measured as a dichotomous variable, it is not meaningful to inquire about the power-efficiency of the binomial test when used with such data.

If a continuous variable is dichotomized and the binomial test is used on the resulting data, the test may be wasteful of data. In such cases, the binomial test has power-efficiency (in the sense as defined in Chap. 3) of 95 percent for $N = 6$, decreasing to an asymptotic efficiency of $2/\pi = 63$ percent as N increases. However, if the data are basically dichotomous, even though the variable has an underlying continuous distribution, the binomial test may have no more powerful and practicable alternative.

4.1.5 References

For other discussions of binomial distribution and its applications, see Hays (1981) or Bailey (1971).

4.2 THE CHI-SQUARE GOODNESS-OF-FIT TEST

4.2.1 Function and Rationale

Frequently research is undertaken in which the researcher is interested in the number of subjects, objects, or responses which fall into various categories. For example, a group of patients may be classified according to their preponderant type of Rorschach response, and the investigator may predict that certain types will be more frequent than others. Or children may be categorized according to their most frequent modes of play, the hypothesis being that these modes will differ in frequency in a prescribed way. Or persons may be categorized according to whether they are "in favor of," "indifferent to," or "opposed to" an opinion to enable the researcher to test the hypothesis that these responses will differ in frequency.

The chi-square test is suitable for analyzing data like these. The number of categories may be two or more. The technique is of the goodness-of-fit type in that it may be used to test whether a significant difference exists between an *observed* number of objects or responses falling in each category and an *expected* number based upon the null hypothesis. That is, the chi-square test assesses the degree of correspondence between the observed and expected observations in each category.

4.2.2 Method

To compare an observed with an expected group of frequencies, we must be able to state what frequencies would be expected. The hypothesis H_0 states the proportion of objects falling in each of the categories in the presumed population. That is, from the null hypothesis we may deduce what are the expected frequencies. The chi-square technique gives the probability that the observed frequencies could have been sampled from a population with the given expected values.

The null hypothesis H_0 may be tested by using the following statistic:

$$X^2 = \sum_{i=1}^{k} \frac{(O_i - E_i)^2}{E_i} \tag{4.5}$$

where O_i = the observed number of cases in the ith category
E_i = the expected number of cases in the ith category when H_0 is true
k = the number of categories

Thus Eq. (4.5) directs one to sum over k categories the squared differences between each observed and expected frequency divided by the corresponding expected frequency.

If the agreement between the observed and expected frequencies is close, the differences $(O_i - E_i)$ will be small and, consequently, X^2 will be small. However, if the divergence is large, the value of X^2 as computed from Eq. (4.5) also will be large. Roughly speaking, the larger the value of X^2, the less likely it is that the observed frequencies came from the population on which the hypothesis H_0 and the expected frequencies are based.

Although Eq. (4.5) is useful for understanding the X^2 statistic, it is often cumbersome to compute because of the number of subtractions involved. After some manipulation, a somewhat more convenient computing formula can be found:

$$X^2 = \sum_{i=1}^{k} \frac{(O_i - E_i)^2}{E_i} \tag{4.5}$$

$$= \sum_{i=1}^{k} \frac{O_i^2}{E_i} - N \tag{4.5a}$$

where N is the total number of observations.

It can be shown that the sampling distribution of X^2 under H_0, as computed from Eq. (4.5), follows the chi-square distribution[3] with degrees of freedom $df = k - 1$. The notion of degrees of freedom is discussed in more detail below. Appendix Table C contains the sampling distribution of chi square, and gives the probability associated with certain values. At the top of each column in Appendix Table C are selected probabilities of occurrence of values of chi square when H_0 is true. The values in any column are the values of chi square which have the associated probability of occurrence under H_0 given at the top of that column. There is a different value of chi square for each df. For example, when $df = 1$ and H_0 is true, the probability of observing a value of chi square as large as 3.84 (or larger) is .05. That is, $P[\chi^2 \geq 3.84] = .05$.

There are a number of different sampling distributions for chi square, one for each value of df, the degrees of freedom. The size of df reflects the number of "observations" which are free to vary after certain restrictions have been placed on the data. For example, if the data for 50 cases are classified into two categories, then as soon as we know that, say, 35 cases fall into one category, we also know that 15 must fall into the other. For this example, $df = 1$, because with two categories and any fixed value of N, as soon as the number of cases in one category is ascertained, then the number of cases in the other category is determined.

In general, for the one-sample goodness-of-fit test, when H_0 fully specifies the E_i's, $df = k - 1$, where k is the number of categories in the classification.

To use chi square in testing an hypothesis in the one-sample goodness-of-fit situation, cast each observation into one of k cells. The total number of such observations should be N, the number of cases in the sample. That is, each observation must be independent of every other; thus one may not make several observations on the same person and count each as independent. To do so produces an "inflated" N. For each of the k cells, the expected frequency must also be entered. If H_0 is that there is an equal proportion of cases in each category in the population, then $E_i = N/k$. With the various values of E_i and O_i known, one may compute the value of X^2 by the application of Eq. (4.5). The significance of this

[3] Some texts use the greek symbol χ^2 to designate both the chi-square distribution and the X^2 statistic. However, there is a difference. The X^2 statistic *asymptotically* has a chi-square or χ^2 distribution. We shall maintain a distinction between the statistic and its sampling distribution.

obtained value of X^2 may be determined by reference to Appendix Table C. If the probability associated with the occurrence under H_0 of the obtained X^2 for $df = k - 1$ is equal to or less than the previously determined value of α, then H_0 may be rejected. If not, H_0 cannot be rejected.

Example 4.2a Horse-racing fans often maintain that in a race around a circular track significant advantages accrue to the horses in certain post positions. Any horse's post position is its assigned post in the starting lineup. Position 1 is closest to the rail on the inside of the track; position 8 is on the outside, farthest from the rail in an eight-horse race. We may test the effect of post position by analyzing the race results, given according to post position, for the first month of racing in the season at a particular circular track.[4]

i. Null hypothesis. H_0: there is no difference in the expected number of winners starting from each of the post positions, and any observed differences are merely chance variations to be expected in a random sample from a uniform distribution. H_1: the theoretical frequencies are not all equal.

ii. Statistical test. Since we are comparing the data from one sample with some presumed population, the chi-square goodness-of-fit test is appropriate. The chi-square test is chosen because the hypothesis under test concerns a comparison of observed and expected frequencies in discrete categories. In this example the eight post positions comprise the categories.

iii. Significance level. Let $\alpha = .01$ and $N = 144$, the total number of winners in 18 days of racing.

iv. Sampling distribution. The sampling distribution of the statistic X^2 as computed from Eq. (4.5) follows the chi-square distribution with $df = k - 1 = 8 - 1 = 7$.

v. Rejection region. H_0 will be rejected if the observed value of X^2 is such that the probability associated with the computed value under H_0 for $df = 7$ is $\leq .01$.

vi. Decision. The sample of 144 winners yielded the data shown in Table 4.2. The observed frequencies of wins are given in the center of each cell; the expected frequencies are given in italics in the corner of each cell. For example, 29 wins accrued to horses in position 1, whereas under H_0 only 18 wins would have been expected. Only 11 wins accrued to horses in position 8, whereas under H_0 18 would have been expected.

TABLE 4.2
Wins accrued on a circular track by horses from eight post positions

	Post positions								
	1	**2**	**3**	**4**	**5**	**6**	**7**	**8**	**Total**
No. of wins	29	19	18	25	17	10	15	11	144
Expected	*18*	*18*	*18*	*18*	*18*	*18*	*18*	*18*	

[4] These data were published in the *New York Post*, August 30, 1955, p. 42.

The computation of X^2 is straightforward:

$$X^2 = \sum_{i=1}^{8} \frac{(O_i - E_i)^2}{E_i}$$

$$= \frac{(29-18)^2}{18} + \frac{(19-18)^2}{18} + \frac{(18-18)^2}{18}$$

$$+ \frac{(25-18)^2}{18} + \frac{(17-18)^2}{18} + \frac{(10-18)^2}{18}$$

$$+ \frac{(15-18)^2}{18} + \frac{(11-18)^2}{18}$$

$$= \frac{121}{18} + \frac{1}{18} + 0 + \frac{49}{18} + \frac{1}{18} + \frac{64}{18} + \frac{9}{18} + \frac{49}{18}$$

$$= 16.3$$

Appendix Table C shows that $P[X^2 \geq 16.3]$ for $df = 7$ has probability of occurrence between $p = .05$ and $p = .02$. That is, $.05 > p > .02$. Inasmuch as that probability is larger than the previously set level of significance, $\alpha = .01$, we cannot reject H_0 at that significance level. We notice that the null hypothesis could have been rejected had we set $\alpha = .05$. It would seem that more data are necessary before any definite conclusions concerning H_1 can be made.

Example 4.2b A researcher gave a vocabulary test to a group of $N = 103$ children. On the basis of previous research and the theory underlying the test, the distribution of scores should follow a normal distribution. The sample mean was 108 and the standard deviation 12.8. In order to apply the one-sample chi-square goodness-of-fit test, categories must be defined and expected frequencies determined. We shall choose $k = 10$ intervals for the frequencies. The cutoff values (denoted X_{cut}) will correspond to the deciles of the normal distribution with mean and standard deviation as given by the data. The deciles of the unit normal distribution (denoted z_{cut}) can be obtained from Appendix Table A:

Category	z_{cut}	Cumulative p	X_{cut}
1	−1.2816	.10	91.60
2	−.8416	.20	97.23
3	−.5244	.30	101.29
4	−.2534	.40	104.76
5	0.0000	.50	108.00
6	.2534	.60	111.24
7	.5244	.70	114.71
8	.8418	.80	118.77
9	1.2816	.90	124.40
10	∞	1.00	No limit

These values must then be transformed to the cut points in the observed distribution. This may be done with the following general formula:

$$X_{\text{cut}} = \bar{X} + s_x z_{\text{cut}} \qquad \text{in general}$$

and

$$X_{\text{cut}} = 108 + 12.8 z_{\text{cut}} \qquad \text{for this example}$$

For the given problem, these values are summarized in the above table. Thus, if an observed datum is less than 91.60, it would be counted in category 1, whereas if the observed datum were 103, it would be counted in category 4. The researcher classified all scores into categories and obtained the following frequencies: 8, 10, 13, 15, 10, 14, 12, 8, 7, 6. The expected frequency in each category is $N/k = \frac{103}{10} - 10.3$. The investigator wishes to test the hypothesis by using $\alpha = .05$. The obtained value of X^2 is

$$\begin{aligned} X^2 &= \frac{(8 - 10.3)^2}{10.3} + \frac{(10 - 10.3)^2}{10.3} + \frac{(13 - 10.3)^2}{10.3} \\ &\quad + \frac{(15 - 10.3)^2}{10.3} + \frac{(10 - 10.3)^2}{10.3} + \frac{(14 - 10.3)^2}{10.3} \\ &\quad + \frac{(12 - 10.3)^2}{10.3} + \frac{(8 - 10.3)^2}{10.3} + \frac{(7 - 10.3)^2}{10.3} + \frac{(6 - 10.3)^2}{10.3} \\ &= 8.36 \end{aligned}$$

In calculating the expected values, we used two pieces of information from the sample. This was because we cannot specify probabilities associated with a normal distribution without estimating the population mean and standard deviation (or variance) using the sample data. For each parameter estimated from the data we "use up" a degree of freedom. For this example, the number of parameters estimated was $n_p = 2$. Thus, the df for the chi square distribution is $df = k - n_p - 1 = 10 - 2 - 1 = 7$. Now in testing H_0 at the .05 level, the critical value of X^2 is 14.07. Since the obtained value of X^2 was 8.36, we cannot reject the hypothesis H_0 that the data were sampled from a normal distribution.

SMALL EXPECTED FREQUENCIES. When $df = 1$, that is, where $k = 2$, each *expected* frequency should be at least 5. When $df > 1$, that is, when $k > 2$, the chi-square test for the one-sample goodness-of-fit test should not be used if more than 20 percent of the expected frequencies are less than 5 or when any expected frequency is less than 1. This is because the sampling distribution of X^2 is only asymptotically chi-square, i.e., the sampling distribution of X^2 is the same as the chi-square distribution as the expected frequencies become large (infinite). For practical purposes, the approximation is good when the expected frequencies are greater than 5. When the expected frequencies are small, the probabilities associated with the chi-square distribution may not be sufficiently close to the probabilities in the sampling distribution of X^2 for appropriate inferences to be made. Expected frequencies sometimes can be increased by combining adjacent categories into a single pooled category. This is desirable only if combinations of categories can meaningfully be made (and, of course, if there are more than two categories to begin with).

For example, a sample of people may be categorized according to whether their response to a statement of opinion is "strongly support," "support," "indifferent," "oppose," or "strongly oppose." To increase E_i's, adjacent categories could be combined, and the people categorized as "support," "indifferent," or "oppose," or possibly as "support," "indifferent," and "strongly oppose." However, if categories are combined, it should be noted that the meanings of the labels attached to the remaining categories may be different from the original meanings.

If one starts with but two categories and has an expected frequency of less than 5, or if after combining adjacent categories one ends up with only two categories and still has an expected frequency of less than 5, then the binomial test (Sec. 4.1) could be used rather than the chi-square test to determine the probability associated with the occurrence of the observed frequencies under H_0.

4.2.3 Summary of Procedure

In this discussion of the method for using the chi-square test in the one-sample goodness-of-fit case, we have shown that the procedure for using the test involves these steps:

1. Cast the observed frequencies into the k categories. The sum of the frequencies should be N, the number of independent observations.
2. From H_0, determine the expected frequencies (the E_i's) for each of the k cells. When $k > 2$, and more than 20 percent of the E_i's are less than 5, combine adjacent categories where this is reasonable, thereby reducing the value of k and increasing the values of some of the E_i's. Where $k = 2$, the chi-square test for the one-sample goodness-of-fit test is accurate only if each expected frequency is 5 or larger.
3. Use Eq. (4.5) to compute the value of X^2.
4. Determine the degrees of freedom, $df = k - n_p - 1$, where n_p is the number of parameters estimated from the data and used in calculating the expected frequencies.
5. By reference to Appendix Table C, determine the probability associated with the occurrence of X^2 under H_0 of a value as large as the observed value of X^2 for the degrees of freedom df appropriate for the data. If that probability is less than or equal to α, reject H_0.

4.2.4 Power

Inasmuch as this test is most commonly used when we do not have a clear alternative available, we are not usually in a position to compute the exact power of the test. When nominal or categorical measurement is used or when the data consist of frequencies in inherently discrete categories, then the notion of power-efficiency is not meaningful, for in such cases there is no parametric test that is suitable.

In cases where the power of the chi-square goodness-of-fit test has been studied, there is an interaction between the number of categories k and the number of observations N. Although specific recommendations depend upon the theoretical distribution to be fit, the following rules of thumb are appropriate:

1. Choose interval boundaries and categories so that expected frequencies are equal to N/k.
2. The number of categories should be chosen so that the expected frequencies are between about 6 and 10, with the lower value appropriate for large N (greater than about 200).

It also should be noted that when $df > 1$, the chi-square test is insensitive to the effects of ordering of categories, and, thus, when an hypothesis takes order into account, the chi-square test may not be the best test. For methods that strengthen the common chi-square tests when H_0 is tested against specific alternatives, see Cochran (1954) or Everitt (1977). More information concerning the chi-square goodness-of-fit test is given in Sec. 4.3.4.

4.2.5 References

Useful discussions of the chi-square goodness-of-fit test are contained in Cochran (1954), Dixon and Massey (1983), McNemar (1969), and Everitt (1977).

4.3 THE KOLMOGOROV-SMIRNOV ONE-SAMPLE TEST

4.3.1 Function and Rationale

The Kolmogorov-Smirnov one-sample test is another test of goodness-of-fit. That is, it is concerned with the degree of agreement between the distribution of a set of sample values (observed scores) and some specified theoretical distribution. It determines whether the scores in a sample can reasonably be thought to have come from a population having the theoretical distribution.

Briefly, the test involves specifying the *cumulative* frequency distribution which would occur given the theoretical distribution and comparing that with the observed cumulative frequency distribution. The theoretical distribution represents what would be expected under H_0. The point at which these two distributions, theoretical and observed, show the greatest divergence is determined. Reference to the sampling distribution indicates whether such a large divergence is likely to occur on the basis of chance. That is, the sampling distribution indicates the likelihood that a divergence of the observed magnitude would occur if the observations were really a random sample from the theoretical distribution. The Kolmogorov-Smirnov test assumes that the distribution of the underlying variable being tested is continuous, as specified by the cumulative frequency distribution. Thus, the test is appropriate to test the goodness-of-fit for variables which are measured on at least an ordinal scale.

4.3.2 Method

Let $F_0(X)$ be a completely specified cumulative relative frequency distribution function, the theoretical distribution under H_0. That is, for any value of X, the value of $F_0(X)$ is the proportion of cases expected to have scores equal to or less than X.

Let $S_N(X)$ be the observed cumulative relative frequency distribution of a random sample of N observations. If X_i is any possible score, then $S_N(X_i) = F_i/N$, where F_i is the number of observations which are equal to or less than X_i. $F_0(X_i)$ is the expected proportion of observations which are less than or equal to X_i.

Now under the null hypothesis that the sample has been drawn from the specified theoretical distribution, it is expected that for every value X_i, $S_N(X_i)$ should be fairly close to $F_0(X_i)$. That is, when H_0 is true, we would expect the differences between $S_N(X_i)$ and $F_0(X_i)$ to be small and within the limits of random error. The Kolmogorov-Smirnov test focuses on the *largest* of the deviations. The largest absolute value of $F_0(X_i) - S_N(X_i)$ is called the *maximum deviation D*:

$$D = \max|F_0(X_i) - S_N(X_i)| \qquad i = 1, 2, \ldots, N \tag{4.6}$$

The sampling distribution of D under H_0 is known. Table F of the Appendix gives certain critical values from that sampling distribution. Notice that the significance of a given value of D depends upon N.

For example, suppose one found by application of Eq. (4.6) that $D = .325$ when $N = 15$. Appendix Table F shows that the probability of $D \geq .325$ is between .05 and .10.

If N is greater than 35, the critical values of D can be determined by the last row in Appendix Table F. For example, suppose a researcher had a sample of size $N = 43$ and chose $\alpha = .05$. Appendix Table F shows that any $D \geq 1.36/\sqrt{N}$ will be significant. That is, any D, as defined by Eq. (4.6), which is equal to or greater than $1.36/\sqrt{43} = .207$ will be significant at the .05 level (two-tailed test).

Example 4.3. During the past several years researchers have been studying the duration of a variety of events such as jobs, strikes, and wars. As a part of such research, precise assumptions concerning individual actions and the course of events has led to mathematical models of the events which make predictions about their distribution.[5] While details of the mathematical models are not of special interest here, assessing the agreement between the data and the model predictions provides a good illustration of the Kolmogorov-Smirnov one-sample goodness-of-fit test. Data concerning the duration of strikes which began in 1965 in the United Kingdom were collected, analyzed, and predictions were made with the use of the mathematical model. Table 4.3 contains the cumulative frequency distribution of the $N = 840$ strike durations. Also given in the table are the cumulative frequencies predicted by the mathematical model.

i. *Null hypothesis.* H_0: the distribution of strike durations follows the mathematical model predictions. That is, the difference between observed and predicted strike durations

[5] Morrison, D. G., and Schmittlein, D. C. (1980). Jobs, strikes, and wars: Probability models for duration. *Organizational Behavior and Human Performance*, **25**, 224–251.

TABLE 4.3
United Kingdom strike data ($N = 840$)

Maximum duration (days)	Cumulative frequency		Cumulative relative frequency		$\lvert F_0(X) - S_N(X) \rvert$
	Observed	Predicted	Observed	Predicted	
1–2	203	212.81	.242	.253	.011
2–3	352	348.26	.419	.415	.004
3–4	452	442.06	.538	.526	.012
4–5	523	510.45	.623	.608	.015
5–6	572	562.15	.681	.669	.012
6–7	605	602.34	.720	.717	.003
7–8	634	634.27	.755	.755	.000
8–9	660	660.10	.786	.786	.000
9–10	683	681.32	.813	.811	.002
10–11	697	698.97	.830	.832	.002
11–12	709	713.82	.844	.850	.006
12–13	718	726.44	.855	.865	.010
13–14	729	737.26	.868	.878	.010
14–15	744	746.61	.886	.889	.003
15–16	750	754.74	.893	.899	.006
16–17	757	761.86	.901	.907	.006
17–18	763	768.13	.908	.914	.006
18–19	767	773.68	.913	.921	.008
19–20	771	778.62	.918	.927	.009
20–25	788	796.68	.938	.948	.010
25–30	804	807.86	.957	.962	.005
30–35	812	815.25	.967	.971	.004
35–40	820	820.39	.976	.977	.001
40–50	832	826.86	.990	.984	.006
>50	840	840.01	1.000	1.000	.000

does not exceed the differences which would be expected to occur by chance. H_1: the observed strike durations do not coincide with those predicted by the mathematical model.

ii. *Statistical test.* The Kolmogorov-Smirnov one-sample test is chosen because the researcher wishes to compare an observed distribution of scores from an ordinal scale with a theoretical distribution of scores.

iii. *Significance level.* Let $\alpha = .05$ and N is the number of strikes which began in the United Kingdom in 1965 = 840.

iv. *Sampling distribution.* Critical values of D, the maximum absolute deviation between observed and predicted cumulative distributions, are presented in Appendix Table F, together with their associated probabilities of occurrence when H_0 is true.

v. *Rejection region.* The region of rejection consists of all values of D [computed from Eq. (4.6)], which are so large that the probability associated with their occurrence when H_0 is true is less than or equal to $\alpha = .05$.

vi. *Decision.* In this study, the difference between the observed cumulative relative frequency distribution $S_N(X)$ and the predicted cumulative relative frequency distribution

$F_0(X)$ is calculated. These differences are summarized in Table 4.3. The value of D, the maximum difference between the cumulative frequencies is $|F_0(X) - S_N(X)| = |510.45/840 - 523/840| = .015$. Since $N > 35$, we must use the large-sample approximation. With $N = 840$ the critical value of D is $1.36/\sqrt{840} = .047$. Since the observed value of D, .015, is less than the critical value, we cannot reject H_0, the hypothesis that the observed data are from a population specified by the theoretical model summarized in Table 4.3.

4.3.3 Summary of Procedure

In the application of the Kolmogorov-Smirnov test, these are the steps:

1. Specify the theoretical cumulative distribution, i.e., the cumulative distribution expected under H_0.
2. Arrange the observed scores into a cumulative distribution and convert the cumulative frequencies into cumulative relative frequencies $[S_N(X_i)]$. For each interval find the expected cumulative relative frequency $F_0(X_i)$.
3. With the use of Eq. (4.6), find D.
4. Refer to Appendix Table F to find the probability (two-tailed) associated with the occurrence under H_0 of values as large as the observed value of D. If that probability is equal to or less than α, reject H_0.

4.3.4 Power

The Kolmogorov-Smirnov one-sample goodness-of-fit test treats individual observations separately and, thus, unlike the chi-square test discussed in Sec. 4.2, need not lose information through the combining of categories, although it may be convenient to use groupings of the variables. When samples are small and adjacent categories must be combined for proper use of the X^2 statistic, the chi-square test is definitely less powerful than the Komogorov-Smirnov test. Moreover, for very small samples the chi-square test cannot be used, but the Kolmogorov-Smirnov test may. These facts suggest that the Kolmogorov-Smirnov test may in all cases be more powerful than its alternative, the chi-square test.

However, it is possible for the tests to yield similar results, particularly when the sample size is large. If we apply the Kolmogorov-Smirnov test to the racing data of Sec. 4.2, we find that $D = \max|S_N(X) - F_0(X)| = |\frac{91}{144} - \frac{72}{144}| = .132$. If we test at $\alpha = .05$, then we can reject H_0 if $D \geq 1.36/\sqrt{144} = .113$. As with the chi-square test, we may reject H_0.

The chi-square test assumes that the distributions are nominal, whereas the Kolmogorov-Smirnov test assumes an underlying continuous distribution. In principle, both tests could be applied to ordinal data; however, the grouping which is necessary for application of the chi-square test makes it less precise than the Kolmogorov-Smirnov test.

The choice between them is difficult. It is difficult to compare the power of the two tests because they each depend on different quantities. When either test could be applied, the choice may depend on ease of computation or another preference. However, with small samples, the Kolmogorov-Smirnov test is exact, while the chi-square goodness-of-fit test is only approximately (asymptotically) exact. In such cases, preference should be given to the Kolmogorov-Smirnov test.

4.3.5 References

Discussions of the Kolmogorov-Smirnov test and other tests of goodness-of-fit may be found in Gibbons (1976) and Hays (1981).

4.4 TEST FOR DISTRIBUTIONAL SYMMETRY

4.4.1 Function and Rationale

The tests discussed thus far in this chapter have dealt with two aspects of a distribution. The binomial test deals with the question of whether dichotomous data can reasonably be thought to be generated by a hypothesized binomial distribution. The next two tests considered the fit of an empirical distribution to an hypothesized distribution. Another sort of hypothesis about a set of data may be about the *shape* of a distribution. The test described in this section is a test for distributional symmetry. That is, can we infer that a set of data was generated by an unknown but *symmetrical* distribution? The hypothesis H_0 is that the observations are from the same symmetrical distribution with an unknown median. The alternative hypothesis is that the distribution is not symmetrical.

The test involves the examination of subsets of three variables (or triples) to determine the likelihood that the distribution is skewed to the left or the right. The test involves a fair amount of computation, but is relatively straightforward.

4.4.2 Method

To apply the test, each subset of size 3 from the sample must be examined and coded. Each triple X_i, X_j, X_k is coded as a right or left triple (or as neither). Although it is possible to classify the triples by inspection, a more formal specification will be given. The following table gives the coding for the triples:

Right triple	X--X------X	$(X_i + X_j + X_k)/3 > \text{med}(X_i, X_j, X_k)$
Left triple	X------X--X	$(X_i + X_j + X_k)/3 < \text{med}(X_i, X_j, X_k)$
Neither	X----X----X	$(X_i + X_j + X_k)/3 = \text{med}(X_i, X_j, X_k)$

Each of the $N(N-1)(N-2)/6$ possible triples must be coded as left, right, or neither. The statistic of interest is

$$T = \#\text{ right triples} - \#\text{ left triples} \tag{4.7}$$

Now, when H_0 is true, $\mu_T = 0$, that is, the X's are symmetric about the median. To complete the test, we need to define the following statistics:

$$B_i = \#\text{ right triples involving } X_i - \#\text{ left triples involving } X_i$$

$$B_{jk} = \#\text{ right triples involving both } X_j \text{ and } X_k - \#\text{ left triples involving both } X_j \text{ and } X_k$$

Then H_0 can be tested by using the statistic $z = T/\sigma_T$, where

$$\sigma_T^2 = \frac{(N-3)(N-4)}{(N-1)(N-2)} \sum_{i=1}^{N} B_i^2 + \frac{N-3}{N-4} \sum_{1 \le j < k \le N} B_{jk}^2 + \frac{N(N-1)(N-2)}{6} - \left[1 - \frac{(N-3)(N-4)(N-5)}{N(N-1)(N-2)}\right] T^2 \tag{4.8}$$

The statistic z is asymptotically normally distributed with mean zero and unit variance. The significance of z may be determined by using Appendix Table A and the critical value determined for a two-tailed test using $\alpha/2$. Compared to alternative procedures, this test is satisfactory for N greater than about 20; that is, it maintains the chosen significance level while maintaining good power for detecting asymmetric distributions.

Example 4.4. In a study of saltiness suppression,[6] subjects tasted a mixture of salt and sucrose for the purpose of scaling saltiness judgments as a function of the salt concentration in the solution. There were substantial individual differences in the judgments of saltiness. Of interest to the researcher was the distribution of saltiness judgments. Four different concentrations were used and separate subjects were run at each concentration. The data are summarized in Table 4.4. For purposes of illustrating the test of distributional symmetry, the data for the saltiness concentration ratio of .5 will be analyzed.

i. Null hypothesis. H_0: the distribution of saltiness judgments is symmetric. The alternative hypothesis is that the distribution of judgments is asymmetric. That is, the null hypothesis is that the deviations from symmetry are those that would be expected to occur by chance.

ii. Statistical test. The number of observations is $N = 9$. (Strictly speaking, our example violates the recommendation that the test is appropriate when $N > 20$. A small sample example was chosen to illustrate the procedure.) The first step involves calculating the triples and determining whether they are right triples, left triples, or neither. The total number of triples for $N = 9$ is $N(N-1)(N-2)/6 = 84$. For the first three points (13.53, 28.42, 48.11) the median is 28.42 and the mean is 30.03. Since the mean is greater than the median, the triple (X_1, X_2, X_3) is classified as a right triple. The triple (X_1, X_3, X_4) is a left triple, since the median is 48.11 and is greater than the mean $(13.53 + 48.11 + 48.64)/3 = 36.76$. The number of right triples is 44 and the number of left triples is 40. Thus the value of T is $44 - 40 = 4$.

---

[6] Kroeze, J. H. A. (1982). The influence of relative frequencies of pure and mixed stimuli on mixture suppression in taste. *Perception & Psychophysics*, **31**, 276–278.

TABLE 4.4
Saltiness judgments for one level of salt concentration

13.53
28.42
48.11
48.64
51.40
59.91
67.98
79.13
103.05

Next the variance of T must be found. To do this, the intermediate quantities B_i and B_{jk} must be calculated. Then these quantities are used in Eq. (4.8) to determine the variance. (The two sums of squares of B_i and B_{jk} are 320 and 364 respectively.) The variance is then 680.04. Finally, the statistic $z = T/\sigma_T = 4/\sqrt{680.04} = .154$ is calculated.

iii. *Significance level and decision.* Let $\alpha = .05$. The significance level for z may be determined by reference to Appendix Table A, the table of the unit normal distribution. We cannot reject the hypothesis of symmetry at the .05 (or even greater) level of significance.

It should be remembered that the test is reasonably good for $N \geq 20$. As the sample sizes become larger, the computation of the triples, while straightforward, is relatively time consuming. Therefore, this technique is perhaps best used when a computer algorithm is available. Program 1 (see Appendix II) gives the coding for a general program for computing T and σ_T for any sample size. For this statistic, the use of a program is recommended.

4.4.3 Summary of Procedure

These are the steps in the application of the symmetry test to a sequence of observations:

1. For each subset of size 3 in the sequence of observations determine whether it is a right or left triple (or neither).
2. Calculate the quantities B_i and B_{jk} for each variable X_i and pair of variables X_j and X_k.
3. Calculate T, the number of right triples minus the number of left triples, and the variance of T by using Eq. (4.8).
4. Test H_0 by using the statistic $z = T/\sigma_T$, which is asymptotically normally distributed with mean 0 and standard deviation 1. The significance of T may be found by use of Appendix Table A. Since the alternative hypothesis is two-tailed, the critical value of T is determined using $\alpha/2$. Because of the relatively large number of computations involved, the use of a computer program like Program 1 in Appendix II is desirable.

4.4.4 Power

The power of the symmetry test has been studied by means of Monte Carlo procedures with the use of a large number of simulated samples from various distributions. On the basis of such studies, the test has reasonable power for samples greater than about 20. Other tests have been proposed, but most have very low power.

4.4.5 References

There are several tests for distributional symmetry. The one presented here is due to Randles, Fligner, Policello, and Wolfe (1980).

4.5 THE ONE-SAMPLE RUNS TEST OF RANDOMNESS

4.5.1 Function and Rationale

If an experimenter wishes to arrive at some conclusion about a population by using the information contained in a sample from that population, then the sample must be random. That is, successive observations must be independent. Several techniques have been developed to enable us to test the hypothesis that a sample is random. These techniques are based on the *order* or *sequence* in which the individual scores or observations originally were obtained.

The techniques to be presented here are based on the number of runs which a sample exhibits. A *run* is defined as a succession of identical symbols which are followed and preceded by different symbols or by no symbols at all.

For example, suppose a series of binary events (indicated by pluses and minuses) occurred in this order:

$$+ \quad + \quad - \quad - \quad - \quad + \quad - \quad - \quad - \quad - \quad + \quad + \quad - \quad +$$

This sample of scores begins with a run of two pluses. A run of three minuses follows. Then comes another run which consists of one plus. It is followed by a run of four minuses, after which comes a run of two pluses, etc. We can group these scores into runs by underlining and numbering each succession of identical symbols:

$$\underbrace{+ \quad +}_{1} \quad \underbrace{- \quad - \quad -}_{2} \quad \underbrace{+}_{3} \quad \underbrace{- \quad - \quad - \quad -}_{4} \quad \underbrace{+ \quad +}_{5} \quad \underbrace{-}_{6} \quad \underbrace{+}_{7}$$

We observe seven runs in all: r is number of runs $= 7$.

The total number of runs in a sample of any given size gives an indication of whether or not the sample is random. If very few runs occur, a time trend or some bunching owing to lack of independence is suggested. If a great many runs occur, systematic short-period cyclical fluctuations seem to be influencing the scores.

For example, suppose a coin were tossed 20 times and the following sequence of heads (H) and tails (T) was observed:

H H H H H H H H H H T T T T T T T T T T

Only two runs occurred in 20 tosses. This would seem to be too few for a "fair" coin (or a fair tosser!). Some lack of independence in the events is suggested. On the other hand, suppose the following sequence occurred:

H T H T H T H T H T H T H T H T H T H T

Here too many runs are observed. In this case, with $r = 20$, when $N = 20$, it also would seem reasonable to reject the hypothesis that the coin is "fair." Neither of the above sequences seems to be a random series of H's and T's. That is, the successive observations do not seem to be independent.

Notice that our analysis, which is based on the *order* of the events, gives us information which is not indicated by the *frequency* of the events. In both of the above cases, 10 tails and 10 heads occurred. If the scores were analyzed according to their frequencies, e.g., by use of the chi-square test or the binomial test, we would have no reason to suspect the "fairness" of the coin. It is only a runs test, focusing on the order of the events, which reveals the striking lack of randomness of the scores and, thus, the possible lack of "fairness" in the coin.

The sampling distribution of the values of r which we could expect from repeated random samples is known. Using this sampling distribution, we may decide whether a given observed sample has more or fewer runs than would be expected to occur by chance in a random sample.

4.5.2 Method

Let m be the number of elements of one kind, and n be the number of elements of the other kind in a sequence of $N = m + n$ binary events. That is, m might be the number of heads and n the number of tails in a series of coin tosses; or m might be the number of pluses and n the number of minuses in a series of responses to a questionnaire.

To use the one-sample runs test, first observe the m and n events in the sequence in which they occurred and determine the value of r, the number of runs.

SMALL SAMPLES. If both m and n are less than or equal to 20, then Table G of the Appendix gives the critical values of r under H_0 for $\alpha = .05$. These are critical values from the sampling distribution of r under H_0 when it is assumed that the sequence is random. If the observed value of r falls between the critical values, we cannot reject H_0. If the observed value of r is equal to or more extreme than one of the critical values, we reject H_0.

There are two entries for each value of m and n in Appendix Table G. The first entry gives the maximum of those values of r which are so *small* that the probability associated with their occurrence under H_0 is $p = .025$ or less. The second entry gives the minimum of the values of r which are so *large* that the probability associated with their occurrence under H_0 is $p = .025$ or less.

Any observed value of r which is *equal to or less than* the top value shown in Table G *or* is *equal to or larger than* the bottom value shown in Table G is in the region of rejection for $\alpha = .05$.

For example, in the first tossing of the coin discussed above, we observed two runs; one run of 10 heads followed by one run of 10 tails. Here $m = 10$, $n = 10$, and $r = 2$. Appendix Table G shows that for these values of m and n a random sample would contain between 7 and 15 runs 95 percent of the time. Any observed r of 6 or less or of 16 or more is in the regions of rejection for $\alpha = .05$. The observed $r = 2$ is smaller than 6, so at the .05 significance level we can reject the null hypothesis that the coin is producing a random series of heads and tails.

If a one-tailed test is desired, i.e., if the direction of the deviation from randomness is predicted in advance, then only one of the two entries need be used. If the prediction is that too few runs will be observed, Appendix Table G gives the critical values of r. If the observed r under such a one-tailed test is equal to or smaller than the upper value shown in Table G, H_0 may be rejected at $\alpha = .025$. If the prediction is that too many runs will be observed, the lower values in Table G are the critical values of r which are significant at the .025 level.

For example, take the case of the second sequence of coin tosses reported above. Suppose we had predicted in advance, for some reason, that the coin would produce too many runs. We observe that $r = 20$ for $m = 10$ and $n = 10$. Since our observed value of r is equal to or larger than the lower value shown in Appendix Table G, we may reject H_0 at $\alpha = .025$, and conclude that the coin is "unfair" in the predicted direction.

In developing the alternative hypothesis for the runs test, a researcher might conclude that the data are grouped or clustered together. In that case, the alternative hypothesis would be that there would be fewer runs than expected if the data were random. On the other hand, the researcher might hypothesize that the data should be more variable than one might expect on the basis of random assignment. In this case, the alternative hypothesis would be that there would be more runs than expected if the data were random. In each of these cases, the test of H_0 would be a one-tailed test.

Example 4.5a For small samples. In a study of the dynamics of aggression in young children, an experimenter observed pairs of children in a controlled play situation.[7] Most of the 24 children who served as subjects in the study came from the same nursery school and thus played together daily. Since the experimenter was able to arrange to observe only two children on any day, she was concerned that biases might be introduced into the study by discussions among those children who had already served as subjects and those who were to serve later. If such discussions had any effect on the level of aggression in the play sessions, this effect might show up as lack of randomness in the aggression scores in the order in which they were collected. After the study was completed, the randomness of the sequence of scores was tested by converting each child's aggression score to a plus or minus, depending upon whether it fell above or below the group median, and then applying the one-sample runs test to the observed sequence of pluses and minuses.

i. *Null hypothesis.* H_0: the pluses and minuses occur in random order. That is, the null hypothesis is that the aggression scores occur randomly above and below the median

---

[7] Siegel, Alberta E. (1955). The effect of film-mediated fantasy aggression on strength of aggressive drive in young children. Unpublished doctoral dissertation, Stanford University.

throughout the experiment. H_1: the order of the pluses and minuses deviates from randomness.

ii. Statistical test. Since the hypothesis concerns the randomness of a single sequence of observations, the one-sample runs test is chosen.

iii. Significance level. Let $\alpha = .05$ and N be the number of subjects $= 24$. Since the scores will be characterized as plus or minus depending upon whether they fall above or below the middlemost score in the group, $m = n = 12$.

iv. Sampling distribution. Appendix Table G gives the critical values of r from the sampling distribution.

v. Rejection region. Since H_1 does not predict the direction of the deviation from randomness, a two-tailed test is used. Since $m = n = 12$, reference to Table G shows that H_0 should be rejected at the .05 level of significance if the observed r is either equal to or less than 7 or equal to or larger than 19.

vi. Decision. Table 4.5 shows the aggression scores for each child in the order in which the scores were obtained. The median of the set of scores is 25.5. All scores falling below the median are designated as minus in Table 4.5; all scores above the median are

TABLE 4.5
Aggression scores in order of occurrence

Child	Score	Position of score with respect to median
1	31	+
2	23	−
3	36	+
4	43	+
5	51	+
6	44	+
7	12	−
8	26	+
9	43	+
10	75	+
11	2	−
12	3	−
13	15	−
14	18	−
15	78	+
16	24	−
17	13	−
18	27	+
19	86	+
20	61	+
21	13	−
22	7	−
23	6	−
24	8	−

designated as plus. From the column showing the sequence of +'s and −'s it is readily seen that 10 runs occurred in the series of observations, that is, $r = 10$.

Reference to Appendix Table G reveals that $r = 10$ for $m = n = 12$ does not fall in the rejection region. Thus we cannot reject the hypothesis that the series of observations occurred in random order.

LARGE SAMPLES. If either m or n is larger than 20, Appendix Table G cannot be used. For such large samples, a good approximation to the sampling distribution of r is the normal distribution with

$$\text{Mean} = \mu_r = \frac{2mn}{N} + 1$$

and

$$\text{Standard deviation} = \sigma_r = \sqrt{\frac{2mn(2mn - N)}{N^2(N-1)}}$$

Therefore, when either m or n is greater than 20, H_0 may be tested by

$$z = \frac{r - \mu_r}{\sigma_r} = \frac{r + h - 2mn/N - 1}{\sqrt{[2mn(2mn - N)]/[N^2(N-1)]}} \tag{4.9}$$

where $h = +.5$ if $r < 2mn/N + 1$, and $h = -.5$ if $r > 2mn/N + 1$. Since the values of z which are obtained using Eq. (4.9) are approximately normally distributed with mean 0 and standard deviation 1 when H_0 is true, the significance of any observed value of z computed by using the equation may be determined from a normal-distribution table such as Appendix Table A. That is, Table A gives the one-tailed probabilities associated with the occurrence under H_0 of values as extreme as the observed z.

The large-sample example which follows uses this normal-distribution approximation to the sampling distribution of r.

Example 4.5b For large samples. A researcher was interested in ascertaining whether the arrangement of men and women in the queue in front of the box office of a theater was a random arrangement. The data were obtained by simply tallying the sex of each of a succession of 50 people as they approached the box office.

i. *Null hypothesis.* H_0: the order of males and females in the queue is random. H_1: the order of males and females in the queue is not random.
ii. *Statistical test.* The one-sample runs test is chosen because the hypothesis concerns the randomness in a sequence of observations. Since the sample size is large, the large-sample test will be used.
iii. *Significance level.* Let $\alpha = .05$ and N is the number of people observed $= 50$. The values of m and n can be determined only after the data are collected.
iv. *Sampling distribution.* For large samples, the values of z computed from Eq. (4.9) when H_0 is true are approximately normally distributed with mean 0 and standard deviation 1. Appendix Table A gives the one-tailed probability associated with the occurrence when H_0 is true of values as extreme as an observed z.

TABLE 4.6
Order of 30 males (M) and 20 females (F) in queue before theater box office*

M F M F MMM FF M F M F
M F MMMM F M F M F MM
FFF M F M F M F MM F
MM F MMMM F M F MM

* Runs are indicated by underlining.

v. Rejection region. Since H_1 does not predict the direction of the deviation from randomness, a two-tailed rejection region is used. It consists of all values of z, as computed from Eq. (4.9), which are so extreme that the probability associated with their occurrence when H_0 is true is less than or equal to $\alpha = .05$. Thus the rejection region includes all values of z more extreme than ± 1.96.

vi. Decision. The males (M) and females (F) were queued in front of the box office in the order shown in Table 4.6. The reader may verify that there were $m = 30$ males and $n = 20$ females in the sample. The count of the number of runs is $r = 35$.

To determine whether $r \geq 35$ might readily have occurred under H_0, we compute the value of z by using Eq. (4.9):

$$z = \frac{r - \mu_r}{\sigma_r} = \frac{r + h - 2mn/N - 1}{\sqrt{[2mn(2mn - N)]/[N^2(N - 1)]}}$$

$$z = \frac{r - \mu_r}{\sigma_r} = \frac{35 - .5 - 2(30)(20)/50 - 1}{\sqrt{\{2(30)(20)[2(30)(20) - 50]\}/[50^2(50 - 1)]}}$$

$$= 2.83$$

Since 2.83 is greater than the critical value of z (1.96), we may reject the hypothesis of randomness. Indeed, the probability of obtaining a value of $z \geq 2.83$ when H_0 is true is $p = 2(.0023) = .0046$. (The probability obtained from Table A is doubled because we are using a two-tailed test.) As a result of the test, we may conclude that the order of males and females in the box office queue is not random.

4.5.3 Summary of Procedure

The following are the steps in the use of the one-sample runs test:

1. Arrange the m and n observations in their order of occurrence.
2. Count the number of runs r.
3. Determine the probability p under H_0 associated with a value as extreme as the observed value of r. If that probability is equal to or less than α, reject H_0. The technique for determining the value of p depends on the number of observations, m and n, in the two groups:
   (*a*) If m and n are both 20 or less, refer to Appendix Table G. For a two-tailed test with $\alpha = .05$, if the observed number of runs is less than or equal to the

upper entry or equal to or larger than the lower entry, reject H_0. For a one-tailed test with $\alpha = .025$, reject H_0 if the number of runs is less than or equal to (or greater than or equal to) the table entry.
(*b*) If either m or n is larger than 20, determine the value of z by using Eq. (4.9). Appendix Table A gives the one-tailed probability associated with the occurrence under H_0 of values as extreme as an observed z. For a two-tailed test, double the probability obtained from the table.

If the probability associated with the observed value of r is equal to or less than α, reject H_0.

4.5.4 Power-Efficiency

Because there are no parametric tests for the randomness of a sequence of events in a sample, the concept of power-efficiency is not meaningful in the case of the one-sample runs test. The runs test is used to test the null hypothesis that the sequence of observations is random. Unlike the techniques to be discussed in the next two chapters, this form of the runs test is not useful for estimating differences between groups. However, for the particular hypothesis of interest the test is useful and direct.

4.6 THE CHANGE-POINT TEST

4.6.1 Function and Rationale

There are many experimental situations in which an experimenter observes a sequence of events and, as one of the research hypotheses, wants to determine whether there has been a change in the underlying process which generates the sequence of events. However, for any of a number of possible reasons, the researcher does not know the point at which a change actually occurs. Although the experimenter might have induced a change in the experimental situation at a particular time, there may be no certainty about when a corresponding change actually occurs in the observed behavior. Another example might be a perceptual learning task in which a subject performs at one level until some sort of cognitive consolidation takes place after which there is a shift in the performance level. In such cases, normal sampling variation in the task may obscure the actual change point.

The tests to be described in this section assume that the observations form an ordered sequence, and that, initially, the distribution of responses has one median, and at some point there is a shift in the median of the distribution. The alternative hypothesis could be one-tailed, e.g., there is an upward shift in the distribution, or two-tailed, e.g., there was a shift in the distribution, but no prediction is made about the direction of change. That is, H_0 is the hypothesis that there is no change in the location parameter, i.e., the median, of the sequence of observations, and H_1 is the hypothesis that there is a change in the location parameter of the sequence.

Two tests will be presented. One is appropriate when the data are binary and are observations of some binomial process. The second test assumes that the data are continuous. The logic of the tests is similar although the computational formulas are different.

4.6.2 Method for Binomial Variables

In a series of N binary observations, $X_1, X_2, \ldots, X_N$, the data for each observation X_i is coded as $X_i = 1$ for one value of the variable (a success) and $X_i = 0$ for the other value (a failure). Of the N observations, let m be the number of successes (or events of one type) and n be the number of failures (or events of the other type). Then

$$m = \sum_{i=1}^{N} X_i \qquad \text{and} \qquad n = N - m$$

The cumulative number of successes ($X_i = 1$) at each point in the sequence is then determined. This frequency will be designated as

$$S_j = \sum_{i=1}^{j} X_i \qquad j = 1, 2, \ldots, N$$

The statistic for testing the hypothesis of change is

$$D_{m,n} = \max \left| \frac{N}{mn} \left(S_j - \frac{jm}{N} \right) \right| \tag{4.10}$$

The expression is evaluated for all values of j from 1 to $N - 1$. $D_{m,n}$ is the largest absolute difference observed in the sequence. The sampling distribution of $D_{m,n}$ has been tabled and some values are given in Appendix Table L_{II} and is a form of the Kolmogorov-Smirnov test. If $D_{m,n}$ equals or exceeds the tabled value, we may reject H_0 at the specified level of significance and conclude that there has been a change in the distribution.

If the sample size is large, the critical values should be determined from Appendix Table L_{III}. For example, if $N = 60$ and $m = 45$, $n = 15$, we may reject H_0 at the .05 level if $D_{m,n} \geq 1.36\sqrt{N/mn} = 1.36(.298) = .41$.

Example 4.6a In a study of the effect of change in payoff in a two-choice probability learning task,[8] the payoff or reward given to a subject was changed (or not changed) after an individual's performance had stabilized at an asymptote (or steady performance level). The hypothesis was that a change in payoff for correct responses would affect the level of responding by the subject. The experiment consisted of 300 trials on each of which the subject made a binary response. Since a subject's response pattern cannot be thought to have stabilized until some learning takes place, only the last 240 trials are analyzed here. At trial 120 (trial 180 in the original sequence) one-half of the subjects experienced a change in payoff. The experimenter wished to determine whether there was a change in the parameter of the binary sequence of responses over the last 240 trials. If there was a change for

---

[8] Castellan, N. J., Jr. (1969). Effect of change of payoff in probability learning. *Journal of Experimental Psychology*, **79**, 178–182.

TABLE 4.7
Data for two subjects in probability learning experiment

Response sequence for subject *A*–no change in payoff
1 1 1 1 0 0 1 1 1 1 0 0 1 1 1 1 1 1 1 1 1 1 1 0 1 1 0 0 1 1 1 0 0 1 1 1 1 1 0 1 1 1 0 0 1 1 1 1 1 1 1 1 0 1 1 1 0 0 1 1
0 1 1 0 1 1 1 1 0 0 1 0 1 1 1 1 0 1 1 1 0 0 1 1 1 1 1 1 1 0 0 0 0 1 1 1 1 1 0 1 1 1 1 1 1 1 0 1 1 1 0 0 0 0 1 1 1 1 0 1 1
0 1 1 0 1 1 1 1 0 0 1 1 1 1 1 1 1 1 1 1 1 0 1 1 0 1 1 1 1 1 1 1 1 1 1 1 1 0 0 1 1 1 1 0 0 1 1 1 0 0 1 1 1 1 0 1 1 0 1
0 0 1 1 1 1 0 1 0 1 1 1 1 1 1 1 1 1 0 0 1 1 1 1 1 1 1 0 0 0 1 1 1 1 1 1 1 1 1 1 1 1 0 1 1 1 1 0 0 1 1 1 1 1 1 1 1 1 1 0 0 1 1

Response sequence for subject *B*–change in payoff
0 0 1 1 0 1 1 1 1 1 1 1 1 1 1 1 1 1 1 1 1 1 1 1 1 1 1 1 1 1 1 1 1 1 1 1 1 1 1 1 1 1 1 1 1 1 1 1 1 1 1 1 1 1 0 1 1 1 1 1 0
1 1 0 1 1 0 0 1 1 1 1 0 0 0 0 1 1 1 1 1 0 1 1 1 0 0 1 0 1 1 1 1 1 0 0 1 1 1 1 0 1 1 0 1 1 1 0 0 1 1 1 1 0 0 0 0 0 1 0 1
1 1 0 1 1 0 1 1 1 1 0 0 0 0 0 0 0 1 1 1 1 1 0 1 1 1 1 1 1 1 0 1 1 1 1 1 1 1 1 1 1 1 0 1 1 1 1 1 1 1 0 0 1 1 0 0 1 1 1 1 1 0 0 1 1 1
1 0 0 0 0 1 1 1 1 0 1 1 0 1 1 0 0 0 0 1 1 1 0 0 0 1 1 1 1 1 1 1 0 0 0 0 1 1 1 1 0 1 1 0 1 0 0 1 0 0 0 0 0 1 1 1 0 0 1 1

those subjects who experienced a change in payoff, then it might be concluded that the change in payoff induced a change in response level.

To illustrate the test, response sequences for two subjects will be analyzed. Subject *A* received 10 cents for each correct response throughout the experiment. Subject *B* received 10 cents until trial 120, after which the payoff was reduced to 1 cent for each correct response. The data are summarized in Table 4.7.

i. Null hypothesis. H_0: there is no change in p, the probability that $X_i = 1$ over the sequence of trials. H_1: there is a change in p over the sequence of trials.

ii. Statistical test. The change-point test for binomial variables will be used because the researcher wishes to determine whether a change in the observed distribution of binary responses occurred during the last 240 trials.

iii. Significance level. Let $\alpha = .05$ and N is the number of observations $= 240$.

iv. Sampling distribution. Critical values of $D_{m,n}$ from the sampling distribution are presented in Appendix Tables L_{II} and L_{III}, together with their associated probabilities of occurrence when H_0 is true.

v. Rejection region. The rejection region consists of all values of $D_{m,n}$ computed from Eq. (4.10) which are so large that the probability associated with their occurrence when H_0 is true is less than or equal to $\alpha = .05$.

vi. Decision. Since the hypothesis in this example concerns individual subjects, each will be analyzed separately. For subject *A* the differences

$$\left|\frac{N}{mn}\left(S_j - \frac{jm}{N}\right)\right|$$

were computed for each trial j. S_j is the number of $X_i = 1$ responses up to and including trial j, m is the number of $X_i = 1$ responses throughout the entire N trials, and $n = N - m$ is the number of $X_i = 0$ responses. For this subject, $N = 240$, $m = 178$, and $n = 62$. The maximum difference was $D_{178,62} = .096$.

Since m and n are large, we must use the large-sample values from Appendix Table L_{III}. The critical value of $D_{m,n}$ for $\alpha = .05$, $m = 178$, and $n = 62$ is $1.36\sqrt{N/mn} = 1.36\sqrt{240/(178)(62)} = .201$. Since the observed value of D (.096) is less than the critical value (.201), we do not reject H_0 and, thus, conclude that there was no change point in the sequence of responses over the last 240 trials for subject A.

For subject B the differences

$$\left|\frac{N}{mn}\left(S_j - \frac{jm}{N}\right)\right|$$

were computed for each trial j. For this subject, $N = 240$, $m = 167$, and $n = 73$. The maximum difference was $D_{167,73} = .275$.

Since m and n are large, we must use the large-sample values from Appendix Table L_{III}. The critical value of $D_{m,n}$ for $\alpha = .05$, $m = 167$, $n = 73$ is $1.36\sqrt{N/mn} = 1.36\sqrt{240/(167)(73)} = .191$. Since the observed value of D (.275) is greater than the critical value (.191) we may reject H_0 and conclude that there was a change point in the sequence of responses over the last 240 trials for subject B.

Thus, for the subject who experienced no change in payoff level during the experiment, we may conclude that there was no change in performance level, whereas for the subject who experienced a decrement in payoff, we may conclude that there was a change in the performance level.

Summary of Procedure These are the steps in the application of the change-point test to a sequence of binomial variables:

1. Code each of the N observations as 1 or 0 for "success" and "failure" respectively.
2. Calculate the total number of successes, m, in the N observations. Let $n = N - m$.
3. Calculate the statistic $D_{m,n}$ by using Eq. (4.10) which is the maximum difference between the observed and "predicted" cumulative successes at each point in the sequence.
4. Consult Appendix Table L_{II} (for small samples) or Appendix Table L_{III} (for large samples) to determine whether H_0: (there is no change in the sequence) should be rejected in favor of H_1: (there is a change in the sequence).

4.6.3 Method for Continuous Variables

First, each of the observations $X_1, X_2, \ldots, X_N$ must be ranked from 1 to N. Let r_i be the rank associated with the datum X_i. Then at each place j in the series, we calculate

$$W_j = \sum_{i=1}^{j} r_i \qquad j = 1, 2, \ldots, N-1$$

which is the sum of the ranks of the variables at or before point j. Next for each point in the sequence, calculate $2W_j - j(N+1)$. Then set

$$K_{m,n} = \max|2W_j - j(N+1)| \qquad j = 1, 2, \ldots, N-1 \tag{4.11}$$

The value of j where the maximum in Eq. (4.11) occurs is the estimated change point in the sequence and is denoted m. $N - m = n$ is the number of observations after the change point. Thus, $K_{m,n}$ is the statistic which divides the sequence into m and n observations occurring before and after the change respectively.

Whether this value of $K_{m,n}$ is larger than we would expect by chance when there is no change in the sequence can be tested by referring to a table of the sampling distribution of W_j, the sum of ranks. The sampling distribution of W is summarized in Appendix Table J for various values of m and n. If W exceeds the tabled value of W at the appropriate significance level, we may reject H_0 that there is no change in distribution.

TIES. The test assumes that the scores are from a population with an underlying continuous distribution. If the measurements are precise, the probability of a tie is zero. However, with the measures usually used in the behavioral sciences, tied scores may occur. When tied ranks occur, give each of the tied observations the average of the ranks they would have had if no ties had occurred. Thus, if two observations are equal and are tied for ranks 3 and 4, each should be assigned the average rank $(3 + 4)/2 = 3.5$.

LARGE SAMPLES. Under the assumption of no change in distribution, the mean of W is $m(N + 1)/2$ and its variance is

$$\text{Variance of } W = \sigma_W^2 = \frac{mn(N+1)}{12}$$

and, as N becomes large, W is approximately normally distributed with mean and variance given above. Thus, when the series is long, the test for change may be done and tested using Appendix Table A by transforming W into a z:

$$z = \frac{W + h - m(N+1)/2}{\sqrt{mn(N+1)/12}} \tag{4.12}$$

where $h = -\frac{1}{2}$ if $W > m(N + 1)/2$ and $h = +\frac{1}{2}$ if $W < m(N + 1)/2$. If there are ties, the variance should be adjusted by using Eq. (6.12) of Chap. 6.

Example 4.6b In a study of the effects of amphetamine on neuronal activity,[9] two researchers were measuring the firing rate of neurons in the caudate nucleus as a function of time after injection of various isomers of amphetamine. The data in Table 4.8 summarize the neuronal firing rate as a percentage of base rate as a function of time since injection in one condition. The researchers wanted to know whether there was a change in firing rate during the time that the measurements were being taken. If a change occurred, it would be evidence for action of the drug at the site where measurements were made.

[9] Rebec, G. V., and Groves, P. M. (1975). Differential effects for the optical isomers of amphetamine on neuronal activity in the reticular formation and caudate nucleus of the rat. *Brain Research*, **83**, 301–318.

TABLE 4.8
Neuronal firing rate as a percentage of base line for 25 time periods following injection of amphetamine

Time period	Firing rate	Rank	W_j	$\lvert 2W_j - j(N+1) \rvert$
1	112	23.5	23.5	21
2	102	14.5	38.0	24
3	112	23.5	61.5	45
4	120	25	86.5	69
5	105	19	105.5	81
6	105	19	124.5	93
7	100	11	135.5	89
8	105	19	154.5	101
9	97	6	160.5	87
10	102	14.5	175.0	90
11	91	4	179.0	72
12	97	6	185.0	58
13	89	3	188.0	38
14	85	1	189.0	14
15	101	12	201.0	12
16	98	8.5	209.5	3
17	102	14.5	224.0	6
18	99	10	234.0	0
19	102	14.5	248.5	3
20	110	22	270.5	21
21	97	6	276.5	7
22	88	2	278.5	15
23	107	21	299.5	1
24	98	8.5	308.0	8
25	104	17	325.0	0

i. Null hypothesis. H_0: there is no change in the neuronal firing rate as a function of time. H_1: there is a change in firing rate.

ii. Statistical test. The change-point test for continuous variables will be used because the researchers wish to detect a change in the observed distribution of neuronal firing rates during the 25 time periods.

iii. Significance level. Let $\alpha = .01$ and N is the number of observations or time periods = 25.

iv. Sampling distribution. Critical values of the sampling distribution of W are presented in Appendix Table J for selected significance levels and selected values of m and n. However, since for this experiment $m > 10$, Appendix Table J cannot be used and the large sample approximation (and, hence, Appendix Table A) must be used.

v. Rejection region. The rejection region consists of all values of W computed from Eq. (4.11) which are so large that the probability associated with their occurrence when H_0 is true is less than or equal to .01.

vi. Decision. The firing rates were first ranked from 1 to 25. These ranks are summarized in Table 4.8, together with W_j, the cumulative sum of ranks up to time period j. Next the values $|2W_j - j(N + 1)|$ were computed for each time period. Examination of these values (also listed in Table 4.8) shows that the maximum is $K_{8,17} = 101$. That is, the maximum occurred at time 8. The test statistic is W, the sum of ranks where the function K is maximized, $W = 154.5$. Since the distribution of W for $m = 8$, $n = 17$ is not given in Appendix Table J, the normal approximation must be found by using Eq. (4.12):

$$z = \frac{W + h - m(N + 1)/2}{\sqrt{mn(N + 1)/12}} \tag{4.12}$$

$$= \frac{154.5 - .5 - 8(25 + 1)/2}{\sqrt{8(17)(25 + 1)/12}}$$

$$= 50/17.166$$

$$= 2.91$$

Using Appendix Table A and $\alpha = .01$, we find that the critical value of z is 2.58. Since the observed value is greater than the critical value, we can reject H_0, and conclude that there was a change in neuronal firing rate during the measurement period.

Summary of Procedure In the application of the change-point test for continuous variables, the following steps are followed:

1. Rank order the observations in the sequence of N observations.
2. Calculate the sum of ranks W_j for each point j in the sequence of observations.
3. For each point in the sequence use Eq. (4.11) to calculate the difference between the observed and "predicted" sum of ranks. $K_{m,n}$ is the maximum and divides the sequence into the m observations before the change and into the n observations after the change.
4. Depending upon the values of m and n, the method for testing varies.
   (*a*) *Small samples.* At the point m at which the maximum occurs, use the values W_m, m, and n to enter Appendix Table J to determine whether to reject the null hypothesis H_0 that there is no change in the sequence in favor of H_1 that there is a change in the sequence of observations.
   (*b*) *Large samples* ($m > 10$ or $n > 10$). Use the observed value of W_m, m, and n to calculate the value of z by using Eq. (4.12). If the observed value of z exceeds the critical value of z found in Appendix Table A, reject the null hypothesis H_0 that there is no change in the sequence.

4.6.4 Power-Efficiency

For the binomial change-point test, the concept of efficiency is not meaningful when the variable is binomial. However, the comments concerning the Kolmogorov-Smirnov goodness-of-fit test (Sec. 4.3.4 and Chap. 6) are relevant to this test when a continuous variable has been dichotomized to form a binary variable in order to apply the test.

For the change-point test for continuous variables, Monte Carlo procedures suggest that the test is robust with respect to changes in distributional form. The efficiency of the procedure has not been analyzed explicitly. However, the relation between this test and the Mann-Whitney-Wilcoxon test (Chap. 6) suggest that the test may be highly efficient.

4.6.5 References

The tests presented here have been presented by Pettitt (1979). An earlier test for binomial sequences owing to Page (1955) has been widely used, but it made additional assumptions about the initial parameters of the binomial distribution.

4.7 DISCUSSION

In this chapter we have presented six nonparametric statistical tests of use in a one-sample design. Three of these tests are of the goodness-of-fit type, one is a test for the symmetry versus nonsymmetry of a distribution, one is a test of the randomness of the sequence of events in a sample, and one is a test for the change in a distribution. This discussion, which briefly compares and contrasts these tests, may aid the reader in choosing the test which will best handle the data of a given study.

In testing hypotheses about whether a sample was drawn from a population with a specified distribution, the investigator may use one of three goodness-of-fit tests: The binomial test, the one-sample chi-square test, or the Kolmogorov-Smirnov one-sample test. The choice among these three tests should be determined by (1) the number of categories in the measurements, (2) the level of measurement used, (3) the size of the sample, and (4) the power of the statistical test.

The binomial test is appropriate when there are just two categories in the classification of the data. It is uniquely useful when the sample size is so small that the chi-square test is inappropriate.

The chi-square test should be used when the data are in discrete categories and when the expected frequencies are sufficiently large. When $k = 2$, each E_i should be 5 or larger. When $k > 2$, no more than about 20 percent of the E_i's should be smaller than 5 and none should be less than 1.

Both the binomial test and the chi-square test may be used with data measured on either a nominal or an ordinal scale.

The chi-square test discussed in this chapter is insensitive to the effects of order when $df > 1$, and thus may not be the best test when a hypothesis assumes that the variables are ordered.

The Kolmogorov-Smirnov test should be used when one can assume that the variable under consideration has a continuous distribution. However, if this test is used when the population distribution $F_0(X)$ is discontinuous, the error that occurs in the resulting probability statement is in the "safe" direction

(Goodman, 1954). That is, if the tables which assume that $F_0(X)$ is continuous are used to test a hypothesis about a discontinuous variable, the test is a conservative one; if H_0 is rejected by that test we can have real confidence in that decision.

It has already been mentioned that the Kolmogorov-Smirnov test treats individual observations separately and thus does not lose information because of grouping, as the chi-square test sometimes must. With a continuous variable, if the sample is small and, therefore, adjacent categories must be combined for the chi-square test, the chi-square test is definitely less powerful than the Kolmogorov-Smirnov test. It would seem that in all cases where it is applicable the Kolmogorov-Smirnov test is the more powerful goodness-of-fit test of those presented.

In cases where parameters must be estimated from the sample the chi-square goodness-of-fit test is easily modified for use by reducing the degrees of freedom. However, for the Kolmogorov-Smirnov test, the distribution of D is not known for the case when certain parameters of the population have been estimated from the sample. There is some evidence which suggests that, if the Kolmogorov-Smirnov test is applied in such cases (e.g., for testing goodness of fit to a normal distribution with mean and standard deviation estimated from the sample), the use of Appendix Table F will lead to a conservative test. That is, if the critical value of D (as shown in Table F) is exceeded by the observed value in these circumstances, we may with considerable confidence reject H_0.

The test for distributional symmetry is useful in determining the shape of a distribution. The shape (or skewness) of a distribution is of special interest when one suspects that, because some observations are "extreme," the distribution is not symmetric about its median.

The one-sample runs test is concerned with the randomness of the temporal occurrence or sequence of the scores in a sample. Thus it could also be used to test hypotheses concerning the clustering or dispersion of dichotomous observations. No general statement about the efficiency of tests of randomness based on runs can be meaningful; in this case the question of efficiency has meaning only in the context of a specific problem.

The change-point test is useful when one wishes to test the hypothesis that there has been a change in the distribution of a sequence of events. In order to use the test appropriately it is not necessary to know *a priori* when the change occurred. The test assesses the likelihood that a change in fact occurred in the sequence of observations and whether the observed change exceeds the fluctuation expected due to chance. Two change-point tests were described: one for observations based upon a binomial or binary process and the other for samples from a continuous distribution.

CHAPTER 5

THE CASE OF ONE SAMPLE, TWO MEASURES OR PAIRED REPLICATES

One-sample statistical tests involving two measures or paired replicates are used when the researcher wishes to establish whether two treatments are different or whether one treatment is "better" than another. The "treatment" may be any of a wide variety of conditions: injection of a drug, training, acculturation, propaganda, separation from family, surgical alteration, introduction of a new element into the economy, etc. In each case, the group that has undergone the treatment is compared with one that has not, or that has undergone a different treatment.

In such comparisons of two groups, sometimes significant differences are observed which are not the result of the treatment. For instance, a researcher may attempt to compare two teaching methods by having one group of students taught by one method and a different group taught by another. Now, if one of the groups has abler or more motivated students, the performance of the two groups after the different learning experiences may not accurately reflect the relative effectiveness of the two teaching methods at all, because other variables are producing the observed differences in performance.

One way to overcome the difficulty imposed by extraneous differences between groups is to use two related samples in the research. That is, one may "match" or otherwise relate the two samples studied. This matching may be achieved by using each subject as its own control or by pairing subjects and then assigning the two members of each pair to the two conditions. The subject who "serves as its own control" is exposed to both treatments at different times. When the pairing method is used, the goal is to select pairs of subjects which are as much alike as possible with respect to any extraneous variables which might influence the outcome of the research. In the example mentioned above, the pairing method would require that a number of pairs of students be selected, each pair composed of two students of substantially equal ability and motivation. One member of each pair, chosen from the two by some random procedure, would be assigned to the class taught by one of the methods and the matched "partner" would be assigned to the class taught by the other method.

Wherever it is feasible, the method of using each subject as its own control (and counterbalancing the order in which the treatments are assigned) is preferable to the pairing method. The reason for this is that our ability to match people is limited by our ignorance of the relevant variables which underlie the behavior being studied. Moreover, even when we do know what variables are important and, therefore, should be controlled by the pairing process, our tools for measuring these variables are rather gross or inexact and, thus, our pairing based on such measures may be faulty. A matching design is only as good as the experimenter's ability to determine how to match the pairs, and this ability is frequently very limited. This problem is circumvented when each subject is used as its own control; no more precise matching is possible than that achieved by identity.

The usual parametric technique for analyzing data from two related samples is to apply a t test to the difference scores. A difference score may be obtained from the two scores of the two members of each matched pair or from the two scores of each subject under the two conditions. The t test assumes that the difference scores are independently drawn from a normal distribution, which implies that the variables be measured on at least an interval scale.

Sometimes, the t test is not appropriate. The researcher may find:

1. The assumptions and requirements of the t test are unrealistic for the data.
2. It is desirable to avoid making the assumptions or testing the requirements of the t test and, thus, give greater generality to his or her conclusions.
3. The differences among matched pairs are not represented as scores but rather as "signs" (i.e., one can tell which member of any pair is "greater than" the other but cannot tell *how much* greater).
4. The scores are simply classificatory—the two members of the matched pair can either respond in the same way or in entirely different ways which do not stand in any order or quantitative relation to each other.

In such instances, the experimenter may choose from one of the nonparametric statistical tests for two measures from one sample, or paired replicates, which are presented in this chapter. In addition to being suitable for the cases mentioned above, these tests have the further advantage that they do not require that all pairs be drawn from the same population. Four tests are presented; the discussion at the end of the chapter indicates the special features and uses of each. This discussion should aid the reader in selecting the technique that would be most appropriate to use in a particular situation.

5.1 THE McNEMAR CHANGE TEST

5.1.1 Function

The *McNemar test* for the significance of changes is particularly applicable to "before and after" designs in which each subject is used as its own control and in which the measurements are made on either a nominal or ordinal scale. Thus it might be used to test the effectiveness of a particular treatment (meeting, newspaper editorial, campaign speech, personal visit, etc.) on voters' preferences among candidates for elective office. Or it might be used to test the effect of rural-to-city moves on people's political affiliations. Notice that these are studies in which people could serve as their own controls and in which nominal or categorical measurement would be appropriate for assessing the "before to after" change.

5.1.2 Rationale and Method

To test the significance of any observed change by this method, a fourfold table of frequencies is used to represent the first and second sets of responses from the same individuals. The general features of such a table are illustrated in Table 5.1, in which + and − are used to denote different responses. Notice that those cases that show changes between the first and second response appear in the upper left (+ to −) and lower right (− to +) cells of the table. The entries in the table are the frequencies of occurrence of the associated outcomes. Thus, A denotes the number of individuals whose responses were + on the first measure and − on the second measure. Similarly, D is the number of individuals who changed from − to +. B is the frequency of individuals who responded the same (+) on each occasion, and C is the number of individuals who responded the same (−) both before and after.

Thus, $A + D$ is the total number of people whose responses changed. The null hypothesis is that the number of changes in each direction is equally likely. That is, of the $A + D$ individuals who changed, we would expect $(A + D)/2$ individuals to change from + to − and $(A + D)/2$ individuals to change from − to +. In other words, when H_0 is true, the expected frequency in each of the two cells is $(A + D)/2$.

		After	
		−	+
Before	+	A	B
	−	C	D

TABLE 5.1
Fourfold table for use in testing significance of changes

It will be recalled from Chap. 4 that

$$X^2 = \sum_{i=1}^{k} \frac{(O_i - E_i)^2}{E_i} \tag{4.5}$$

where O_i = the observed number of cases in the ith category
E_i = the expected number of cases in the ith category when H_0 is true
k = the number of categories

In the McNemar test for the significance of changes, we are interested only in cells in which changes may occur. Therefore, if A is the observed number of cases for which the responses change from $+$ to $-$, D is the observed number of cases which change $-$ to $+$, and $(A + D)/2$ is the expected number of cases in each cell A and D, then

$$X^2 = \sum_{i=1}^{2} \frac{(O_i - E_i)^2}{E_i}$$

$$= \frac{[A - (A + D)/2]^2}{(A + D)/2} + \frac{[D - (A + D)/2]^2}{(A + D)/2}$$

Expanding and collecting terms, we have

$$X^2 = \frac{(A - D)^2}{A + D} \qquad \text{with } df = 1 \tag{5.1}$$

The sampling distribution of X^2 calculated from Eq. (5.1) when H_0 is true is asymptotically distributed as chi square with $df = 1$.

CORRECTION FOR CONTINUITY. The approximation by the chi-square distribution of the sampling distribution of X^2 becomes more precise if a correction for continuity is made. The correction is necessary because a continuous distribution (chi square) is used to approximate a discrete distribution (X^2). When all expected frequencies are small, the approximation may be poor. The purpose of the correction for continuity (Yates, 1934) is to remove this source of imprecision.

With the correction for continuity included,

$$X^2 = \frac{(|A - D| - 1)^2}{A + D} \qquad \text{with } df = 1 \tag{5.2}$$

The evaluation of the numerator in Eq. (5.2) directs one to subtract 1 from the absolute value of the difference between A and D (i.e., the difference between A and D irrespective of sign) before squaring. The significance of any observed value of X^2, computed from Eq. (5.2), is determined by reference to Table C of the Appendix, which gives various critical values of the chi-square distribution for df's from 1 to 30. That is, if the observed value of X^2 is greater than or equal to the critical value given in Appendix Table C for a particular significance level and $df = 1$, one may reject the hypothesis that the two types of changes were equally likely.

TABLE 5.2
Form of fourfold table to show changes in preference for Presidential candidates

Preference before TV debate	Preference after TV debate	
	Reagan	Carter
Carter	A	B
Reagan	C	D

Example 5.1 During Presidential campaigns (and some other campaigns for elective office) there have been television debates between two or more candidates. A researcher in communication techniques—as well as the candidates—was interested in determining whether or not a particular debate between two candidates in the 1980 Presidential election was effective in changing viewers' preferences for the candidates. It was predicted that, if the candidates (Jimmy Carter and Ronald Reagan) were equally effective, there should have been comparable changes in the preferences for each candidate of viewers of the debate. However, if one candidate were more effective or persuasive during the debate, there would be a differential shift in preference from one candidate to the other. To assess the effectiveness of the debate, the researcher selected 70 adults at random before the debate and asked them to indicate their preferences for the two candidates. Upon the conclusion of the debate, he asked the *same* people for their preference for the two candidates. Thus, in each case he knows the preference of each person before and after the debate. He may cast the data in the form shown in Table 5.2.

i. Null hypothesis. H_0: among those viewers *who change* their preferences, the probability that a viewer will switch from Reagan to Carter will be the same as the probability that a viewer will switch from Carter to Reagan.[1] The alternative hypothesis is H_1: there is a differential change in preference. The hypotheses may be summarized as follows:

$$H_0: \quad P[\text{Reagan} \longrightarrow \text{Carter}] = P[\text{Carter} \longrightarrow \text{Reagan}]$$

$$H_1: \quad P[\text{Reagan} \longrightarrow \text{Carter}] \neq P[\text{Carter} \longrightarrow \text{Reagan}]$$

ii. Statistical test. The McNemar test for the significance of changes is chosen because the study uses two related samples (the same subjects measured twice); this test is of the "before and after" type and uses nominal (categorical) measurement.

iii. Significance level. Let $\alpha = .05$ and N is the number of people queried before and after viewing the Presidential debate = 70.

iv. Sampling distribution. Appendix Table C gives critical values of the chi-square distribution for various levels of significance. The sampling distribution of X^2 computed from Eq. (5.2) is asymptotically distributed as chi square with $df = 1$.

---

[1] This statement of H_0 suggests a straightforward application of the binomial test (Sec. 4.1). The relation between the McNemar test and the binomial test is outlined in the discussion of small expected frequencies (below).

TABLE 5.3
Subject's preference for Presidential candidates before and after TV debate

Preference before TV debate	Preference after TV debate	
	Reagan	Carter
Carter	13	28
Reagan	27	7

v. Rejection region. Since H_1 does not specify the direction of the difference in preference, the region of rejection is nondirectional. The region of rejection consists of all values of X^2 which are so large that they have a nondirectional probability associated with their occurrence when H_0 is true of .05 or less.

vi. Decision. The data from this study are shown in Table 5.3. It shows that $A = 13 =$ the number of viewers who switched their preferences from Carter to Reagan, and $D = 7 =$ the number of viewers who switched their preferences from Reagan to Carter. $B = 28$ and $C = 27$ are the numbers of viewers who did not change their preferences. We are interested in those viewers who changed their preferences; they are represented in A and D.

For these data,

$$X^2 = \frac{(|A - D| - 1)^2}{A + D} \quad \text{with } df = 1 \tag{5.2}$$

$$= \frac{(|13 - 7| - 1)^2}{13 + 7}$$

$$= 5^2/20$$

$$= 1.25$$

Reference to Appendix Table C reveals that, when H_0 is true and $df = 1$, the probability that $X^2 \geq 3.84$ is .05.

Since the observed value of X^2 (1.25) is less than the critical value of chi square (3.84), we cannot reject the hypothesis that the candidates were equally effective in changing viewers' preferences.

Note. In this example the researcher was interested in whether or not there was a change in preference. The candidates might be interested in the same question; however, for them the appropriate alternative hypothesis would be that the debate would be effective in changing preferences in a particular direction. That is, H_1 would be one-tailed. In that case, Appendix Table C should be used with the probability values halved since the table entries are based on a two-tailed or nondirectional test.

SMALL EXPECTED FREQUENCIES. It was noted earlier that the sampling distribution of X^2 in the chi-square test (and, hence, the McNemar change test) is well approximated by the chi-square distribution only when the sample size is large. For small samples, the approximation is poor. However, there is an alternative procedure when N is small. If the expected frequency for the McNemar test, $(A + D)/2$, is very small—less than 5—, the binomial test (Sec. 4.1) should be used rather than the McNemar test. To use the binomial test, let $N = A + D$ and x be the smaller of the two observed frequencies, either A or D, and use Appendix Table D to test the significance of x.

It should be noted that we could have analyzed the data in Table 5.3 by using the binomial test. In that case, the null hypothesis would be that the sample of $N = A + D$ cases came from a binomial population where $p = q = \frac{1}{2}$. For the above data, $N = 20$ and $x = 7$, the smaller of the two frequencies observed. Appendix Table D gives the probability under H_0 of observing seven or fewer changes in one direction (one-tail). That probability is .132, which, when doubled, yields the probability associated with the two-tailed change test, which, for this example, is .264. Thus, the result is essentially the same as that obtained by using the McNemar change test. The difference between the two is due mainly to the fact that the chi-square table does not include probability values between .20 and .30. Had the table of the chi-square distribution (Appendix Table C) been more complete, it would still be unlikely that we could have obtained a probability equal to that of the binomial test; the reason is that the sampling distribution of X^2 is only asymptotically that of the chi-square distribution. Of course, with small samples, we do not expect close correspondence in the probabilities when using the two tests.

5.1.3 Summary of Procedure

These are the steps in the computation of the McNemar change test:

1. Cast the observed frequencies in a fourfold table of the form illustrated in Table 5.1.
2. Determine the total number of "changes," $A + D$. If the total number of changes is less than 10, use the binomial test (Sec. 4.1) rather than the McNemar test.
3. If the total frequency of changes exceeds 10, compute the value of X^2 by using Eq. (5.2).
4. Determine the probability associated with a value as large as the observed value of X^2 by referring to Appendix Table C. If a one-tailed test is called for, halve the probability shown in the table. If the probability shown by Appendix Table C for the observed value of X^2 with $df = 1$ is less than or equal to α, reject H_0 in favor of H_1.

5.1.4 Power-Efficiency

When the McNemar test is used with nominal measures, the concept of power-efficiency is not meaningful since there is no alternative with which to compare the test. However, when the measurements and other aspects of the data are such that it is possible to apply the parametric t test, the McNemar test, like the binomial test, has power-efficiency of about 95 percent for $A + D = 6$, and the power-efficiency declines as $A + D$ increases to an asymptotic efficiency of about 63 percent.

5.1.5 References

Discussions of this test are presented in McNemar (1969) and Everitt (1977).

5.2 THE SIGN TEST

5.2.1 Function

The *sign test* gets its name from the fact that it is based upon the direction of differences between two measures rather than quantitative measures as its data. It is particularly useful for research in which quantitative measurement is impossible or infeasible, but in which it is possible to determine, for each pair of observations, which is the "greater" (in some sense).

The sign test is applicable to the case of two related samples when the experimenter wishes to establish that two conditions are different. The only assumption underlying this test is that the variable under consideration has a continuous distribution. The test does not make any assumptions about the form of the distribution of differences nor does it assume that all subjects are drawn from the same population. The different pairs may be from different populations with respect to age, sex, intelligence, etc.; the only requirement is that within each pair the experimenter has achieved matching with respect to the relevant extraneous variables. As noted earlier in this chapter, perhaps the best way to accomplish this is to use each subject as its own control.

5.2.2 Method

The null hypothesis tested by the sign test is that

$$P[X_i > Y_i] = P[X_i < Y_i] = \tfrac{1}{2}$$

where X_i is the judgment or score under one condition (or before the treatment) and Y_i is the judgment or score under the other condition (or after the treatment). That is, X_i and Y_i are the two "scores" for a matched pair. Another way of stating H_0 is that the median difference between X and Y is zero.

In applying the sign test, we focus on the direction of the difference between every X_i and Y_i, noting whether the *sign* of the difference is positive or negative (+ or −). When H_0 is true, we would expect the number of pairs which have $X_i > Y_i$ to be equal to the number of pairs which have $X_i < Y_i$. That is, if the null hypothesis were true, we would expect about half of the differences to be negative and half to be positive. H_0 is rejected if too few differences of one sign occur.

5.2.3 Small Samples

The probability associated with the occurrence of a particular number of +'s and −'s can be determined by reference to the binomial distribution with $p = q = \frac{1}{2}$, where N is the number of pairs. If a matched pair shows no difference (i.e., the difference is zero and has no sign), it is dropped from the analysis and N is reduced accordingly. Appendix Table D gives the probabilities associated with the occurrence under H_0 of values as small as x for $N \leq 35$. To use this table, let x be the number of fewer signs.

For example, suppose 20 pairs are observed. Sixteen show differences in one direction (+) and the other four show differences in the other direction (−). In this case, $N = 20$ and $x = 4$. Reference to Appendix Table D reveals that the probability of this few or fewer −'s when H_0 is true (i.e., that $p = \frac{1}{2}$) is .006 (one-tailed).

The sign test may be either one-tailed or two-tailed. In a one-tailed test, the alternative hypothesis states which sign (+ or −) will occur more frequently. In a two-tailed test, the prediction is simply that the frequencies with which the two signs occur will be significantly different. For a two-tailed test, the probability values in Appendix Table D are doubled.

Example 5.2*a* For small samples. A researcher was studying husband-wife decision-making processes.[2] A sample of husband-wife pairs was intensively studied to determine the perceived role of each spouse in a major purchase decision—in this case, a home. At one time, each spouse completed a questionnaire concerning the perceived influence that each spouse (in their own marriage) should have in various aspects of the purchase decision. The response to the question was on a scale from husband-dominant to equality to wife-dominant. For each husband-wife pair, the difference between their ratings was determined and was coded as + if the husband judged that the husband should have greater influence than the influence accorded to the husband by the wife. The difference was coded as − if the husband's rating accorded greater influence to the wife than that rated by the wife. The difference was coded as 0 if the couple were in complete agreement on the degree of influence appropriate in the decision.

i. *Null hypothesis.* H_0: husbands and wives agree on the degree of influence each should have in one aspect of the home purchase decision. H_1: husbands judge that they should have greater influence in the purchase decision than their wives judge that they should.
ii. *Statistical test.* The rating scale used in this study constitutes at best a partially ordered scale. The information contained in the ratings is preserved if the difference between each couple's two ratings is expressed by a sign (+ or −). Each couple in this study constitutes a matched pair; they are matched in the sense that each responded to the same question concerning spousal influence in the purchase decision and each is a member of the same family. The sign test is appropriate for measures of the sort described and, of course, is appropriate for a case of two related or matched samples.
iii. *Significance level.* Let $\alpha = .05$ and N is the number of couples in one of the conditions = 17. (N may be reduced if ties occur.)

---

[2] This example is motivated by Qualls, W. J. (1982). A study of joint decision making between husbands and wives in a housing purchase decision. Unpublished D.B.A. dissertation, Indiana University.

TABLE 5.4
Judged influence in decision making

Couple	Rating of influence: Husband	Rating of influence: Wife	Direction of difference	Sign
A	5	3	$X_H > X_W$	+
B	4	3	$X_H > X_W$	+
C	6	4	$X_H > X_W$	+
D	6	5	$X_H > X_W$	+
E	3	3	$X_H = X_W$	0
F	2	3	$X_H < X_W$	−
G	5	2	$X_H > X_W$	+
H	3	3	$X_H = X_W$	0
I	1	2	$X_H < X_W$	−
J	4	3	$X_H > X_W$	+
K	5	2	$X_H > X_W$	+
L	4	2	$X_H > X_W$	+
M	4	5	$X_H < X_W$	−
N	7	2	$X_H > X_W$	+
O	5	5	$X_H = X_W$	0
P	5	3	$X_H > X_W$	+
Q	5	1	$X_H > X_W$	+

iv. Sampling distribution. The associated probability of occurrence of values as large as x is given by the binomial distribution for $p = q = \frac{1}{2}$. The binomial distribution is tabled for selected values of N in Appendix Table D.

v. Rejection region. Since H_1 predicts the direction of the differences, the rejection region is one-tailed. It consists of all values of x (where x is the number of pluses, since the prediction for H_1 is that the positive differences will predominate) for which the one-tailed probability of occurrence when H_0 is true is equal to or less than $\alpha = .05$.

vi. Decision. The influence judgments of each spouse were rated on a seven-point rating scale. On this scale, a rating of 1 represents a judgment that the wife should have complete authority for the decision, a rating of 7 represents a judgment that the husband should have complete authority for the decision, and intermediate values indicate intermediate degrees of influence. Table 5.4 shows the influence ratings assigned by each husband (H) and wife (W) among the 17 couples. The signs of the differences between each couple's ratings are shown in the final column. Note that three couples showed differences opposite to the predicted difference; these are coded with a minus sign. Three other couples were in complete agreement about the influence and, thus, there was no difference; these are coded with a zero and the sample size is reduced from $N = 17$ to $N = 17 - 3 = 14$. The remaining couples showed differences in the predicted direction.

For the data in Table 5.4, x is the number of positive signs $= 11$, and N is the number of matched pairs $= 14$. Appendix Table D shows that for $N = 14$ the probability of observing $x \geq 11$ has a one-tailed probability when H_0 is true of .029. Since this value is in the region of rejection for $\alpha = .05$, our decision is to reject H_0 in favor of H_1. Thus we conclude that husbands believe that they should have greater influence in the home purchase decision than their wives believe that they should.

TIES. For the sign test, a "tie" occurs when it is not possible to discriminate between the values of a matched pair or the two values are equal. In the case of the couples, three ties occurred: the researcher judged that three couples agreed on the degree of influence that each spouse should have in the home purchase decision.

All tied cases are dropped from the analysis for the sign test, and the N is correspondingly reduced. Thus N is the number of matched pairs whose difference score *has a sign*. In the example, 14 of the 17 couples had difference scores with a sign, so for that study $N = 14$.

RELATION TO THE BINOMIAL EXPANSION. In the study just discussed, we should expect that when H_0 is true the frequency of pluses and minuses would be the same as the frequency of heads and tails in a toss of 14 unbiased coins. (More exactly, the analogy is to the toss of 17 unbiased coins, 3 of which rolled out of sight and, thus, could not be included in the analysis.) The probability of getting as extreme an occurrence as 11 heads and 3 tails in a toss of 14 coins is given by the binomial distribution as

$$\sum_{i=x}^{N} \binom{N}{i} p^i q^{N-i}$$

where N = the total number of coins tossed = 14
x = the observed number of heads = 11

and
$$\binom{N}{i} = \frac{N!}{i!(N-i)!}$$

In the case of 11 or more heads when 14 coins are tossed, this is

$$P[x \geq 11] = \frac{\binom{14}{11} + \binom{14}{12} + \binom{14}{13} + \binom{14}{14}}{2^{14}}$$

$$= \frac{364 + 91 + 14 + 1}{16{,}284}$$

$$= .029$$

The probability found by this method is, of course, identical to that found by the method used in the example.

5.2.4 Large Samples

If N is larger than 35, the normal approximation to the binomial distribution can be used. This distribution has

$$\text{Mean} = \mu_x = Np = \frac{N}{2}$$

and
$$\text{Variance} = \sigma_x^2 = Npq = \frac{N}{4}$$

That is, the value of z is given by

$$z = \frac{x - \mu_x}{\sigma_x} = \frac{x - N/2}{.5\sqrt{N}} \tag{5.3}$$

$$= \frac{2x - N}{\sqrt{N}} \tag{5.3a}$$

This expression is approximately normally distributed with zero mean and unit variance. Equation (5.3*a*) is computationally more convenient; however, it does somewhat obscure the form of the test.

The approximation becomes better when a *correction for continuity* is employed. The correction is effected by reducing the difference between the observed number of pluses (or minuses) and the expected number (i.e., the mean) when H_0 is true by .5. (See p. 43 for a more complete discussion of this point.) That is, with the correction for continuity,

$$z = \frac{(x \pm .5) - N/2}{.5\sqrt{N}} \tag{5.4}$$

where $x + .5$ is used when $x < N/2$ and $x - .5$ is used when $x > N/2$. A computationally simpler form of Eq. (5.4) is the following:

$$z = \frac{2x \pm 1 - N}{\sqrt{N}} \tag{5.4a}$$

Here we use $+1$ when $x < N/2$ and -1 when $x > N/2$. The value of z obtained by the application of Eq. (5.4) may be considered to be normally distributed with zero mean and unit variance. Therefore, the significance of an obtained z may be determined by reference to Appendix Table A. That is, Appendix Table A gives the one-tailed probability associated with the occurrence when H_0 is true of values as extreme as an observed x. If a two-tailed test is required, the probability obtained from Table A should be doubled.

Example 5.2*b* For large samples. Suppose an experimenter were interested in determining whether a certain film about juvenile delinquency would change the opinions of the members of a particular community about how severely juvenile delinquents should be punished. He draws a random sample of 100 adults from the community and conducts a "before and after" study, having each subject serve as his or her own control. He asks each subject to take a position on the amount or degree of punitive actions which should be taken against juvenile delinquents. He then shows the film to the 100 adults, after which he repeats the question.

i. Null hypothesis. H_0: the film has no systematic effect on attitudes. That is, of those whose opinions change after seeing the film, just as many decrease as increase the amount of punishment they believe to be appropriate, and any difference observed is of a magnitude which might be expected in a random sample from a population on which the film would have no systematic effect. H_1: the film has a systematic effect on attitudes.

TABLE 5.5
Adult opinions concerning degree of severity of punishment for juvenile delinquents

Judged attitude	Number
Increase in severity	26
Decrease in severity	59
No change	15

ii. *Statistical test.* The sign test is chosen for this study of two related groups because the study uses ordinal measures within paired replicates, and, therefore, the differences may appropriately be represented by plus and minus signs.

iii. *Significance level.* Let $\alpha = .01$ and N is the number of adults (out of 100) who show a difference in their attitudes.

iv. *Sampling distribution.* When H_0 is true, z as computed from Eq. (5.4*a*) [or Eq. (5.4)] is approximately normally distributed for $N > 35$. Appendix Table A gives the probability associated with the occurrence of values as extreme as an obtained z.

v. *Rejection region.* Since H_1 does not state the direction of the predicted differences, the region of rejection is two-tailed. It consists of all values of z which are so extreme that their associated probability of occurrence when H_0 is true is equal to or less than $\alpha = .01$.

vi. *Decision.* The results of this study of the effect of a film upon opinion are summarized in Table 5.5. Did the film have any effect? The data show that there were 15 adults who did not change and 85 who did. The analysis is based only on those subjects who did change. If the film had no systematic effect, we would expect about half of those whose attitudes changed after viewing the film to have increased their judgment and about half to have decreased their judgment. That is, of the 85 people whose attitudes changed, we would expect about 42.5 to show one kind of change and 42.5 to show the other change. Now we observe that 59 *decreased* and 26 *increased*. We may determine the probability that, when H_0 is true, a split as extreme or more extreme could occur by chance. Using Eq. (5.4), and noting that $x > N/2$ (that is, $59 > 42.5$), we have

$$z = \frac{2x \pm 1 - N}{\sqrt{N}} \tag{5.4a}$$

$$z = \frac{118 - 1 - 85}{\sqrt{85}}$$

$$= 3.47$$

Reference to Appendix Table A reveals that the probability $|z| \geq 3.47$ when H_0 is true is $2(.0003) = .0006$. (The probability shown in the table is doubled because the tabled values are for a one-tailed test, whereas the region of rejection in this case is two-tailed.) Since .0006 is smaller than $\alpha = .01$, the decision is to reject the null hypothesis in favor of the alternative hypothesis. We conclude from these data that the film had a significant systematic effect on adults' attitudes regarding the severity of punishment desirable for juvenile delinquents.

This example was included not only because it demonstrates a useful application of the sign test but also because data of this sort are often analyzed incorrectly. The data in Table 5.5 are cast in terms of the variables of interest. A fourfold table could be constructed which contained the same information, but would require that we also know the separate frequencies B and C.[3] It is not too uncommon for researchers to analyze such data by using the row and column totals as if they represented independent samples. This is not the case; the row and column totals are separate but not independent representations of the same data.

This example could also have been analyzed by the McNemar test for the significance of changes (Sec. 5.1). With the use of the data in Table 5.5,

$$X^2 = \frac{(|A - D| - 1)^2}{A + D} \qquad \text{with } df = 1 \tag{5.2}$$

$$= \frac{(|59 - 26| - 1)^2}{59 + 26}$$

$$= 12.05$$

Appendix Table C shows that $X^2 \geq 12.05$ with $df = 1$ has a probability of occurrence when H_0 is true of less than .001. This finding is not in conflict with that yielded by the sign test. The slight difference between the two results is due to the limitations of the table of the chi-square distribution used. It should be noted that, if z is computed by using Eq. (5.3) and if X^2 is computed by using Eq. (5.1) (that is, no correction for continuity is made in either case), then z^2 will be identical to X^2 for any set of data. The same is true if the calculations are made by using the correction for continuity [Eqs. (5.2) and (5.4)].

5.2.5 Summary of Procedure

These are the steps in the use of the sign test:

1. Determine the sign of the difference between the two members of each pair.
2. By counting, determine the value of N equal to the number of pairs whose differences show a sign (ties are ignored).
3. The method for determining the probability of occurrence of data as extreme or more extreme when H_0 is true depends on the size of N:
   (*a*) If N is 35 or smaller, Appendix Table D shows the one-tailed probability associated with a value as small as the observed value of x = the number of fewer signs. For a two-tailed test, double the probability value obtained from Appendix Table D.
   (*b*) If N is larger than 35, compute the value of z by using Eq. (5.4*a*). Appendix Table A gives one-tailed probabilities associated with values as extreme as

---

[3] The reader is urged to construct the fourfold table as an exercise using $B = 7$ and $C = 8$.

various values of z. For a two-tailed test, double the probability values shown in Appendix Table A.

4. If the probability yielded by the test is less than or equal to α, reject H_0.

5.2.6 Power-Efficiency

The power-efficiency of the sign test is about 95 percent for $N = 6$, but it declines as the size of the sample increases to an eventual (asymptotic) efficiency of 63 percent. Discussions of the power-efficiency of the sign test for large samples may be found in Lehmann (1975).

5.2.7 References

For other discussions of the sign test, the reader should consult Dixon and Massey (1983), Lehmann (1975), Moses (1952), and Randles and Wolfe (1979).

5.3 THE WILCOXON SIGNED RANKS TEST

The sign test discussed in the previous section utilizes information only about the *direction* of the differences within pairs. If the relative *magnitude* as well as the direction of the differences is considered, a more powerful test can be used. The *Wilcoxon signed ranks test* does just that—it gives more weight to a pair which shows a large difference between the two conditions than to a pair which shows a small difference.

The Wilcoxon signed ranks test is a very useful test for the behavioral scientist. With behavioral data, it is not uncommon that the researcher can (1) tell which member of a pair is "greater than," i.e., tell the sign of the difference between any pair, and (2) rank the differences in order of absolute size. That is, the researcher can make the judgment of "greater than" between any pair's two values as well as between any two difference scores arising from any two pairs. With such information the experimenter may use the Wilcoxon signed ranks test.

5.3.1 Rationale and Method

Let d_i be the difference score for any matched pair, representing the difference between the pair's scores under two treatments X and Y. That is, $d_i = X_i - Y_i$. To use the Wilcoxon signed ranks test, rank all of the d_i's without regard to sign: give the rank of 1 to the smallest $|d_i|$, the rank of 2 to the next smallest, etc. When ranking scores without regard to sign, a d_i of -1 is given a lower rank than a d_i of either $+2$ or -2.

Then to each *rank* affix the sign of the difference. That is, indicate which ranks arose from negative d_i's and which ranks arose from positive d_i's.

The null hypothesis is that treatments X and Y are equivalent, i.e., they are samples from populations with the same medians and the same continuous distribution. If H_0 is true, we should expect to find some of the larger d_i's favoring treatment X and some favoring treatment Y. That is, when there is no difference between X and Y, some of the larger ranks would come from positive d_i's whereas others would come from negative d_i's. Thus, if we summed those ranks having plus signs and summed those ranks having minus signs, we would expect the two sums to be about equal when H_0 is true. But if the sum of the positive ranks is very much different from the sum of the negative ranks, we would infer that treatment X differs from treatment Y, and, thus, we would reject H_0. That is, we reject H_0 if either the sum of the ranks for the negative d_i's *or* the sum of the ranks for the positive d_i's is too small.

To develop a test, we shall define two statistics:

$$T^+ = \text{the sum of the ranks of the positive } d_i\text{'s}$$

and

$$T^- = \text{the sum of the ranks of the negative } d_i\text{'s}$$

Since the sum of all of the ranks is $N(N + 1)/2$, $T^- = N(N + 1)/2 - T^+$.

TIES. Occasionally the two scores of any pair are equal. That is, no difference between the two treatments is observed for that pair, so that $X_i - Y_i = d_i = 0$. Such pairs are dropped from the analysis and the sample size is reduced accordingly. This is the same practice we followed for the sign test. Thus, N is the number of matched pairs minus the number of pairs for which $X = Y$.

Another sort of tie can occur. Two or more d's can be of the same magnitude. We assign such tied cases the same rank. The rank assigned is the *average of the ranks* which would have been assigned if the d's had differed slightly. Thus three pairs might yield d's of -1, -1, and $+1$. Each pair would be assigned the rank of 2, for $(1 + 2 + 3)/3 = 2$. Then the next d in order would receive the rank of 4, because ranks 1, 2, and 3 have already been assigned. If two pairs had yielded d's of 1, both would receive the rank of 1.5 since $(1 + 2)/2 = 1.5$, and the next largest d would receive a rank of 3. The practice of giving tied observations the average of the ranks they would otherwise have gotten has a negligible effect on T^+, the statistic on which the Wilcoxon signed ranks test is based, but is essential if proper use is to be made of the test.

For applications of these principles for the handling of ties, see the example for large samples in Sec. 5.3.3.

5.3.2 Small Samples

Let T^+ be the sum of the ranks for which the differences d_i are positive. Appendix Table H gives various values of T^+ and their associated probabilities of occurrence under the assumption of no difference between the X and Y groupings. That is, if an observed T^+ is equal to the value given in Appendix Table H for a particular sample size N, the probability of a T^+ as large (or larger) is tabulated. If that probability is less than or equal to the significance level chosen, the null hypothesis may then be rejected at that level of significance.

Appendix Table H may be used with both one-tailed and two-tailed tests. A one-tailed test is appropriate if the experimenter has predicted in advance the direction of the differences. For a two-tailed test, double the tabled entry.

For example, if $T^+ = 42$ were the sum of the positive ranks when $N = 9$, one could reject H_0 at the $\alpha = .02$ level if H_1 had been that the two variables would differ, and one could reject H_0 at the .01 level if H_1 had been that the median of X is greater than the median of Y.

Example 5.3*a*   For small samples. There is considerable evidence that adults are able to use visual cues in processing auditory information. In normal conversation, people are able to utilize lip movements in processing speech. The congruence between lip movements and speech sounds is particularly beneficial in noisy environments. Additional research has shown that the processing of speech is impaired when the auditory and visual cues are not congruent. In infants, the ability to discriminate and localize the source of complex auditory and visual stimuli is established by the age of 6 months.

An experiment was designed to determine whether 10- to 16-week-old infants are aware of the synchrony between lip movements and speech sounds in normal speech.[4] Infants were placed in a soundproof room with a window through which they could see a person speaking. That person spoke into a microphone and the sound was delivered directly into the room (in-synchrony) or after a 400-millisecond delay (out-of-synchrony). The amount of time the infant watched the face in the window was measured in each condition. It was argued that, if an infant is able to discriminate the two conditions, the amount of time spent looking at the face in the window would be different, although there was no *a priori* hypothesis concerning which condition would elicit the greater amount of attention in-synchrony because it is consistent with experience or out-of-synchrony because of its novelty.

There are substantial individual differences among infants in the amount of time they may be able to attend to any stimulus. However, the *difference* in the time spent looking in the in-synchrony condition and the time spent looking in the out-of-synchrony condition should be a reliable indicator of the ability to discriminate. If the infant spends more time looking at the in-synchrony presentation, the difference would be positive. If the infant spends more time looking at the out-of-synchrony presentation, the difference would be negative. If the infant can discriminate, the differences should tend to be in one direction. Moreover, any differences in the opposite direction should be relatively small.

Although the experimenter is confident that differences in the percentage of time spent looking indicate differences in attention, she is not sure that the scores are sufficiently exact to be treated other than in an ordinal manner. That is, she is not willing to say more than that larger differences in looking reflect increased attention; for example, a difference in looking of 30 indicates a greater difference in attention than a difference of 20. Thus, although the interpretation of the numerical magnitudes of differences in looking does not directly reflect the numerical magnitudes of differences in attention, the *rankings* of the differences in looking do reflect the order of differences in attention.

[4] Dodd, B. (1979). Lip reading in infants: Attention to speech presented in- and out-of-synchrony. *Cognitive Psychology*, **11**, 478–484.

i. *Null hypothesis.* H_0: the amount of time the infant spends looking at the window does not depend upon the type of presentation. In terms of the Wilcoxon signed ranks test, the sum of the positive ranks does not differ from the sum of the negative ranks. The alternative hypothesis is H_1: the amount of time the infant spends looking does depend upon the type of presentation, i.e., the sum of the positive ranks differs from the sum of the negative ranks.

ii. *Statistical test.* The Wilcoxon signed ranks test is chosen because the study employs two related samples and it yields difference scores which may be ranked in order of absolute magnitude.

iii. *Significance level.* Let $\alpha = .01$ and N is the number of pairs (12) minus any pairs whose $d_i = 0$.

iv. *Sampling distribution.* Appendix Table H gives upper-tail probability values from the sampling distribution for T^+ for $N \leq 15$.

v. *Rejection region.* Since the direction of the difference is not predicted in advance, a two-tailed region of rejection is appropriate. The region of rejection consists of all values of T^+ (the sum of the positive ranks) which are so large that the probability associated with their occurrence when H_0 is true is less than or equal to $\alpha = .01$ for a two-tailed test.

vi. *Decision.* In this study, 12 infants served as subjects. The percentage of time spent looking at each presentation is given in Table 5.6. The table shows that only two infants (*RH* and *CW*) showed differences in the direction of greater attention paid to the in-synchrony presentations. These difference scores are among the smallest; their ranks are 1 and 4.

The sum of the positive ranks is $T^+ = 10 + 12 + 6 + 3 + 8 + 5 + 11 + 9 + 2 + 7 = 73$. Appendix Table H shows that when $N = 12$ and $T^+ = 73$, we may reject the null hypothesis at $\alpha = .01$ for a two-tailed test since the tabled probability (.0024) corresponds to .0048 for a two-tailed test. Therefore we reject H_0 in favor of H_1 in this study, and conclude that infants are able to discriminate between in-synchrony and out-of-synchrony speech and lip movements.

TABLE 5.6
Percentage inattention to in- and out-of-synchrony presentation

Subject	In-synchrony	Out-of-synchrony	d	Rank of d
DC	20.3	50.4	30.1	10
MK	17.0	87.0	70.0	12
VH	6.5	25.1	18.6	6
JM	25.0	28.5	3.5	3
SB	5.4	26.9	21.5	8
MM	29.2	36.6	7.4	5
RH	2.9	1.0	−1.9	−1
DJ	6.6	43.8	37.2	11
JD	15.8	44.2	28.4	9
ZC	8.3	10.4	2.1	2
CW	34.0	29.9	−4.1	−4
AF	8.0	27.7	19.7	7

$N = 12$, $T^+ = 73$, $T^- = 5$.

It is worth noting that the data in Table 5.6 could be analyzed with the sign test (Sec. 5.2), a less powerful test. For that test, $x = 2$ and $N = 12$. Appendix Table D gives the probability associated with such an occurrence when H_0 is true as $2(.019) = .038$ for a two tailed test. Therefore, using the sign test, our decision would be to *not reject* H_0 when $\alpha = .01$, whereas the Wilcoxon signed rank test enabled us to *reject* H_0 at that level. This difference is not surprising, for the Wilcoxon signed ranks test takes into account the fact that the two negative d's are among the smallest d's observed, whereas the sign test is unaffected by the relative magnitude of the d_i's.

5.3.3 Large Samples

When N is larger than 15, Appendix Table H cannot be used. However, it can be shown that in such cases the sum of the ranks, T^+, is approximately normally distributed with

$$\text{Mean} = \mu_{T^+} = \frac{N(N+1)}{4}$$

and

$$\text{Variance} = \sigma^2_{T^+} = \frac{N(N+1)(2N+1)}{24}$$

Therefore,

$$z = \frac{T^+ - \mu_{T^+}}{\sigma_{T^+}} = \frac{T^+ - N(N+1)/4}{\sqrt{N(N+1)(2N+1)/24}} \tag{5.5}$$

is approximately normally distributed with mean zero and unit variance. Thus, Appendix Table A may be used to find the probability associated with the occurrence when H_0 is true of values as extreme as an observed z computed from Eq. (5.5).

Although the large-sample test appears to be a good approximation even for relatively small samples, the correspondence between the exact and approximate probabilities for a given sample size depends on the value of T^+. The approximation does improve as the sample size gets larger.

Example 5.3*b* For large samples. Inmates in a Federal prison served as subjects in a decision-making study.[5] First the prisoners' utility (subjective value) for cigarettes was measured individually, cigarettes being negotiable in prison society. Using each subject's utility function, the experimenter then attempted to predict the decisions the man would make in a game in which he repeatedly had to choose between two different (varying) gambles, and in which cigarettes might be won or lost.

[5] Hurst, P. M., and Siegel, S. (1956). Prediction of decisions from a higher ordered metric scale. *Journal of Experimental Psychology*, **52**, 138–144.

The first hypothesis tested was that the experimenter could better predict the subjects' decisions by means of their utility functions than he could by assuming that their utility for cigarettes was equal to the cigarette's objective value and, therefore, predicting the "rational" choice in terms of objective value. This hypothesis was confirmed.

However, as was expected, some responses were not predicted successfully by this hypothesis of maximization of expected utility. Anticipating this outcome, the experimenters had hypothesized that such errors in prediction would be due to the indifference of the subjects as to the two gambles offered. That is, a prisoner might find two gambles either equally attractive or equally unattractive, and, therefore, be indifferent in the choice between them. Such choices would be difficult to predict. But in such choices, it was reasoned that the subject might vacillate considerably before stating a decision. That is, the latency between the offer of the gamble and his statement of a decision would be long. The second hypothesis, then, was that the latencies or response times for those choices that would not be predicted successfully by maximization of expected utility would be longer than the latency times for those choices that would be successfully predicted.

i. *Null hypothesis.* H_0: there is no difference between the latencies or response times of incorrectly predicted and correctly predicted decisions. H_1: the latencies of incorrectly predicted decisions are longer than the latencies of correctly predicted decisions.

ii. *Statistical test.* The Wilcoxon signed ranks test is selected because the data are difference scores from two related samples (correctly predicted choices and incorrectly predicted choices made by the same prisoners), where each subject is used as his own control.

iii. *Significance level.* Let $\alpha = .01$ and N is the number of prisoners who served as subjects $= 30$. (This N will be reduced if any prisoner's d is zero.)

iv. *Sampling distribution.* When H_0 is true, the values of z computed by using Eq. (5.5) are asymptotically normally distributed with a mean of zero and variance of one. Thus Appendix Table A gives the probability associated with the occurrence under H_0 of values as extreme as an obtained z.

v. *Rejection region.* Since the direction of the difference is predicted, the region of rejection is one-tailed. T^+, the sum of the postive rank orders, will be the sum of the ranks of those prisoners whose d's are in the direction predicted. The region of rejection consists of all z's (obtained from T^+) which are so extreme that the probability associated with their occurrence when H_0 is true is equal to or less than $\alpha = .01$.

vi. *Decision.* A difference score ($d_i = X_i - Y_i$) was obtained for each subject by subtracting his median time in coming to correctly predicted decisions Y_i from his median time in coming to incorrectly predicted decisions X_i. Table 5.7 gives these values of d for 30 prisoners as well as the other information necessary to complete the Wilcoxon signed ranks test. A negative d_i indicates that the prisoner's median time in coming to correctly predicted decisions was *longer* than his median time in coming to incorrectly predicted decisions.

For the data in Table 5.7, $T^+ = 298$. We apply Eq. (5.5):

$$z = \frac{T^+ - \mu_{T^+}}{\sigma_{T^+}} = \frac{T^+ - N(N+1)/4}{\sqrt{N(N+1)(2N+1)/24}} \tag{5.5}$$

$$= \frac{298 - (26)(27)/4}{\sqrt{(26)(27)(53)/24}}$$

$$= 3.11$$

TABLE 5.7
Difference in median time between prisoners' correctly and incorrectly predicted decisions

Prisoner	d	Rank of d
1	−2	−11.5
2	0	—
3	0	—
4	1	4.5
5	0	—
6	0	—
7	4	20.
8	4	20.
9	1	4.5
10	1	4.5
11	5	23.
12	3	16.5
13	5	23.
14	3	16.5
15	−1	−4.5
16	1	4.5
17	−1	−4.5
18	5	23.
19	8	25.5
20	2	11.5
21	2	11.5
22	2	11.5
23	−3	−16.5
24	−2	−11.5
25	1	4.5
26	4	20.
27	8	25.5
28	2	11.5
29	3	16.5
30	−1	−4.5

$N = 26$, $T^+ = 298$, $T^- = 53$.

Notice that we have $N = 26$, since four of the prisoners' median times were the same for both correctly and incorrectly predicted decisions and thus their d's were zero. Notice also that our T^+ is the sum of the ranks of those prisoners whose d's are in the direction predicted under H_1, and, therefore, we are justified in proceeding with a one-tailed test. Appendix Table A shows that a z as extreme as $+3.11$ has a one-tailed probability associated with its occurrence when H_0 is true of .0009. Inasmuch as this probability is less than $\alpha = .01$ and the value of z is in the region of rejection, our decision is to reject H_0 in favor of H_1. We conclude that the prisoners' latencies for incorrectly predicted decisions were significantly longer than their latencies for correctly predicted decisions. This conclusion lends some support to the idea that the incorrectly predicted decisions concerned gambles which were equal, or approximately equal, in expected utility to the subjects.

TIED RANKS AND LARGE SAMPLES. If there are tied ranks, then it is necessary to adjust the test statistic to account for the decrease in variability of T. The correction involves counting the ties and reducing the variance accordingly. If there are tied ranks, then

$$\sigma^2_{T^+} = \frac{N(N+1)(2N+1)}{24} - \frac{1}{2}\sum_{j=1}^{g} t_j(t_j-1)(t_j+1) \tag{5.6}$$

where g = the number of groupings of different tied ranks
t_j = the number of tied ranks in grouping j

For the data in the above example, there are a large number of ties. There are $g = 6$ groupings of ties; eight tied at rank 4.5, six tied at rank 11.5, etc. The correction factor for the variance is 414. It was computed by using Eq. (5.6) in the following way:

Grouping	Rank	t_j
1	4.5	8
2	11.5	6
3	16.5	4
4	20	3
5	23	3
6	25.5	2

The uncorrected variance is 1550.25, the corrected variance with the use of Eq. (5.6) is $1550.25 - 414 = 1136.25$. The value of z corrected for ties is, thus, $z = 3.63$. Recall that the unadjusted z was 3.11. The correction of the Wilcoxon signed ranks statistic will *always* increase the value of z when there are ties; therefore, if H_0 is rejected without the correction, it will be rejected with the correction. It should also be noted that use of the correction when there are no ties produces no change in the variance (all groupings would be "ties" of size 1).

5.3.4 Summary of Procedure

These are the steps in the use of the Wilcoxon signed ranks test:

1. For each matched pair of observations, X_i and Y_i, determine the signed difference $d_i = X_i - Y_i$ between the two variables.
2. Rank these d_i's without respect to sign. For tied d_i's, assign the average of the tied ranks.
3. Affix to each rank the sign (+ or −) of the d which it represents.
4. Determine N, the number of nonzero d_i's.
5. Determine T^+, the sum of the ranks which have a positive sign.

6. The procedure for determining the significance of the observed value of T^+ depends on the size of N:

(*a*) If N is 15 or less, Appendix Table H gives probabilities associated with various values of T^+. If the probability associated with the observed value of T^+ is less than or equal to the chosen significance level, reject H_0.

(*b*) If N is larger than 15, compute the value of z by using Eq. (5.5) and, if there are tied ranks, correct the variance by using Eq. (5.6). Determine its associated probability when H_0 is true by referring to Appendix Table A.

For a two-tailed test, double the probability value given. If the probability thus obtained is less than or equal to α, reject H_0.

5.3.5 Power-Efficiency

When the assumptions of the parametric t test are, in fact, met, the asymptotic efficiency near H_0 of the Wilcoxon signed ranks test compared with the t test is $3/\pi = 95.5$ percent (Mood, 1954). This means that $3/\pi$ is the limiting ratio of sample sizes necessary for the Wilcoxon signed ranks test and the t test to attain the same power. For small samples, the efficiency is nearly 95 percent.

5.3.6 References

The reader may find other discussions of the Wilcoxon signed ranks test in Wilcoxon (1945; 1947; 1949), Lehmann (1975), and Randles and Wolfe (1979).

5.4 THE PERMUTATION TEST FOR PAIRED REPLICATES

5.4.1 Function

Permutation tests are nonparametric tests that not only have practical value in the analysis of data but also have heuristic value in that they help expose the underlying nature of nonparametric tests in general. With a permutation test, we can obtain the exact probability when H_0 is true of the occurrence of the observed data, and we can do this without making any assumptions about normality, homogeneity of variance, or the precise form of the underlying distribution. Permutation tests, under certain conditions, are the most powerful of the nonparametric techniques, and are appropriate whenever measurement is so precise that the values of the scores have numerical meaning.

5.4.2 Rationale and Method

The *permutation test* assumes that when we make the paired observations for each subject or the observations for each paired replicate, the two scores observed are randomly assigned to the two conditions. That is, we assume that the subject (or pair) would have given us these two scores *regardless of condition*. This is what we would expect if the null hypothesis of no difference between the conditions is true. Thus, if we had measured subjects on each of two occasions, it is assumed that the scores, say X and Y, could have been observed in the order X then Y or in the order Y then X. If we would calculate the difference scores between the conditions, that difference, under the assumption of random assignment, would be just as likely to be negative as positive. Let $d_i = X_i - Y_i$ be the difference for the ith subject; this is a measure of the difference between conditions. Thus, if H_0 were true, we presume that the sign of this d_i is plus rather than minus simply because we happened to observe the scores in a particular order. It is as if we knew that the subject would give us scores X and Y, and we tossed a coin to determine which score would be the first. If we apply this reasoning to all of the subjects, and if H_0 were true, then every difference we observe could equally likely have had the opposite sign.

Suppose our sample consisted of $N = 8$ pairs, and that the difference scores that we observed happened to be

$$+19 \quad +27 \quad -1 \quad +6 \quad +7 \quad +13 \quad -4 \quad +3$$

When H_0 is true, if our coin tosses had been different, they might just as probably have been

$$-19 \quad -27 \quad +1 \quad -6 \quad -7 \quad -13 \quad +4 \quad -3$$

or if the coins had fallen still another way the observations could have been

$$+19 \quad -27 \quad +1 \quad -6 \quad -7 \quad -13 \quad -4 \quad +3$$

As a matter of fact, if the null hypothesis is true, there are $2^N = 2^8 = 256$ equally likely outcomes, and the one which we observe depends entirely on how the coin landed for each of the eight tosses when we assigned the observations to the two conditions. This means that associated with the sample of scores we observed there are many other possible ones, the total being $2^8 = 256$. When H_0 is true, any one of these 256 possible outcomes is just as likely to occur as the one that actually did occur.

For each of the possible outcomes there is a sum of the differences—Σd_i. Now many of the possible Σd_i are near zero, about what we should expect if H_0 were true. A few Σd_i are far from zero. These are for those combinations which we also would expect if the population median under one of the treatments exceeds that of the other, that is, if H_0 is *false*.

If we wish to test H_0 against some H_1, we set up a region of rejection consisting of the combinations where Σd_i is largest. Suppose $\alpha = .05$. Then the region of rejection would consist of that 5 percent of the possible combinations which contain the most extreme values of Σd_i.

In the example under discussion, 256 possible outcomes are equally likely when H_0 is true. The region of rejection thus consists of the 12 most extreme possible outcomes, for $(.05)(256) = 12.8$. When the null hypothesis is true, the probability that we would observe one of these 12 extreme outcomes is $\frac{12}{256} = .047$. If we actually observe one of those extreme outcomes included in the region of rejection, we may reject H_0 in favor of H_1. Basically, if one of those extreme outcomes actually occurs, we reject H_0, arguing that the probability of the observed outcome (or one more extreme) is so small that the hypothesis must have been incorrect.

When a two-tailed test is appropriate, as in the case of the following example, the region of rejection consists of the most extreme possible outcomes at both the positive and negative ends of the distribution of Σd_i's. That is, in the example, the 12 outcomes in the region of rejection would include the 6 which yield the largest *positive* Σd_i and the 6 which yield the largest *negative* Σd_i (or the smallest sums).

Example 5.4 Suppose a child psychologist wished to test whether nursery school attendance has any effect on children's social perceptiveness. He or she scores social perceptiveness by rating children's responses to a group of pictures which depict a variety of social situations by asking a standard group of questions about each picture. By this means he or she obtains a score between 0 and 100 for each child.

By means of careful standardization procedures the researcher is reasonably confident that the index of social perceptiveness is on an interval scale. That is, the researcher is able to interpret the numerical magnitudes of the differences observed.

To test the effect of nursery school attendance on children's social perceptiveness scores, the psychologist obtains eight pairs of identical twins to serve as subjects. At random, one twin from each pair is assigned to attend nursery school for a term. At the end of the term, the 16 children are each given the test of social perceptiveness.

i. *Null hypothesis.* H_0: the two treatments are equivalent. That is, there is no difference in social perceptiveness under the two conditions (attendance at nursery school or staying at home). In social perceptiveness, all 16 observations (8 pairs) are from a common population. H_1: the two treatments are not equivalent.

ii *Statistical test.* The permutation test for paired replicates is chosen because of its appropriateness to this design (two matched samples or paired replicates), and because for these data we are willing to consider that its requirement of an interval scale of measurement is met.

iii. *Significance level.* Let $\alpha = .05$ and N is the number of pairs = 8.

iv. *Sampling distribution.* The sampling distribution consists of the permutation of the signs of the differences to include all possible (2^N) occurrences of Σd_i. In this case, $2^N = 2^8 = 256$.

v. *Rejection region.* Since H_1 does not predict the direction of the differences, a two-tailed test is used. The region of rejection consists of those 12 outcomes that have the most extreme Σd_i's, the 6 largest and the 6 smallest.

vi. *Decision.* The data of this study are shown in Table 5.8. The d's observed, in order of absolute magnitude, were

$$+27 \quad +19 \quad +13 \quad +7 \quad +6 \quad -4 \quad +3 \quad -1$$

For these d's, the sum is $+70$. For ease of computation of the permutation distribution, the d's are listed in order of decreasing magnitude in Table 5.9. The first row of the table shows each d with a positive value, resulting in the largest Σd_i. Starting at the right side of the list (with the smallest value), we begin to alternate the signs. Thus the signs in the

TABLE 5.8
Social perceptiveness scores of "nursery school" and "home" children

Pair	Social perceptiveness of twin at: Nursery school	Home	d
a	82	63	19
b	69	42	27
c	73	74	−1
d	43	37	6
e	58	51	7
f	56	43	13
g	76	80	−4
h	85	82	3

TABLE 5.9
The six most extreme possible positive outcomes for the *d*'s shown in Table 5.8

	Outcome								Σd_i
(1)	+27	+19	+13	+7	+6	+4	+3	+1	80
(2)	+27	+19	+13	+7	+6	+4	+3	−1	78
(3)	+27	+19	+13	+7	+6	+4	−3	+1	74
(4)	+27	+19	+13	+7	+6	+4	−3	−1	72
(5)	+27	+19	+13	+7	+6	−4	+3	+1	72
(6)*	+27	+19	+13	+7	+6	−4	+3	−1	70

* Observed outcome.

last *column* for successive rows would be + − + − + − ⋯. For the next *column* the pattern of signs would be + + − − + + − − + + ⋯. The next *column* would alternate + + + + − − − − + ⋯. The pattern would continue. If we then sum the differences for each pattern, we find that they will be in decreasing order of magnitude of Σd_i. For this example, the first six are in the rejection region at the .05 level (two-tailed). Since the observed Σd_i is in the rejection region, we may reject H_0 that there is no difference between the groups. (Note that outcome 6 is in fact the observed outcome.) The probability of its occurrence or the occurrence of a Σd_i as extreme or more extreme when H_0 is true is .047. Since the probability is less than .05, we may reject H_0.

In applying the permutation test, an orderly layout of data as in Table 5.9 facilitates computation. With this sort of layout, it is easy to obtain the critical sum without enumerating all of them. Knowing the number of permutations (2^N) and the significance level chosen enables the researcher to know which sum (but not its value) is at the critical level. Once the outcome entry is specified, the associated sum may then be computed as the critical value.[6]

LARGE SAMPLES. If the number of pairs exceeds about 12, the permutation test is tedious to compute by hand. For example, if $N = 13$, the number of possible outcomes is $2^{13} = 8192$. The rejection region for $\alpha = .05$ would consist of $(.05)(8192) = 410$ possible extreme outcomes. Although only the extreme sums need be calculated, the procedure can be tedious. The computer program in Appendix II can facilitate the use of the permutation test.

Because of the computational cumbersomeness of the permutation test when N is at all large, it is suggested that the Wilcoxon signed ranks test be used in such cases. In the Wilcoxon signed ranks test, ranks are substituted for numbers. It provides a very efficient alternative to the permutation test—indeed, it is *exactly* the permutation test based on ranks.[7]

5.4.3 Summary of Procedure

When N is small and when measurement is on, at least, an interval scale, the permutation test for paired replicates or matched pairs may be used. These are the steps:

1. Observe the values of the various d_i's and their signs.
2. Arrange the observed d_i's in order of decreasing magnitude.
3. Determine the number of possible outcomes when H_0 is true, 2^N.
4. Determine the number of possible outcomes in the region of rejection, $(\alpha)(2^N)$.
5. Identify those possible outcomes which are in the region of rejection by choosing from the possible outcomes those with the largest Σd_i's by using the method described in the example or with a computer program. For a one-tailed test, the outcomes in the region of rejection are at one end of the distribution. For a two-tailed test, half of the outcomes in the region of rejection are those with the largest positive Σd_i's and half are those with the smallest Σd_i's.
6. Determine whether the observed outcome is one of those in the region of rejection. If it is, reject H_0 in favor of H_1.

---

[6] Because there may be duplicate values of Σd_i for different outcomes near the boundary of the region of rejection, the value of Σd_i for successive entries *outside* the critical region should be calculated to ensure that there are no duplicates which cross the boundary. If there are, the region of rejection should be adjusted accordingly.

[7] In a permutation test on ranks, all 2^N permutations of the signs of the ranks are considered, and the most extreme possible constitute the region of rejection. For the data shown in Table 5.6, there are $2^{12} = 4096$ possible and equally likely combinations of signed ranks when H_0 is true. The curious reader should be able to determine that the sample of signed ranks is among the $(.05)(4096) = 204$ most extreme possible outcomes and thus leads us to reject H_0 at $\alpha = .05$, which was our decision based upon Appendix Table H. Indeed, by this permutation method Appendix Table H, the table of the sampling distribution of T^+, can be constructed.

When N is large, the Wilcoxon signed ranks test is recommended for use rather than the permutation test.

5.4.4 Power-Efficiency

The permutation test for matched pairs or paired replicates, because it uses all of the information in the sample, has power-efficiency of 100 percent. It is among the most powerful of all statistical tests.

5.4.5 References

Discussions of the permutation method are contained in Fisher (1973), Moses (1952), Pitman (1937*a*, 1937*b*, 1937*c*), and Scheffé (1943). Moses discusses an alternative method for determining the significance of Σd_i when N is large.

5.5 DISCUSSION

In this chapter we have presented four nonparametric statistical tests for the case of one sample with two measures—either matched pairs or paired replicates. The comparison and contrast of these tests outlined below may aid the reader in choosing from among these tests the one which will be most appropriate to the data of a particular experiment.

All of the tests but the McNemar test for the significance of changes assume that the variable under consideration has a continuous distribution underlying the observations. Notice that there is no requirement that the measurement itself be continuous; the requirement concerns the variable of which the measurement gives some gross or approximate representation.

The McNemar test for the significance of changes may be used when one or both of the conditions under study has been measured only in the sense of a nominal scale. For the case of a matched pair, the McNemar test is unique in its suitability for such data. That is, this test should be used when the data are in frequencies which can only be classified by separate categories which have no relation to each other of the "greater than" type. No assumption of a continuous variable need be made, because this test is equivalent to a test using the binomial distribution with $p = q = \frac{1}{2}$, and N is the number of changes.

If ordinal measurement within pairs is possible (i.e., if the score of one member of a pair can be ranked as "greater than" the score of the other member of the same pair), then the sign test is applicable. That is, the sign test is useful for data on a variable which has underlying continuity but which can be measured in only a very gross way. When the sign test is applied to data which meet the conditions of the parametric alternative (the t test), it has power-efficiency of about 95 percent for $N = 6$, but its power-efficiency declines as N increases to about 63 percent for very large samples.

When the measurement is in an ordinal scale both *within* and *between* paired observations, the Wilcoxon signed ranks test should be used; that is, it is applicable when the researcher can meaningfully rank the differences observed for the various matched pairs. It is not uncommon for behavioral scientists to be able to rank difference scores in the order of absolute size without being able to give truly numerical scores to the observations within each pair. When the Wilcoxon signed ranks test is used for data which, in fact, meet the condition of the t test, its power-efficiency is about 95 percent for large samples and not much less for smaller samples.

The permutation test should be used whenever N is sufficiently small to make it computationally feasible and when the measurement of the variable is at least on an interval scale. The permutation test uses all of the information in the sample and, thus, is 100 percent efficient on data which may be properly analyzed by the t test. A computer program makes the permutation test feasible for moderate sample sizes.

In summary, we conclude that the McNemar test for the significance of changes should be used for both large and small samples when the measurement of at least one of the variables is merely nominal. For the crudest of ordinal measurements, the sign test should be used; for more refined measurement, the Wilcoxon signed ranks test may be used in all cases. If interval measurement is achieved, the permutation test should be used for small to moderate N.

CHAPTER 6

TWO INDEPENDENT SAMPLES

In studying differences between two groups, we first must determine whether they are related or independent groups. Chapter 5 contained statistical tests for use in designs having two related groups or paired replicates. This chapter presents statistical tests for use in designs having two independent groups. Like those presented in Chap. 5, the tests presented here determine whether differences in the samples constitute convincing evidence of a difference in the processes applied to them.

Although the merits of using two related samples or paired replicates in a research design are great, to do so is frequently impracticable. Often the nature of the dependent variable precludes using the subjects as their own controls, as is the case when the dependent variable is the length of time spent solving an unfamiliar problem. A problem can be unfamiliar only once. It also may be impossible to design a study which uses matched pairs, perhaps because of the researcher's inability to discover useful matching variables, or because of an inability to obtain adequate measures (to use in selecting matched pairs) of some variable known to be relevant, or finally because good "matches" are simply unavailable.

When the use of two related samples is impracticable or inappropriate, one may use two independent samples. In this design the two samples may be obtained by either of two methods: (1) they may each be drawn at random from two populations or (2) they may arise from the assignment at random of two treatments to the members of some sample the origins of which are arbitrary. In either case it is not necessary that the two samples be of the same size.

An example of random sampling from two populations would be the drawing of every tenth Democrat and every tenth Republican from an alphabetical list of registered voters.[1] This would result in a random sample of registered Democrats and Republicans from the voting area covered by the list, and the number of Democrats would equal the number of Republicans only if the registration of the two parties happened to be substantially equal in that area. Another example would be the drawing of every eighth freshman and every twelfth senior from a list of students in a college.

An example of the random assignment method might occur in a study of the effectiveness of two instructors in teaching the same course. A registration card might be collected from every student enrolled in the course, and at random one-half of these cards would be assigned to one instructor and one-half to the other.

The usual parametric technique for analyzing data from two independent samples is to apply a t test to the means of the two groups. The t test assumes that the scores (which are summed in the computing of the means) in the samples are independent observations from normally distributed populations with (usually) equal variances. The t test assumes that the observations are measured on at least an interval scale.

For a given piece of research, the t test may be inapplicable for a variety of reasons. The researcher may find that: (1) the assumptions of the t test are unrealistic for the data; (2) he or she prefers to avoid making the assumptions and thus to give the conclusions greater generality; or (3) the "scores" may not be truly *numerical* and, therefore, fail to meet the measurement requirement of the t test. In instances like these, the researcher may analyze the data with one of the nonparametric statistical tests for two independent samples which are presented in this chapter. The comparison and contrast of these tests in the discussion at the conclusion of the chapter may assist the researcher in choosing from among the tests presented that one which is best suited to the data at hand.

6.1 THE FISHER EXACT TEST FOR 2 × 2 TABLES

6.1.1 Function

The *Fisher exact probability test* for 2 × 2 tables is an extremely useful technique for analyzing discrete data (either nominal or ordinal) when the two independent samples are small. It is used when the scores from two independent random samples all fall into one or the other of two mutually exclusive classes. In other words, every subject in each group obtains one of two possible scores. The scores are represented by frequencies in a 2 × 2 contingency table, like Table 6.1. Groups I and

---

[1] Technically, for the sample to be considered a truly *random sample*, we would take each successive group of 10 Democrats (or Republicans) and select at random 1 person from each set.

TABLE 6.1
2 × 2 contingency table

	Group		
Variable	**I**	**II**	Combined
+	A	B	$A+B$
−	C	D	$C+D$
Total	$A+C$	$B+D$	N

II might be any two independent groups, such as experimentals and controls, males and females, employed and unemployed, Democrats and Republicans, fathers and mothers, etc. The row headings, here arbitrarily indicated as plus (+) and minus (−), may be any two classifications: above and below the median, passed and failed, science majors and arts majors, agree and disagree, etc. The test determines whether the two groups differ in the proportions with which they fall into the two classifications. For the data in Table 6.1 (where A, B, C, and D denote frequencies) it would determine whether group I and group II differ significantly in the proportion of pluses and minuses attributed to them.

6.1.2 Method

The exact probability of observing a particular set of frequencies in a 2 × 2 table, when the marginal totals are regarded as fixed, is given by the hypergeometric distribution:

$$p = \frac{\binom{A+C}{A}\binom{B+D}{B}}{\binom{N}{A+B}}$$

$$= \frac{[(A+C)!/A!\,C!][(B+D)!/B!\,D!]}{N!/[(A+B)!\,(C+D)!]}$$

and, thus,

$$p = \frac{(A+B)!\,(C+D)!\,(A+C)!\,(B+D)!}{N!\,A!\,B!\,C!\,D!} \tag{6.1}$$

Appendix Table W may be helpful in calculating the factorials.

To illustrate the use of Eq. (6.1), suppose we observe the data shown in Table 6.2. In that table, $A = 5$, $B = 4$, $C = 0$, and $D = 10$. The marginal totals are $A + B = 9$, $C + D = 10$, $A + C = 5$, and $B + D = 14$. N, the total number of independent observations, is 19. The exact probability that these 19 cases should fall in the 4 cells as they did if the assignment were random may be determined

TABLE 6.2

Variable	Group I	Group II	Combined
+	5	4	9
−	0	10	10
Total	5	14	19

by substituting the observed values into Eq. (6.1):

$$p = \frac{9!\,10!\,5!\,14!}{19!\,5!\,4!\,0!\,10!}$$

$$= .0108$$

We determine that the probability of such an outcome when H_0 is true (that the assignment is random) is $p = .0108$.

Now the above example was a comparatively simple one to compute because one of the cells (the lower left) had a frequency of 0. But if none of the cell frequencies is zero, we must remember that more extreme deviations from the distribution assumed under H_0 could occur with the same marginal totals, and we must take into account these possible more extreme deviations, for a statistical test of the null hypothesis asks: "What is the probability when H_0 is true of the occurrence of the observed outcome *or one more extreme*?"

For example, suppose the data from a particular study were those given in Table 6.3*a*. With the marginal totals unchanged, a more extreme occurrence would be that in Table 6.3*b*. Thus, if we wish to apply a statistical test of the null hypothesis to the data given in Table 6.3*a*, we must sum the probability of its occurrence with the probability of the more extreme possible outcome shown in Table 6.3*b*. We compute each p by using Eq. (6.1). Thus we have

$$p = \frac{5!\,7!\,5!\,7!}{12!\,4!\,1!\,1!\,6!}$$

$$= .04419$$

TABLE 6.3

(*a*)

Group I	Group II	
4	1	5
1	6	7
5	7	12

(*b*)

Group I	Group II	
5	0	5
0	7	7
5	7	12

HIGH ROYDS HOSPITAL
MEDICAL LIBRARY

and
$$p = \frac{5!\,7!\,5!\,7!}{12!\,5!\,0!\,0!\,7!}$$
$$= .00126$$

for Tables 6.3*a* and 6.3*b* respectively. Thus the probability of the occurrence of Table 6.3*a* or of one which is even more extreme (Table 6.3*b*) is

$$p = .04419 + .00126$$
$$= .04545$$

That is, $p = .04545$ is the probability we would use in deciding whether the data in Table 6.3*a* permit us to reject H_0.

The reader can readily see that, if the smallest cell value in the contingency table is even moderately large, the Fisher exact test becomes computationally very tedious. For example, when the alternative hypothesis H_1 is one-tailed, if the smallest cell value is 2, then three exact probabilities must be determined by using Eq. (6.1) and summed; if the smallest cell is 3, then four exact probabilities must be found and summed, etc.

To facilitate calculation of the probability associated with 2×2 contingency tables, Appendix Table I may be used. Table I is applicable to 2×2 contingency tables for which $N \leq 15$. Because of its size and arrangement, we shall discuss the use of Table I in some detail.

These are the steps in using Table I:

1. Determine the row and column totals. Denote the smallest row or column total as S_1. Denote the second smallest row or column total as S_2. Table 6.4 can help in visualizing the procedure. The reader should note that, if S_1 is a row total, S_2 will be a column total.
2. X is the observed frequency in the cell where the row and column containing the smallest and second smallest marginal frequencies intersect.
3. Locate the row (N, S_1, S_2, X) in Table I. There are three entries. The first entry "Obs." is the one-tailed probability of observing a difference equal to or more extreme than the one observed. The second entry is the probability of observing a difference as great or greater in the *opposite* direction. Finally, the third entry "Total" is the two-tailed probability of observing a difference as great or greater than that observed in either direction.

TABLE 6.4

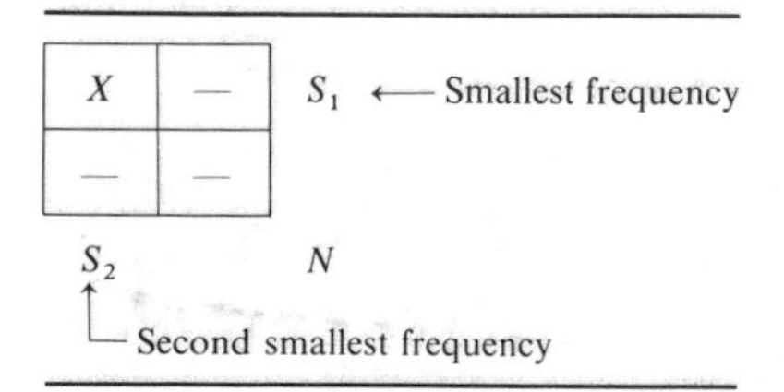

4. Orient and label the observed table to ensure that the table entries are consistent with the hypotheses.

Although the computation of one-tailed and two-tailed probabilities associated with the Fisher exact test is greatly facilitated by the use of Table I, it is important that the user understand the rationale of the test in order to use the table effectively. We shall use Table 6.5 to illustrate its application.

Suppose a researcher has sampled two groups and has the null hypothesis that there are no differences between the two groups on a measured dichotomous variable which is coded, for convenience, + and −. The alternative hypothesis is that group 1 exceeds group 2 in the proportion of + responses. If we let p_1 be the probability that a randomly selected subject from group 1 will respond + and p_2 be the probability that a randomly selected subject from group 2 will respond +, then the null and alternative hypotheses may be written

$$H_0: p_1 = p_2$$

$$H_1: p_1 > p_2$$

Suppose that $N = 15$ subjects were sampled, seven from group 1 and eight from group 2, and five subjects in group 1 responded + while one subject in group 2 responded +. The data may be represented as in the outcome arrangement II in Table 6.5. Thus, in the *sample* $P_1 = \frac{5}{7} = .714$ and $P_2 = \frac{1}{8} = .125$. To test the hypothesis H_0, the probability of observing a 2 × 2 contingency table as extreme or more extreme must be determined. In Table 6.5 all of the possible outcomes having the same marginal totals are listed. For each of these seven possible outcomes, P_1 and P_2 are given together with the probability of sampling that outcome arrangement when H_0 is true [using Eq. (6.1)]. Note that the probability of sampling the outcome actually observed is $P[\text{II}] = .0336$. Inspection of Table 6.5 shows only one other outcome arrangement with a more extreme result (i.e., $P_1 - P_2 > .714 - .125 = .589$), that is, outcome I which has probability .0014. Thus the probability of the observed outcome or one more extreme is

$$\begin{aligned} p &= P[\text{II}] + P[\text{I}] \\ &= .0336 + .0014 \\ &= .035 \end{aligned}$$

Note that this is the entry Obs. in Table 6.5 and Appendix Table I for outcome II.

Suppose the alternative hypothesis had been two-tailed, that is,

$$H_1: p_1 \neq p_2$$

Then the outcome arrangements which exhibit differences in possible p's greater than the observed outcome II are outcomes I and VII. Outcome VII is more extreme than the observed outcome, but in the "other" direction. The probability of that outcome is $P[\text{VII}] = .0056$. It is this value (rounded) which is tabled in the "Other" entry in Table 6.5 and Appendix Table I associated with outcome II. Thus the probability of observing an outcome as extreme as outcome II in *either*

TABLE 6.5
Example of computation of one- and two-tailed probabilities for the Fisher exact test

	Table	P_1	P_2	$P_1 - P_2$	P(table)	Obs.	Other	Total
I:	1 2 + 6 0 6 − 1 8 9 7 8 15	.857	0	.857	.0014	.001	.000	.001
II:	1 2 + 5 1 6 − 2 7 9 7 8 15	.714	.125	.589	.0336	.035	.006	.041
III:	1 2 + 4 2 6 − 3 6 9 7 8 15	.571	.250	.321	.1958	.231	.084	.315
IV:	1 2 + 3 3 6 − 4 5 9 7 8 15	.429	.375	.054	.3916	.622	.378	1.000
V:	1 2 + 2 4 6 − 5 4 9 7 8 15	.286	.500	−.214	.2937	.378	.231	.608
VI:	1 2 + 1 5 6 − 6 3 9 7 8 15	.143	.625	−.482	.0783	.084	.035	.119
VII:	1 2 + 0 6 6 − 7 2 9 7 8 15	0	.750	−.750	.0056	.006	.001	.007

direction is

$$P[\text{II}] + P[\text{I}] + P[\text{VII}] = .0336 + .0014 + .0056$$
$$= .041$$

This is the entry "Total" in Table 6.5 and Appendix Table I. If we performed a two-tailed test on the observed data at the $\alpha = .05$ level, we would reject H_0 since the observed probability is .041.

Suppose outcome III had been observed. Then the observed proportions would be $P_1 = \frac{4}{7} = .571$ and $P_2 = \frac{2}{8} = .250$. The difference is $P_1 - P_2 = .321$. The more extreme outcomes (in the same direction) are I and II. Therefore the probability associated with the one-tailed test is

$$P[\text{III}] + P[\text{I}] + P[\text{II}] = .1958 + .0014 + .0336 = .231$$

For the two-tailed test, outcomes VI and VII are more extreme in the opposite direction. In this case, the probability of an outcome as extreme or more extreme in either direction is

$$P[\text{III}] + P[\text{I}] + p[\text{II}] + P[\text{VI}] + P[\text{VII}]$$
$$= .1958 + .0014 + .0366 + .0783 + .0056$$
$$= .315$$

The reader should test his or her understanding of the use of the table to compute entries in the last three columns of Table 6.5 (which correspond to those in Appendix Table I).

Example 6.1 In a study of situations in which people threatened suicide by jumping from a building, bridge, or tower, it was noted that jeering or baiting by a crowd of onlookers occurs in some cases and not in others. Several theories propose that a psychological state of diminished identity and self-awareness, known as *deinviduation*, can contribute to the baiting phenomenon. Some factors known to elicit reactions from crowds include temperature, noise, and fatigue. In an effort to test various hypotheses concerning baiting by crowds, Mann[2] examined 21 published accounts of suicide and examined the relation between baiting by the crowd and month of year, the latter being a crude index of temperature. The hypothesis is that there should be increased baiting by the crowd when it is warm.

i. Null hypothesis. H_0: baiting and nonbaiting by crowds does not vary as a function of temperature as measured by time of year. H_1: there is increased baiting by crowds during warmer months.

ii. Statistical test. This study calls for a test to determine the significance of difference between two independent samples—crowds that baited victims and crowds that did not. The dependent variable, time of year, is dichotomous. Since N is small, the Fisher exact test is appropriate.

iii. Significance level. Let $\alpha = .10$ and $N = 21$.

---

[2] Mann, L. (1981). The baiting crowd in episode of threatened suicide. *Journal of Personality and Social Psychology*, **41**, 703–709.

TABLE 6.6
Incidence of baiting by crowds in episodes of threatened suicide

	Crowd		
Month	**Baiting**	**Nonbaiting**	Combined
June–September	8	4	12
October–May	2	7	9
Total	10	11	21

iv. Sampling distribution. The probability of the occurrence when H_0 is true of an observed set of values in a 2×2 table may be found by use of Eq. (6.1). Since $N > 15$, Appendix Table I cannot be used.

v. Rejection region. Since H_1 predicts the direction of the difference between the groups, the region of rejection is one-tailed. H_0 will be rejected if the observed cell values differ in the predicted direction and if they are of such magnitude that the probability associated with their occurrence (or the occurrence of more extreme tables) when H_0 is true is equal to or less than $\alpha = .10$.

vi. Decision. The information from the newspaper accounts is summarized in Table 6.6. In this study there were 10 crowds that baited victims and 11 crowds that did not bait victims. Examination of the table shows that there are two additional tables that would produce a more extreme (one-tailed) result. Thus the probability of observing a set of cell frequencies as extreme or more extreme than the one actually observed is determined by use of Eq. (6.1):

$$p = \frac{(A + B)!\,(C + D)!\,(A + C)!\,(B + D)!}{N!\,A!\,B!\,C!\,D!}$$

for each possible table. Thus

$$p = \frac{12!\,9!\,10!\,11!}{21!\,8!\,4!\,2!\,7!} + \frac{12!\,9!\,10!\,11!}{21!\,9!\,3!\,1!\,8!} + \frac{12!\,9!\,10!\,11!}{21!\,10!\,2!\,0!\,9!}$$

$$= .0505 + .0056 + .0002$$

$$= .0563$$

Since the obtained probability .0563 is less than the chosen significance level $\alpha = .10$, we may reject H_0 in favor of H_1. We conclude that baiting by crowds in suicide attempts is affected by temperature (as measured by month of year).

6.1.3 Summary of Procedure

These are the steps in the use of the Fisher exact test:

1. Cast the observed frequencies in a 2×2 table.
2. Determine the marginal totals. Let N be the total number of observations, S_1 be the smallest row or column total, S_2 be the second smallest row or column

total, and X be the cell frequency at the intersection of the row and column with totals S_1 and S_2.

3. Using the values N, S_1, S_2, X, determine from Appendix Table I the one-tailed probability of observing data as extreme or more extreme than that observed (the "Obs." entry), or for a two-tailed test, determine the probability using the "Total" entry.
4. If $N > 15$, use Eq. (6.1) recursively to determine the probability or use the approximate chi-square test (Sec. 6.2.2).

6.1.4 Power

The Fisher exact test is one of the most powerful one-tailed tests for data of the sort for which the test is appropriate—dichotomous, nominally scaled variables.

6.1.5 References

Other discussions of the Fisher exact test may be found in Cochran (1952) and McNemar (1969).

6.2 THE CHI-SQUARE TEST FOR TWO INDEPENDENT SAMPLES

6.2.1 Function

When the data consist of frequencies in discrete categories, the *chi-square test* may be used to determine the significance of differences between two independent groups. The measurement involved may be as weak as nominal or categorical scaling.

The hypothesis being tested is usually that the two groups differ with respect to some characteristic and, therefore, with respect to the relative frequency with which group members fall in several categories; i.e., there is a group by variable interaction. To test this hypothesis, we count the number of cases from each group which fall in the various categories and compare the proportion of cases from one group in the various categories with the proportion of cases from the other group. If the proportions are the same, then there is no interaction; if the proportions differ, there is an interaction. The focus of the test is on whether the differences in proportions exceed those expected as chance or random deviations from proportionality. For example, we might test whether two political groups differ in their agreement or disagreement with some opinion, or we might test whether the sexes differ in the frequency with which they choose certain leisure time activities, etc.

6.2.2 Method

First, the data are arranged into a frequency or *contingency* table in which the columns represent groups and each row represents a category of the measured

TABLE 6.7
3 × 2 contingency table

	Group		
Variable	**1**	**2**	Combined
1	n_{11}	n_{12}	R_1
2	n_{21}	n_{22}	R_2
3	n_{31}	n_{32}	R_3
Total	C_1	C_2	N

variable. Table 6.7 depicts such a table. In that table there is one column for each group and the measured variable may take on three values. The observed frequency of occurrence of the ith value or category for the jth group is denoted n_{ij}.

The null hypothesis that the groups are sampled from the same population may be tested by

$$X^2 = \sum_{i=1}^{r} \sum_{j=1}^{c} \frac{(n_{ij} - E_{ij})^2}{E_{ij}} \tag{6.2}$$

or

$$X^2 = \sum_{i=1}^{r} \sum_{j=1}^{c} \frac{n_{ij}^2}{E_{ij}} - N \tag{6.2a}$$

where n_{ij} = observed number of cases categorized in the ith row of the jth column
E_{ij} = number of cases expected in the ith row of the jth column when H_0 is true

and the double summation is over all rows and columns of the table (i.e., summation over all cells). The values of X^2 yielded by Eq. (6.2) are distributed asymptotically (as N gets large) as chi square with $df = (r - 1)(c - 1)$, where r is the number of rows and c is the number of columns in the contingency table. Although the X^2 statistic is easier to compute by using Eq. (6.2*a*), we shall usually use Eq. (6.2) in this book because it reflects more naturally the intuitive aspects of the statistic.

Under the assumption of independence, the expected frequency of observations in each cell should be proportional to the distribution of row and column totals. This expected frequency is estimated as the product of the corresponding row and column totals divided by the total number of observations. We begin by finding the row and column totals. The total frequency in the ith row is

$$R_i = \sum_{j=1}^{c} n_{ij}$$

Similarly, the total frequency in the jth column is

$$C_j = \sum_{i=1}^{r} n_{ij}$$

TABLE 6.8
Height and leadership

	Short	Tall	Combined
Follower	22	14	36
Unclassifiable	9	6	15
Leader	12	32	44
Total	43	52	95

Thus, in Table 6.7, $R_1 = n_{11} + n_{12}$, and $C_1 = n_{11} + n_{21} + n_{31}$. To find the expected frequency in each cell (E_{ij}), multiply the two marginal totals common to a particular cell and then divide this product by the total number of cases N. Thus,

$$E_{ij} = \frac{R_i C_j}{N}$$

We may illustrate this method of finding expected values by a simple example with the use of artificial data. Suppose we wished to test whether tall and short people differ with respect to leadership qualities. Table 6.8 shows the frequencies with which 43 short people and 52 tall people are categorized as "leaders," "followers," and as "unclassifiable." Now the null hypothesis is that height is independent of leader-follower position, i.e., that the proportion of tall people who are leaders is the same as the proportion of short people who are leaders, that the proportion of tall people who are followers is the same as the proportion of short people who are followers, etc. With such an hypothesis, we may determine the expected frequency for each cell by the method outlined above. In each case we multiply the two marginal totals common to a particular cell, and then divide this product by N to obtain the expected frequency. Thus, for example, the expected frequency for the lower right-hand cell in Table 6.8 is $E_{32} = (44)(52)/95 = 24.1$. Table 6.9 shows the expected frequencies for each of the six cells for the data shown in Table 6.8. In each cell the expected frequencies are shown in italics together with the various observed frequencies.

TABLE 6.9
Height and leadership: observed and expected frequencies

	Short		Tall		Combined
Follower	22	*16.3*	14	*19.7*	36
Unclassifiable	9	*6.8*	6	*8.2*	15
Leader	12	*19.9*	32	*24.1*	44
Total	43		52		95

Now if the observed frequencies are in close agreement with the expected frequencies, the differences $(n_{ij} - E_{ij})$ will, of course, be small and, consequently, the value of X^2 will be small. With a small value of X^2 we may not reject the null hypothesis that the two variables are independent of each other. However, if some or many of the differences are large, then the value of X^2 will also be large. The larger the value of X^2 the more likely it is that the two groups differ with respect to the classifications.

The sampling distribution of X^2 as defined by Eq. (6.2) is approximately distributed as chi square[3] with degrees of freedom

$$df = (r - 1)(c - 1)$$

The probabilities associated with various values of chi square are given in Appendix Table C. If an observed value of X^2 is equal to greater than the value given in Appendix Table C for a particular level of significance, at a particular df, then H_0 may be rejected at that level of significance.

Notice that there is a different sampling distribution of X^2 for every value of df. That is, the significance of any particular value of X^2 depends on the number of df in the data from which it was computed. The size of df reflects the number of observations that are free to vary after certain restrictions have been placed on the data. (Degrees of freedom are discussed in Chap. 4.)

The df for an $r \times c$ contingency table may be found by

$$df = (r - 1)(c - 1)$$

where r = number of classifications (rows)
c = number of groups (columns)

For the data in Table 6.9, $r = 3$ and $c = 2$, for we have three classifications (follower, unclassifiable, and leader) and two groups (tall and short). Thus the $df = (3 - 1)(2 - 1) = 2$.

The computation of X^2 for the data in Table 6.9 is straightforward:

$$X^2 = \sum_{i=1}^{r} \sum_{j=1}^{c} \frac{(n_{ij} - E_{ij})^2}{E_{ij}} \tag{6.2}$$

$$= \frac{(22 - 16.3)^2}{16.3} + \frac{(14 - 19.7)^2}{19.7} + \frac{(9 - 6.8)^2}{6.8} + \frac{(6 - 8.2)^2}{8.2} + \frac{(12 - 19.9)^2}{19.9} + \frac{(32 - 24.1)^2}{24.1}$$

$$= 1.99 + 1.65 + .71 + .59 + 3.14 + 2.59$$

$$= 10.67$$

[3] In this book, we distinguish between a variable which asymptotically has a chi-square distribution and the distribution itself. Thus, the statistic X^2 has a sampling distribution which is asymptotically that of the chi-square distribution.

By using Eq. (6.2a) we would compute the following:

$$X^2 = \sum_{i=1}^{r} \sum_{j=1}^{c} \frac{n_{ij}^2}{E_{ij}} - N \qquad (6.2a)$$

$$= \frac{22^2}{16.3} + \frac{14^2}{19.7} + \frac{9^2}{6.8} + \frac{6^2}{8.2} + \frac{12^2}{19.9} + \frac{32^2}{24.1} - 95$$

$$= 10.67$$

To determine the significance of $X^2 = 10.67$ when $df = 2$, we turn to Appendix Table C. The table shows that this value of X^2 is significant beyond the .01 level. Therefore we could reject the null hypothesis of no difference between the groups at $\alpha = .01$.

Example 6.2*a* In a study of exsmokers, Shiffman collected data on relapse crises.[4] Relapse crises include actual lapses in cessation and situations in which a lapse in abstinence was imminent but successfully avoided. These crisis episodes were collected from exsmokers who called a relapse crisis hotline. Various data were collected including the strategy used in an attempt to avoid a relapse. Coping strategies were categorized as behavioral (e.g., leaving the situation) or cognitive (e.g., mentally reviewing the reasons why the person had decided to stop smoking). Some subjects reported using one kind of coping strategy, some reported using both, and others reported using none. The hypothesis was that utilization of coping strategies would differ among those who were successful and those who were not successful in avoiding a relapse.

i. Null hypothesis. H_0: there is no difference in coping strategies employed in those who successfully avoided a lapse in abstinence and those who did not. H_1: the two groups differ in the coping strategies employed during the crisis.

ii. Statistical test. Since the behaviors reported (behavioral and/or cognitive coping, and no coping) are categorical variables, and because there were two groups (those who lapsed and those who did not), and because the categories are mutually exclusive and exhaustive, the chi-square test for independent groups is appropriate to test H_0.

iii. Significance level. Let $\alpha = .01$ and N is the number of subjects for which data were reported = 159.

iv. Sampling distribution. The sampling distribution of X^2 is approximated by chi square with 3 df. The df are determined by $df = (r - 1)(c - 1)$, where r is the number of categories (4) and c is the number of groups (2). Hence $(4 - 1)(2 - 1) = 3$.

v. Rejection region. Since H_1 simply predicts a difference between the two groups, the region of rejection consists of those values of X^2 that exceed the critical value of the chi-square distribution for $df = 3$. Appendix Table C indicates that the critical value of X^2 is 11.34 when $\alpha = .01$.

---

[4] Shiffman, S. (1982). Relapse following smoking cessation: A situational analysis. *Journal of Counseling and Clinical Psychology*, **50**, 71–86.

TABLE 6.10
Effect of coping strategies on relapse crises in smoking cessation

	Outcome group		
Coping	**Smoked**	**Did not smoke**	Combined
Behavioral	15	24	39
Cognitive	15	21	36
Behavioral and cognitive	13	43	56
None	22	6	28
Total	65	94	159

vi. Decision. Table 6.10 summarizes the data obtained on the crisis hotline. It shows that 65 people lapsed and 94 people successfully abstained during the crisis. The expected values for each cell were obtained by using the formula $E_{ij} = R_i C_j/N$. Thus, $E_{11} = (39)(65)/159 = 15.94$, $E_{21} = 14.72$, etc. By using Eq. (6.2), the obtained value of X^2 was 23.78.

$$X^2 = \sum_{i=1}^{4} \sum_{j=1}^{2} \frac{(n_{ij} - E_{ij})^2}{E_{ij}} \tag{6.2}$$

$$= \frac{(15 - 15.94)^2}{15.94} + \frac{(24 - 23.06)^2}{23.06} + \cdots + \frac{(6 - 16.55)^2}{16.55}$$

$$= 23.78$$

Since the observed value of X^2 exceeds the critical value, we reject the hypothesis that coping strategy is independent of whether a person lapsed or not during a crisis.

6.2.3 2 × 2 Contingency Tables

Perhaps the most common of all uses of the chi-square test is the test of whether an observed set of frequencies in a 2 × 2 contingency table could have occurred when H_0 is true. We are familiar with the form of such a table; an example is given in Table 6.1. When applying the X^2 test to data where both r and c equal 2, the following equation should be used:

$$X^2 = \frac{N(|AD - BC| - N/2)^2}{(A + B)(C + D)(A + C)(B + D)} \qquad df = 1 \tag{6.3}$$

This equation is somewhat easier to apply than Eq. (6.2), inasmuch as only one division is necessary in the computation. It has the additional advantage of incorporating a correction for continuity which markedly improves the approximation of the sampling distribution of the computed X^2 by the chi-square distribution.

Example 6.2*b* Another variable recorded in the smoking cessation study reported in Sec. 6.2.2 was whether or not alcohol consumption was a factor during the relapse crisis. Subjects were asked whether they were consuming alcohol prior to or during the crisis. The hypothesis was that alcohol consumption is related to whether or not the subject lapsed or abstained during the crisis.

i. Null hypothesis. H_0: alcohol consumption is unrelated to the outcome of the crisis. H_1: alcohol consumption is related to the success or nonsuccess in abstaining during the crisis.

ii. Statistical test. Since both variables (group and alcohol consumption) are categorical and since the measures are mutually exclusive and exhaustive, a chi-square test is appropriate. Moreover, since both variables are dichotomous, the chi-square test for 2×2 tables will be employed.

iii. Significance level. Let $\alpha = .01$ and N is the number of subjects who responded $= 177$.

iv. Sampling distribution. The sampling distribution of X^2 determined from Eq. (6.3) is asymptotically distributed as chi square with $df = 1$.

v. Rejection region. The rejection region for this test consists of all values of X^2 for which the probability of observing a value as large or larger when H_0 is true is less than $\alpha = .01$.

vi. Decision. Table 6.11 summarizes the observed data. Twenty of 68 people who lapsed (29 percent) consumed alcohol during the crisis and 13 of 109 (12 percent) of those who did not lapse consumed alcohol during the crisis. The value of X^2 was computed by using Eq. (6.3):

$$X^2 = \frac{N(|AD - BC| - N/2)^2}{(A+B)(C+D)(A+C)(B+D)} \qquad df = 1 \qquad (6.3)$$

$$= \frac{177(|(20)(96) \quad (13)(48)| - \frac{177}{2})^2}{(33)(144)(68)(109)}$$

$$= 7.33$$

Reference to Appendix Table C shows that $X^2 \geq 7.33$ with $df = 1$ has probability of occurrence when H_0 is true of less than .01. Since the observed value of X^2 exceeds the critical value 6.64, we reject the hypothesis that alcohol consumption has no effect on relapse or abstinence during a smoking cessation crisis.

TABLE 6.11
Effect of alcohol consumption on relapse crises in smoking cessation

Alcohol consumption	Outcome group: Smoked	Outcome group: Did not smoke	Combined
Yes	20	13	33
No	48	96	144
Total	68	109	177

6.2.4 Partitioning the Degrees of Freedom in $r \times 2$ Tables

Once a researcher determines that the value of X^2 for particular contingency table is significant, he or she knows that there is a difference between the two groups on the measured variable. However, he or she does not know *where* the differences are. Since the measured variable takes on several values, it is possible that the difference found may be reflected for some values but not for others. The question of where the differences are in the contingency table may be answered by means of *partitioning* the contingency table into subtables and analyzing each of them. One might consider constructing a number of 2×2 subtables which could be analyzed by means of the Fisher exact test; however, such tables are not independent and interpretation of them is difficult. Fortunately, it is possible to construct 2×2 subtables which are independent and which are interpretable by constructing them by using the methods outlined below. Any contingency table may be partitioned into as many 2×2 subtables as there are degrees of freedom in the original table. The method of constructing the tables is relatively straightforward and is best understood through examples. For the 3×2 table in Table 6.7, there are two partitions; these are illustrated in Table 6.12.

These tables each have 1 *df*. To test the independence between the two groups in such tables, the X^2 test must be modified to reflect the fact that these are *subtables* obtained from a larger table and, hence, reflect characteristics of the entire sample. The formulas for the partitions in Table 6.12 are the following:

$$X_1^2 = \frac{N^2(n_{22}n_{11} - n_{21}n_{12})^2}{C_1C_2R_2R_1(R_1 + R_2)} \tag{6.4a}$$

$$X_2^2 = \frac{N[n_{32}(n_{11} + n_{21}) - n_{31}(n_{12} + n_{22})]^2}{C_1C_2R_3(R_1 + R_2)} \tag{6.4b}$$

TABLE 6.12
Additive partitions of a 3×2 contingency table

n_{11}	n_{12}	R_1
n_{21}	n_{22}	R_2
C_1	C_2	N

(1)

n_{11} + n_{21}	n_{12} + n_{22}	R_1 + R_2
n_{31}	n_{32}	R_3
C_1	C_2	N

(2)

Each of these X^2 statistics is asymptotically distributed as chi square with 1 *df*. The reader may notice that these formulas are similar to that for the 2×2 contingency table. An important difference is that the marginal distributions reflect the marginal distributions for the *entire* sample, not just the particular 2×2 subtable. Also, the first subtable appears to be "collapsed" into the second table.

For the general $r \times 2$ tables discussed in this section, $r - 1$ partitions may be formed. The general equation for the tth partition of an $r \times 2$ table is the following:

$$X_t^2 = \frac{N^2\left(n_{t+1,2}\sum_{i=1}^{t} n_{i1} - n_{t+1,1}\sum_{i=1}^{t} n_{i2}\right)^2}{C_1 C_2 R_{t+1}\left(\sum_{i=1}^{t} R_i\right)\left(\sum_{i=1}^{t+1} R_i\right)} \qquad t = 1, 2, \ldots, r-1 \tag{6.5}$$

The formula for partitioning has each table being collapsed to form the next table. The arrangement proceeds from top to bottom. This is merely for convenience in writing the equation. The researcher must arrange the table so that the collapsing and combining of categories make sense. For the example in Table 6.8, the focus is on leaders *versus* nonleaders. Therefore, one might first compare the short and tall people who are either followers or unclassifiable; then these two variables would be collapsed to form the second partition which would compare leaders and nonleaders. These partitions are summarized in Table 6.13.

TABLE 6.13
Additive partitions for example 3 × 2 contingency table (Table 6.8)

	Stature		
	Short	**Tall**	Combined
Followers	22	14	36
Unclassifiable	9	6	15
Total	43	52	95

(1)

	Stature		
	Short	**Tall**	Combined
Follower or unclassifiable	31	20	51
Leader	12	32	44
Total	43	52	95

(2)

For the first partition in Table 6.13 we calculate X^2 by using Eq. (6.4*a*):

$$X_1^2 = \frac{N^2(n_{22}n_{11} - n_{21}n_{12})^2}{C_1C_2R_2R_1(R_1 + R_2)} \tag{6.4a}$$

$$= \frac{95^2[(6)(22) - (9)(14)]^2}{(43)(52)(15)(36)(51)}$$

$$= .005$$

This is distributed as chi square with $df = 1$ and is clearly not significant. The researcher may thus safely conclude that there is no relation between stature and people who are either followers or not classifiable in terms of leadership. Thus, it is reasonable to combine these two categories to form the first row of the second table. These two categories are collapsed to form the second partition in Table 6.13. The value of the partitioned X^2 is obtained by using Eq. (6.4*b*):

$$X_2^2 = \frac{N[n_{32}(n_{11} + n_{21}) - n_{31}(n_{12} + n_{22})]^2}{C_1C_2R_3(R_1 + R_2)} \tag{6.4b}$$

$$= \frac{95[32(22 + 9) - 12(14 + 6)]^2}{(43)(52)(44)(51)}$$

$$= 10.707$$

Since this value exceeds the critical value of the chi-square distribution for $\alpha = .05$, the researcher may conclude that the distribution of leaders and nonleaders differs as a function of stature. The reader will note that this result is similar to what was found when we analyzed the overall 3×2 table. However, it is strengthened in that we have been able to say that the followers and unclassifiable people are essentially similar. It should be noted that the two partitioned X^2 values sum to approximately the value of the overall chi square: $10.707 + .005 = 10.71$ for the partitions *versus* 10.67 for the overall table. The partitioned X^2 values asymptotically sum to the overall X^2. Thus, in a sample the sum of the partitioned X^2's should be approximately equal to the overall value, and this serves as a rough check on one's computations.

Example 6.2c In the study of exsmokers described on p. 115 and summarized in Table 6.10, it was found that there were significant differences in coping behaviors between those who smoked and did not smoke as a result of relapse crises. In that section it was found that $X^2 = 23.78$ with $df = 3$. It would be desirable to determine which of the behaviors were effective during relapse crises. To determine this, we shall partition the obtained X^2. It is necessary to determine *a priori* in what order to partition the table. Since $df = 3$, there are three partitions which may be constructed. Examination of the levels of the variables suggests the most useful partitions. The first partition contrasts the two types of coping when employed singly, i.e., behavioral *versus* cognitive coping. The second partition compares the utilization of a *single* coping behavior with the utilization of *two* coping behaviors. The third partition compares the use of *any* coping behavior with the failure to use any coping behavior. The resulting partitioned tables are summarized in Table 6.14.

TABLE 6.14
Additive partitions of contingency table for smoking for smoke cessation example (Table 6.10)

Coping	Outcome group: Smoked	Outcome group: Did not smoke	Combined
Behavioral	15	24	39
Cognitive	15	21	36
Total	65	94	159

(1)

Coping	Outcome group: Smoked	Outcome group: Did not smoke	Combined
Behavioral or cognitive	30	45	75
Behavioral and cognitive	13	43	56
Total	65	94	159

(2)

Coping	Outcome group: Smoked	Outcome group: Did not smoke	Combined
Behavioral and/or cognitive	43	88	131
None	22	6	28
Total	65	95	159

(3)

For each of these partitions, the associated X^2 value is determined by using Eq. 6.5. For the first partition ($t = 1$) we find:

$$X_t^2 = \frac{N^2\left(n_{t+1,2}\sum_{i=1}^{t} n_{i1} - n_{t+1,1}\sum_{i=1}^{t} n_{i2}\right)^2}{C_1 C_2 R_{t+1}\left(\sum_{i=1}^{t} R_i\right)\left(\sum_{i=1}^{t+1} R_i\right)} \tag{6.5}$$

$$X_1^2 = \frac{159^2[(21)(15) - (15)(24)]^2}{(65)(94)(36)(39)(75)}$$

$$= .08$$

Next, we find the value of X^2 for the second partition:

$$X_2^2 = \frac{159^2[(43)(30) - (13)(45)]^2}{(65)(94)(56)(75)(131)}$$

$$= 3.74$$

Finally, for the third partition,

$$X_3^2 = \frac{159^2[(6)(43) - (22)(88)]^2}{(65)(94)(28)(131)(159)}$$

$$= 19.98$$

Each of these X^2 values is distributed asymptotically as chi square with 1 *df*. In the overall test, the significance level $\alpha = .01$ was chosen. Using the same level, the critical value of X^2 is 6.64. Thus, only the third partition is significant. The researcher may conclude that there are no differences in effectiveness among the coping behaviors, and that the difference between the two groups depends on whether or not *any* coping behavior was employed. That is, the coping behaviors are equally effective and are significantly more effective than using no coping behavior during relapse crises.

In partitioning any table, the researcher must examine the measured variable *a priori* to determine which variables may be appropriately combined as part of the partitioning scheme. Once these combinations are determined, the table can be arranged so that Eq. (6.5) may be applied to each partition. If the original variable was nominally scaled or categorical, the rows may be easily arranged into the proper order for partitioning. If the variable represents ordered categories, such rearrangement may not make particular sense for the variable under study; however, one may still arrange the table in order to begin the partitioning at either "end" of the table. It is important, however, for the researcher to use partitions which result in 2×2 tables which are interpretable in the context of the particular research.

6.2.5 Summary of Procedure

These are the steps in the use of the chi-square test for two independent samples:

1. Cast the observed frequencies into an $r \times c$ contingency table, using the c columns for the groups and the r rows for the conditions. Thus for this test $c = 2$.
2. Calculate the row totals R_i and the column totals C_j.
3. Determine the expected frequency for each cell by finding the product of the marginal totals common to it and divide this by N (where N represents the total number of *independent* observations); thus $E_{ij} = R_i C_j / N$. Note that inflated N's invalidate the test. Steps 2 and 3 are unnecessary if the data are in a 2×2 table for which either Appendix Table I may be used if $N \leq 15$ or Eq. (6.3) if $N > 15$. If r or c is greater than 2, use Eq. (6.2).
4. Determine the significance of the observed X^2 by reference to Appendix Table C. If the probability given by Table C is equal to or smaller than α, reject H_0 in favor of H_1.

5. If the table is larger than 2 × 2 and if H_0 is rejected, the contingency table may be partitioned into independent subtables to determine just where the differences are in the original table. Use Eq. (6.5) [or Eqs. (6.4*a*) and (6.4*b*) if the table is 3 × 2] to calculate the value of X^2 for each partition. Test the significance of each X^2 by reference to the distribution of chi square with $df = 1$ in Appendix Table C. Use of the computer program in Appendix II may speed computation.

6.2.6 When to Use the Chi-Square Test

As we have already noted, the chi-square test requires that the expected frequencies E_{ij} in each cell should not be too small. When they are too small, the test may not be properly or meaningfully used. Cochran (1954) and others make these recommendations:

THE 2 × 2 CASE. If the frequencies are in a 2 × 2 contingency table, the decision concerning the use of chi square should be guided by these considerations:

1. When $N \leq 20$, always use the Fisher exact test.
2. When N is between 20 and 40, the X^2 test [Eq. (6.3)] may be used *if* all expected frequencies are 5 or more. If the smallest expected frequency is less than 5, use the Fisher exact test (Sec. 6.1).
3. When $N > 40$, use X^2 corrected for continuity, i.e., use Eq. (6.3).

CONTINGENCY TABLES WITH *df* LARGER THAN 1. When r is larger than 2 (and thus $df > 1$), the X^2 test may be used if fewer than 20 percent of the cells have an expected frequency of less than 5 and if no cell has an expected frequency of less than 1. If these requirements are not met by the data in the form in which they were originally collected, the researcher should combine adjacent categories to increase the expected frequencies in the various cells. Only after combining categories to meet the above requirement may the tabled significance values for the chi-square distribution be sufficiently close to the actual sampling distribution of X^2.

When $df > 1$, chi-square tests are insensitive to the effects of order, and thus when an hypothesis takes order into account, the chi-square test may not be the best test. Tests which may be used are discussed later in this chapter and in Chap. 9.

SMALL EXPECTED VALUES. The chi-square test is applicable to data in a contingency table only if the expected frequencies are sufficiently large. The size requirements for expected frequencies were discussed above. When the expected frequencies do not meet these requirements, one may increase their values by combining cells, i.e., by combining adjacent classifications and, thereby, reducing the number of cells. This may be properly done only if such combining does not rob the data of their meaning. In our example of height and leadership, of course, any combining of categories would have rendered the data useless for testing our hypothesis. The researcher may usually avoid this problem by planning in advance to collect a sufficient number of cases relative to the number of classifications used in the analysis.

6.2.7 Power

When the chi-square test is used there is usually no clear alternative and, thus, the exact power of the test is difficult to compute. However, Cochran (1952) has shown that the limiting power distribution of X^2 tends to 1 as N becomes large.

6.2.8 References

For other discussions of the chi-square test, the reader may refer to Cochran (1952, 1954), Everitt (1977), McNemar (1969), a classic paper on the use and "misuse" of chi square by Lewis and Burke (1949), and a derivative paper by Delucchi (1983). Extended discussion of partitioning procedures may be found in Castellan (1966).

6.3 THE MEDIAN TEST

6.3.1 Function

The *median test* is a procedure for testing whether two independent groups differ in central tendencies. More precisely, the median test will give information as to whether it is likely that two independent groups (not necessarily of the same size) have been drawn from populations with the same median. The null hypothesis is that the two groups are from populations with the same median; the alternative hypothesis may be that the median of one population is *different* from that of the other (two-tailed test) or that the median of one population is *higher* than that of the other (one-tailed test). The test may be used whenever the scores for the two groups are measured on at least an ordinal scale. It should be noted that there may be no alternative to the median test, even for interval-scale data. This would occur when one or more of the observations are "off the scale" and are truncated to the maximum (or minimum) previously assigned to the observations.

6.3.2 Rationale and Method

To perform the median test, we first determine the median score for the combined group (i.e., the median for all scores in both samples). We then dichotomize both sets of scores at that combined median and cast these data in a 2×2 table like Table 6.15.

Now if both group I and group II are samples from populations whose medians are the same, we would expect about half of each group's scores to be above the combined median and about half to be below. That is, we would expect frequencies A and C to be about equal and B and D to be about equal.

It can be shown (Mood, 1950) that, if A is the number of the m cases in group I that fall above the combined median, and if B is the number of the n cases in group II that fall above the combined median, then the sampling distribution

TABLE 6.15
Median test: form for data

	Group		
	I	II	Combined
No. scores above combined median	A	B	$A + B$
No. scores below combined median	C	D	$C + D$
Total	m	n	$N = m + n$

of A and B under the null hypothesis (H_0 is that the medians are the same) is the hypergeometric distribution

$$P[A, B] = \frac{\binom{m}{A}\binom{n}{B}}{\binom{m+n}{A+B}} \tag{6.6}$$

Therefore, if the total number of cases in both groups $(m + n)$ is small, one may use the Fisher exact test (Sec. 6.1) to test H_0. If the total number of cases is sufficiently large, the chi-square test with $df = 1$ [Eq. (6.3)] may be used to test H_0.

When analyzing data split at the median, the researcher should be guided by these considerations in choosing between the Fisher exact test and the chi-square test for 2 × 2 tables:

1. When $N = m + n$ is larger than 20, use X^2 corrected for continuity [Eq. (6.3)].
2. When $N = m + n = 20$ or less, use the Fisher exact test.

One difficulty may arise in the computation of the median test; several scores may fall right at the combined median. If this happens, the researcher has two alternatives:

1. The groups may be dichotomized as those scores that *exceed* the median and those that do not.
2. If $m + n$ is large, and if only a few cases fall at the combined median, those few cases may be dropped from the analysis.

The first alternative is preferable.

Example 6.3 In a cross-cultural test of some behavior theory hypotheses adapted from psychoanalytic theory,[5] Whiting and Child studied the relation between child-rearing practices and customs related to illness in various nonliterate cultures. One hypothesis of their

[5] Whiting, J. W. M., and Child, I. L. (1953). *Child training and personality.* New Haven: Yale University Press.

study, derived from the notion of negative fixation, was their oral explanations of illness: Illness results from eating poison, from drinking certain liquids, and from verbal spells and incantations performed by others. Judgments of the typical oral socialization anxiety in any society were based on the rapidity of oral socialization, the severity of oral socialization, the frequency of punishment typical in oral socialization, and the severity of emotional conflict typically evidenced by the children during the period of oral socialization.

Excerpts from ethnological reports of nonliterate cultures were used in the collection of the data. By using only excerpts concerning customs relating to illness, judges classified the societies into two groups—those with oral explanations of illness present and those with oral explanations absent. Other judges, using the excerpts concerning child-rearing practices, rated each society on the degree of oral socialization anxiety typical in its children. For the 39 societies for which judgments of the presence or absence of oral explanations were possible, these ratings ranged from 6 to 17.

i. Null hypothesis. H_0: there is no difference between the median oral socialization anxiety in societies which give oral explanations of illness and the median oral socialization anxiety in societies which do not give oral explanations of illness. H_1: the median oral socialization anxiety in societies with oral explanations present is higher than the median in societies with oral explanations absent.

ii. Statistical test. The ratings constitute ordinal measures at best; thus a nonparametric test is appropriate. For the data from the two independent groups of societies, the median test may be used to test H_0.

iii. Significance level. Let $\alpha = .01$ and N is the number of societies for which ethnological information on both variables was available $= 39$; m is the number of societies with oral explanations absent $= 16$; n is the number of societies with oral explanations present $=$ 23.

iv. Sampling distribution. Since the sample size is large, the X^2 approximation to the Fisher exact test will be used [Eq. (6.3)]. The sampling distribution of X^2 is asymptotically chi square with 1 *df*.

v. Rejection region. Since H_1 predicts the direction of the difference, the region of rejection is one-tailed. It consists of all outcomes in a median-split table which are in the predicted direction and are so extreme that the probability associated with their occurrence when H_0 is true (as determined by the appropriate test) is equal to less than $\alpha = .01$.

vi. Decision. Table 6.16 shows the ratings assigned to each of the 39 societies. These are divided at the combined median for the $m + n$ ratings. (We have followed Whiting and Child in calling 10.5 the median of the 39 ratings.) Table 6.17 shows these data cast in the form for the median test. Since none of the expected frequencies is less than 5, and since $m + n > 20$, we may use the X^2 test to test H_0:

$$X^2 = \frac{N(|AD - BC| - N/2)^2}{(A + B)(C + D)(A + C)(B + D)} \tag{6.3}$$

$$= \frac{N(|AD - BC| - N/2)^2}{(A + B)(C + D)(m)(n)}$$

$$= \frac{39(|(3)(6) - (17)(13)| - \frac{39}{2})^2}{(20)(19)(16)(23)}$$

$$= 9.39$$

TABLE 6.16
Oral socialization anxiety and oral explanations of illness*†

	Societies with oral explanations absent	Societies with oral explanations present
Societies above median on oral socialization anxiety	13 Lapp 12 Chamorro 12 Samoans	17 Marquesans 16 Dobuans 15 Baiga 15 Kwoma 15 Thonga 14 Alorese 14 Chagga 14 Navaho 13 Dahomeans 13 Lesu 13 Masai 12 Lepcha 12 Maori 12 Pukapukans 12 Trobrianders 11 Kwakiutl 11 Manus
Societies below median on oral socialization anxiety	10 Arapesh 10 Balinese 10 Hopi 10 Tanala 9 Paiute 8 Chenchu 8 Teton 7 Flathead 7 Papago 7 Venda 7 Warrau 7 Wogeo 6 Ontong-Javanese	10 Chiricahua 10 Comanche 10 Siriono 8 Bena 8 Slave 6 Kurtatchi

* Reproduced from table 4 of Whiting, J. W. M., and Child, I. L. (1953). *Child training and personality*. New Haven: Yale University Press, p. 156, with the kind permission of the authors and the publisher.

† The name of each society is preceded by its rating on oral socialization anxiety.

TABLE 6.17
Oral socialization anxiety and oral explanations of illness

	Societies with oral explanations absent	Societies with oral explanations present	Combined
Societies above median on oral socialization anxiety	3	17	20
Societies below median on oral socialization anxiety	13	6	19
Total	16	23	39

Reference to Appendix Table C shows that $X^2 > 9.39$ with $df = 1$ has probability of occurrence when H_0 is true of $p < .5(.01) = .005$ for a one-tailed test. Thus our decision is to reject H_0 for $\alpha = .01$. We conclude that the median oral socialization anxiety is higher in societies with oral explanations of illness present than is the median in societies with oral explanations absent.

6.3.3 Summary of Procedure

These are the steps in the use of the median test:

1. Determine the combined median of the $m + n$ scores.
2. Split each group's scores at that combined median. Enter the resultant frequencies into a 2×2 table like Table 6.15. If many scores fall at the combined median, split the scores into these categories—those which exceed the median and those which do not.
3. Find the probability of the observed values by either the Fisher exact test if $m + n \leq 20$ or its chi-square approximation [Eq. (6.3)] if $m + n > 20$.
4. If the probability yielded by that test is equal to or less than α, reject H_0.

6.3.4 Power-Efficiency

Mood (1954) has shown that, when the median test is applied to data measured in at least an interval scale from normal distributions with common variance (i.e., data that might properly be analyzed by the t test), it has the same power-efficiency as the sign test. That is, its power-efficiency is about 95 percent for $m + n$ as low as 6. This power-efficiency decreases as the sample size increases, reaching an asymptotic efficiency of $2/\pi = 63$ percent.

6.3.5 References

Discussions of the median test are found in the same sources mentioned in Sec. 6.1 on the Fisher exact test. Other discussions are found in Mood (1950).

6.4 THE WILCOXON-MANN-WHITNEY TEST

6.4.1 Function

When at least ordinal measurement has been achieved for the variables being studied, the *Wilcoxon-Mann-Whitney*[6] *test* may be used to test whether two independent groups have been drawn from the same population. This is one of the

[6] Mann, Whitney, and Wilcoxon (among others) independently proposed nonparametric tests which are essentially the same as the one presented in this section. The first edition presented the test in the form proposed by Mann and Whitney. The form used in this edition follows that of Wilcoxon. For convenience, we often shall refer to the test as the Wilcoxon test.

most powerful of the nonparametric tests, and it is a very useful alternative to the parametric t test when the researcher wishes to avoid the t test's assumptions or when the measurement in the research in weaker than interval scaling.

Suppose we have samples from two populations, X and Y. The null hypothesis is that X and Y have the same distribution. The alternative hypothesis H_1 against which we test H_0 is that X is stochastically larger than Y—a directional hypothesis. We may accept H_1 if the probability that a score from X is larger than a score from Y is greater than one-half. That is, if X is one observation from population X and Y is an observation from the population Y, then H_1 is that $P[X > Y] > \frac{1}{2}$. If the evidence supports H_1, this implies that the "bulk" of the elements of population X are larger than the bulk of the elements of population Y. Using this approach, the null hypothesis is H_0: $P[X > Y] = \frac{1}{2}$.

Of course, our hypothesis might instead be that Y is stochastically larger than X. In that case, the alternative hypothesis H_1 would be that $P[X > Y] < \frac{1}{2}$. Confirmation of this assertion would imply that the bulk of Y is larger than the bulk of X.

For a two-tailed test, i.e., for a prediction of differences which does not state the direction of the differences, H_1 would be that $P[X > Y] \neq \frac{1}{2}$.

Another way of stating the alternative hypothesis is that the median of X is greater than the median of Y, that is, H_1: $\theta_x > \theta_y$. In a similar fashion, the other hypotheses may be stated in terms of medians.

6.4.2 Method

Let m be the number of cases in the sample from group X and n be the number of cases in the sample from group Y. We assume that the two samples are independent. To apply the Wilcoxon test, we first combine the observations or scores from both groups and rank them in order of increasing size. In this ranking, algebraic size is considered, i.e., the lowest ranks are assigned to the largest negative values, if any.

Now focus on one of the groups, say, the group X with m cases. The value of W_x (the statistic used in this test) is the sum of the ranks in the first group.

For example, suppose we had an experimental group of three cases and a control group of four cases. Here $m = 3$ and $n = 4$. Suppose these were the scores:

Experimental scores X:	9	11	15	
Control scores Y:	6	8	10	13

To find W_x, we first rank these scores in order of increasing size, being careful to retain each score's identity as either an X or Y score:

Score:	6	8	9	10	11	13	15
Group:	Y	Y	X	Y	X	Y	X
Rank:	1	2	3	4	5	6	7

Now consider the experimental group, and calculate the sum of the ranks for that group. Thus,

$$W_x = 3 + 5 + 7 = 15$$

In a similar fashion,

$$W_y = 1 + 2 + 4 + 6 = 13$$

The reader should recall that the sum of the first N integers is

$$1 + 2 + 3 + \cdots + N = \frac{N(N + 1)}{2} \tag{6.7}$$

Therefore, for our sample of size $N = m + n = 7$, the sum of ranks is $7(7 + 1)/2 = 28$. Also, the sums of the ranks for the two groups should be equal to the sum of the ranks for the combined group. That is,

$$W_x + W_y = \frac{N(N + 1)}{2} \tag{6.8}$$

If H_0 is true, we would expect the average ranks in each of the two groups to be about equal. If the sum of ranks for one group is very large (or very small), then we may have reason to suspect that the samples were not drawn from the same population. The sampling distribution of W_x when H_0 is true is known, and with this knowledge we can determine the probability associated with the occurrence under H_0 of any W_x as extreme as the observed value.

6.4.3 Small Samples

When m and n are less than or equal to 10, Appendix Table J may be used to determine the exact probability associated with the occurrence when H_0 is true of any W_x as extreme as an observed value of W_x. The reader will observe that Appendix Table J is made up of separate subtables, one for each value of m from 1 to 10, and each one of these subtables has entries for $n = m$ to 10. (Actually $n = m$ to 12 for $m = 3$ or 4.) To determine the probability under H_0 associated with the data, the researcher needs to know m (the size of the smaller group), n (the size of the larger group), and W_x. With this information the probability associated with W_x may be read from the subtable appropriate to hypothesis H_1.

In our example, $m = 3$, $n = 4$, and $W_x = 15$. The subtable for $m = 3$ in Appendix Table J shows that for $n = 4$, the probability of observing a value of $W_x \geq 15$ when H_0 is true is .200. This value is found by choosing the critical upper limit (c_U) to be 15 and locating that entry in the column for $n = 4$. The value to the left of $c_U = 15$ is the required probability. If the probability that $W_x \leq c_L$ is desired (c_L is the critical lower limit), the table is entered from the corresponding entry in the first column.

For convenience and economy, Appendix Table J is arranged for $m \leq n$, that is, the group associated with the X scores is the smaller. This restriction poses no problem in the use of the Wilcoxon test since the group identification labels may be interchanged and the table used for the transformed groups. However, the researcher must remember to ensure that the alternative hypothesis is stated correctly if the variable labels are interchanged.

Example 6.4*a* **For small samples.** Solomon and Coles[7] studied whether rats would generalize learned imitation when placed under a new drive in a new situation. Five rats were trained to imitate leader rats in a T maze. They were trained to follow the leaders when hungry in order to attain a food incentive. Then the five rats were each transferred to a shock-avoidance situation, where imitation of leader rats would have enabled them to avoid electric shock. Their behavior in the shock-avoidance situation was compared to that of four controls who had no previous training to follow leaders. The hypothesis was that the five rats who had already been trained to imitate would transfer this training to the new situation and, thus, would reach the learning criterion in the shock-avoidance situation sooner than would the four control rats. The comparison is in terms of how many trials each rat took to reach a criterion of 10 correct responses in 10 trials.

i. *Null hypothesis.* H_0: the number of trials needed to reach the criterion in the shock-avoidance situation is the same for rats previously trained to follow a leader to a food incentive as for rats not previously trained. H_1: rats previously trained to follow a leader to a food incentive will reach the criterion in the shock-avoidance situation in fewer trials than will rats not previously trained.
ii. *Statistical test.* The Wilcoxon test is chosen because this study employs two independent samples, uses small samples, and uses measurement (number of trials to criterion as an index of speed of learning) which is probably, at most, in an ordinal scale.
iii. *Significance level.* Let $\alpha = .05$, $m = 4$ (control rats), and $n = 5$ (experimental rats).
iv. *Sampling distribution.* The probabilities associated with the occurrence under H_0 of values as large as an observed W_x for small m and n are given in Appendix Table J.
v. *Rejection region.* Since H_1 states the direction of the predicted difference, the region of rejection is one-tailed. It consists of all values of W_x which are so large that the probability associated with their occurrence when H_0 is true is equal to or less than $\alpha = .05$. (Since the control group is denoted X, the alternative hypothesis is H_1: $\theta_x > \theta_y$, that is, the median of control group is greater than the median of the experimental group.)
vi. *Decision.* The number of trials to criterion required by the experimental and control rats were:

Control rats:	110	70	53	51	
Experimental rats:	78	64	75	45	82

We arrange these scores in the order of their magnitude, retaining the identity of each:

Score:	45	51	53	64	70	75	78	82	110
Group:	Y	X	X	Y	X	Y	Y	Y	X
Rank:	1	2	3	4	5	6	7	8	9

[7] Solomon, R. L., and Coles, M. R. (1953). A case of failure of generalization of imitation across drives and across situations. *Journal of Abnormal and Social Psychology*, **49**, 7–13. Only two of the groups studied are included in this example.

From these data we find that the sum of the ranks for the control group is $W_x = 2 + 3 + 5 + 9 = 19$. In Appendix Table J, we locate the subtable for $m = 4$. Since the alternative hypothesis is that W_x should be large, we use the right (upper) tail of the distribution. When H_0 is true, we see that $P[W_x \geq 19] = .6349$. Our decision is that the data do not give evidence which justify rejecting H_0 at the previously set level of significance.

The conclusion is that these data do not support the hypothesis that previous training to imitate will generalize across situations and across drives.[8]

6.4.4 Large Samples

Appendix Table J cannot be used if $m > 10$ or $n > 10$ ($n > 12$ if $m = 3$ or 4). However, it has been shown that as m and n increase in size, the sampling distribution of W_x rapidly approaches that of the normal distribution with

$$\text{Mean} = \mu_{W_x} = \frac{m(N+1)}{2} \tag{6.9}$$

and

$$\text{Variance} = \sigma^2_{W_x} = \frac{mn(N+1)}{12} \tag{6.10}$$

That is, when $m > 10$ or $n > 10$, we may determine the significance of an observed value W_x by

$$z = \frac{W_x \pm .5 - \mu_{W_x}}{\sigma_{W_x}} = \frac{W_x \pm .5 - m(N+1)/2}{\sqrt{mn(N+1)/12}} \tag{6.11}$$

which is asymptotically normally distributed with zero mean and unit variance. That is, the probability associated with the occurrence when H_0 is true of value as extreme as an observed z may be determined by reference to Appendix Table A. The value $+.5$ is added if we wish to find probabilities in the *left* tail of the distribution and $-.5$ is added if we wish to find probabilities in the *right* tail of the distribution.

Example 6.4*b* For large samples. For our example, we shall reexamine the Whiting and Child data that we have already analyzed by the median test (pp. 125–128).

i. *Null hypothesis.* H_0: oral socialization anxiety is equally severe in both societies with oral explanations of illness present and societies with oral explanations absent. H_1: societies with oral explanations of illness present are (stochastically) higher in oral socialization anxiety than societies which do not have oral explanations of illness.
ii. *Statistical test.* The two groups of societies constitute two independent groups, and the measure of oral socialization anxiety (rating scale) constitutes an ordinal measure at best. For these reasons the Wilcoxon test is appropriate for analyzing these data.
iii. *Significance level.* Let $\alpha = .01$, m is the number of societies with oral explanations absent = 16, and n is the number of societies with oral explanations present = 23.

---

[8] Solomon and Coles report the same conclusion. The test used in their paper was not reported.

iv. Sampling distribution. For $n > 10$, Eq. (6.11) yields values of z. The probability associated with the occurrence under H_0 of values as extreme as an observed z may be determined by reference to Appendix Table A.

v. Rejection region. Since H_1 predicts the direction of the difference, the region of rejection is one-tailed. It consists of all values of z which are so extreme (in the predicted direction) that the associated probability under H_0 is equal to or less than $\alpha = .01$.

vi. Decision. The ratings assigned to each of the 39 societies are shown in Table 6.18 together with the rank of each in the combined group. Notice that tied rankings are assigned the average of the tied ranks. For these data $W_x = 200.0$ and $W_y = 580.0$. We may find the value of z by substituting into Eq. (6.11):

$$z = \frac{W_x \pm .5 - m(N + 1)/2}{\sqrt{mn(N + 1)/12}} \tag{6.11}$$

$$= \frac{200 + .5 - 16(39 + 1)/2}{\sqrt{(16)(23)(39 + 1)/12}}$$

$$= -3.41$$

TABLE 6.18
Oral socialization anxiety and oral explanation of illness

Societies with oral explanations absent	Rating on oral socialization anxiety	Rank	Societies with oral explanations present	Rating on oral socialization anxiety	Rank
Lapp	13	29.5	Marquesans	17	39
Chamorro	12	24.5	Dobuans	16	38
Samoans	12	24.5	Baiga	15	36
Arapesh	10	16	Kwoma	15	36
Balinese	10	16	Thonga	15	36
Hopi	10	16	Alorese	14	33
Tanala	10	16	Chagga	14	33
Paiute	9	12	Navaho	14	33
Chenchu	8	9.5	Dahomeans	13	29.5
Teton	8	9.5	Lesu	13	29.5
Flathead	7	5	Masai	13	29.5
Papago	7	5	Lepcha	12	24.5
Venda	7	5	Maori	12	24.5
Warrau	7	5	Pukapukans	12	24.5
Wogeo	7	5	Trobrianders	12	24.5
Ontong-Javanese	6	1.5	Kwakiutl	11	20.5
		$W_x = 200.0$	Manus	11	20.5
			Chiricahua	10	16
			Comanche	10	16
			Siriono	10	16
			Bena	8	9.5
			Slave	8	9.5
			Kurtatchi	6	1.5
					$W_y = 580.0$

Reference to Appendix Table A reveals that $z \leq -3.41$ has a one-tailed probability when H_0 is true of $p < .0003$. Since this p is smaller than $\alpha = .01$, our decision is to reject H_0 in favor of H_1. We conclude that societies with oral explanations of illness present are (stochastically) higher in oral socialization anxiety than societies with oral explanations absent.

It is important to notice that for these data the Wilcoxon test exhibits greater power to reject H_0 than the median test. Testing a similar hypothesis about these data, the median test yielded a value which permitted rejection of H_0 at the $p < .005$ level (one-tailed test), whereas the Wilcoxon test yielded a value which permitted rejection of H_0 at the $p < .0003$ level (one-tailed test). The fact that the Wilcoxon test is more powerful than the median test is not surprising, inasmuch as it considers the rank value of each observation rather than simply its location with respect to the combined median, and, thus, uses more of the information in the data. The use of a more powerful test is justified if its assumptions are satisfied.

TIES. The Wilcoxon test assumes that the scores are sampled from a distribution which is continuous. With very precise measurement of a continuous variable, the probability of a tie is zero. However, with the relatively crude measures which we typically employ in behavioral science research, ties may well occur. We assume that the two (or more) observations which result in tied scores are really different, but that this difference is simply too refined or minute to be detected by our measurements.

When tied scores occur, we give each of the tied observations the average of the ranks they would have had if no ties had occurred.[9]

If the ties occur between two or more observations in the same group, the value of W_x is not affected. But if the ties occur between two or more observations involving both groups, the value of W_x (and W_y) is affected. Although the effect is usually negligible, a correction for ties is available and should be used whenever we employ the large-sample approximation to the sampling distribution of W_x.

The effect of tied ranks is to change the variability of the set of ranks. Thus the correction for ties must be applied to the variance of the sampling distribution of W_x. Corrected for ties, the variance becomes

$$\sigma_{W_x}^2 = \frac{mn}{N(N-1)}\left(\frac{N^3 - N}{12} - \sum_{j=1}^{g} \frac{t_j^3 - t_j}{12}\right) \tag{6.12}$$

[9] If two or more scores are tied at the same rank, the rank assigned is the *average of the tied ranks* which would have been assigned if the scores had differed slightly. Thus, if three scores are tied for the first (lowest) position, each score would be assigned the rank of 2 for $(1 + 2 + 3)/3 = 2$. The next score would then be assigned the rank of 4 because ranks 1, 2, and 3 have already been assigned. If two scores were tied for the first position, both would receive a rank of 1.5 since $(1 + 2)/2 = 1.5$, and the next largest score would receive a rank of 3.

where $N = m + n$, g is the number of groupings of different tied ranks, and t_j is the number of tied ranks in the jth grouping. Using this correction for ties, the value of z becomes

$$z = \frac{W_x \pm .5 - m(N+1)/2}{\sqrt{[mn/N(N-1)]\left[(N^3 - N)/12 - \sum_{j=1}^{g} (t_j^3 - t_j)/12\right]}} \tag{6.13}$$

It may be seen that, if there are no ties, the above expression reduces directly to that given originally in Eq. (6.11).

The use of the correction for ties in the Wilcoxon test may be illustrated by applying that correction to the data in Table 6.18. For those data,

$$m + n = 16 + 23 = 39 = N$$

We observed the following tied groups:

Grouping	Value	Rank	t_j
1	6	1.5	2
2	7	5	5
3	8	9.5	4
4	10	16	7
5	11	20.5	2
6	12	24.5	6
7	13	29.5	4
8	14	33	3
9	15	36	3

In order to find the variance, we need to calculate the correction factor for the $g = 9$ groupings of ties:

$$\begin{aligned}\sum_{j=1}^{9} \frac{t_j^3 - t_j}{12} &= \frac{2^3 - 2}{12} + \frac{5^3 - 5}{12} + \frac{4^3 - 4}{12} + \cdots + \frac{3^3 - 3}{12} \\ &= .5 + 10.0 + 5.0 + 28.0 + \cdots + 2.0 \\ &= 70.5\end{aligned}$$

Using this correction factor and $m = 16$, $n = 23$, $N = 39$, we have

$$\begin{aligned} z &= \frac{W_x \pm .5 - m(N+1)/2}{\sqrt{[mn/N(N-1)]\left((N^3 - N)/12 - \sum_{j=1}^{g} (t_j^3 - t_j)/12\right)}} \qquad (6.13) \\ &= \frac{200 + .5 - 16(39+1)/2}{\sqrt{[(16)(23)]/[39(39-1)]\,[(39^3 - 39)/12 - 70.5]}} \\ &= -3.44 \end{aligned}$$

The value of z when corrected for ties is a little larger than that found earlier when the correction was not used. The difference between $z \leq -3.41$ and $z \leq -3.44$, however, is negligible in so far as the probability given by Appendix Table A is concerned. Both z's result in $p < .0003$ (one-tailed test).

As this example demonstrates, ties have only a slight effect. Even when many of the scores are tied (this example had over 90 percent of its observations involved in ties) the effect is very small. Observe, however, that the magnitude of the correction factor depends importantly on the *number of ties* at each grouping of ties. Thus a tie of "size" 4 contributes 5.0 to the correction factor, whereas two ties of size 2 contribute together only 1.0 (that is, .5 + .5); and a tie of size 6 contributes 17.5, whereas two of size 3 contribute together only 2.0 + 2.0 = 4.0.

When the correction is employed, it always *increases* the magnitude of z slightly, making it more significant. Therefore, when we do not correct for ties our test is "conservative" in that the associated probability will be slightly inflated compared to that for the corrected z. That is, the value of the probability associated with the observed data when H_0 is true will be slightly larger than that which would be found were the correction employed. Our recommendation is that one should correct for ties only if the proportion of ties is quite large, if some of the t's are large, or if the probability obtained without the correction is very close to the previously set value of α.

6.4.5 Summary of Procedure

These are the steps in the use of the Wilcoxon test:

1. Determine the value of m and n. The number of cases in the smaller group (denoted X) is m; the number of cases in the larger group (denoted Y) is n.
2. Rank together the scores for both groups, assigning the rank of 1 to the score that is algebraically lowest. The ranks will range from 1 to $m + n = N$. Assign tied observations the average of the tied ranks.
3. Determine the value of W_x by summing the ranks in group X.
4. The method for determining the significance of W_x depends upon the size of m and n:
   (*a*) If $m \leq 10$ and $n \leq 10$ (or $n \leq 12$ for $m = 3$ or 4), the exact probability associated with a value as large (or as small) as an observed W_x is given in Appendix Table J. The tabled values are one-tailed probabilities. For a two-tailed test, double the tabled values.[10]
   (*b*) If $m > 10$ or $n > 10$, the probability associated with a value as extreme as the observed value of W_x may be determined by computing the normal approximation by using Eq. (6.11) and assessing the significance of z by referring to

[10] It may not be possible to achieve an exact probability level with a two-tailed test because of the discrete nature of the sampling distribution. To achieve greater precision, the region of rejection can be chosen with two different critical values from each tail so that $\alpha_1 + \alpha_2 = \alpha$.

Appendix Table A. For a two-tailed test, the probability shown in that table is doubled. If the number of ties is large or if the obtained probability is very close to the chosen significance level (α), apply the correction for ties, i.e., use Eq. (6.13).

5. If the observed value of W_x has an associated probability equal to or less than α, reject H_0 in favor of H_1.

6.4.6 Power-Efficiency

If the Wilcoxon test is applied to data which might properly be analyzed by the more powerful parametric test, the t test, its power-efficiency approaches $3/\pi = 95.5$ percent as N increases and is close to 95 percent even for moderate-sized samples. It is, therefore, an excellent alternative to the t test, and, of course, it does not have all of the restrictive assumptions and requirements associated with the t test.

In some cases, it has been shown that the Wilcoxon test has power greater than 1, that is, it is more powerful than the t test.

6.4.7 References

For useful discussions of the Wilcoxon-Mann-Whitney test, the reader should refer to Mann and Whitney (1947), Whitney (1948), Wilcoxon (1945), and Lehmann (1975).

6.5 ROBUST RANK-ORDER TEST

6.5.1 Function

The Wilcoxon-Mann-Whitney test described in the previous section was used to test the hypothesis that two independent groups were sampled from the same population. That test assumed that the variables X and Y were sampled from the same continuous distribution. Thus the variables were measured on at least an ordinal scale. One way of stating the null hypothesis is H_0: $\theta_x = \theta_y$. That is, the median of the distribution X is equal to the median of the distribution Y. It should be recalled that, when we assume that the distributions are the same, we are implying that the variability or *variances* of the distributions are equal. The alternative hypothesis specifies only that there is a difference in medians and, like the null hypothesis, assumes that the variabilities of the distributions are *the same*.

Sometimes we wish to test the hypothesis H_0: $\theta_x = \theta_y$ without assuming that the underlying distributions are the same. Perhaps because of some known differences between the groups, a restriction in range, or some other factor, the researcher has reason to believe that the underlying distributions of X and Y are not equal, but still wishes to test H_0. This sort of testing problem is known to statisticians as the *Behrens-Fisher* problem. In such cases, the Wilcoxon test is not appropriate. The *robust rank-order test* discussed in this section is a useful alternative to the Wilcoxon test.

6.5.2 Method

Let m be the number of cases in the sample from group X and n be the number of cases in the sample from group Y. We assume that the two samples are independent. To apply the robust rank-order test, we first combine the observations or scores from both groups, and rank them in order of increasing size. In this ranking, algebraic size is considered, i.e., the lowest ranks are assigned to the largest negative values, if any.

Now focus on one of the groups, say, the group X with m cases. For ease of computation, we shall calculate a statistic which is different from the ranking, called $\grave{U}$. For comparison with the Wilcoxon test, we shall use the same data to illustrate the computation of the statistic. In that example, there was an experimental group of $m = 3$ cases and a control group of $n = 4$ cases. The scores were the following:

Experimental scores X:	9	11	15	
Control scores Y:	6	8	10	13

Although we shall not use the rank-order statistic, it is still necessary to rank the data, retaining each score's identity as either an X or Y score:

Score:	6	8	9	10	11	13	15
Group:	Y	Y	X	Y	X	Y	X

For each X_i we count the number of observations of Y with a lower rank. This number represents the *placement* of the X scores and will be denoted $U(YX_i)$. For this example we have

X_i	$U(YX_i)$
9	2
11	3
15	4

We then find the mean of the $U(YX_i)$:

$$U(YX) = \sum_{i=1}^{m} \frac{U(YX_i)}{m} \tag{6.14a}$$

$$= \frac{2 + 3 + 4}{3}$$

$$= 3$$

Similarly, we find the *placements* of each Y. That is, we find $U(XY_j)$, the number of observations from X which precede each Y_j.

Y_j	$U(XY_j)$
6	0
8	0
10	1
13	2

We then find the mean:

$$U(XY) = \sum_{j=1}^{n} \frac{U(XY_j)}{n} \tag{6.14b}$$

$$= \frac{0 + 0 + 1 + 2}{4}$$

$$= .75$$

Next, we must find an index of variability of $U(YX_i)$ and $U(XY_j)$. Define the two indexes to be

$$V_x = \sum_{i=1}^{m} [U(YX_i) - U(YX)]^2 \tag{6.15a}$$

and

$$V_y = \sum_{j=1}^{n} [U(XY_j) - U(XY)]^2 \tag{6.15b}$$

For the data from this example,

$$V_x = (2 - 3)^2 + (3 - 3)^2 + (4 - 3)^2$$
$$= 1 + 0 + 1$$
$$= 2$$

and

$$V_y = (0 - .75)^2 + (0 - .75)^2 + (1 - .75)^2 + (2 - .75)^2$$
$$= 2.75$$

Finally, we calculate the test statistic $\grave{U}$:

$$\grave{U} = \frac{mU(YX) - nU(XY)}{2\sqrt{V_x + V_y + U(XY)U(YX)}} \tag{6.16}$$

$$= \frac{3(3) - 4(.75)}{2\sqrt{2 + 2.75 + (.75)(3)}}$$

$$= 1.13$$

The sampling distribution of $\grave{U}$ has been tabled and is found in Appendix Table K for small sample sizes ($m \leq n \leq 12$). As the sample sizes increase, the distribution of $\grave{U}$ approaches that of the unit normal distribution, so that Appendix Table A may be used to determine the significance of values of the statistic $\grave{U}$ calculated by using Eq. (6.16).

For the data in the above example, $m = 3$, $n = 4$, and $\grave{U} = 1.13$. Reference to Appendix Table K shows that the probability of obtaining a sample value of $\grave{U}$ as large as 1.13 when H_0 is true exceeds .10. Since the sample sizes are small the sampling distribution of $\grave{U}$ is such that it is not possible to achieve precisely the "traditional" .05 and .01 significance levels. Therefore, the table consists of those values of $\grave{U}$ that are closest to the desired significance level. If the alternative hypothesis is two-tailed, the probabilities in Appendix Table K should be doubled.

Example 6.5 Many contemporary hypotheses concerning the etiology of schizophrenia have suggested a role for dopamine. There is evidence which indicates increased dopamine activity at some central-nervous-system sites in schizophrenic patients compared to nonschizophrenic patients. Some antipsychotic drugs appear to block dopamine receptors, and some drugs that increase central dopamine function aggravate schizophrenic symptoms. One hypothesis is that neuroleptic medications act by decreasing the central transmission of dopamine resulting in a decrease in schizophrenic activity.

In a study involving 25 hospitalized schizophrenics,[11] each was treated with antipsychotic (neuroleptic) medication, observed over a period of time, and classified as nonpsychotic or psychotic by the professional nursing staff at the hospital. Fifteen were judged nonpsychotic during treatment and ten remained psychotic. From each patient samples of cerebrospinal fluid were drawn and assayed for dopamine *b*-hydroxylase (DBH) activity. The results are shown in Table 6.19. The researchers wished to determine whether the difference in DBH activity between the two groups was significant.

i. Null hypothesis. H_0: the DBH activity in the cerebrospinal fluid of schizophrenic patients who became nonpsychotic during treatment is the same as the DBH activity in patients who remained schizophrenic. H_1: the DBH activity levels in the two groups are different.

ii. Statistical test. The robust rank-order test is chosen because this study involves two independent samples and uses measurement (DBH activity in cerebrospinal fluid as an index of activity at central-nervous-systems sites) which is probably at most in an ordinal scale. In addition, because the groups may differ in terms of variability, the robust rank-order test is appropriate.

iii. Significance level. Let $\alpha = .05$, m are patients judged nonpsychotic $= 15$, and n are patients who remained psychotic $= 10$.

iv. Sampling distribution. The probabilities associated with the occurrence when H_0 is true of values as large as $\grave{U}$ may be determined by the normal distribution (Appendix Table A).

v. Rejection region. Since H_1 does not state a direction of difference, a two-tailed test is appropriate. Therefore, since $\alpha = .05$, the rejection region consists of all values of $\grave{U}$ which are greater than 1.96 or less than -1.96, using the normal distribution approximation to the sampling distribution of $\grave{U}$.

[11] Sternberg, D. E., Van Kammen, D. P., and Bunney, W. E. (1982). Schizophrenia: Dopamine *b*-hydoxylase activity and treatment response. *Science*, **216**, 1423–1425.

TABLE 6.19
Dopamine *b*-hydroxylase activity in the cerebrospinal fluid of schizophrenic patients after treatment with antipsychotic medication

Judged nonpsychotic	Remained psychotic
$m = 15$	$n = 10$
.0252	.0320
.0230	.0306
.0210	.0275
.0200	.0270
.0200	.0245
.0180	.0226
.0170	.0222
.0156	.0208
.0154	.0204
.0145	.0150
.0130	
.0116	
.0112	
.0105	
.0104	

Note: Measurements are in nmol/(ml)(hr)/(mg) of protein.

vi. *Decision.* To calculate the statistic $\acute{U}$, we need to calculate the placements of the X and Y scores. Table 6.20 summarizes the calculation of $U(YX_i)$ and $U(XY_j)$. With the values found in Table 6.20, we find, by using the two Eqs. (6.14*a*) and (6.14*b*), that

$$U(YX) = \sum_{i=1}^{m} \frac{U(YX_i)}{m} \qquad (6.14a)$$

$$= \frac{20}{15}$$

$$= 1.33$$

and

$$U(XY) = \sum_{j=1}^{n} \frac{U(XY_j)}{n} \qquad (6.14b)$$

$$= \frac{130}{10}$$

$$= 13$$

Next, by using Eq. (6.15), we must find the index of variability for $U(YX_i)$ and $U(XY_j)$.

$$V_x = \sum_{i=1}^{m} [U(YX_i) - U(YX)]^2 \qquad (6.15a)$$

$$= 49.33$$

TABLE 6.20
Placements for observations in Table 6.19

X_i	$U(YX_i)$	$U(YX_i) - U(YX)$	Y_j	$U(XY_j)$	$U(XY_j) - U(XY)$
.0104	0	$\frac{4}{3}$			
.0105	0	$\frac{4}{3}$			
.0112	0	$\frac{4}{3}$			
.0116	0	$\frac{4}{3}$			
.0130	0	$\frac{4}{3}$			
.0145	0	$\frac{4}{3}$			
			.0150	6	7
.0154	1	$\frac{1}{3}$			
.0156	1	$\frac{1}{3}$			
.0170	1	$\frac{1}{3}$			
.0180	1	$\frac{1}{3}$			
.0200	1	$\frac{1}{3}$			
.0200	1	$\frac{1}{3}$			
			.0204	12	1
			.0208	12	1
.0210	3	$\frac{5}{3}$			
			.0222	13	0
			.0226	13	0
.0230	5	$\frac{11}{3}$			
			.0245	14	1
.0252	6	$\frac{14}{3}$			
			.0270	15	2
			.0275	15	2
			.0306	15	2
			.0320	15	2
	20			130	
	$U(YX) = \frac{20}{15} = \frac{4}{3} = 1.33$			$U(XY) = \frac{130}{10} = 13$	

and

$$V_y = \sum_{j=1}^{n} [U(XY_j) - U(XY)]^2 \tag{6.15b}$$

$$= 68$$

Finally, we calculate the test statistic $\grave{U}$:

$$\grave{U} = \frac{mU(YX) - nU(XY)}{2\sqrt{V_x + V_y + U(XY)U(YX)}} \tag{6.16}$$

$$= \frac{15(1.33) - 10(13)}{2\sqrt{49.33 + 68 + (1.33)(13)}}$$

$$= -4.74$$

Since the observed value $\grave{U}$ exceeds the critical value (-1.96), we may reject the hypothesis H_0 that there is no difference between the two groups in DBH activity.

TIES. As is sometimes the case with observed data, tied observations may occur. In the calculation of the robust rank-order statistic, the adjustment for ties is straightforward. The adjustment is made in calculating the placements:

$U(YX_i) =$ the number of Y observations in the sample that are less than X_i $+\frac{1}{2}$ of the number of Y observations in the sample that are equal to X_i.

$U(XY_j) =$ the number of X observations in the sample that are less than Y_j $+\frac{1}{2}$ of the number of X observations in the sample that are equal to Y_j.

The calculation of $U(YX)$, $U(XY)$, V_x, V_y, and $\grave{U}$ are then completed using the adjusted placements.

6.5.3 Summary of Procedure

These are the steps in the use of the robust rank-order test:

1. Order the scores in the combined X and Y groups. For each score in each group, calculate the placements $U(YX_i)$ and $U(XY_j)$. If necessary, make adjustments for tied observations.
2. Calculate the mean placements $U(YX)$ and $U(XY)$, the variability indices V_x and V_y, and the statistic U by using Eq. (6.16).
3. The method for determining the significance of $\grave{U}$ depends upon the size of m and n:
   (*a*) If m and n are less than 12, the significance probabilities associated with large values of $\grave{U}$ are given in Appendix Table K. The tabled values are one-tailed probabilities. For a two-tailed test, the probabilities are doubled.
   (*b*) If m or n are greater than 12, the probability associated with a value as extreme as the observed value of $\grave{U}$ may be determined by referring to Appendix Table A since, for large m and n, the sampling distribution of $\grave{U}$ is approximately normal.
4. If the observed value of $\grave{U}$ has an associated probability equal to or less than α, reject H_0 in favor of H_1.

6.5.4 Power-Efficiency

The test procedures have *exact* significance levels equal to α for testing the hypothesis that X and Y have identical distributions. The significance levels are approximate when we test the hypothesis H_0: $\theta_x = \theta_y$ without requiring equal variances for the two populations. In general, the test has essentially the same power as the Wilcoxon test (when the assumptions of that test are met); however, the test appears to approach the normal distribution somewhat faster as m and n get large.

6.5.5 References

The Behrens-Fisher problem (comparing two groups with unequal variances) has a long history in statistics. Nonparametric tests for this situation are relatively new, and some that have been proposed are difficult to compute. For additional discussion, see Lehmann (1975) and Randles and Wolfe (1979). The test described in this chapter is due to Fligner and Policello (1981).

6.6 THE KOLMOGOROV-SMIRNOV TWO-SAMPLE TEST

6.6.1 Function and Rationale

The *Kolmogorov-Smirnov two-sample test* is a test of whether two independent samples have been drawn from the same population (or from populations with the same distribution). The two-tailed test is sensitive to any kind of difference in the distributions from which the two samples were drawn—differences in location (central tendency), in dispersion, in skewness, etc. The one-tailed test is used to decide whether or not the data values in the population from which one of the samples was drawn are stochastically larger than the values of the population from which the other sample was drawn, e.g., to test the prediction that the scores of an experimental group will be higher than those of the control group.

Like the Kolmogorov-Smirnov one-sample test (Sec. 4.3) the two-sample test is concerned with the agreement between two cumulative distributions. The one-sample test is concerned with the agreement between the distribution of a set of sample values and some specified theoretical distribution. The two-sample test is concerned with the agreement between two sets of sample values.

If the two samples have, in fact, been drawn from the same population distribution, then the cumulative distributions of both samples may be expected to be fairly close to each other, inasmuch as they both should show only random deviations from the common population distribution. If the two-sample cumulative distributions are "too far apart" at any point, this suggests that the samples come from different populations. Thus a large enough deviation between the two-sample cumulative distributions is evidence for rejecting H_0.

6.6.2 Method

To apply the Kolmogorov-Smirnov two-sample test, we determine the cumulative frequency distribution[12] for each sample of observations by using the same intervals for both distributions. Then, for each interval we subtract one step function from the other. The test focuses on the largest of these observed deviations.

---

[12] In this section we shall use the term *cumulative frequency distribution* to refer to the empirical distribution function which is the *proportion* of observations which are less than or equal to a particular value. In some texts this function is called the *cumulative relative frequency distribution*.

Let $S_m(X)$ be the observed cumulative distribution for one sample (of size m), that is, $S_m(X) = K/m$, where K is the number of data equal to or less than X. And let $S_n(X)$ be the observed cumulative distribution of the other sample, that is, $S_n(X) = K/n$. Now the Kolmogorov-Smirnov two-sample test statistic is

$$D_{m,n} = \max[S_m(X) - S_n(X)] \tag{6.17}$$

for a one-tailed test, and

$$D_{m,n} = \max|S_m(X) - S_n(X)| \tag{6.18}$$

for a two-tailed test.

In each case, the sampling distribution of $D_{m,n}$ is known. The probabilities associated with the occurrence of values as large as an observed $D_{m,n}$ under the null hypothesis (that the two samples have come from the same distribution) have been tabled. Actually, there are *two* sampling distributions, depending upon whether the test is one-tailed or two-tailed. Notice that for a one-tailed test we find the $D_{m,n}$ *in the predicted direction* [using Eq. (6.17)], and for a two-tailed test we find the maximum *absolute* difference $D_{m,n}$ [using Eq. (6.18)] irrespective of direction. This is because in the one-tailed test, H_1 means that the population values from which one of the samples was drawn are stochastically larger than the population values from which the other sample was drawn, whereas in the two-tailed test, H_1 means simply that the two samples are from different populations.

In the use of the Kolmogorov-Smirnov test on data for which the size and number of the intervals are arbitrary, it is well to use as many intervals as are feasible. When too few intervals are used, information may be wasted. That is, the maximum vertical deviation $D_{m,n}$ of the two cumulative distributions may be obscured by casting the data with too few intervals.

For instance, in the example presented below for the case of small samples, only eight intervals were used to simplify the exposition. As it happens, eight intervals were sufficient to yield a $D_{m,n}$ which enabled us to reject H_0 at the predetermined level of significance. If it had happened that with these eight intervals the observed $D_{m,n}$ had not been large enough to permit us to reject H_0, before we could accept H_0 it would have been necessary to increase the number of intervals in order to ascertain whether the maximum deviation $D_{m,n}$ had been obscured by the use of too few intervals. It is advisable then to use as many intervals as are feasible to start with, so as not to waste information inherent in the data.

6.6.3 Small Samples

When both m and n are 25 or less, Appendix Table L_I may be used to test the null hypothesis against a one-tailed alternative, and Appendix Table L_{II} may be used to test the null hypothesis against a two-tailed alternative. The body of these tables gives values of $mnD_{m,n}$ which are significant at various significance levels. Knowing the values m, n, $mnD_{m,n}$ and whether the test is one-tailed or two-tailed, one may find critical values of the statistic. For example, in a one-tailed test where $m = 6$ and $n = 8$, one would reject H_0 at the $\alpha = .01$ level when $mnD_{m,n} \geq 38$.

TABLE 6.21
Percentage of total errors in first half of series

Eleventh-grade subjects	Seventh-grade subjects
35.2	39.1
39.2	41.2
40.9	45.2
38.1	46.2
34.4	48.4
29.1	48.7
41.8	55.0
24.3	40.6
32.4	52.1
—	47.2

Example 6.6*a* Lepley compared the serial learning of 10 seventh-grade students with the serial learning of 9 eleventh-grade students.[13] His hypothesis was that the primacy effect should be less prominent in the learning of the younger subjects. The primacy effect is the tendency for the material learned early in a series to be remembered more efficiently than the material learned later in the series. He tested this hypothesis by comparing the percentage of errors made by the two groups in the first half of the series of learned material, predicting that the older group (the eleventh-graders) would make relatively fewer errors in repeating the first half of the series than would the younger group.

i. Null hypothesis. H_0: there is no difference in the proportion of errors made in recalling the first half of a learned series between eleventh-grade students and seventh-grade students. H_1: eleventh-graders make proportionally fewer errors than seventh-graders in recalling the first half of a learned series.

ii. Statistical test: Since two small independent samples are being compared and the alternative hypothesis is one-tailed, the Kolmogorov-Smirnov two-sample one-tailed test will be applied to the data.

iii. Significance level. Let $\alpha = .01$, $m = 9$, and $n = 10$.

iv. Sampling distribution. Appendix Table L_I gives critical values for the sampling distribution of $mnD_{m,n}$ for m and n less than 25.

v. Region of rejection. Since H_1 predicts the direction of the difference, the region of rejection is one-tailed. H_0 will be rejected if the value of $D_{m,n}$ (the largest deviation in the predicted direction) is so large that the probability associated with its occurrence when H_0 is true is less than or equal to $\alpha = .01$.

vi. Decision. Table 6.21 gives the percentage of each student's errors which were committed in the recall of the first half of the serially learned material. For analysis by the Kolmogorov-Smirnov test, these data were cast in two cumulative frequency distributions shown in Table 6.22. Here $m = 9$ eleventh-graders, and $n = 10$ seventh-graders.

[13] Lepley, W. M. (1934). Serial reactions considered as conditioned reactions. *Psychological Monographs*, **46**, whole number 205.

TABLE 6.22
Data in Table 6.21 cast for Kolmogorov-Smirnov test

	Percent of total errors in first half of series							
	24–27	**28–31**	**32–35**	**36–39**	**40–43**	**44–47**	**48–51**	**52–55**
$S_m(X)$	$\frac{1}{9}$	$\frac{2}{9}$	$\frac{5}{9}$	$\frac{7}{9}$	$\frac{9}{9}$	$\frac{9}{9}$	$\frac{9}{9}$	$\frac{9}{9}$
$S_n(X)$	$\frac{0}{10}$	$\frac{0}{10}$	$\frac{0}{10}$	$\frac{1}{10}$	$\frac{3}{10}$	$\frac{6}{10}$	$\frac{8}{10}$	$\frac{10}{10}$
$S_m(X) - S_n(X)$	.111	.222	.556	.678	.700	.400	.200	0

Observe that the largest discrepancy between the two cumulative distributions is $D_{m,n} = .70$. Thus, $mnD_{m,n} = (9)(10)(.70) = 63$. Reference to Table L_I reveals that the critical value for $\alpha = .01$ is 61; therefore, since the observed value exceeds the critical value, we reject H_0 in favor of H_1. We conclude that eleventh-graders make proportionally fewer errors than seventh-graders in recalling the first half of a learned series.

6.6.4 Large Samples: Two-Tailed Test

When either m or n are larger than 25, Appendix Table L_{III} may be used for the Kolmogorov-Smirnov two-sample test. To use this table, determine the value of $D_{m,n}$ for the observed data by using Eq. (6.18). Then compare that observed value with the critical value which is obtained by entering the observed values of m and n in the expression given in Table L_{III}. If the observed $D_{m,n}$ is equal to or larger than that computed from the expression in the table, H_0 may be rejected at the level of significance (two-tailed) associated with that expression.

For example, suppose $m = 55$ and $n = 60$, and that a researcher wishes to perform a two-tailed test at $\alpha = .05$. In the row in Table L_{III} for $\alpha = .05$, the researcher finds the value of $D_{m,n}$ which must be equaled or exceeded in order to reject H_0. By computation, the researcher finds that $D_{m,n}$ must be at least .254 in order to reject H_0, for

$$1.36\sqrt{\frac{m+n}{mn}} = 1.36\sqrt{\frac{55+60}{(55)(60)}} = .254$$

6.6.5 Large Samples: One-Tailed Test

When m and n are large, we may make a one-tailed test by using

$$D_{m,n} = \max[S_m(X) - S_n(X)] \tag{6.17}$$

We test the null hypothesis that the two samples have been drawn from the same population against the alternative hypothesis that the values of the population from which one of the samples was drawn are stochastically larger than the values of the population from which the other sample was drawn. For example, we may wish to test not simply whether an experimental group is different from a control group but whether the experimental group is "higher" than the control group.

It has been shown (Goodman, 1954) that

$$X^2 = 4D_{m,n}^2 \frac{mn}{m+n} \tag{6.19}$$

is approximated by the chi-square distribution with $df = 2$ as the sample sizes (m and n) increase. That is, we may determine the significance of an observed $D_{m,n}$, as computed from Eq. (6.17), by using Eq. (6.19) and referring to the chi-square distribution with $df = 2$ (Appendix Table C).

Example 6.6*b* For large samples. In a study of correlates of authoritarian personality structure,[14] one hypothesis was that people high in authoritarianism would show a greater tendency to possess stereotypes about members of various national and ethnic groups than would those low in authoritarianism. This hypothesis was tested with a group of 98 randomly selected college women. Each subject was given 20 photographs and asked to "identify" (by matching) as many or as few photographs as they wished. Since, unknown to the subjects, all photographs were of Mexican nationals—either candidates for the Mexican legislature or winners in a Mexican beauty contest—and since the matching list of 20 different national and ethnic groups did not include "Mexican," the number of photographs which any subject "identified" constitutes an index of that subject's tendency to stereotype.

Authoritarianism was measured by the F scale of authoritarianism, and the subjects were grouped as "high" and "low" scorers. High scorers were those who scored at or above the median on the F scale; low scorers were those who scored below the median. The prediction was that these two groups would differ in the number of photographs they identified.

i. *Null hypothesis.* H_0: women at this university who score low in authoritarianism stereotype as much (identify as many photographs) as women who score high in authoritarianism. H_1: women who score high in authoritarianism stereotype more (identify more photographs) than women who score low in authoritarianism.

ii. *Statistical test.* Since the low scorers and the high scorers constitute two independent groups, a test for two independent samples was chosen. Because the number of photographs identified by a subject cannot be considered more than an ordinal measure of that subject's tendency to stereotype, a nonparametric test is desirable. The Kolmogorov-Smirnov two-sample test compares two-sample cumulative frequency distributions and determines whether the observed $D_{m,n}$ indicates that they have been drawn from two populations, one of which is stochastically larger than the other.

iii. *Significance level.* Let $\alpha = .01$. The sample sizes m and n may be determined only after the data are collected, because subjects will be grouped according to whether they score at or above the median on the F scale or score below the median on the F scale.

iv. *Sampling distribution.* The sampling distribution of

$$X^2 = 4D_{m,n}^2 \frac{mn}{m+n}$$

[14] Siegel, S. (1954). Certain determinants and correlates of authoritarianism. *Genetic and Psychological Monographs*, **49**, 187–229.

TABLE 6.23
Number of low and high authoritarians "identifying" various numbers of photographs

Number of photographs "identified"	Low scorers	High scorers
0–2	11	1
3–5	7	3
6–8	8	6
9–11	3	12
12–14	5	12
15–17	5	14
18–20	5	6

where $D_{m,n}$ is computed from Eq. (6.17), is approximated by the chi-square distribution with $df = 2$. The probability associated with an observed value of $D_{m,n}$ when H_0 is true may be determined by referring to Appendix Table C.

v. Rejection region. Since H_1 predicts the direction of the difference between low and high F scorers, a one-tailed test is used. The region of rejection consists of all values of X^2, as computed from Eq. (6.19), which are so large that the probability associated with their occurrence when H_0 is true is equal to or less than $\alpha = .01$.

vi. Decision. Of the 98 college women, 44 obtained F scores below the median; thus, $m = 44$. The remaining 54 women obtained scores at or above the median; thus $n = 54$. The number of photographs identified by each of the subjects in the two groups is given in Table 6.23. To apply the Kolmogorov-Smirnov test, we recast these data into two cumulative frequency distributions, as in Table 6.24. By subtraction, we find the differences between the two sample distributions at the various intervals. The largest of these differences in the predicted direction is .406. That is,

$$D_{m,n} = \max[S_m(X) - S_n(X)]$$
$$D_{44,54} = \max[S_{44}(X) - S_{54}(X)]$$
$$= .406$$

TABLE 6.24
Data in Table 6.23 cast for Kolmogorov-Smirnov test

	Number of photographs "identified"						
	0–2	3–5	6–8	9–11	12–14	15–17	18–20
$S_{44}(X)$	$\frac{11}{44}$	$\frac{18}{44}$	$\frac{26}{44}$	$\frac{29}{44}$	$\frac{34}{44}$	$\frac{39}{44}$	$\frac{44}{44}$
$S_{54}(X)$	$\frac{1}{54}$	$\frac{4}{54}$	$\frac{10}{54}$	$\frac{22}{54}$	$\frac{34}{54}$	$\frac{38}{54}$	$\frac{54}{54}$
$S_{44}(X) - S_{54}(X)$	.232	.355	.406	.252	.143	.182	.0

With $D_{44,54} = .406$, we compute the value of X^2 as defined by Eq. (6.19):

$$X^2 = 4D_{m,n}^2 \frac{mn}{m+n} \qquad (6.19)$$

$$= \frac{4(.406)^2(44)(54)}{44+54}$$

$$= 15.99$$

Reference to Appendix Table C reveals that the probability associated with $X^2 = 15.99$ for $df = 2$ is $p < .001$ (one-tailed test). Since this value is smaller than $\alpha = .01$, we may reject H_0 in favor of H_1.[15] We conclude that women who score high on the authoritarianism scale stereotype more (identify more photographs) than do women who score low on the scale.

It is interesting to notice that the chi-square approximation may also be used with small samples, but in this case it leads to a conservative test. That is, the error in the use of the chi-square approximation with small samples is always in the "safe" direction (Goodman, 1954, p. 168). In other words, if H_0 is rejected with the use of the chi-square approximation with small samples, we may surely have confidence in the decision. Thus, the chi-square approximation may be used for small samples, but the test is conservative and the use of Appendix Table L_I is preferred.

6.6.6 Summary of Procedure

These are the steps in the use of the Kolmogorov-Smirnov two-sample test:

1. Arrange each of the two groups of scores in a cumulative frequency distribution by using the same intervals (or classifications) for both distributions. Use as many intervals as feasible.
2. By subtraction, determine the difference between the two-sample cumulative distributions at each listed point.
3. Determine the largest of these differences, $D_{m,n}$. For a one-tailed test, $D_{m,n}$ is the largest difference in the predicted direction. For a two-tailed test, $D_{m,n}$ is the largest difference in either direction.
4. The method for determining the significance of the observed $D_{m,n}$ depends on the sample sizes and the nature of H_1:
   (*a*) When m and n are both ≤ 25, Appendix Table L_I is used for a one-tailed test and Appendix Table L_{II} is used for a two-tailed test. In either table, the entry $mnD_{m,n}$ is used.
   (*b*) For a two-tailed test when either m or n is larger than 25, Appendix Table L_{III} is used. Critical values of $D_{m,n}$ for any given large values of m or n may be computed by using the formulas in that table.

---

[15] With the use of a parametric test, Siegel made the same decision. He found that $t = 3.55$, $p < .001$ (one-tailed test).

(*c*) For a one-tailed test when either m or n is larger than 25, the value of X^2 computed by using Eq. (6.19) is distributed as chi square with $df = 2$. Its significance may be determined with the use of Appendix Table C. (The chi-square approximation may also be employed for small m and n, but it is conservative and the use of Table L_I is preferred.)

5. If the observed value is equal to or larger than that given in the appropriate table for a particular level of significance, H_0 may be rejected in favor of H_1.

6.6.7 Power-Efficiency

When compared with the t test, the Kolmogorov-Smirnov test has high power-efficiency (about 95 percent) for small samples. As the sample size increases the power-efficiency decreases slightly.

The Kolmogorov-Smirnov test is more powerful in all cases than either the chi-square test or the median test.

The evidence seems to indicate that, whereas for very small samples the Kolmogorov-Smirnov test is slightly more efficient than the Wilcoxon-Mann-Whitney test, for large samples the converse holds.

6.6.8 References

For other discussions of the Kolmogorov-Smirnov two-sample test, the reader may consult Goodman (1954), Kolmogorov (1941), and Smirnov (1948).

6.7 THE PERMUTATION TEST FOR TWO INDEPENDENT SAMPLES

6.7.1 Function

The *permutation test* for two independent samples is a useful and powerful nonparametric technique for testing the significance of the difference between the means of two independent samples when the sample sizes m and n are small. The test employs the numerical values of the scores and, therefore, requires at least interval measurement of the variable being studied. With the permutation test we can determine the exact probability associated with our observations under the assumption that H_0 is true, and can do so without making any special assumptions about the underlying distributions in the populations involved.

6.7.2 Rationale and Method

Consider the case of two small independent samples, either drawn at random from two populations or arising from the random assignment of two treatments to the members of a group whose origins are arbitrary. Group X includes five subjects; $m = 5$. Group Y includes four subjects; $n = 4$. We observe the following scores:

Scores for group X:	16	19	22	24	29
Scores for group Y:	0	11	12	20	

With these scores,[16] we wish to test the null hypothesis of no difference between the means against the alternative hypothesis that the mean of the population from which group X was drawn is larger than the mean of the population from which group Y was drawn. That is, H_0: $\mu_x = \mu_y$ and H_1: $\mu_x > \mu_y$.

Now under the null hypothesis, all of the $m + n$ observations may be considered to be from the same population. That is, it is merely a matter of chance that certain observations are labeled X and others are labeled Y. The assignment of the labels X and Y to the scores in the particular way observed may be conceived as one of many equally likely outcomes if H_0 is true. When H_0 is true, the labels could have been assigned to the scores in any of 126 equally likely ways:

$$\binom{m+n}{n} = \binom{5+4}{4} = 126$$

When H_0 is true, only once in 126 "experiments" would it happen that the five largest scores of the $N = m + n = 9$ would all acquire the label X, while the four smallest acquire the label Y.

Now if just such a result should occur in an actual single-trial experiment, we could reject H_0 at the $p = \frac{1}{126} = .008$ level of significance, by applying the reasoning that, if the two groups were really from a common population, i.e., if H_0 were really true, there is no good reason to think that the most extreme of 126 possible outcomes should occur on just the trial that constitutes our experiment. That is, we would decide that the likelihood that the observed event would occur when H_0 is true is very small and, therefore, we would reject H_0. This is part of the familiar logic of statistical inference.

The permutation test specifies a number of the most extreme possible outcomes which could occur with $N = m + n$ scores and designates these as the region of rejection. When we have $\binom{m+n}{n}$ equally likely occurrences under H_0, for some of these the difference between ΣX (the sum of group X's scores) and ΣY (the sum of group Y's scores) will be extreme. The cases for which these differences are largest constitute the region of rejection.

If α is the significance level, then the region of rejection consists of the $\alpha\binom{m+n}{n}$ most extreme among the possible occurrences. That is, the *number* of possible outcomes constituting the region of rejection is $\alpha\binom{m+n}{n}$. The particular outcomes chosen to constitute that number are those for which the *difference* between the mean of the X's and the mean of the Y's is the largest. These are the occurrences in which the difference between ΣX and ΣY is greatest. Now if the

[16] This example is taken from Pitman, E. J. G. (1937*a*). Significance tests which may be applied to samples from any population. *Journal of the Royal Statistical Society*, **4**, 122.

sample we obtain is among those cases included in the region of rejection, we reject H_0 at significance level α.

In the above example of $N = 9$ scores, there are $\binom{5+4}{4} = 126$ possible differences between ΣX and ΣY. If $\alpha = .05$, then the region of rejection consists of $\alpha\binom{m+n}{n} = .05(126) = 6.3$ extreme outcomes. Since the alternative hypothesis is directional, the region of rejection consists of the six most extreme possible outcomes in the specified direction.

Since the alternative hypothesis is H_1: $\mu_x > \mu_y$, the six most extreme possible outcomes constituting the region of rejection of $\alpha = .05$ (one-tailed test) are those given in Table 6.25. The third of these possible extreme outcomes, the one denoted with a dagger, is the sample we obtained. Since our observed set of scores is in the region of rejection, we may reject H_0 at $\alpha = .05$. The exact probability (one-tailed) of the occurrence of the observed scores of a set more extreme when H_0 is true is $p = \frac{3}{126} = .024$.

Now if the alternative hypothesis had not predicted the direction of the difference, then, of course, a two-tailed test of H_0 would have been appropriate. In that case, the six sets of possible outcomes in the region of rejection would consist of the three most extreme possible outcomes in one direction and of the three most extreme possible outcomes in the other direction. Thus it would include the six possible outcomes where the difference between ΣX and ΣY was greatest in absolute value. For illustrative purposes, the six most extreme possible outcomes for a two-tailed test at $\alpha = .05$ for the nine scores presented earlier are given in Table 6.26. With our observed scores H_0 would have been rejected in favor of the alternative hypothesis H_1: $\mu_x \neq \mu_y$, because the obtained sample (shown with a dagger in Table 6.26) is one of the six most extreme of the possible outcomes in either direction. The exact probability (two-tailed) associated with the occurrence

TABLE 6.25
The six most extreme possible outcomes in the predicted direction*

Possible scores for five X cases					Possible scores for four Y cases				$\Sigma X - \Sigma Y$
29	24	22	20	19	16	12	11	0	$114 - 39 = 75$
29	24	22	20	16	19	12	11	0	$111 - 42 = 69$
29	24	22	19	16	20	12	11	0	$110 - 43 = 67$†
29	24	20	19	16	22	12	11	0	$108 - 45 = 63$
29	24	22	20	12	19	16	11	0	$107 - 46 = 61$
29	22	20	19	16	24	12	11	0	$106 - 47 = 59$

* These constitute the region of rejection for the permutation test when $\alpha = .05$.

† The observed sample.

TABLE 6.26
The six most extreme possible outcomes in either direction*

Possible scores for five X cases	Possible scores for four Y cases	$\lvert\Sigma X - \Sigma Y\rvert$
29 24 22 20 19	16 12 11 0	$\lvert 114 - 39\rvert = 75$
29 24 22 20 16	19 12 11 0	$\lvert 111 - 42\rvert = 69$
29 24 22 19 16	20 12 11 0	$\lvert 110 - 43\rvert = 67$†
22 16 12 11 0	29 24 20 19	$\lvert 61 - 92\rvert = 31$
20 16 12 11 0	29 24 22 19	$\lvert 59 - 94\rvert = 35$
19 16 12 11 0	29 24 22 20	$\lvert 58 - 95\rvert = 37$

* These constitute the two-tailed region of rejection for the permutation test when $\alpha = .05$.

† The observed sample.

when H_0 is true of a set as extreme (or more extreme) as the one observed is $p = \frac{6}{126} = .048$.

6.7.3 Large Samples

When m and n are large, the computations necessary for the permutation test can become extremely tedious. It is possible to write a simple computer program which can calculate the possible outcomes. However, as $N = m + n$ become large, the computations become time consuming for the computer as well. However, the computations may be avoided because it can be shown that, if m and n are large and the kurtosis of the combined samples is small, then the permutation distribution of $\binom{m+n}{n}$ possible outcomes is closely approximated by the t distribution. That is, if the above conditions are satisfied, then the t test for differences between two means may be used to test the hypothesis

$$t = \frac{\bar{X} - \bar{Y}}{\sqrt{\Sigma(X_i - \bar{X})^2/(m-1) + \Sigma(Y_i - \bar{Y})^2/(n-1)}} \tag{6.20}$$

which has approximately a Student t distribution. The expression for the degrees of freedom is complicated,[17] but a conservative test would have $df = m + n - 2$. Therefore, the probability associated with the occurrence when H_0 is true of any values as extreme as an observed t may be determined by reference to Appendix Table B.

[17] In the case of unequal population variances, the degrees of freedom for the t test is a function of both the sample sizes and the sample variances. The correct value for the degrees of freedom lies between the smaller sample size minus 1 and $m + n - 2$. Thus, using $df = m + n - 2$ yields a conservative test since, if H_0 is rejected with the maximum possible degrees of freedom, it will be rejected with fewer.

The reader should note that even though Eq. (6.20) is a form of the t test, the test is not used in this case as a parametric statistical test, since the test relies on the central limit theorem for the sampling distribution of the sample means to have an asymptotically normal distribution when the individual observations do not. However, its use assumes not only that the two conditions mentioned above be met but also that the scores represent measurement in at least an interval scale.

When m and n are large, another alternative to the permutation test is the Wilcoxon test, which may be regarded as a permutation test applied to the *ranks* of the observations and, thus, constitutes a good approximation to the permutation test. It can be shown that there are situations for which the Wilcoxon test is more powerful than the t test and, thus, is the better alternative.

6.7.4 Summary of Procedure

These are the steps in the use of the permutation test for two independent samples:

1. Determine the number of possible outcomes in the region of rejection: $\alpha\binom{m+n}{n}$.
2. Specify as belonging to the region of rejection that number of the most extreme possible outcomes. The extremes are those that give the largest difference between ΣX and ΣY. For a one-tailed test, all of these are in the predicted direction. For a two-tailed test, half of the number are the most extreme possible outcomes in one direction and half are the most extreme possible outcomes in the other direction.
3. If the observed scores comprise one of the outcomes listed in the region of rejection, reject H_0 at the α level of significance.

For samples which are so large that the enumeration of the possible outcomes in the region of rejection is too tedious, a computer program (see Appendix II) or Eq. (6.20) may be used as an approximation if the conditions for its use are met by the data. Alternatives which need not meet such conditions and, thus, may be more satisfactory, are the Wilcoxon test or the robust rank-order test.

6.7.5 Power-Efficiency

Because it uses all of the information in the samples, the permutation test for two independent samples has power-efficiency (in the sense defined in Chap. 3) of 100 percent.

6.7.6 References

Discussions of the permutation test for two independent samples may be found in Moses (1952a), Pitman (1937*a*, 1937*b*, 1937*c*), and Lehmann (1975).

6.8 THE SIEGEL-TUKEY TEST FOR SCALE DIFFERENCES

6.8.1 Function and Rationale

In the behavioral sciences, we sometimes expect that an experimental condition will cause some subjects to show extreme behavior in one direction while it causes others to show extreme behavior in the opposite direction. Thus we may think that economic depression and political instability will cause some people to become extremely reactionary and others to become extremely "left-wing" in their political opinions. Or we may expect environmental unrest to create extreme excitement in some mentally ill people while it creates extreme withdrawal in others. In psychological research utilizing a perceptual approach to personality, there are theoretical reasons to predict that "perceptual defense" may manifest itself in either an extremely rapid "vigilant" perceptual response or an extremely slow "repressive" perceptual response.

The *Siegel-Tukey test* is specifically designed for use with data measured on at least an ordinal scale collected to test such hypotheses. It should be used when it is expected that one group will have higher variability than another but the medians (or means) of the two groups are the same (or known). In studies of perceptual defense, for example, we expect control subjects to evince medium or normal responses, whereas we expect experimental subjects to give either vigilant or repressive responses, thus receiving either high or low scores compared to subjects in the control group.

In such studies, statistical tests addressed to differences in central tendency will shield rather than reveal group differences. They lead to acceptance of the null hypothesis when it should be rejected, because when some of the experimental subjects show vigilant responses and thus obtain very low latency scores while others show repressive responses and thus obtain very high latency scores, the average of the scores of the experimental group may be quite close to the average score of the control group (each member of which may have obtained scores which are medium).

The Siegel-Tukey test is specifically designed for the sort of situation described above. It is uniquely valuable when there exist *a priori* grounds for believing that the experimental condition will lead to extreme scores in either direction while maintaining the same median. Thus, if σ^2 is the variance of the variables and if X denotes the experimental group and Y denotes the control group, we can write the hypotheses as

$$H_0\colon \sigma_x^2 = \sigma_y^2$$

and

$$H_1\colon \sigma_x^2 > \sigma_y^2$$

The Siegel-Tukey test focuses on the *range* or spread of one group compared to another, and is often called a test for scale differences between two groups. That is, if there are m cases in the X group and n cases in the Y group, and the $N = m + n$ scores are arranged in order of increasing size, and if the null hypothesis (the X scores and the Y scores are from the same population) is true, then we should expect that the X's and Y's will be well mixed in the ordered series. We should expect under H_0 that some of the extremely high scores will be X's and some will be Y's, that some of the extremely low scores will be X's and some will be Y's, and that the middle range of scores will include a mixture of X's and Y's. However, if the alternative hypothesis is true (X scores represent extreme responses), then we would expect that a considerable proportion of the X's will be high or low while there will be relatively few X's in the middle of the combined distribution. That is, the Y's will be relatively congested, and their range or variability will be small relative to the X scores. The Siegel-Tukey test determines whether the Y scores are so closely compacted or congested relative to all of the $N = m + n$ scores as to lead us to reject the null hypothesis that both X and Y come from the same distribution.

6.8.2 Method

To compute the Siegel-Tukey test, combine the scores from the X and Y groups and arrange these scores in a single ordered series, retaining the group identity of each score. We then assign rank orders to the scores in the sequence, *assigning ranks alternately from the extremes of the sequence.* Thus, in the Siegel-Tukey test, rankings proceed from the extreme (or atypical) scores to the central (or typical) ones. The reader should note that, in accord with the avowed logic of the test, this procedure would separate "extreme-scoring" groups from "normal" ones. For example, suppose a set of X and Y scores were observed with $m = 7$ and $n = 6$, and then ordered from smallest to largest:

Group:	X	X	Y	X	Y	X	Y	Y	Y	X	Y	X	X
Rank:	1	4	5	8	9	12	13	11	10	7	6	3	2

We then calculate the sum of the ranks of the X and Y groups.

$$W_x = 1 + 4 + 8 + 12 + 7 + 3 + 2 = 37$$

and

$$W_y = 5 + 9 + 13 + 11 + 10 + 6 = 54$$

Now if the null hypothesis that the dispersion of the two groups is the same is true, we would expect the sum of ranks (adjusted for sample size) to be about the same for each group. However, if the alternative hypothesis that the X scores are more variable than the Y scores is true, then we would expect W_x to be small and W_y to be large, reflecting the smaller rank numbers assigned to the tails. The reader will note that this is precisely the logic of the Wilcoxon test (Sec. 6.4). Therefore, to test the null hypothesis, we determine the probability associated with the observation of rank sums as large or larger than the obtained W_y for our sample sizes by using Appendix Table J. (Alternatively, we could compute the probability of observing rank sums as small or smaller than the obtained W_x.) For these data, the probability of observing a W_y as large or larger than 54 is $p = .051$.

Therefore, if $\alpha = .05$, we may reject the hypothesis of equal dispersion or variance for the two groups.

Example 6.8 In a study of duration discrimination, Eisler[18] examined various forms of power functions relating objective and subjective durations. These functions were used to test a parallel-clock model for duration discrimination. Two groups of subjects were used. One group's task involved (among other things) the estimation of short durations and the other's involved long durations. It was argued that, although certain parameters may vary as a function of condition, the exponent of the power functions should not be a function of the duration. However, some researchers have argued that individual differences should vary as a function of duration and that there should be greater variability in the exponents associated with long durations. There were eight subjects in the group which performed with long durations (.9 to 1.2 s) and nine subjects in the group which performed with short durations (.07 to .16 s).

The hypothesis was that, for the models tested, the exponent of the power function would not be a function of duration and the variability of the exponent would not vary.

i. Null hypothesis. H_0: the variability of the estimate of the exponents of the power function in duration judgments is unaffected by the duration sets used. H_1: the variability of the exponent of the power function does vary with the durations used.

ii. Statistical test. Since the hypothesis concerns scale parameters (variances) of distributions and since the medians of the distributions are assumed to be equal, the Siegel-Tukey test is appropriate.

iii. Significance level. Let $\alpha = .05$, $m = 8$, and $n = 9$.

iv. Sampling distribution. The sampling distribution of the Siegel-Tukey test is the same as that for the Wilcoxon test. Thus, the logic of that test may be applied to the rank orders assigned by the procedure.

v. Rejection region. Since the alternative hypothesis does state the direction of the difference, a one-tailed test is used. The region of rejection consists of all values of rank sums as large as (or larger than) that observed in the data.

vi. Decision. The values of the estimated exponent are summarized in Table 6.27. In the lower part of the table the data from the two groups are ranked together and rank orders are assigned to the data. From that table, $W_x = 72$ and $W_y = 81$. Reference to Appendix Table J shows that the (one-tailed) probability of observing a value of W_x as small or smaller than the observed value of 72 is $p = .519$. Thus, we cannot reject the hypothesis that the distribution of the power function exponents is the same under the two conditions.

ASSIGNING RANK ORDERS. Although we assign rank orders from the "outside" of the distribution to the median, there are several alternative procedures. To illustrate the method, consider a situation in which there are seven scores that are

[18] Eisler, H. (1981). Applicability of the parallel-clock model to duration discrimination. *Perception and Psychophysics*, **29**, 225–233.

TABLE 6.27
Exponent values for parallel-clock model of duration discrimination

Group X: Long durations ($m = 8$)
.62 1.10 .82 .68 .78 .75 .76 .47

Group Y: Short durations ($n = 9$)
.89 .70 .80 .74 .85 .67 .69 .89 .77

Combined data			
Score	**Group**	**Ranking**	**Adjusted ranking**
.47	X	1	1
.62	X	4	4
.67	Y	5	5
.68	X	8	8
.69	Y	9	9
.70	Y	12	12
.74	Y	13	13
.75	X	16	16
.76	X	17	17
.77	Y	15	15
.78	X	14	14
.80	Y	11	11
.82	X	10	10
.85	Y	7	7
.89	Y	6	4.5
.89	Y	3	4.5
1.10	X	2	2

$W_x = 72$, $W_y = 81$.

already ordered. The ranks may be assigned thus:

1 4 5 7 6 3 2

In assigning ranks to alternating sides we cannot have the same ranks assigned to scores on each side of the median. However, the method employed has the advantage that the *sum of ranks* for any two adjacent scores on one side of the median is equal to the sum of ranks for the two scores which are the same distance from the median on the other side. Thus, in the above example, $1 + 4 = 3 + 2$, $4 + 5 = 6 + 3$, etc. If, instead of assigning rank orders from the smallest score to the largest, we assigned rank orders to the data from the largest score to the smallest, then the values of W_x and W_y will be different. Although the resultant values of W_x and W_y should not be very different for moderate sample sizes, the researcher should decide which ordering to use *before* examining the data. For the data in Table 6.27, if we ranked the data beginning with the largest score, we would obtain $W_x = 76$ and $W_y = 77$ for which the associated (one-tailed) probability is .336. The change would not affect our conclusion.

It also should be pointed out that some researchers assign the rank orders from the inside to the outside. Thus, for the above data, the rank orders could be

$$7 \quad 4 \quad 3 \quad 1 \quad 2 \quad 5 \quad 6$$

or

$$6 \quad 5 \quad 2 \quad 1 \quad 3 \quad 4 \quad 7$$

Either method may be used. However, in the latter method, we would expect the extreme rankings to be larger than the middle rankings, and the test must be adjusted accordingly.

MEDIANS KNOWN. If the medians of the two distributions are known, the test may be applied by subtracting the median from the scores in each group before obtaining the combined ranking. The effect of this is to render the medians equal so that the test may be applied properly. However, this correction is appropriate when the *population* medians *are known*, and it is not appropriate to use the sample medians to render the distributions similar in central tendency.

6.8.3 Summary of Procedure

These are the steps in the use of the Siegel-Tukey test:

1. In advance of the collection of data, determine the order in which the rankings will be assigned.
2. After the scores are collected, rank them in a single series, retaining the group identity of each score. If the population medians are known and unequal, subtract the median from each score before pooling the data into one ordered group. Assign rank orders to the scores in the sequence, assigning ranks alternately from the extremes of the sequence as described earlier.
3. Determine the value W_x and W_y.
4. For small samples, determine the significance of the observed W_x by using Appendix Table J. If the sample size is large, determine the significance of W_x by using Eq. (6.11) [or Eq. (6.13) if there are tied ranks].
5. If the probability determined in step 4 is less than α, reject H_0.

6.8.4 Power

The power of the Siegel-Tukey test is relatively low. When used on data which have a normal distribution, the power is .61 for small N. It must be stressed that, unless the assumption of equal medians is satisfied, the Siegel-Tukey test cannot be interpreted since a significant value can be obtained simply as a result of a difference in medians.

6.8.5 References

Good discussions of this test may be found in Siegel and Tukey (1960, 1961), Moses (1963), and Lehmann (1975).

6.9 THE MOSES RANK-LIKE TEST FOR SCALE DIFFERENCES

6.9.1 Function and Rationale

As noted in the last section, in the behavioral and social sciences there is often interest in testing for differences in dispersion between two groups. Although researchers desire to know about differences in central tendency, differences in scale can be of theoretical importance and practical value. For example, determining that a particular group is more homogeneous than another could be of value in developing special instructional materials for that group. Differences in the heterogeneity of groups could be of interest to the social psychologist studying the factors involved in adjustment to new environments. The Siegel-Tukey test is a useful test for comparing differences in scale or variability. However, proper use of the test requires that the medians of the two groups be the same or known. That is, the Siegel-Tukey test assumes that the two medians are equal or, if they are known, that the population medians may be subtracted from each score to render the "adjusted" medians equal. As many readers may suspect, there are many situations in which these assumptions cannot be justified. The *Moses rank-like test* is useful in cases in which the medians are either unknown or cannot be assumed equal. Unlike the Siegel-Tukey test, the Moses rank-like test assumes that the observations are measured on at least an interval scale.

The hypotheses to be tested can be written as

$$H_0\colon \sigma_x^2 = \sigma_y^2$$

and

$$H_1\colon \sigma_x^2 \neq \sigma_y^2$$

if a two-tailed alternative is to be tested, or

$$H_1\colon \sigma_x^2 > \sigma_y^2$$

if we wish to test the one-tailed alternative that the variability of the X variable is greater than the variability of the Y variable. Of course, the alternative hypothesis could be

$$H_1\colon \sigma_x^2 < \sigma_y^2$$

6.9.2 Method

To compute the Moses rank-like test it is necessary to divide the observations in the two groups into subsets of equal size. Each subset must have at least two observations in it. If the division is such that there are observations left over, they are discarded from the analysis. It is important to divide the data randomly into subsets; this is best accomplished with a table of random numbers. For example, if there are $m = 25$ observations in the set X, and $n = 21$ observations in the set Y, then subsets of size 5 could be used which would result in $m' = 5$ subsets of X and $n' = 4$ subsets of Y, with one of the Y scores discarded. Or the data could be divided into subsets of size 4, with $m' = 6$ subsets of X and $n' = 5$ subsets of Y, with one score from each set discarded. Of course, other subset sizes could be used.

For each subset, calculate the sum of the squared differences of each datum from the subset mean. The procedure is rather straightforward but many computations are required. To provide notation, we shall resort to double subscripts so that individual subsets may be identified. First, let k be the number of observations in each subset, m' be the number of subsets of X, and n' be the number of subsets of Y. Then the data for the jth subset of X can be listed as

$$X_{j1}, X_{j2}, \ldots, X_{jk} \qquad j = 1, 2, \ldots, m'$$

and the data for the jth subset of Y can be listed as

$$Y_{j1}, Y_{j2}, \ldots, Y_{jk} \qquad j = 1, 2, \ldots, n'$$

For the subsets of X we calculate a dispersion index $D(X_j)$:

$$D(X_j) = \sum_{i=1}^{k} (X_{ji} - \bar{X}_j)^2 \qquad j = 1, 2, \ldots, m' \tag{6.21}$$

where

$$\bar{X}_j = \frac{\sum_{i=1}^{k} X_{ji}}{k}$$

is the mean of the observations in the jth subset of X. In a similar fashion, for each of the subsets of Y we calculate a dispersion index $D(Y_j)$:

$$D(Y_j) = \sum_{i=1}^{k} (Y_{ji} - \bar{Y}_j)^2 \qquad j = 1, 2, \ldots, n' \tag{6.22}$$

where

$$\bar{Y}_j = \frac{\sum_{i=1}^{k} Y_{ji}}{k}$$

is the mean of the observations in the jth subset of Y.

Now if the null hypothesis of equal variability for the groups X and Y is true, we would expect that the values of $D(X_j)$ and $D(Y_j)$ should be well mixed in that the dispersion measures for the subsets should be similar. However, if the alternative hypothesis is true, then we would expect that the values $D(X_j)$ would generally tend to be smaller than the $D(Y_j)$ if the X data are less variable than the Y data [or the values of $D(X_j)$ would tend to be larger than the $D(Y_j)$ if the X data are more variable than the Y data]. To test the hypothesis of equal dispersion, we then apply the Wilcoxon test to the dispersion indices calculated for each of the subsets. In applying that test in this situation, the sample sizes are m' and n'. That is, once we compute the D's, the logic of the Wilcoxon test may be applied. If we reject the hypothesis of equal D's, then we reject the hypothesis of equal dispersion for the variables X and Y.

Example 6.9 Research has found that insulin receptors vary as a function of variation in physiologically or pharmacologically induced changes in glucose metabolism. However, it is not known whether changes in the insulin receptors induce change in glucose metabolism.

TABLE 6.28
Insulin binding to monocytes

Normal subjects	DMD subjects
2.50	2.10
2.48	2.00
2.45	1.80
2.32	1.70
2.32	1.60
2.31	1.55
2.28	1.40
2.27	1.40
2.25	1.30
2.22	1.25
2.22	1.10
2.18	1.03
2.16	.98
2.12	.86
2.12	.85
2.05	.70
1.90	.65

In an effort to examine this question, researchers analyzed situations in which glucose metabolism could be measured as a function of modification of insulin receptors.[19] People who have Duchenne muscular dystrophy (DMD) have marked membrane defects which would be expected to result in modification of the insulin receptors. However, such people generally have normal carbohydrate metabolism, which suggests that there is no alteration in the insulin receptors. The research literature does not show defects in insulin receptors in the absence of overt changes in carbohydrate metabolism.

A group of 17 normal subjects and a group of 17 DMD subjects were selected for the study. All subjects were put on the same diet. As part of the study, insulin binding to monocytes was measured for each subject. The results are summarized in Table 6.28. Although differences in insulin binding is expected, the variability in binding should be different in the DMD group compared with the controls. That is, the group of normal subjects would be expected to be more homogeneous in insulin binding than DMD subjects who would be expected to show variation over a relatively wide range.

i. Null hypothesis. H_0: normal and DMD subjects show equal variation in insulin binding. H_1: DMD subjects show greater variability in insulin binding than normal subjects.

ii. Statistical test. Since the hypothesis concerns differences in scale parameters (variances) of distributions and since the medians of the distributions are not assumed to be equal, and since the underlying distributions cannot be assumed to be normally distributed, the Moses rank-like test is appropriate.

---

[19] De Pirro, R., Lauro, R., Testa, I., Ferretti, G., De Martinis, C., and Dellantonio, R. (1982). Decreased insulin receptors but normal glucose metabolism in Duchenne mucular dystrophy. *Science*, **216**, 311–313.

iii. Significance level. Let $\alpha = .05$, $m = 17$, and $n = 17$.

iv. Sampling distribution. The sampling distribution of the statistics associated with the Moses rank-like test is the same as that of the Wilcoxon test. Therefore the logic of the Wilcoxon test may be applied to the derived statistics.

v. Rejection region. Since the alternative hypothesis specifies the direction of difference in the scale parameters, a one-tailed test will be used. The region of rejection consists of all values of rank sums as large or larger than the observed value.

vi. Decision. It was decided to use subsets of size $k = 4$. This was done because only one datum from each group would have to be discarded. (If we used $k = 3$ or 5, two data would have to be discarded from each group.) By using a table of random numbers, the 16th and 15th observations from the normal and DMD groups were eliminated, respectively. Again referring to a table of random numbers, the data in each group were divided into four subsets. Table 6.29 lists the observations assigned to each subset. By using Eq. (6.21), the indices $D(X_j)$ were computed for each of the subsets of normal subjects, and Eq. (6.22) was used to calculate the indices $D(Y_j)$ for the DMD subsets. These values are also summarized in Table 6.29.

Now the Wilcoxon test is applied to the eight dispersion indices. That is, $m' = n' = 4$. To apply the test, the D's are ordered from smallest to largest:

D score:	.0145	.0261	.0563	.1646	.3275	.3857	.4212	1.1706
Rank:	1	2	3	4	5	6	7	8
Group:	X	X	X	X	Y	Y	Y	Y

With the use of these rankings, we calculate the sums of ranks:

$$W_x = 1 + 2 + 3 + 4 = 10$$

and

$$W_y = 5 + 6 + 7 + 8 = 26$$

TABLE 6.29

Data from Table 6.28 arranged into subsets for calculation of the Moses rank-like test

Data from normal subjects arranged into subsets					
Set		**Scores**			$D(X_j)$
1	2.18	2.31	1.90	2.45	.1646
2	2.28	2.25	2.12	2.22	.0145
3	2.22	2.48	2.50	2.30	.0563
4	2.16	2.12	2.27	2.32	.0261
Data from DMD subjects arranged into subsets					
Set		**Scores**			$D(Y_j)$
1	1.55	1.25	1.03	.70	.3857
2	2.10	.98	1.10	.65	1.1706
3	1.30	2.00	1.40	1.80	.3275
4	1.40	1.60	.86	1.70	.4212

Since the alternative hypothesis is that the DMD subjects (the Y group) should show greater variability, the alternative hypothesis is

$$H_1: \sigma_x^2 < \sigma_y^2$$

Therefore, we should reject H_0 if the probability associated with a W_x as small as 10 (or alternatively the probability associated with a W_y as large as 26) is less than .05. Referring to Appendix Table J we find that the associated probability is .014; therefore, we may reject H_0 and conclude that the variability in the DMD subjects is greater than the variability in the normal subjects.

TIES. Although ties in the original data are no problem in the application of the Moses rank-like test, adjustment for ties must be made if there are ties in the $D(X_j)$ and the $D(Y_j)$. The usual correction for ties associated with the Wilcoxon test should be applied (see Sec. 6.4.4).

LARGE SAMPLES. When the sample sizes are large, the large-sample approximation for the Wilcoxon test should be used (Sec. 6.4.4).

6.9.3 Summary of Procedure

These are the steps in the application of the Moses rank-like test for scale differences:

1. Depending upon the sample sizes in each group of data, divide the data in each group into random samples of size $k \geq 2$ with the use of a table of random numbers. Discard any extra data. The subset sizes should be chosen to minimize the number of discarded data. Let m' be the number of subsets of X and n' be the number of subsets of Y.
2. Use Eqs. (6.21) and (6.22) to calculate the dispersion indices $D(X_j)$ and $D(Y_j)$ for each subset.
3. Arrange the D's in order and assign rank orders. Calculate the rank sums W_x and W_y.
4. Use the subset sample sizes m' and n' and refer to Appendix Table J to determine the significance of W_x. If the associated probability is less than α, reject H_0. If the sample sizes m' and n' are large, use the large-sample approximation [Eq. (6.11) or Eq. (6.13)].

6.9.4 Power-Efficiency

The efficiency of the Moses rank-like test is a function of the size of the subsets used. The efficiency increases with increasing sample size. If the underlying distribution is normal, the relative efficiency is .61 for subsets of size 4, .80 for subsets of size 9, and is asymptotically .95 (when the subsets become infinitely large). Of course, there is a tradeoff, since increasing the sample size decreases the number of samples used in the Wilcoxon test. It should be noted that the parametric F test for equality of variances is extremely sensitive to violation of the assumption of normality.

6.9.5 References

Further discussion of the Moses rank-like test may be found in Moses (1963) and Hollander and Wolfe (1971). Discussions of the power and efficiency of the test may be found in the Moses paper and Schorak (1969).

6.10 DISCUSSION

In this chapter we have presented nine statistical tests that are useful in testing for the "significance of the difference" between two independent samples. In choosing among these tests the researcher may be aided by the following discussion, in which any unique advantages of the tests are pointed out and contrasts among them are noted.

All of the nonparametric tests for two independent samples test the hypothesis that the two independent samples came from the same population. But the various tests we have presented are more or less sensitive to different kinds of differences between samples. For example, if one wishes to test whether two samples represent populations that differ in location (central tendency), the following tests are most sensitive to such differences and, therefore, should be chosen: The median test (or the Fisher exact test when N is small), the Wilcoxon test, the robust rank-order test, the Kolmogorov-Smirnov two-sample test (one-tailed), and the permutation test. On the other hand, if the researcher is interested in determining whether the two samples are from populations that differ in any respect at all, i.e., in location *or* dispersion *or* skewness, etc., one of the following tests is appropriate: The chi-square test or the Kolmogorov-Smirnov test (two-tailed). The remaining techniques—the Siegel-Tukey test and the Moses rank-like dispersion test—are suitable for testing whether one group is exhibiting extreme responses in comparison with the responses exhibited by an independent group.

The choice among the tests which are sensitive to differences in location is determined by the kind of measurement achieved in the research and by the sample sizes. The most powerful test of location is the permutation test. However, this test can be used only when we have some confidence in the *numerical* nature of the measurement obtained and is feasible only when the sample sizes are small. With larger samples or weaker measurement (ordinal measurement), the suggested alternative is either the Wilcoxon test, which is almost as powerful as the permutation test if the dispersion between the two groups is the same, or the robust rank-order test if one cannot assume equal dispersion (or variance) for the two groups. If the samples are very small, the Kolmogorov-Smirnov test is slightly more efficient than the Wilcoxon test. If the measurement is such that it is meaningful only to dichotomize the observations as above or below the combined median, then the median test is applicable. This test is not as powerful as the Wilcoxon test in guarding against differences in location, but it is more appropriate than the

Wilcoxon test or the robust rank-order test when the data are observations which cannot be completely ranked. If the combined sample sizes are very small, the researcher, when applying the median test, should do the analysis by using the Fisher exact test. It should be noted that the median test may sometimes be the only viable alternative even for interval scale data. For example, if the observations are cut off or truncated so that the full range of values is not observed, then the *t* test is not appropriate, whereas the median test is appropriate since it counts only those scores as above (or below) the median.

The choice among the tests which are sensitive to all kinds of differences (the second group mentioned above) is predicated on the strength of the measurement obtained, the size of the two samples, and the relative power of the available tests. The chi-square test is suitable for data which are in nominal or stronger scales. If the chi-square test is done and H_0 is rejected, then the contingency table and the degrees of freedom may be partitioned into additive components to determine exactly where the differences appear in the table. When N is small and the data are in a 2×2 contingency table, the Fisher exact test should be used rather than the chi-square test. In many cases the chi-square test may not make efficient use of all of the information in the data. If the populations of scores are continuously distributed, we may choose the Kolmogorov-Smirnov (two-tailed) test in preference to the chi-square test. Of all tests for any kind of difference, the Kolmogorov-Smirnov test is the most powerful. If it is used with data which do not meet the assumption of continuity, it is still suitable but it is more conservative, i.e., the obtained value of p in such cases will be slightly higher than it should be and, therefore, the probability of a Type II error will be increased somewhat. If H_0 is rejected with such data, we can surely have confidence in the decision.

Two points should be emphasized about the use of the second group of tests. First, if one is interested in testing the alternative hypothesis that the groups differ in central tendency, i.e., that one population has a larger median than the other, then one should use a test specifically designed to guard against differences in location—one of the tests in the first group listed above. Second, when one rejects H_0 on the basis of a test which guards against any kind of difference (one of the tests in the second group), one can then assert that the two groups are from different populations but one cannot say *in what specific way(s)* the populations differ.

Finally, in testing differences in dispersion or variance, the Seigel-Tukey test assumes that the medians for the two groups are the same (or known). If the medians for the two groups are unequal, the Moses rank-like dispersion test is appropriate; however, in addition to assuming interval scale data, it requires additional computations and the subdivision of each group into random subgroups.

Taken together, the tests in this chapter form a useful set of procedures for analyzing differences between two independent groups.

CHAPTER 7

THE CASE OF k RELATED SAMPLES

In the earlier chapters we presented statistical tests for (1) testing differences between a single sample and some specified population and (2) testing differences between two samples, either related or independent. In this and the following chapter, procedures will be presented for testing differences among three or more groups. That is, statistical tests will be presented for testing the null hypothesis that k (three or more) samples have been drawn from the same population or identical populations. This chapter will present tests for the case of k *related* samples; the following chapter will present tests for the case of k *independent* samples.

Circumstances sometimes require that we design an experiment so that more than two samples or conditions can be studied simultaneously. When three or more samples or conditions are to be compared in an experiment, it is necessary to use a statistical test which will indicate whether there is an *overall* difference among the k samples or conditions before one picks out any pair of samples to test the significance of the difference between them.

If we wished to use a two-sample statistical test to test for differences among, say, five groups, we would need to compute, in order to compare each pair of samples, ten statistical tests. [Five samples taken two at a time = $\binom{5}{2} = 5!/2!\,3! = 10$.] Such a procedure is not only tedious but also it may lead to fallacious conclusions as well because it capitalizes on chance. That is, suppose we wish to use a significance level of, say, $\alpha = .05$. Our hypothesis is that there is a difference among $k = 5$ samples. If we test that hypothesis by comparing each of the five samples with every other sample, using a two-sample test (which would require ten comparisons in all), we are giving ourselves ten chances rather than one chance to reject H_0. Now when we choose .05 as our level of significance, we are taking the risk of rejecting H_0 erroneously (making a Type I error) 5 percent of the time. But if we make ten statistical tests of the same hypothesis, we increase the probability to .40 that a two-sample statistical test will find one or more "significant" differences—even though $\alpha = .05$ for each individual test. That is, the *actual* significance level in such a procedure becomes $\alpha = .40$.

Cases have been reported in the research literature in which an overall test of five samples yields nonsignificant results (leads to acceptance of H_0) but two-sample tests of the larger differences among the five samples yield significant results. Such *a posteriori* selection tends to capitalize on chance and, therefore, we can have no confidence in a decision involving k samples in which the analysis consisted of only testing two samples at a time.

It is only when an overall test (a k-sample test) allows us to reject the null hypothesis that we are justified in employing a procedure for testing for differences between any two of the k samples.

The parametric technique for testing whether several samples have come from identical populations is the *analysis of variance* and associated F statistics. The assumptions associated with the statistical mode underlying the analysis of variance are:

1. The scores or observations are independently drawn from normally distributed populations.
2. The populations all have the same variance.
3. The means in the normally distributed populations are linear combinations of "effects" due to rows and columns, i.e., the effects are additive.

In addition, the F test assumes at least interval measurement of the variables involved.

If a researcher finds such assumptions unrealistic, finds that the scores do not meet the measurement requirements, or wishes to avoid making the assumptions in order to increase the generality of the findings, one of the nonparametric statistical tests presented in this and the following chapter would be appropriate. In addition to avoiding the assumptions and requirements mentioned, these nonparametric k-sample tests have the further advantage of enabling analysis to be done on data which are only categorical or ordinal in nature.

There are two basic designs for comparing k groups. In the first design, k samples of equal size are *matched* according to some criterion or criteria which may affect the values of the observations. In some cases, the matching is achieved by comparing the same individuals or cases under all k conditions. Or each of N individuals may be measured under all k conditions. For such designs, the statistical tests for k related samples (presented in this chapter) should be used. The second design involves k *independent* random samples, not necessarily of the same size, and one sample from each population. For that design, the statistical tests for k independent samples (presented in Chap. 8) should be employed.

The above distinction is, of course, exactly that made in the parametric case. The first design is known as the *two-way analysis of variance*, or *repeated measures* analysis of variance, and sometimes called the *randomized blocks* design.[1] The second design is known as the *one-way analysis of variance*.

The distinction is similar to the one we made between the case of two related samples discussed in Chap. 5 and the case of two independent samples discussed in Chap. 6.

In this chapter we shall present nonparametric statistical tests which parallel the two-way or repeated measures analysis of variance. We shall begin with a test appropriate for categorical (nominally scaled) data. The second test is suitable for data measured on at least an ordinal scale. The third test permits an hypothesis about the ordering of the effects for ordinal variables to be tested. At the conclusion of the chapter we shall compare and contrast these tests for k related samples and offer further guidance to the researcher in the selection of the test best suited to the data at hand.

7.1 THE COCHRAN Q TEST

7.1.1 Function

The McNemar test for two related samples, presented in Chap. 5, can be extended for use in studies involving more than two samples. The extension, the *Cochran Q test* for k related samples, provides a method for testing whether three or more matched sets of frequencies or proportions differ significantly among themselves. The matching may be based on relevant characteristics of the different subjects or on the fact that the same subjects are used under different conditions. The Cochran Q test is particularly suitable when the data are categorical (measured on a nominal scale) or are dichotomized ordinal (or interval) observations.

One may imagine a wide variety of research hypotheses for which the data might be analyzed by the Cochran Q test. For example, one might test whether the various items on a test differ in difficulty by analyzing data consisting of pass-fail information on k items for N individuals. In this design, the k groups are considered "matched" because each person answers all k items.

On the other hand, we might have only one item to be analyzed, and wish to compare the responses of N subjects under k different conditions. Here again the matching is achieved by having the same subjects in every group, but now the "groups" differ in that each is observed under a different condition. This would test whether there is a difference in the responses of subjects in each of the k conditions. For example, one might ask each member of a panel of voters which

---

[1] The term *randomized blocks* derives from agricultural experimentation, in which plots of land may be used as experimental units. A block consists of adjacent plots of land, and it is assumed that plots of land adjacent to each other are more alike (i.e., are better matched) than are plots remote from each other. The k treatments (for example, k varieties of fertilizer or k varieties of seed) are assigned at random, one to each of the k plots in a block; this is done with independent random assignment in each block.

of two candidates they prefer at $k = 5$ times during the election season—before the campaign, at the peak of Smith's campaign, at the peak of Miller's campaign, immediately before the balloting, and immediately after the results are announced. The Cochran Q test would determine whether these conditions have a significant effect on the voters' preferences for the candidates.

Again, we might compare the responses to one item from N sets having k matched persons in each set. That is, we would have responses from k matched groups.

7.1.2 Method

If the data from studies like those described above are arranged in a two-way table consisting of N rows and k columns, it is possible to test the null hypothesis that the proportion (or frequency) of responses of a particular kind is the same in each column except for chance differences. Cochran (1950) has shown that, if the null hypothesis is true, i.e., if there is no difference in the probability of, say, "success" under each condition (which is to say that the "successes" and "failures" are randomly distributed in the rows and columns of the two-way table), and if the number of rows is not too small, the statistic

$$Q = \frac{k(k-1)\sum_{j=1}^{k}(G_j - \bar{G})^2}{k\sum_{i=1}^{N} L_i - \sum_{i=1}^{N} L_i^2} \tag{7.1}$$

is distributed approximately as χ^2 with $df = k - 1$,

where G_j = total number of "successes" in the jth column
$\bar{G}$ = mean of the G_j
L_i = total number of "successes" in the ith row

An equation equivalent to and easily derivable from Eq. (7.1) but which simplifies computations is

$$Q = \frac{(k-1)\left[k\sum_{j=1}^{k} G_j^2 - \left(\sum_{j=1}^{k} G_j\right)^2\right]}{k\sum_{i=1}^{N} L_i - \sum_{i=1}^{N} L_i^2} \tag{7.2}$$

Inasmuch as the sampling distribution of Q is approximated by the χ^2 distribution with $df = k - 1$, the probability associated with the occurrence under H_0 of values as large as an observed Q may be determined by reference to Appendix Table C for a particular significance level and a particular value of $df = k - 1$. The implication is that the proportion (or frequency) of successes differs significantly among the various samples. That is, H_0 may be rejected at that particular level of significance.

Example 7.1 Suppose we were interested in the influence of interviewer friendliness upon householders' responses in an opinion survey. We might train an interviewer to conduct three kinds of interviews: interview 1, showing interest, friendliness, and enthusiasm; interview 2, showing formality, reserve, and courtesy; and interview 3, showing disinterest, abruptness, and harsh formality. The interviewer would be assigned to visit 3 groups of 18 houses, and told to use interview 1 with one group, interview 2 with another, and interview 3 with the third. That is, we would obtain 18 sets of householders with 3 matched householders (equated on relevant variables) in each set. For each set, the three members would be assigned randomly to the three conditions (types of interviews). Thus we would have 3 matched samples ($k = 3$) with 18 members in each ($N = 18$). We could then test whether the gross differences among the three styles of interviews influenced the number of "yes" responses given to a particular item by the three matched groups. With the use of artificial data, a test of this hypothesis follows.

i. Null hypothesis. H_0: the probability of a "yes" response is the same for all three types of interviews. H_1: the probabilities of "yes" responses differ according to the style of the interview.

ii. Statistical test. The Cochran Q test is chosen because the data are from more than two related groups ($k = 3$) and are dichotomized as "yes" and "no."

iii. Significance level. Let $\alpha = .01$. N is the number of cases in each of the k matched sets or groups = 18.

iv. Sampling distribution. When the null hypothesis is true, Q [as determined from Eq. (7.1) or Eq. (7.2)] is distributed approximately as χ^2 with $df = k - 1$. That is, the probability associated with the occurrence under H_0 of any values as large as an observed value of Q may be determined by reference to Appendix Table C.

v. Region of rejection. The region of rejection consists of all values of Q which are so large that the probability associated with their occurrence when H_0 is true is equal to or less than $\alpha = .01$.

vi. Decision. For this example, we will represent "yes" responses by 1s and "no" responses by 0s. The data of the study are given in Table 7.1. As is the practice, the scores have been arranged in $N = 18$ rows and $k = 3$ columns. Also shown in that table are the values of L_i (the total number of "yes" responses for each row) and the values of L_i^2. For example, in the first matched set all of the householders responded negatively, regardless of the interview style. Thus, $L_1 = 0 + 0 + 0 = 0$, and $L_1^2 = 0^2 = 0$. In the second matched set of three householders, the responses to interviews 1 and 2 were affirmative but the response to interview 3 was negative, so that $L_2 = 1 + 1 + 0 = 2$, and thus $L_2^2 = 2^2 = 4$.

We observe that $G_1 = 13$ is the total number of "yes" responses to interview 1. $G_2 = 13$ is the total number of "yes" responses to interview 2. $G_3 = 3$ is the total number of "yes" responses to interview 3.

The total number of "yes" responses in all three interviews is

$$\sum_{j=1}^{3} G_j = 13 + 13 + 3 = 29$$

Observe that

$$\sum_{i=1}^{18} L_i = 29$$

TABLE 7.1
"Yes" (1) and "no" (0) responses by householders under three types of interviews (artificial data)

Set	Response to interview 1	Response to interview 2	Response to interview 3	L_i	L_i^2
1	0	0	0	0	0
2	1	1	0	2	4
3	0	1	0	1	1
4	0	0	0	0	0
5	1	0	0	1	1
6	1	1	0	2	4
7	1	1	0	2	4
8	0	1	0	1	1
9	1	0	0	1	1
10	0	0	0	0	0
11	1	1	1	3	9
12	1	1	1	3	9
13	1	1	0	2	4
14	1	1	0	2	4
15	1	1	0	2	4
16	1	1	1	3	9
17	1	1	0	2	4
18	1	1	0	2	4
Total	$G_1 = 13$	$G_2 = 13$	$G_3 = 3$	$\sum_{i=1}^{18} L_i = 29$	$\sum_{i=1}^{18} L_i^2 = 63$

(The column and row totals are equal.) The sum of squares of the row totals is

$$\sum_{i=1}^{18} L_i^2 = 63$$

the sum in the final column.

Entering these values in Eq. (7.2) we have

$$Q = \frac{(k-1)\left[k \sum_{j=1}^{k} G_j^2 - \left(\sum_{j=1}^{k} G_j\right)^2\right]}{k \sum_{i=1}^{N} L_i - \sum_{i=1}^{N} L_i^2} \tag{7.2}$$

$$= \frac{(3-1)[3(13^2 + 13^2 + 3^2) - 29^2]}{(3)(29) - 63}$$

$$= 16.7$$

Reference to Appendix Table C reveals that $Q \geq 16.7$ has probability of occurrence when H_0 is true of $p < .001$ when $df = k - 1 = 3 - 1 = 2$. This probability is smaller than the significance level, $\alpha = .01$. Thus the value of Q is in the region of rejection and, therefore, our decision is to reject H_0 in favor of H_1. On the basis of these data, we conclude that the probabilities of "yes" responses are different under interviews 1, 2, and 3.

It should be noted that Q is distributed as χ^2 with $df = k - 1$ *if* the number of rows (the size N of the sample) is not too small—generally $N \geq 4$—and if the product Nk is greater than about 24. Actually, since rows which consist only of 0s or 1s do not affect the value of Q, the "effective" sample size for approximating the χ^2 distribution is N', the number of rows which are not all 0s or all 1s. For very small samples, the exact sampling distribution of Q can be constructed from permutation arguments. However, because the relevant calculations are especially tedious and the distribution is relatively quickly approximated by the χ^2 distribution, details will not be given here.

7.1.3 Summary of Procedure

These are the steps in the use of the Cochran Q test:

1. For the dichotomous data, assign a score of 1 to each "success" and a score of 0 to each "failure".
2. Cast the scores into an $N \times k$ table by using N rows and k columns. N is the number of cases in each of the k groups or conditions.
3. Determine the value of Q by using Eq. (7.1) or Eq. (7.2).
4. The significance of the observed value of Q may be determined by reference to Appendix Table C, since Q is distributed approximately as χ^2 with $df = k - 1$. If the probability associated with the occurrence when H_0 is true of a value as large as the observed value of Q is equal to or less than α, reject H_0.

7.1.4 Power and Power-Efficiency

The notion of power-efficiency is meaningless when the Cochran Q test is used for categorical or naturally dichotomous data, because parametric tests are not applicable to such data. When the Cochran Q test is used with data which are not categorical or naturally dichotomous, it may be wasteful of information. As noted earlier, the χ^2 distribution approximates the exact sampling distribution of Q well when $N \geq 4$, and $Nk > 24$.

7.1.5 References

The reader may find discussions of the Cochran Q test in Cochran (1950) and Marascuilo and Sweeney (1977). Tables of the exact sampling distribution for small N and k may be found in Patil (1975).

7.2 THE FRIEDMAN TWO-WAY ANALYSIS OF VARIANCE BY RANKS

7.2.1 Function

When the data from k matched samples are in at least an ordinal scale, the *Friedman two-way analysis of variance by ranks* is used to test the null hypothesis that the k samples have been drawn from the same population.

Since the k samples are matched, the number of cases N is the same in each of the samples. That matching may be achieved by studying the same group of subjects under each of the k conditions. Or the researcher may obtain N sets, each consisting of k matched subjects, and then randomly assign one subject in each set to the first condition, one subject in each set to the second condition, etc. For example, if one wished to study the differences in learning achieved under four teaching methods, one might obtain N sets of $k = 4$ pupils, each set consisting of children who are matched on the relevant variables (age, previous learning, intelligence, socioeconomic status, motivation, etc.), and then at random assign one child from each of the N sets to teaching method A, another from each set to method B, another from each set to C, and the fourth to D.

The Friedman two-way analysis of variance by ranks tests the null hypothesis that the k repeated measures or matched groups come from the same population or populations with the same median. To specify the null hypothesis more explicitly, let θ_j be the population median in the jth condition or group. Then we may write the null hypothesis that the medians are the same as H_0: $\theta_1 = \theta_2 = \cdots = \theta_k$. The alternative hypothesis is then H_1: $\theta_i \quad \theta_j$ for at least two conditions or groups i and j. That is, if the alternative hypothesis is true, at least one pair of conditions has different medians. Under the null hypothesis, the test assumes that the variables have the same underlying continuous distribution; thus it requires at least ordinal measurement of that variable.

7.2.2 Rationale and Method

For the Friedman test, the data are cast in a two-way table having N rows and k columns. The rows represent the subjects or matched sets of subjects, and the columns represent the various conditions. If the scores of subjects serving under all conditions are under study, then each row gives the scores of one subject under each of the k conditions.

The data of the test are ranks. The scores in each *row* are ranked separately. That is, with k conditions being studied, the ranks in any row range from 1 to k. The Friedman test determines the probability that the different *columns* of ranks (samples) come from the same population, that is, that the k variables have the same median.

For example, suppose we wish to study the scores of three groups under four conditions. Here $N = 3$ and $k = 4$. Each group contains four matched subjects, one being assigned to each of the four conditions. Suppose our scores for this study were those given in Table 7.2. To perform the Friedman test on those data, we first rank the scores *in each row*. We may give the lowest score in each row a rank of 1, the next lowest score in each row the rank of 2, etc. By doing this we obtain the data shown in Table 7.3. Observe that the ranks in each row of Table 7.3 range from 1 to $k = 4$.

Now if the null hypothesis (that all of the samples—columns—came from the same population) is in fact true, then the distribution of ranks *in each column* would be a matter of chance and, thus, we would expect the ranks of 1, 2, 3, and 4 to appear in each column with about equal frequency. That is, if the data were

TABLE 7.2
Scores of three matched groups under four conditions

	Conditions			
Groups	**I**	**II**	**III**	**IV**
A	9	4	1	7
B	6	5	2	8
C	9	1	2	6

TABLE 7.3
Ranks of three matched groups under four conditions

	Conditions			
Groups	**I**	**II**	**III**	**IV**
A	4	2	1	3
B	3	2	1	4
C	4	1	2	3
R_j	11	5	4	10

random, we would expect the sum of ranks in each column to be $N(k + 1)/2$. For the data in Table 7.3, the expected column sums would be $3(4 + 1)/2 = 7.5$. This indicates that for any group it is a matter of chance under which condition the highest score occurs and under which condition the lowest occurs—which would be the case if the conditions really did not differ.

If the subjects' scores were independent of the condition, the set of ranks in each column would represent a random sample from the discrete rectangular distribution of rank numbers 1, 2, 3, and 4, and the rank totals for the various columns would be about equal. If the subjects' scores were dependent on the conditions (i.e., if H_0 were false), then the rank totals would vary from one column to another. Inasmuch as the columns all contain an equal number of cases, an equivalent statement would be that under H_0 the average of the ranks in the various columns would be about equal.

The Friedman test determines whether the rank totals (denoted R_j) for each condition or variable differ significantly from the values which would be expected by chance. To do this test, we compute the value of the statistic which we shall denote as F_r.

$$F_r = \left[\frac{12}{Nk(k + 1)} \sum_{j=1}^{k} R_j^2 \right] - 3N(k + 1) \tag{7.3}$$

where N = number of rows (subjects)
k = number of columns (variables or conditions)
R_j = sum of ranks in the jth column
(i.e., the sum of ranks for the jth variable)

and $\sum_{j=1}^{k}$ directs one to sum the squares of the sums of ranks over all conditions.

Probabilities associated with various values of F_r when H_0 is true have been tabulated for various sample sizes and various numbers of variables. Appendix Table M gives the probabilities associated with values of F_r as large or larger than the tabled values for various values of N and k. If the observed value of F_r is larger than the tabled value of F_r at the chosen significance level, then H_0 may be rejected in favor of H_1.

If the number of variables k exceeds five or the sample size N exceeds that for the tabled entries in Appendix Table M, then a large-sample approximation may be used. When the number of rows and/or columns is large, it can be shown that the statistic F_r as given in Eq. (7.3) is distributed approximately as χ^2 with $df = k - 1$. Thus, Appendix Table C may be used to determine the significance probability.

If the value of F_r as computed from Eq. (7.3) is equal to or larger than that given in Appendix Table M or Appendix Table C for a particular level of significance, then the implication is that the sums of ranks (or, equivalently, the average rank R_j/N) for the various columns differ significantly (which is to say that the size of the scores depends on the conditions under which the scores were obtained), and thus H_0 may be rejected at that level of significance.

To illustrate the computation of F_r and the use of Appendix Table M, we may test for significance of differences in the data shown in Table 7.3. By referring to that table, the reader may see that the number of conditions is $k = 4$ and the number of rows is $N = 3$. The successive sums of ranks R_j are 11, 5, 4, and 10 respectively. We may compute the value of F_r for the data in Table 7.3 by substituting these values into Eq. (7.3):

$$F_r = \left[\frac{12}{Nk(k+1)} \sum_{j=1}^{k} R_j^2\right] - 3N(k+1) \qquad (7.3)$$

$$= \frac{12}{(3)(4)(4+1)}(11^2 + 5^2 + 4^2 + 10^2) - (3)(3)(4+1)$$

$$= 7.4$$

We may determine the probability of occurrence when H_0 is true of $F_r \geq 7.4$ by turning to Appendix Table M which gives the selected critical values of observed F_r for $k = 4$. Reference to that table shows that the probability associated with $F_r \geq 6.5$ when $N = 3$ and $k = 4$ is $p \leq .05$. Thus, for these data, we may reject the null hypothesis that the four samples were drawn from a population with the same medians at the .05 level of significance since the observed value of F_r exceeds the critical value.

Example 7.2*a* **For N and k large.** In a study of the effect of three different patterns of reinforcement upon the extent of discrimination learning in rats[2] three matched samples ($k = 3$) of 18 rats ($N = 18$) were trained under three patterns of reinforcement. Matching was achieved by the use of the 18 sets of litter mates, 3 in each set. Although all of the 54 rats received the same quantity of reinforcement (reward), the patterning of the administration of reinforcement was different for each of the groups. One group was trained with 100 percent reinforcement (RR), a second matched group was trained with partial reinforcement in which each sequence of trials ended with an unreinforced trial (RU), and the third

[2] Grosslight, J. H. and Radlow, R. (1956). Patterning effect of the nonreinforcement-reinforcement sequence in a discrimination situation. *Journal of Comparative and Physiological Psychology*, **49**, 542–546.

matched group was trained with partial reinforcement in which each sequence of trials ended with a reinforced trial (UR).

After this training, the extent of learning was measured by the speed at which the various rats learned an "opposing" behavior—whereas they had been trained to run to white, the rats were now rewarded for running to black. The better the initial learning, the slower should be this transfer of learning. The prediction was that the different patterns of reinforcement used would result in differential learning as exhibited by ability to transfer.

i. *Null hypothesis.* H_0: the different patterns of reinforcement have no differential effect on the observed behavior. H_1: the different patterns of reinforcement have a differential effect.

ii. *Statistical test.* Because the number of errors in transfer of learning is probably not an interval measure of the strength of original learning, the Friedman two-way analysis of variance by ranks was chosen. Moreover, the use of the parametric analysis of variance is precluded because examination of the experimental situation suggested that one of the basic assumptions of the F test was probably untenable.

iii. *Significance level.* Let $\alpha = .05$ and N is the number of rats in each of the $k = 3$ matched groups $= 18$.

iv. *Sampling distribution.* As computed by Eq. (7.3) and because the sample size is large, F_r is distributed approximately as χ^2 with $df = k - 1$. Thus the probability associated with the occurrence under H_0 of a value as large as the observed value of F_r may be determined by reference to Appendix Table C.

v. *Rejection region.* The region of rejection consists of all values of F_r which are so large that the probability associated with their occurrence when H_0 is true is equal to or less than $\alpha = .05$.

vi. *Decision.* The number of errors committed by each rat in the transfer-of-learning situation was determined, and those scores were ranked for each of the 18 sets of 3 matched rats. These ranks are given in Table 7.4.

Observe that the sum of ranks for the RR groups is 39.5, the sum of ranks for the RU group is 42.5, and the sum or ranks for the UR groups is 26.0. A low rank signifies a high number of errors in transfer, i.e., strong original learning. We may compute the value of F_r by substituting our observed values into Eq. (7.3):

$$F_r = \left[\frac{12}{Nk(k+1)} \sum_{j=1}^{k} R_j^2\right] - 3N(k+1) \qquad (7.3)$$

$$= \frac{12}{(18)(3)(3+1)}(39.5^2 + 42.5^2 + 26^2) - (3)(18)(3+1)$$

$$= 8.58$$

Reference to Appendix Table C indicates that $F_r = 8.58$ when $df = k - 1 = 3 - 1 = 2$ is significant at between the .02 and .01 levels. Therefore, since $p < .02$ is less than our previously established significance level of $\alpha = .05$, the decision is to reject H_0. The conclusion is that the rats' scores on transfer of learning depend on the pattern of reinforcement in the original learning trials.

TIES When there are ties among the ranks for any given group (or row) the statistic F_r must be corrected to account for changes in the sampling distribution. Equation

TABLE 7.4
Ranks of 18 matched groups in transfer after training under three conditions of reinforcement

	Type of reinforcement		
Group	**RR**	**RU**	**UR**
1	1	3	2
2	2	3	1
3	1	3	2
4	1	2	3
5	3	1	2
6	2	3	1
7	3	2	1
8	1	3	2
9	3	1	2
10	3	1	2
11	2	3	1
12	2	3	1
13	3	2	1
14	2	3	1
15	2.5	2.5	1
16	3	2	1
17	3	2	1
18	2	3	1
R_j	39.5	42.5	26.0

(7.4) gives the value of F_r which is appropriate when ties occur. Although Eq. (7.4) can be used in general, that is, when there are no ties as well as when there are ties, the computation is somewhat more tedious.

$$F_r = \frac{12 \sum_{j=1}^{k} R_j^2 - 3N^2k(k+1)^2}{Nk(k+1) + \dfrac{\left(Nk - \sum_{i=1}^{N} \sum_{j=1}^{g_i} t_{i.j}^3\right)}{(k-1)}} \tag{7.4}$$

where g_i is the number of sets of tied ranks in the ith group and $t_{i.j}$ is the size of the jth set of tied ranks in the ith group. We include the sets of size 1 in the count. As is the case with other corrections for tied data, the effect of tied ranks is to increase the size of the Friedman statistic F_r. If the correction for ties is made in the example given above, we note that there are two tied ranks in the 15th group. We note that there are 52 ties of size 1 and one tie of size 2. Therefore,

$$\begin{aligned}\sum_{i=1}^{N} \sum_{j=1}^{g_i} t_{i.j}^3 &= 1 + 1 + 1 + \cdots + 1 + 8 + 1 + \cdots + 1 \\ &= 60\end{aligned}$$

By using Eq. (7.4), we get $F_r = 8.70$, which is larger than the value (8.58) obtained without the correction. Obviously, since H_0 was rejected without the correction, it would be rejected with the correction as well. It should be remarked that in this example the effect of ties was very small; however, as the number of ties increases, the greater is the effect on F_r.

7.2.3 Multiple Comparisons between Groups or Conditions

When the obtained value of F_r is significant, it indicates that *at least one* of the conditions differs from *at least one* other condition. It does not tell the researcher which one is different, nor does it tell the researcher how many of the groups are different from each other. That is, when the obtained value of F_r is significant, we would like to test the hypothesis $H_0\colon \theta_u = \theta_v$ against the hypothesis $H_1\colon \theta_u \neq \theta_v$ for some conditions u and v. There is a simple procedure for determining which condition (or conditions) differ. We begin by determining the differences $|R_u - R_v|$ for all pairs of conditions or groups. When the sample size is large, these differences are approximately normally distributed. However, since there are a large number of differences and because the differences are not independent, the comparison procedure must be adjusted appropriately. Suppose the hypothesis of no difference between the k conditions or matched groups was tested and rejected at the α significance level. Then we can test the significance of individual pairs of differences by using the following inequality. That is, if

$$|R_u - R_v| \geq z_{\alpha/k(k-1)} \sqrt{\frac{Nk(k+1)}{6}} \tag{7.5a}$$

or if the data are expressed in terms of average ranks within each condition, and if

$$|\bar{R}_u - \bar{R}_v| \geq z_{\alpha/k(k-1)} \sqrt{\frac{k(k+1)}{6N}} \tag{7.5b}$$

then we may reject the hypothesis $H_0\colon \theta_u = \theta_v$ and conclude that $\theta_u \neq \theta_v$. Thus, if the difference between the rank sums (or average ranks) exceeds the corresponding critical value given in Eq. (7.5*a*) or (7.5*b*), then we may conclude that the two conditions are different. The value of $z_{\alpha/k(k-1)}$ is the abscissa value from the unit normal distribution above which lies $\alpha/k(k-1)$ percent of the distribution. The values of z can be obtained from Appendix Table A.

Because it is often necessary to obtain values based upon extremely small probabilities, especially when k is large, Appendix Table A_{II} may be used in place of Appendix Table A. This is a table of the standard normal distribution which has been arranged so that values used in multiple comparisons may be obtained easily. The table is arranged on the basis of the number of comparisons ($\#c$) that can be made. The tabled values are the *upper-tail* probabilities associated with various values of α. When there are k groups, there are $k(k-1)/2$ comparisons possible.[3]

Example 7.2*b* In the example above which analyzed the differences between patterns of reinforcement, the null hypothesis that there was no difference among the three training methods was rejected, and we concluded that there was a difference among the training methods. However, although we could conclude that there was a difference, we do not know whether there was a difference between one condition and the others or whether all three groups were different from each other. To find where the differences are, we shall determine the multiple comparisons for the three groups.

Since the $\alpha = .05$ level of significance was used in the initial analysis, we shall use the same level here as well. First, we determine the differences among the conditions. For convenience, we shall use the subscripts *RR*, *RU*, and *UR* to refer to the three groups. Then, since $R_{RR} = 39.5$, $R_{RU} = 42.5$, and $R_{UR} = 26.0$, we have the following differences:

$$|R_{RR} - R_{RU}| = |39.5 - 42.5| = 3.0$$

$$|R_{RR} - R_{UR}| = |39.5 - 26.0| = 13.5$$

$$|R_{RU} - R_{UR}| = |42.5 - 26.0| = 16.5$$

We then find the critical difference by using Eq. (7.5*a*). Since $\alpha = .05$ and $k = 3$, the number of comparisons $\#c$ is equal to $k(k-1)/2 = (3)(2)/2 = 3$. Referring to Appendix Table A_{II}, we see that the value of z is 2.394. [Alternatively, we could obtain the value of z from Appendix Table A. To use that table, we first compute $\alpha/k(k-1) = .05/(3)(2) = .00833$. Referring to Appendix Table A, we again find (after interpolation) that $z_{.00833} = 2.394$.] The critical difference is then

$$z_{\alpha/k(k-1)}\sqrt{\frac{Nk(k+1)}{6}} = 2.394\sqrt{\frac{(18)(3)(3+1)}{6}}$$

$$= 2.394\sqrt{36}$$

$$= 14.36$$

Since only the third difference (16.5) exceeds the critical difference, we conclude that only the difference between conditions *RU* and *UR* is significant. Note that the second difference, although large, is not of a magnitude great enough to permit us to conclude that *RR* and *UR* are different when using the significance level we have chosen.

7.2.4 Comparison of Groups or Conditions with a Control

Sometimes a researcher may have a more specific comparison in mind than the set of multiple comparisons described above. For example, suppose one condition or group represented a *baseline* or control condition against which all of the other conditions should be compared. After applying the Friedman two-way analysis of

[3] Some readers will note a seeming discrepancy between the subscript for z, which is $\alpha/k(k-1)$, and the number of comparisons $\#c$, which is $k(k-1)/2$. Note that we are testing absolute differences and, therefore, use only the *upper tail* of tabled distribution. Hence the upper-tail probability, $\alpha/2$, is divided by the number of comparisons $k(k-1)/2$ which yields $\alpha/k(k-1)$.

variance by ranks test and noting that it is significant, the researcher may wish to compare all conditions against one. For convenience, we shall denote the control condition as condition 1. Then the hypothesis that the researcher would like to test is

$$H_0: \theta_1 = \theta_u \qquad \text{for } u = 2, 3, \ldots, k$$

against

$$H_1: \theta_1 \neq \theta_u \qquad \text{for } \textit{some } u = 2, 3, \ldots, k$$

The following procedure permits the researcher to test a set of conditions against a control condition.

As with the multiple-comparison procedure described in the previous section, we compute the differences $|R_1 - R_u|$ between the treatment condition and each of the other conditions. When the sample sizes are moderate to large, these differences are approximately normally distributed. However, the comparisons are not independent and the critical values must be obtained by use of a special table (Appendix Table A_{III}). Then we can test the significance of differences between a treatment condition and other conditions by using the following inequality. That is, if

$$|R_1 - R_u| \geq q(\alpha, \#c)\sqrt{\frac{Nk(k+1)}{6}} \qquad (7.6a)$$

or if the data are expressed in terms of average ranks within each condition, and if

$$|\bar{R}_1 - \bar{R}_u| \geq q(\alpha, \#c)\sqrt{\frac{k(k+1)}{6N}} \qquad (7.6b)$$

then we can reject the hypothesis $H_0: \theta_1 = \theta_u$ in favor of $H_1: \theta_1 \neq \theta_u$. Values of $q(\alpha, \#c)$ are given in Appendix Table A_{III} for selected values of α and $\#c$, where $\#c = k - 1$, which is the number of comparisons.

Example 7.2.c As an example, suppose we had a set of $N = 12$ subjects measured at some baseline and in four other conditions; then $k = 5$. Suppose the values of $R_1 = 33$, $R_2 = 30$, $R_3 = 43$, $R_4 = 14$, and $R_5 = 60$. By using Eq. (7.3), the value of $F_r = 38.47$, which is significant beyond the $\alpha = .05$ level.[4] Suppose we then wish to test the difference between each condition and the baseline. The successive values of $|R_1 - R_u|$ are 3, 10, 19, and 27 respectively. By using Eq. (7.6*a*) we can find the limits for the differences. First, from Appendix A_{III}, we find that $q(\alpha, \#c) = 2.44$ for $\alpha = .05$ and $\#c = k - 1 = 4$. Then,

$$|R_1 - R_u| \geq q(\alpha, \#c)\sqrt{\frac{Nk(k+1)}{6}} \qquad (7.6a)$$

$$\geq 2.44\sqrt{\frac{(12)(5)(5+1)}{6}}$$

$$\geq 18.9$$

[4] The reader is encouraged to calculate the value of F_r in this example to ensure an understanding of its calculation from the data given.

Any difference which exceeds 18.9 will indicate a significant difference between that condition and the control condition. Only two of the differences exceed that limit. Therefore, we may conclude that conditions 4 and 5 are significantly different from control condition 1.

7.2.5 Summary of Procedure

These are the steps in the use of the Friedman two-way analysis of variance by ranks:

1. Cast the scores in a two-way table having N rows (subjects) and k columns (conditions or variables).
2. Rank the data in each row from 1 to k.
3. Determine the sum of the ranks in each column (R_j).
4. Compute the value of F_r with Eq. (7.3) if there are no ties or Eq. (7.4) if there are tied observations in any row.
5. The method for determining the probability of occurrence when H_0 is true of an observed value of F_r depends upon the sizes of N and k:
   (*a*) Appendix Table M gives selected critical values of F_r for small N and k.
   (*b*) For N and/or k larger than those used in Appendix Table M, the associated probability may be determined by reference to the χ^2 distribution (Appendix Table C) with $df = k - 1$.
6. If the probability yielded by the appropriate method in step 5 is equal to or less than α, reject H_0.
7. If H_0 is rejected, use multiple comparisons [Eq. (7.5)] to determine which differences among conditions are significant. If the differences among the various conditions and a control condition are to be tested, use Eq. (7.6).

7.2.6 Relative Efficiency

The power-efficiency of the Friedman two-way analysis of variance test for normally distributed data when compared with its normal counterpart (the F test) is $2/\pi = .64$ when $k = 2$ and increases with k to .80 for $k = 5$, .87 for $k = 10$, and .91 for $k = 20$. When compared with samples from uniform and exponential distributions the efficiency is greater.

7.2.7 References

Early discussion of the Friedman two-way analysis of variance by ranks may be found in Friedman (1937, 1940). More recent discussions include Lehmann (1975) and Randles and Wolfe (1979). The Friedman two-way analysis of variance by ranks is functionally related to another nonparametric test, the Kendall coefficient of concordance (W), which is discussed in Chap. 9.

7.3 THE PAGE TEST FOR ORDERED ALTERNATIVES

7.3.1 Function

The Friedman two-way analysis of variance by ranks tests the hypothesis that k matched groups or k repeated measures are the same versus the alternative hypothesis that one or more of the groups are different. Sometimes a researcher may wish to entertain a more specific alternative hypothesis. For example, in an experiment on learning, the researcher may wish to test the hypothesis of "no learning" against the hypothesis that subjects will recall more on trial 2 than on trial 1, recall more on trial 3 than on trial 2, etc. In this case the alternative hypothesis associated with the Friedman two-way analysis of variance by ranks is too general. The *Page test* for ordered alternatives described in this section tests the hypothesis that the groups (or measures) are the same versus the alternative hypothesis that the groups (or measures) are ordered in a specific sequence. To specify the null hypothesis and its alternative more explicitly, let θ_j be the population median for the jth group or measure. Then we may write the null hypothesis that the medians are the same as

$$H_0: \theta_1 = \theta_2 = \cdots = \theta_k$$

and the alternative hypothesis may be written as

$$H_1: \theta_1 \leq \theta_2 \leq \cdots \leq \theta_k$$

that is, the medians are ordered in magnitude. If the alternative hypothesis is true, at least one of the differences is a strict inequality ($<$). It is important to note that to ensure proper use of the test, the researcher must be able to specify the order of the groups (measures or conditions) *a priori*.

To apply the Page test, the data from the k matched samples or measures must be on at least an ordinal scale. We shall assume that there are N cases or sets of observations. As with the Friedman two-way analysis of variance by ranks, if the k samples are matched, the matching is achieved by obtaining N sets of k matched subjects and then randomly assigning one subject in each set to one of the k conditions.

7.3.2 Rationale and Method

To apply the Page test for ordered alternatives, the researcher must first specify the *a priori* ordering of groups. The data are then cast into a two-way table having N rows and k columns. As with the Friedman two-way analysis of variance by ranks test, the rows represent the subjects or matched sets of subjects and the columns represent the k conditions (groups or measures).

The data of the test are ranks. The scores in each *row* are ranked separately and range from 1 to k. The null hypothesis is that the average rank in each of the columns are the same. The alternative hypothesis is that the average rank increases across groups 1 to k. Rather than use average ranks in the computation, the test statistic uses the rank totals R_j for the jth group. To do the test, we calculate the statistic L:

$$L = \sum_{j=1}^{k} jR_j = R_1 + 2R_2 + \cdots + kR_k \tag{7.7}$$

where R_j is the sum of the ranks in the jth column.

Probabilities associated with various values of L when H_0 is true have been tabulated for various sample sizes N and various numbers of variables k. Appendix Table N gives the probabilities associated with values of L as large or larger than the tabled values for various values of N and k. If the observed value of L is greater than the tabled value for the chosen significance level, then the hypothesis H_0 may be rejected in favor of the alternative hypothesis H_1. For example, consider an experiment in which there are $N = 9$ sets of observations on $k = 4$ measures. A significance level of $\alpha = .01$ is chosen. Referring to Appendix Table N we see that, if $L \geq 246$, we would reject H_0 in favor of H_1.

LARGE SAMPLES. Critical values of L are tabled in Appendix Table N for $N \leq 20$ for $k = 3$, and $N \leq 12$ for $k = 4, 5, 6, 7, 8, 9$, and 10. For larger values of N or k a large-sample approximation is used to test hypotheses concerning the Page test statistic L. For large values of N and k the sampling distribution of L is approximately normally distributed with

$$\mu_L = \frac{Nk(k+1)^2}{4} \tag{7.8}$$

$$\sigma_L^2 = \frac{Nk^2(k^2-1)^2}{144(k-1)} \tag{7.9}$$

Thus, to test the hypothesis H_0 that the medians are equal against the alternative hypothesis that they are ordered, we calculate the statistic z_L:

$$z_L = \frac{12L - 3Nk(k+1)^2}{k(k^2-1)} \sqrt{\frac{k-1}{N}} \tag{7.10}$$

For large N the statistic z_L is approximately normally distributed with zero mean and standard deviation one. Therefore, the significance of z_L and, hence, L may be determined by reference to a table of the standard normal distribution (Appendix Table A). Since the alternatives are ordered, the Page test is a one-tailed test.

Example 7.3 For N and k small. In recent years there has been increasing interest in the ability of people to perceive tactile patterns. Devices have been developed that convert printed characters to vibrotactile patterns, one purpose of which is to enable visually impaired people to "read" text which is tactually presented. One device that has been designed to do this, the Optacon, contains a grid of small pins, each of which may vibrate independently. Letters of the alphabet produce different patterns of pin vibration. In experimental investigations involving temporal integration of such vibrotactile patterns,

TABLE 7.5
Proportion of correct responses as a function of stimulus onset asynchrony (SOA)

	Stimulus onset asynchrony (ms)					
Subject	**204**	**104**	**56**	**30**	**13**	**0**
A	.797	.873	.888	.923	.942	.956
B	.794	.772	.908	.982	.946	.913
C	.838	.801	.853	.951	.883	.837
D	.815	.801	.747	.859	.887	.902

Craig[5] examined the amount of interaction between elements of vibrotactile patterns as a function of the time between the onsets of the individual elements. In a subsequent study, the experimenter manipulated the "stimulus onset asynchrony" (SOA) of parts of patterns and the spacing or gap between rows of vibrating pins which are in contact with the subject's fingertip. The subject's task was to indicate whether a gap was present or not.

Four trained subjects were tested for a large number of trials in which the stimuli varied in onset asynchrony and spacing between stimuli. To evaluate the subjects' accuracy in detecting the presence of a gap, it was necessary to see how accurate subjects were in reporting the absence of a gap when there was no gap or spacing between the successive stimuli but the SOA was varied. For each subject six different SOA's were used. Table 7.5 summarizes the proportion of correct responses for each subject for each of the SOA's. The researcher wished to test the hypothesis that accuracy was inversely related to SOA.

i. Null hypothesis. H_0: the different SOA's have no effect on subjects' accuracy when there is no spatial gap in the vibrotactile pattern. H_1: subjects' accuracy is inversely related to SOA. That is, as the asynchrony decreases, the proportion of correct responses increases.

ii. Statistical test. Because the experimenter hypothesizes an ordering for the response accuracy as a function of SOA, the Page test for ordered alternatives is appropriate. Moreover, the use of the parametric analysis of variance is precluded because the data exhibit a lack of homogeneity of variance and the distributions appear to be skewed. Thus, some of the basic assumptions of the F test are not satisfied. This, coupled with the small sample size suggests that a nonparametric test is appropriate.

iii. Significance level. Let $\alpha = .01$, N is the number of subjects $= 4$, and k is the number of measures on each subject $= 6$.

iv. Sampling distribution. Because of the small values of N and k, the sampling distribution of L as computed from Eq. (7.7) is tabled in Appendix Table N.

v. Rejection region. The region of rejection consists of all values of L which exceed the tabled value of L associated with the appropriate values of α, N, and k.

vi. Decision. The proportion of correct responses for each subject in each condition is summarized in Table 7.5. To do the Page test, it is necessary to rank the data in each

[5] Craig, J. C. (1984). Vibratory temporal integration as a function of pattern discriminability. *Perception & Psychophysics*, **35**, 579–582.

TABLE 7.6
Rank orders of proportion of correct responses for data in Table 7.5

	Stimulus onset asynchrony (ms)					
Subject	**204**	**104**	**56**	**30**	**13**	**0**
A	1	2	3	4	5	6
B	2	1	3	6	5	4
C	3	1	4	6	5	2
D	3	2	1	4	5	6
R_j	9	6	11	20	20	18

row from 1 to 6. These rankings are summarized in Table 7.6. From these rankings, the column sums of ranks R_j were computed.

With the use of these values, the value of L is computed with Eq. (7.7):

$$L = \sum_{j=1}^{k} jR_j = R_1 + 2R_2 + \cdots + kR_k \tag{7.7}$$

$$= 9 + 2(6) + 3(11) + 4(20) + 5(20) + 6(18)$$

$$= 9 + 12 + 33 + 80 + 100 + 108$$

$$= 342$$

Reference to Appendix Table N shows that the critical value of L for $\alpha = .01$, $N = 4$, and $k = 6$ is 331. Since the observed value (342) exceeds the tabled value (331) for the chosen significance level, the experimenter is justified in rejecting H_0 and concluding that response accuracy is inversely related to SOA. (It should be noted that H_0 could, in fact, have been rejected at the $\alpha = .001$ level.)

7.3.3 Summary of Procedure

These are the steps in the use of the Page test for ordered alternatives:

1. Cast the data into a two-way table having N rows (subjects) and k columns (conditions or variables). The ordering of the conditions must be specified *a priori*.
2. Rank the data in each row from 1 to k.
3. Determine the sum of the ranks in each column (R_j).
4. Compute the value of L with Eq. (7.7).
5. The method for determining the probability associated with L when H_0 is true depends upon the sizes of N and k:
   (*a*) Appendix Table N gives selected critical values of L for $N \leq 20$ when $k = 3$, and $N \leq 12$ for $4 \leq k \leq 10$.
   (*b*) If the number of observations and/or variables preclude the use of Appendix Table N, the normal approximation should be used. The value of z_L should

be computed using Eq. (7.10) and Appendix Table A should be used to determine whether z_L, and hence L, is in the region of rejection. Since H_1 specifies an ordered alternative hypothesis, a one-tailed test should be used. If H_0 is rejected, multiple comparison procedures like those outlined in Sec. 7.2.3 could be used. However, when doing comparisons, it must be noted that the tests are one-tailed and the z values must be adjusted accordingly.

7.3.4 Relative Efficiency

The efficiency of the Page test for ordered alternatives when compared with its normal distribution alternative (the t test) is the same as that of the Friedman two-way analysis of variance by ranks test (see Sec. 7.2.6). However, compared to the Friedman test, the Page test is more powerful in its ability to detect ordered alternatives.

7.3.5 References

The Page test was proposed by Page (1963). It is related to the Spearman rank-order correlation coefficient (see Chap. 9). The power of the test has been considered by Hollander (1967).

7.4 DISCUSSION

Three nonparametric statistical tests for testing H_0 in the case of k related samples or matched groups were presented in this chapter. The first, the Cochran Q test, is useful when the measurement of the variable under study is categorical (in a nominal scale with two levels or dichotomized ordinal scale). This test enables the researcher to determine whether it is likely that the k related samples could have come from the same population with respect to the proportion or frequency of "successes" in the various samples or conditions. That is, it is an overall test of whether the k samples exhibit significantly different frequencies of "successes" than would be expected by chance.

The second nonparametric statistical test presented, the Friedman two-way analysis of variance by ranks, F_r, is appropriate when the measurements of the variables are at least ordinal. It tests the probability that the k related samples could have come from the same population with respect to the mean rankings. That is, it is an overall test of whether the values of the data vary as a function of the conditions under which they were observed.

The Friedman test should be used in preference to the Cochran Q test whenever the data are appropriate for its use (i.e., whenever the variables are at least ordered). The Friedman test has the advantage of having tables of exact probabilities for very small samples, whereas the Cochran Q test should not be used when N (the number of rows or sets of observations) is very small.

If, when using the Friedman test, the hypothesis H_0 that there is no difference among medians is rejected, multiple comparisons may be done to determine which conditions are different from each other. If the researcher has a more precise hypothesis concerning the difference between one condition (say, a control condition) and the other conditions, then these specific comparisons may be tested as well.

The last test, the Page test for ordered alternatives, like the Friedman test, assumes that the data are on an ordinal scale. However, for the Friedman two-way analysis of variance by ranks, the alternative hypothesis is that the groups or measures are different. In contrast, the alternative for the Page test is that the groups are ordered *a priori* with respect to their medians. Since the alternative hypothesis is more precise, the Page test should be preferred when the alternative hypothesis is appropriate for the particular experimental investigation. Finally, it should be remarked that the alternative hypothesis specified by the Page test is quite frequently found in experimental studies in the behavioral and social sciences.

CHAPTER 8

THE CASE OF k INDEPENDENT SAMPLES

In the analysis of research data, the investigator often needs to decide whether several independent samples may be regarded as having come from the same population. The research hypothesis is that the k populations are different, and the statistical hypothesis to be tested is H_0: pop 1 = pop 2 = $\cdots$ = pop k. The investigator draws a sample from each population. Sample values almost always differ somewhat, and the problem is to determine whether the observed sample differences signify real differences among populations or whether they are merely the type of differences that are to be expected among random samples from the same population.

In this chapter, procedures will be presented for testing the significance of differences among three or more independent groups or samples. That is, statistical techniques will be presented for testing the null hypothesis that k independent samples have been drawn from the same population or from k identical populations.

In the introduction to Chap. 7, we attempted to distinguish between two types of k-sample tests. The first type of test is used to analyze data from k *matched* samples or repeated observations of a single sample, and nonparametric tests of that sort were presented in Chap. 7. The second kind of k-sample test is appropriate for analyzing data from k *independent* samples. Such tests will be presented in this chapter.

The usual parametric technique for testing whether several independent samples have come from the same population is the one-way analysis of variance or F test. The assumptions associated with the statistical model underlying the F test are that the observations are independently drawn from normally distributed populations, all of which have the same variance. For meaningful interpretation of the results of the F test, the measurement requirement is that the variables be measured on at least an interval scale.

If a researcher finds that such assumptions are unrealistic or inappropriate for the data derived from the problem under investigation, one of the nonparametric statistical tests for k independent samples presented in this chapter may be used. The choice of a particular test depends upon the nature of the data and the assumptions that the researcher must make. Some of the tests described in this chapter deal with data which are inherently only categorical (in a nominal scale), and others deal with data which are in ranks (in an ordinal scale).

We shall present four nonparametric tests for the case of k independent samples, and shall conclude the chapter with a discussion of the comparative use of these tests.

8.1 THE CHI-SQUARE TEST FOR *k* INDEPENDENT SAMPLES

8.1.1 Function

When the experimental data consist of frequencies in discrete categories (either nominal or categorical or sometimes ordinal), the *chi-square test* may be used to assess the significance of differences among k independent groups. The chi-square test for k independent samples or groups is a straightforward extension of the chi-square test for two independent samples presented in Chap. 6. In general, the test is similar for both two and k independent samples or groups.

8.1.2 Method

The method of computing the statistic for the chi-square test for independent samples will be outlined briefly here, together with an example of the application of the test. The reader will find a fuller discussion of this test in Chap. 6.

To apply the chi-square test, one first arranges the frequencies in an $r \times k$ table where the data in each column are the frequencies of each of the r categorical responses for each of the k different groups or samples. The null hypothesis is that the k samples of frequencies have come from the same population or from identical populations. This hypothesis, that the k populations do not differ among themselves, may be tested by applying Eq. (6.2) or Eq. (6.2*a*):

$$X^2 = \sum_{i=1}^{r} \sum_{j=1}^{k} \frac{(n_{ij} - E_{ij})^2}{E_{ij}} \tag{6.2}$$

or

$$X^2 = \sum_{i=1}^{r} \sum_{j=1}^{k} \frac{n_{ij}^2}{E_{ij}} - N \tag{6.2a}$$

where n_{ij} = observed number of cases categorized in the ith row of the jth column
E_{ij} = number of cases expected in the ith row of the jth column when H_0 is true

and the double summation is over all rows and columns of the table (i.e., summation across all cells). The reader will recall from Chap. 6 that the expected values may be determined by calculating $E_{ij} = R_i C_j / N$ for each cell of the table. The values of X^2 obtained by using [Eq. (6.2) or Eq. (6.2*a*)] are distributed asymptotically (as N gets large) as χ^2 with $df = (r - 1)(k - 1)$, where r is the number of rows and k is the number of columns (or independent groups) in the contingency table. Thus, the probability associated with the occurrence of values as large as an observed X^2 is given in Appendix Table C. If an observed value of X^2 is equal to or larger than that given in Appendix Table C for a particular level of significance and for $df = (r - 1)(k - 1)$, then H_0 may be rejected at that level of significance. As we shall see in the examples and in Sec. 8.1.5, it is important that the expected values (the E_{ij}) be not too small in order that a proper interpretation of the statistic may be made.

Example 8.1a In a major project to determine the efficacy of various outpatient treatments for clinical depression, two researchers gave 178 moderately clinically depressed clients 10 weeks of one of four different modes of therapy—psychotherapy, behavior therapy, drug therapy, or relaxation therapy.[1] The researchers carefully screened clients to ensure that each met the selection criteria for the study. These criteria included scoring within or beyond the moderate range on psychometric tests for depression. After assigning subjects randomly to one of the four treatment conditions, each was treated by a therapist. The therapists were licensed psychologists, physicians, or psychiatrists who were selected on the strength of their reputations in the particular treatment they offered.

A fixed time after the 10-week period, client-subjects completed a questionnaire which included the Beck Depression Inventory (BDI), which is a common instrument for measuring depression. Scores on the inventory were collapsed into three categories: normal (score ≤ 7), mild ($7 <$ score < 23), and moderate to severe (score ≥ 23). (A score of 23 or more on the BDI was one of the original selection criteria for the program.)

i. *Null hypothesis.* H_0: the proportion of subjects in each of the score categories of the BDI is the same in each of the treatment groups. H_1: the proportion of subjects in each of the score categories of the BDI differs across the treatment groups.
ii. *Statistical test.* Since the groups in the study are independent and number more than two, a statistical test for k independent groups is appropriate. Since the data are in discrete categories, the chi-square test is appropriate.
iii. *Significance level.* Let $\alpha = .05$ and N is the number of subjects who participated in the study $= 178$.
iv. *Sampling distribution.* Under the null hypothesis, X^2 as computed from Eq. (6.2) is distributed approximately as χ^2 with $df = (r - 1)(k - 1)$. When H_0 is true, the probability associated with the occurrence of values as large as or larger than an observed X^2 is tabled in Appendix Table C.
v. *Rejection region.* The region of rejection consists of all values of X^2 which are so large that the probability associated with their occurrence when H_0 is true is less than or equal to $\alpha = .05$.

---

[1] McLean, P. D., and Hakstian, A. R. (1979). Clinical depression: Comparative efficacy of outpatient treatments. *Journal of Consulting and Clinical Psychology*, **47**, 818–836.

TABLE 8.1
Frequencies of treatment response level

Score range on BDI (posttreatment)	Psychotherapy	Relaxation therapy	Drug therapy	Behavior therapy	Total
Moderate to severe (score $\geq$ 23)	13 *8.40*	8 *8.21*	10 *9.36*	3 *8.02*	34
Mild (7 < score < 23)	20 *21.75*	23 *21.26*	27 *24.22*	18 *20.76*	88
Normal (score $\leq$ 7)	11 *13.84*	12 *13.53*	12 *15.42*	21 *13.21*	56
Total	44	43	49	42	178

vi. Decision. Table 8.1 summarizes the frequency of occurrence of scores within each category for each of the treatment groups. Table 8.1 also shows in italics the number of subjects who might be expected to have scored in each of the BDI categories when H_0 is true, i.e., the expected number scores in each category if there were really no difference in treatment efficacy as a function of type of therapy. (The expected values were determined from the marginal totals by the method described in Sec. 6.2.) For example, whereas 11 of the subjects receiving psychotherapy treatment scored 7 or less on the BDI, when H_0 is true we would expect $(56 \times 44)/178 = 13.84$ subjects to have received scores of 7 or less. And whereas 21 of the subjects in the behavior therapy treatment group scored 7 or below on the BDI, if H_0 were true, we would expect $(56 \times 42)/178 = 13.21$ to have scored that low. Of the 42 subjects in the behavior therapy group, only 3 received scores of 23 or above on the BDI, whereas under H_0 we would expect to find 8.02 with scores of 23 or above.

The size of X^2 reflects the magnitude of the discrepancy between the observed and the expected values in each of the cells. We may compute X^2 for the values in Table 8.1 by the application of Eq. (6.2*a*):

$$X^2 = \sum_{i=1}^{r} \sum_{j=1}^{k} \frac{n_{ij}^2}{E_{ij}} - N \tag{6.2a}$$

$$\begin{aligned}
&= \frac{13^2}{8.40} + \frac{8^2}{8.21} + \frac{10^2}{9.36} + \frac{3^2}{8.02} + \frac{20^2}{21.75} \\
&\quad + \frac{23^2}{21.26} + \frac{27^2}{24.22} + \frac{18^2}{20.76} + \frac{11^2}{13.84} \\
&\quad + \frac{12^2}{13.53} + \frac{12^2}{15.42} + \frac{21^2}{13.21} - 178 \\
&= 20.12 + 7.80 + 10.68 + 1.12 + 18.39 + 24.88 + 30.10 \\
&\quad + 15.61 + 8.74 + 10.64 + 9.34 + 33.38 - 178 \\
&= 12.80
\end{aligned}$$

We observe that for the data in Table 8.1, $X^2 = 12.80$ with

$$df = (r - 1)(k - 1) = (3 - 1)(4 - 1) = 6$$

Reference to Appendix Table C reveals that such a value of X^2 is significant beyond the .05 level. (The critical value for $\alpha = .05$ and $df = 6$ is 12.59). Therefore, our decision is to reject H_0. We conclude that posttreatment scores on the BDI vary as a function of treatment categories.

8.1.3 Partitioning the Degrees of Freedom in $r \times k$ Contingency Tables

If, in analyzing an $r \times k$ contingency table, H_0 is rejected, then the researcher may safely conclude that the k groups differ on the measured (row) variable. However, although one may safely conclude that the k groups are different, the result of the chi-square test by itself does not tell the researcher what the differences are. That is, a significant X^2 only tells one that *somewhere* in the table the observed frequencies are not simply chance deviations from the theoretical or expected frequencies. Most researchers would like to know *just where* in a contingency table the important discrepancies are. The partitioning procedure outlined in this section enables the researcher to do further analysis of a contingency table for which the obtained X^2 is significant. In Chap. 6, partitioning procedures for $r \times 2$ contingency tables were outlined. The procedures for partitioning an $r \times k$ table are similar.

To partition the contingency table, a series of 2×2 subtables are constructed—one for each degree of freedom. For convenience of exposition, the partitioning begins in the upper left-hand corner of the table, and successive partitions are constructed by combining appropriate rows and/or columns. Since the measured variable is nominal and the k groups can be listed in any order without changing the overall X^2, the table should be arranged *a priori* so that the partitions are meaningful in terms of the particular problem under study.

To illustrate the method, we list the partitions for a 3×3 contingency table. The first partition consists of the four frequencies in the upper left-hand corner of the table:

n_{11}	n_{12}
n_{21}	n_{22}

(1)

The second partition is formed by collapsing the columns of the 2×2 first partition to form the first row of the second partition:

$n_{11} + n_{21}$	$n_{12} + n_{22}$
n_{31}	n_{32}

(2)

The remaining partitions for the 3×3 table are the following:

$n_{11} + n_{12}$	n_{13}
$n_{21} + n_{22}$	n_{23}

(3)

$n_{11} + n_{12}$ + $n_{21} + n_{22}$	n_{13} + n_{23}
$n_{31} + n_{32}$	n_{33}

(4)

Although the arrangement may look cumbersome, the system is really straightforward. The lower-right cell of a partition associated with the ijth cell consists of a single frequency (n_{ij}), the upper-left cell is the sum of all of the frequencies "above" and to the "left" of the ijth cell. The lower-left frequency is the sum of the frequencies to the left of the ijth cell, and the upper-right cell is the sum of the frequencies above the ijth cell.

As noted in Chap. 6, each partition is tested by using a chi-square statistic. However, it is not appropriate to use the "usual" formula for X^2 since the expected frequencies must be adjusted for each 2×2 table to reflect the entire table (and population), not just the subset represented in the partition.

The value of the partitioned X^2 for the tth partition is given by the following equation:

$$X_t^2 = \frac{N\left[C_j\left(R_i \sum_{h=1}^{i-1} \sum_{m=1}^{j-1} n_{hm} - \sum_{h=1}^{i-1} R_h \sum_{m=1}^{j-1} n_{im}\right) - \sum_{m=1}^{j-1} C_m\left(R_i \sum_{h=1}^{i-1} n_{hj} - n_{ij} \sum_{h=1}^{i-1} R_h\right)\right]^2}{C_j R_i \sum_{m=1}^{j-1} C_m \sum_{m=1}^{j} C_m \sum_{h=1}^{i-1} R_h \sum_{h=1}^{i} R_h} \tag{8.1}$$

where $t = i + (r - 1)(j - 2) - 1$. That is, X_t^2 is the test for the tth partition associated with the ijth cell. Each of the X_t^2 statistics is distributed as χ^2 with $df = 1$. The X_t^2 for all of the partitions sum to the value of X^2 for the entire table. The calculation of X_t^2 with Eq. (8.1) is straightforward but very cumbersome. Therefore, the program in the Appendix should be used to do the calculations. (This program also may be used to apply the partitioning procedures described in Chap. 6.)

Example 8.1b In the example concerning the efficacy of various outpatient treatments for clinical depression, we found that posttreatment scores on the BDI differed across treatment conditions. ($X^2 = 12.80$ with 6 df for the data in Table 8.1.) Although the researcher may safely conclude that there are indeed differences among the treatments, it is desirable to determine whether the differential efficacy of treatment varied across *all* treatments or whether the dependence is concentrated in one or two treatments.

To determine where the differences in treatment effects lie within Table 8.1, that table was partitioned. The successive partitions are listed in Table 8.2. At the bottom of that table, the partitioned X^2's are summarized. The first two partitions compare psychotherapy and relaxation therapy. The first partition compares moderate-to-severe BDI

TABLE 8.2
Partitions derived from contingency table in Table 8.1

BDI	Psychotherapy	Relaxation therapy
Moderate to severe	13	8
Mild	20	23

(1)

BDI	Psychotherapy	Relaxation therapy
Moderate to severe + mild	33	31
Normal	11	12

(2)

BDI	Psychotherapy + relaxation therapy	Drug therapy
Moderate to severe	21	10
Mild	43	27

(3)

BDI	Psychotherapy + relaxation therapy	Drug therapy
Moderate to severe + mild	64	37
Normal	23	12

(4)

BDI	Psychotherapy + relaxation + drug therapy	Behavior therapy
Moderate to severe	31	3
Mild	70	18

(5)

BDI	Psychotherapy + relaxation + drug therapy	Behavior therapy
Moderate to severe + mild	101	21
Normal	35	21

(6)

Summary of partitioned X^2

Partition	X^2
1	1.62
2	.09
3	.42
4	.06
5	1.84
6	8.76
Overall	12.80

scores against mild BDI scores for these two groups. With the use of Eq. (8.1) (or the computer program), the value $X_1^2 = 1.62$. X_1^2 is distributed as χ^2 with $df = 1$, which is clearly not significant. Next, subjects with moderate-to-severe or mild BDI scores were combined, and the combined treatment group was tested against subjects with normal BDI scores. For this, the second partition $X_2^2 = .09$; again, this value is not significant. We may now conclude that there are no differences between psychotherapy and relaxation therapy treatments as measured by the BDI.

These two treatment groups were then pooled and compared with drug therapy on the posttreatment BDI scores. These partitions resulted in $X_3^2 = .42$ and $X_4^2 = .06$. The results of these partitions permit the researcher to conclude that there were no differences among the three treatments of psychotherapy, relaxation therapy, and drug therapy.

What remains is to compare behavior therapy against the three other therapies. The first three therapy groups are combined and the distribution of BDI scores of this combined group is compared with the distribution of BDI scores for the behavior therapy group. The relevant partitions are (5) and (6) in Table 8.2. The resulting X^2 values are 1.84 and 8.76 respectively. Thus, $X_6^2 = 8.76$ is the only significant X^2 associated with the partitions. It would be appropriate, therefore, for the researcher to conclude that, for this study, psychotherapy, relaxation therapy, and drug therapy produced similar results. However, behavior therapy is different from the other three. Examination of Table 8.1 and the partitioned X^2 values shows the locus of the difference—significantly more subjects in the behavior therapy group scored in the normal range on the BDI.

It should be noted that the sequence of partitioning can have an effect on the resulting X^2's. If the contingency table is partitioned in a different order, i.e., rows and/or columns are rearranged, the values of the partitions will almost certainly vary. It is important for proper use and interpretation of the partitioning analysis that the researcher be able to specify an *a priori* partitioning order which is meaningful for the particular problem under study.

If one wishes to construct the partition *a posteriori*, the partitioning procedures outlined in this chapter may be used. However, the critical value for the significance of each partition must be changed. The tail probability must be changed from α to α/p where $p =$ the number of partitions. Thus, if one wanted to construct the six partitions *a posteriori* in the above example, the critical value of χ^2 would be based on $\alpha/p = .05/6 = .0083$.

ANALYSIS OF RESIDUALS. When the obtained value of X^2 for an $r \times k$ contingency table is significant, the method of partitioning can help the researcher determine where the differences are within the table. The method outlined above will often be sufficient to delineate the differences. However, for some tables, after applying the method of partitioning, the researcher may still desire to analyze the data further in an effort to understand better just where the differences are. It is possible to complement the partitioning method by analyzing the residuals (the discrepancies between the observed and expected values) in order to determine which are larger than might be expected by chance. The residual, e_{ij} for the ijth cell in an $r \times k$ table, is

$$e_{ij} = \frac{n_{ij} - E_{ij}}{\sqrt{E_{ij}}}$$

where $E_{ij} = R_i C_j/N$. The variance of this residual may be estimated by

$$v_{ij} = \frac{1 - R_i/N}{1 - C_j/N} = \frac{N - R_i}{N - C_j}$$

The *adjusted* residual or *standardized* residual for the *ij*th cell may be computed as

$$d_{ij} = \frac{n_{ij} - E_{ij}}{\sqrt{E_{ij}}} \sqrt{\frac{N - C_j}{N - R_i}} \tag{8.2}$$

As the sample size N becomes large, the d_{ij} has approximately a normal distribution with mean 0 and variance 1. Thus, the significance of d_{ij} may be determined by reference to Appendix Table A. The researcher who analyzes the residuals should be cautioned that the d_{ij} are *not* independent. Therefore, the interpretation of the results should be guarded. A prudent procedure is to combine the analysis of residuals with the partitioning analysis.

For the example above, the adjusted residual d_{11} for the upper left-hand cell may be computed by using Eq. (8.2) as

$$d_{11} = \frac{13 - 8.4}{\sqrt{8.4}} \sqrt{\frac{178 - 44}{178 - 34}}$$

$$= 1.53$$

The remaining d_{ij} in the first row are $-.07$, .20, -1.72. The d_{ij} for the second and third rows are $-.46$, .46, .67, $-.75$, $-.80$, $-.44$, $-.89$, and 2.26 respectively. The only significant difference at the $\alpha = .05$ level (two-tailed) is the difference in the lower right-hand cell of Table 8.1 (d_{34}). This result adds additional force to the argument that it is the difference between behavior therapy and the other therapies that has produced the effect found in the table—behavior therapy results in significantly more scores on the BDI in the normal range than do the other therapies used.

8.1.4 Summary of Procedure

These are the steps in the use of the chi-square test for k independent samples or groups:

1. Cast the observed frequencies into an $r \times k$ contingency table, using the k columns for the groups or samples.
2. Determine the expected frequency under H_0 for each cell by finding the product of the marginal totals common to the cell and dividing this product by N. That is, find the expected frequencies $E_{ij} = R_i C_j/N$. (N is the sum of each of the marginal totals and represents the total number of *independent* observations. Inflated N's due to multiple observations of each subject invalidate the test.) If the expected frequencies are small, combine categories as discussed in the next section.

3. Compute X^2 by using Eq. (6.2) or (6.2*a*). Determine the degrees of freedom $df = (r - 1)(k - 1)$.
4. Determine the significance of the observed X^2 by reference to Appendix Table C. If the probability given for the observed value of X^2 for the particular value of df is less than or equal to α, reject the null hypothesis H_0 in favor of H_1.
5. If H_0 is rejected, the overall value of X^2 may be partitioned with the use of Eq. (8.1) to determine where the differences between the groups on the measured variables are in the contingency table. Each of the partitioned X^2's is distributed as χ^2 with $df = 1$ as N gets large. After partitioning the table, the residuals (differences between observed and expected values) may be analyzed by using Eq. (8.2).

8.1.5 When to Use the Chi-Square Test

Proper application of the chi-square test requires that the expected frequencies (the E_{ij}'s) in each cell are not too small. When this requirement is violated, the results of the test cannot be interpreted because the sampling distribution of X^2 is not well approximated by the χ^2 distribution in Appendix Table C. Cochran (1954) recommends that in chi-square tests for which the degrees of freedom are greater than 1 (that is, when either r or k is larger than 2), no more than 20 percent of the cells should have an expected frequency of less than 5, and no cell should have an expected frequency of less than 1.[2]

If these requirements are not met by the data in the form in which they were originally collected and a larger sample cannot be obtained, the researcher should combine categories to increase the E_{ij}'s in the various cells. Only after combining categories so that fewer than 20 percent of the cells have expected frequencies of less than 5 and no cell has an expected frequency of less than 1 may the researcher meaningfully interpret the results of the chi-square test. The combining of categories must be done judiciously. That is, the results of the statistical test may not be interpretable if the combining of categories has been capricious. The categories which are combined must have some common property or mutual identity if interpretation of the outcome of the test after the combining of rows or columns is to be meaningful. The researcher may guard against the necessity of combining categories if a sufficiently large sample is used.

The chi-square test is insensitive to the effects of order. Thus, when either the response categories or the groups (or both) are ordered, the chi-square test may not

---

[2] The reader will note that the "rules of thumb" concerning small expected frequencies appear to be somewhat arbitrary. This is because authorities differ on "how close" the actual sampling distribution of X^2 should be to the χ^2 distribution for the approximation to be good. It does appear that the greater the number of rows and columns in the contingency table, the smaller the expected values may be for the approximation to remain good. (One investigator found that for a table with 50 cells and *all* expected values less than 1, the approximation was very good: however, we would not expect to use such tables in actual practice.)

be the best test. Cochran (1954) has presented methods that strengthen the common chi-square tests when H_0 is tested against specific alternatives.

Finally, it should be noted that the chi-square test is performed on *frequencies*. Thus, it is important to use Eq. (6.2) or (6.2*a*) on the frequencies of the data. It is not correct to use percentages or some other transformation of the data in performing the test.

8.1.6 Power

There is usually no clear alternative to the chi-square test when it is used for categorical data, and thus the exact power of the chi-square test usually cannot be computed. However, Cochran (1952) has shown that the limiting power distribution of the chi-square test tends to 1 as the sample size N becomes large.

8.1.7 References

For other discussions of the chi-square test, the reader is referred to Cochran (1952, 1954), Delucchi (1983), Everitt (1977), Lewis and Burke (1949), and McNemar (1969). Partitioning procedures are discussed in detail by Castellan (1965). Lienert and Netter (1987) describe adjustments to the partitioning procedure when the partitioning order is not determined *a priori*. An alternative to partitioning is discussed by Shaffer (1973). The method for analyzing residuals has been discussed by Haberman (1973).

8.2 THE EXTENSION OF THE MEDIAN TEST

8.2.1 Function

The *extension of the median test* determines whether k independent groups (of not necessarily equal size) have been drawn from the same population or from populations with equal medians. It is useful and appropriate when the variable under study has been measured in at least an ordinal scale. It is particularly appropriate when, for some reason, it has not been possible to observe the exact value of extreme scores, e.g., when some of the observed data are above some cut point.

8.2.2 Method

To apply the extension of the median test, we first determine the median score for the combined k samples of scores, i.e., we find the *common* median for all scores in the k groups. We then replace each score by a plus (+) if the score is larger than the common median and by a minus (−) if it is smaller than the common median. (Should it happen that one or more scores fall at the common median, then the scores may be dichotomized by assigning a plus to those scores which exceed the common median and a minus to those scores which fall at or below the median.)

We may cast the resulting dichotomous sets of scores into a $2 \times k$ contingency table, with the numbers in the body of the table representing the frequencies of pluses (scores above the median) and minuses (scores below the median) in each of the k groups. An example of such a table is the following:

	Group			
	1	**2**	...	k
Observations above median	n_{11}	n_{12}	...	n_{1k}
Observations below median	n_{21}	n_{22}	...	n_{2k}

To test the null hypothesis that the k samples have come from the same population with respect to medians, we compute the value of the X^2 statistic using Eq. (6.2) or (6.2*a*):

$$X^2 = \sum_{i=1}^{2} \sum_{j=1}^{k} \frac{(n_{ij} - E_{ij})^2}{E_{ij}} \tag{6.2}$$

or

$$X^2 = \sum_{i=1}^{2} \sum_{j=1}^{k} \frac{n_{ij}^2}{E_{ij}} - N \tag{6.2a}$$

where n_{ij} = observed number of cases categorized in the ith row of the jth column
E_{ij} = number of cases expected in the ith row of the jth column when H_0 is true

and the double summation is over all rows and columns of the table (i.e., summation over all cells). The values of X^2 yielded by the use of Eq. (6.2) are distributed (for large N) as χ^2 with $df = (r - 1)(k - 1)$, where r is the number of rows and k is the number of columns (groups) in the contingency table. For the median test $r = 2$, thus

$$df = (r - 1)(k - 1) = (2 - 1)(k - 1) = k - 1$$

When H_0 is true, the probability associated with the occurrence of values as large as an observed X^2 are given in Appendix Table C. If the observed X^2 is equal to or larger than that given in Appendix Table C for the previously determined level of significance and for the observed value of $df = k - 1$, then H_0 may be rejected at that level of significance.

If it is possible to dichotomize the scores exactly at the common median, then each E_{ij} is one-half of the marginal total for its column. When the scores are dichotomized as those which do and do not exceed the common median, the method for finding expected frequencies presented in Sec. 6.2.2 must be used.

Once the data have been categorized as pluses and minuses with respect to the common median, and the resulting frequencies have been cast into a $2 \times k$ contingency table, the computation procedures for this test are exactly the same as those for the chi-square test for k independent samples given in Sec. 8.1. They will be illustrated in the following example.

Example 8.2 Suppose an educational researcher wishes to study the influence of amount of education upon mothers' degree of interest in their children's schooling. As a measure of amount of education, he or she uses the highest school grade completed by each mother; as a measure of degree of interest in the child's schooling, the researcher uses the number of voluntary visits each mother makes to the school during the school year, e.g., to class plays, to parent meetings, to self-initiated conferences with teachers and administrators, etc. He or she draws a random sample of 10 percent of the 440 children enrolled in the school; from this the names of 44 mothers are obtained who then comprise the sample. The hypothesis is that the number of visits to the school by a mother will vary according to the number of years of school the mother completed.

i. Null hypothesis. H_0: there is no difference in frequency of school visits among mothers with different amounts of education; that is, the frequency of maternal visits to school is independent of amount of maternal education. H_1: the frequency of school visits by mothers differs for varying amounts of maternal education.

ii. Statistical test. Since the groups of mothers at various educational levels are independent of each other and since several groups will be used, a significance test for k independent groups or samples is in order. Because the number of years of school constitutes at best an ordinal measure of degree of education, and since the number of visits to school constitutes at best an ordered measure of degree of interest in one's child's schooling, the extension of the median test is appropriate for testing the hypothesis concerning differences in the medians for each group.

iii. Significance level. Let $\alpha = .05$ and N is the number of mothers in the sample = 44.

iv. Sampling distribution. Under the null hypothesis, the statistic X^2 computed from Eq. (6.2) is distributed approximately as χ^2 with $df = k - 1$ when $r = 2$. (In the median test, the number of rows r in the associated contingency table is always 2.) The probability associated with the occurrence of values as large as an observed X^2 when H_0 is true is given in Appendix Table C.

v. Rejection region. The region of rejection consists of all values of X^2 which are so large that the probability associated with their occurrence when H_0 is true is less than or equal to $\alpha = .05$.

vi. Decision. In this (fictitious) example, the researcher collected the data presented in Table 8.3. The combined median for these 44 data is 2.5. That is, half of the mothers visited the school two or fewer times during the school year, and half visited three or more times. These data are split at the combined median to obtain the data given in Table 8.4, which gives the number of mothers at each educational level who fall above or below the combined median of the number of visits to school. For example, of those mothers whose education was limited to eight years, five visited the school three or more times during the year, and five visited the school two or fewer times during the year. Of those mothers who had attended some years of college, three visited the school three or more times and one visited two or fewer times.

TABLE 8.3
Number of visits to school by mothers attaining various educational levels (artificial data)

Education completed by mother					
Elementary school (8th grade)	**10th grade**	**High school (12th grade)**	**Some college**	**College graduate**	**Graduate school**
4	2	2	9	2	2
3	4	0	4	4	6
0	1	4	2	5	
7	6	3	3	2	
1	3	8			
2	0	0			
0	2	5			
3	5	2			
5	1	1			
1	2	7			
	1	6			
		5			
		1			

Given in italics in Table 8.4 are the expected number of visits of each group under the assumption that H_0 is true. Observe that with scores dichotomized exactly at the median, the expected frequency in each column is precisely one-half of the sum of the frequencies for the column in which the cell is located. The researcher observed that one-half of the expected frequencies in the contingency table are less than five. The sampling distribution of the X^2 statistic is not well approximated by the χ^2 distribution when more than about 20 percent of the cells have expected frequencies less than five. (See the discussion of when to use the chi-square test in Sec. 8.1.5.) Therefore, the researcher decided to combine categories in order to have expected values sufficiently large. Since the categories with small expected frequencies all involved women with varying amounts of college education, the researcher decided to collapse these three categories into a single category—college (one or more years).[3,4] By doing this, the data

[3] It should be noted that for this particular example, the *a priori* expected value in each cell of the original table is $44/12 = 3.67 < 5$. There are several ways that the small-expected-value problem could have been solved: A larger sample could have been selected, the number of categories of educational attainment could have been reduced, or the categories could be combined after the data are in hand. The researcher chose the latter. Use of a larger sample is not only more costly but also does not ensure that all expected values will be sufficiently large. The *a priori* use of fewer categories or groups not only sacrifices information but also does not ensure that the expected values will be sufficiently large. The choice taken by researcher appears to be the best.

[4] The particular choice for combining groups has the additional advantage of making the expected frequencies in each group nearly equal. The power of the chi-square test is greatest when the expected frequencies in each cell are equal.

TABLE 8.4
Visits to school by mothers attaining various educational levels (artificial data)

	Education completed by mother						
	Elementary school (8th grade)	**10th grade**	**High school (12th grade)**	**Some college**	**College graduate**	**Graduate school**	Total
No. of mothers whose visits were more frequent than common median no. of visits	5 *5*	4 *5.5*	7 *6.5*	*3* *2*	2 *2*	1 *1*	22
No. of mothers whose visits were less frequent than common median no. of visits	5 *5*	7 *5.5*	6 6.5	1 *2*	2 *2*	1 *1*	22
Total	10	11	13	4	4	2	44

TABLE 8.5
Visits to school by mothers attaining various educational levels (artificial data)

	Education completed by mother				
	Elementary school (8th grade)	**10th grade**	**High school (12th grade)**	**College (one or more years)**	Total
No. of mothers whose visits were more frequent than common median no. of visits	5 *5*	4 *5.5*	7 *6.5*	6 *5*	22
No. of mothers whose visits were less frequent than common median no. of visits	5 *5*	7 *5.5*	6 *6.5*	4 *5*	22
Total	10	11	13	10	44

shown in Table 8.5 were obtained. Observe that, in this collapsed table, all of the expected frequencies exceed five.

We may then compute the value of the X^2 statistic by substituting the data in Table 8.5 into Eq. (6.2):

$$X^2 = \sum_{i=1}^{2} \sum_{j=1}^{k} \frac{(n_{ij} - E_{ij})^2}{E_{ij}} \tag{6.2}$$

$$= \frac{(5-5)^2}{5} + \frac{(4-5.5)^2}{5.5} + \frac{(7-6.5)^2}{6.5} + \frac{(6-5)^2}{5}$$

$$+ \frac{(5-5)^2}{5} + \frac{(7-5.5)^2}{5.5} + \frac{(6-6.5)^2}{6.5} + \frac{(4-5)^2}{5}$$

$$= 0 + .409 + .0385 + .2 + 0 + .409 + .0385 + .2$$

$$= 1.295$$

By this computation we determine that $X^2 = 1.295$ and $df = k - 1 = 4 - 1 = 3$. Reference to Appendix Table C reveals that a value of X^2 greater than or equal to 1.295 for $df = 3$ has probability of occurrence between .80 and .70 when H_0 is true. Since this probability is larger than our previously set level of significance, $\alpha = .05$, our decision is that on the basis of these (fictitious) data, we cannot reject the null hypothesis that interest in their children's education (as measured by the number of school visits made by mothers) is independent of the amount of maternal education.

8.2.3 Summary of Procedure

These are the steps in the use of the extension of the median test:

1. Determine the common median of the scores in the k groups.
2. Assign pluses (+) to all scores above the common median and minuses (−) to all scores below the common median, thereby splitting each of the k groups of scores into two categories. Cast the resulting frequencies into a $2 \times k$ contingency table.
3. By using the data in that table, compute the value of X^2 with Eq. (6.2) or (6.2*a*). Determine $df = k - 1$.
4. Determine the significance of the observed value of X^2 by reference to Appendix Table C. If the associated probability given for the values as large as the observed value of X^2 is equal to or less than α, reject H_0 in favor of H_1.

As we have mentioned, the extension of the median test is, in effect, a chi-square test for k independent samples or groups. If there are several groups, the researcher may wish to partition the contingency table to determine where the differences are. For information concerning the conditions under which the test may properly be used, and the power of the test, the reader is referred to the discussion of the topic in Sec. 8.1. In the next section we shall discuss a test which is a more powerful alternative which may be utilized when the data may be completely ordered on the measured variable.

8.2.4 References

Discussions relevant to this test may be found in the references at the end of Sec. 8.1.

8.3 THE KRUSKAL-WALLIS ONE-WAY ANALYSIS OF VARIANCE BY RANKS

8.3.1 Function

The *Kruskal-Wallis one-way analysis of variance by ranks* is an extremely useful test for deciding whether k independent samples are from different populations. Sample values almost invariably differ somewhat, and the question is whether the differences among the samples signify genuine population differences or whether they represent merely the kind of variations that are to be expected among random samples from the same population. The Kruskal-Wallis technique tests the null hypothesis that the k samples come from the same population or from identical populations with the same median. To specify the null hypothesis and its alternative more explicitly, let θ_j be the population median for the jth group or sample. Then we may write the null hypothesis that the medians are the same as H_0: $\theta_1 = \theta_2 = \cdots = \theta_k$; and the alternative hypothesis may be written as $H_1: \theta_i \neq \theta_j$ for some groups i and j. That is, if the alternative hypothesis is true, at least one pair of groups has different medians. Under the null hypothesis, the test assumes that the variables under study have the same underlying continuous distribution; thus it requires at least ordinal measurement of that variable.

8.3.2 Rationale and Method

In applying the Kruskal-Wallis one-way analysis of variance by ranks, the data are cast into a two-way table with each column representing each successive sample or group. Thus the data would be arranged in the following manner:

Group			
1	**2**	$\cdots$	k
X_{11}	X_{12}	$\cdots$	X_{1k}
X_{21}	X_{22}	$\cdots$	X_{2k}
$\vdots$			$\vdots$
$X_{n_1 1}$	$\vdots$		
		$\cdots$	$X_{n_k k}$
	$X_{n_2 2}$		

where X_{ij} is the datum for the ith observation in the jth group and n_j is the number of observations in the jth group.

In the computation of the Kruskal-Wallis test, each of the N observations is replaced by ranks. That is, all of the scores from all of the k samples are combined and ranked in a *single* series. The smallest score is replaced by rank 1, the next smallest score is replaced by rank 2, and the largest score is replaced by rank N, where N is the total number of independent observations in the k samples.

When this is done, the sum of the ranks in each sample (column) is found. From these sums, we could compute the average rank for each sample or group. Now, if the samples are from the same or identical populations, the average ranks should be about the same, whereas if the samples were from populations with different medians, the average ranks should differ. The Kruskal-Wallis test assesses the differences among the average ranks to determine whether they are so disparate that they are not likely to have come from samples which were drawn from the same population.

We will give two forms for the Kruskal-Wallis test and the terms necessary to compute the Kruskal-Wallis statistic:

$$KW = \frac{12}{N(N+1)} \sum_{j=1}^{k} n_j(\bar{R}_j - \bar{R})^2$$

or

$$KW = \left[\frac{12}{N(N+1)} \sum_{j=1}^{k} n_j \bar{R}_j^2\right] - 3(N+1) \tag{8.3}$$

where k = number of samples or groups
n_j = number of cases in the jth sample
N = number of cases in the combined sample (the sum of the n_j's)
R_j = sum of the ranks in the jth sample or group
$\bar{R}_j$ = average of the ranks in the jth sample or group
$\bar{R} = (N+1)/2$ = the average of the ranks in the combined sample (the grand mean)

and the summation is across the k samples.

If the k samples actually are drawn from the same population or from identical populations, that is, if H_0 is true, then the sampling distribution of the statistic KW can be calculated and the probability of observing different values of KW can be tabled. However, when there are more than $k = 3$ groups and when the number of observations in each group exceeds five, the sampling distribution of KW is well-approximated by the χ^2 distribution with $df = k - 1$. The approximation gets better as both the number of groups, k, and the number of observations within each group, n_j, increase. Thus, when there are more than five cases in the various groups, that is, when all $n_j > 5$, and when H_0 is true, the probability associated with values as large as an observed KW may be determined by reference to Appendix Table C. If the observed value of KW is equal to or larger than the tabled value of χ^2 given in Appendix Table C for the previously determined significance level and for the observed $df = k - 1$, then H_0 may be rejected at that level of significance.

When $k = 3$ and the number of cases in each of the three samples is five or fewer, the probabilities associated with each KW may be obtained from Appendix Table O. That table gives selected significance values of KW for small values of n_1, n_2, and n_3, that is, for samples of sizes up to five. These significance probabilities are those associated with the occurrence of values as large as or larger than a tabled value of KW when H_0 is true.

Example 8.3a For small samples. In the experimental study of decision making, researchers have devoted theoretical and empirical effort at understanding decision tasks which are learned in a stepwise fashion. In a series of studies in which subjects were required to learn the relation of two cues to a probabilistic outcome, one task required subjects to learn functional relations of the form $X + Y + c = Z$, in which X and Y were probabilistically related to the criterion Z and c was an arbitrary constant. Subjects learn the task easily when both cues X and Y are given. However, some earlier research suggested that if the task is divided into parts, i.e., learning the relation between *one* cue and the outcome and then learning the relation of *both* cues to the outcome, subjects should have considerable difficulty learning the compound task. In one study,[5] one cue was a valid (but imperfect) predictor of the outcome, while the other cue, Y, was unrelated to the outcome and was not useful unless the cue X was presented at the same time. To assess the ability of people to make predictions in this type of task and to learn complex inference tasks, subjects were divided into three groups—one given *both cues*, one given the *valid cue first*, and one given the *irrelevant cue first*. For this example, the data are the prediction performance of subjects in the final stage of the experiment in which both cues are presented. The index of performance is a statistic which gives the judgmental accuracy of the subject. The research hypothesis was that the three groups would differ in their terminal performance in the prediction task.

[5] Castellan, N.J., Jr., and Jenkins, R. Deprivation conditions in multiple-cue probability learning (working paper).

i. Null hypothesis. H_0: there is no difference in the median performance of subjects in the three prediction tasks. H_1: the groups differ with respect to performance in the prediction task.

ii. Statistical test. Since three independent groups are under study, a test for k indepedent samples is called for. Moreover, since the judgmental accuracy index is measured on an ordinal scale, the Kruskal-Wallis test is appropriate.

iii. Significance level. Let $\alpha = .05$, N is the total number of subjects in the study $= 12$, n_1 is the number of subjects in the irrelevant-cue-first condition $= 3$, n_2 is the number of subjects in the valid-cue-first condition $= 4$, and n_3 is the number of subjects who learned by using both cues $= 5$.

iv. Sampling distribution. For $k = 3$ and n_j being small, the sampling distribution of KW is given in Appendix Table O.

v. Rejection region. The region of rejection consists of all values of KW which are so large that the probability associated with their occurrence when H_0 is true is equal to or less than $\alpha = .05$.

vi. Decision. The judgmental accuracy index for each subject in each condition of the study is summarized in Table 8.6. If we rank these 12 data from lowest to highest, we obtain the ranks shown in Table 8.7. These ranks are summed for the three groups to obtain $R_1 = 17$, $R_2 = 21$, and $R_3 = 40$, as shown in Table 8.7. Also given in that table are the average ranks for each group, 5.67, 5.25, and 8.00 respectively.

Now with these data, we may compute the value of KW by using Eq. (8.3):

$$KW = \left[\frac{12}{N(N+1)} \sum_{j=1}^{k} n_j \bar{R}_j^2\right] - 3(N+1) \tag{8.3}$$

$$= \frac{12}{12(12+1)}[3(5.67)^2 + 4(5.25)^2 + 5(8.00)^2] - 3(12+1)$$

$$= 1.51$$

TABLE 8.6
Judgmental accuracy indexes for subjects learning relation $X + Y + c$

Training		
Irrelevant cue first	**Valid cue first**	**Both cues**
.994	.795	.940
.872	.884	.979
.349	.816	.949
	.981	.890
		.978

TABLE 8.7
Judgmental accuracy indexes for subjects learning relation $X + Y + c$ (ranked data)

	Training		
	Irrelevant cue first	**Valid cue first**	**Both cues**
	12	2	7
	4	5	10
	1	3	8
		11	6
			9
R_j	17	21	40
$\bar{R}_j$	5.67	5.25	8

Reference to Appendix Table O discloses that when the n_j's are 3, 4, and 5, $KW \geq 1.51$ has probability of occurrence under the null hypothesis of no difference among the groups exceeding .10. Thus, we cannot reject H_0 for these data.[6]

TIED OBSERVATIONS. When ties occur between two or more scores (regardless of group), each score is given the mean of the ranks for which it is tied.

Since the variance of the sampling distribution of KW is influenced by ties, one may wish to correct for ties in the calculation of KW. To correct for the effect of ties, KW is computed by using Eq. (8.3) and then divided by

$$1 - \frac{\sum_{i=1}^{g} (t_i^3 - t_i)}{N^3 - N} \tag{8.4}$$

where g = number of groupings of different tied ranks

t_i = number of tied ranks in the ith grouping

N = total number of observations across all samples

As usual, the magnitude of the correction factor depends upon the sizes of the groups of ties, i.e., the values of the t_i as well as the percentage of observations involved. This point was discussed in Sec. 6.6.4.

Thus a general expression for KW corrected for ties is

$$KW = \frac{\left[\frac{12}{N(N+1)} \sum_{j=1}^{k} n_j \bar{R}_j^2\right] - 3(N+1)}{1 - \left[\sum_{i=1}^{g} (t_i^3 - t_i)\right] \Big/ (N^3 - N)} \tag{8.5}$$

The effect of correcting for ties is to increase the value of KW and thus to make the result more significant than it would have been had no correction been made. Therefore, if one is able to reject H_0 without making the correction [i.e., by using Eq. (8.3) for computing KW], one will be able to reject H_0 at an even more stringent level of significance if the correction is used.

Frequently, the effect of the correction is negligible. If no more than about 25 percent of the observations are involved in ties, the probability associated with a KW computed without the correction for ties, i.e., by use of Eq. (8.3), is rarely

[6] The reader should be cautioned concerning the failure to find a significant difference in this (and other examples). Failure to reject H_0 *does not imply* that H_0 may be accepted and that there are no differences between the groups. When the sample sizes are small, only relatively large differences are detected by our statistical procedures which lead to rejection of H_0. This is because when the sample size is small and H_0 is in fact true, the probability of large variation in outcomes is also large. As a consequence, it is difficult to distinguish between outcomes reflecting merely chance deviations (when H_0 is true) and true differences (when H_1 is true). If H_0 is not rejected, then there in fact may be no differences between the groups—or the sample sizes may be so small and/or the variability in the sample so large and/or the true differences so small that true differences can not be detected. Before *accepting* H_0 in such cases the researcher should seek corroborating evidence or obtain additional data. As a final note, this caution does not imply that we should not have confidence in the differences between groups if we are able to reject H_0 at a given significance level. These arguments apply with equal force to both parametric and nonparametric tests.

changed by more than 20 percent when the correction is made, that is, if KW is computed with Eq. (8.5).

In the following example there are ties in observations, and the value of KW is computed with and without the correction to illustrate the effect that ties have on the statistic in this case.

Example 8.3b For large samples. As part of the programmatic research described in the example for small samples in this section, another experiment focused on learning functional relations of the form $aX + bY = Z$. As in the experiment described earlier, cue X was partially valid, cue Y was irrelevant, and a and b were constants. If a subject solved the problem, a correct response could be made on every trial. Subjects were assigned to one of three conditions—the same conditions as in the earlier example. The subjects initially learned with both predictors or with one of the two predictors, either the partially valid cue or the irrelevant cue, and then made predictions by using both predictors for the balance of the experimental session. The experimental hypothesis was that the initial training mode would have an effect on the final performance in the prediction task.

i. *Null hypothesis.* H_0: there is no difference among the three groups in final levels of accuracy in the prediction task. H_1: the groups differ in final levels of performance in the prediction task.

ii. *Statistical test.* Since the three groups are independent, a statistical test for k independent samples is appropriate. Since the index of judgmental accuracy is continuous and on an ordered scale, the assumptions for the Kruskal-Wallis test are satisfied.

iii. *Significance level.* Let $\alpha = .05$ and N is the total number of subjects in the experiment = 18.

iv. *Sampling distribution.* Since the sample sizes exceed five, the sampling distribution of KW is approximately distributed as χ^2 with $df = k - 1$. Thus the probability associated with the occurrence when H_0 is true of values as large as an observed KW may be determined by reference to Appendix Table C.

v. *Rejection region.* The region of rejection consists of all values of KW which are so large that the probability associated with their occurrence when H_0 is true when $df = k - 1 = 2$ is equal to or less than $\alpha = .05$.

vi. *Decision.* The terminal values of the accuracy index are summarized in Table 8.8 for each subject in each condition. If the $N = 18$ data are ranked from lowest to highest, we obtain the ranks shown in Table 8.9. Observe that the data have been ranked in a single series as is required by this test. The smallest score is .21 and is given rank 1. There is a three-way tie for the largest score of .80; thus the highest rank is 17, $[(16 + 17 + 18)/3 = 17]$. Also shown in Table 8.9 are the sums of ranks (the R_j's) for each group and the average ranking within each group (the $\bar{R}_j$'s).

With the data in Table 8.9, we may compute the value of KW, uncorrected for ties, by using Eq. (8.3):

$$KW = \left[\frac{12}{N(N+1)} \sum_{j=1}^{k} n_j \bar{R}_j^2\right] - 3(N+1) \tag{8.3}$$

$$= \frac{12}{18(18+1)} [6(4.17)^2 + 6(10.83)^2 + 6(13.50)^2] - 3(18+1)$$

$$= 66.72 - 57$$

$$= 9.72$$

TABLE 8.8
Judgmental accuracy indexes for subjects learning the relation $aX + bY$

Training		
Irrelevant cue first	Valid cue first	Both cues
.44	.70	.80
.44	.77	.76
.54	.48	.34
.32	.64	.80
.21	.71	.73
.28	.75	.80

TABLE 8.9
Judgmental accuracy indexes for subjects learning the relation $aX + bY$ (ranked data)

	Training		
	Irrelevant cue first	Valid cue first	Both cues
	5.5	10	17
	5.5	15	14
	8	7	4
	3	9	17
	1	11	12
	2	13	17
R_j	25	65	81
$\bar{R}_j$	4.17	10.83	13.50

Reference to Appendix Table *C* indicates that a $KW \geq 5.99$ with $df = 3 - 1 = 2$ has probability of occurrence when H_0 is true of $p < 0.5$. Thus, since the observed value of KW (9.72) exceeds 5.99, the hypothesis of no difference in judgmental accuracy is rejected, and we conclude that there are differences among the groups trained in different ways. Indeed, inspection of Table 8.9 show that subjects in the irrelevant-cue-first condition performed much worse than subjects in either of the other two groups.

CORRECTION FOR TIES. To correct for ties, we must determine how many groups of ties occurred and how many scores were tied in each group. For these data, there are two groups of ties—two scores are tied at .44 (with a rank of 5.5), and three scores are tied at .80 (with a rank of 17). Thus, in applying the correction as given by Eq. (8.4), we have $g = 2$ is the number of groups of ties, $t_1 = 2$ is the number of ties in the first group of ties, and $t_2 = 3$ is the number of ties in the second group of ties. Thus, the correction is

$$1 - \frac{\sum_{i=1}^{g} (t_i^3 - t_i)}{N^3 - N} = 1 - \frac{(2^3 - 2) + (3^3 - 3)}{18^3 - 18} \tag{8.4}$$

$$= 1 - \frac{(8 - 2) + (27 - 3)}{5832 - 18}$$

$$= 1 - .005$$

$$= .995$$

When the correction for ties is applied to the value of KW found earlier, the corrected value is $KW = 8.72/.995 = 8.76$. Of course, since H_0 was rejected with the first value obtained, it will be rejected with the corrected value as well. It should be noted that even with 5 of the 18 observations involved in ties, the correction produced a very small change in KW.

8.3.3 Multiple Comparisons Between Treatments

When the obtained value of KW is significant, it indicates that at least one of the groups is different from at least one of the others. It does not tell the researcher which ones are different, nor does it tell the researcher how many of the groups are different from each other. What is needed is a procedure which will enable us to determine which groups are different. That is, we would like to test the hypothesis H_0: $\theta_u = \theta_v$ against the hypothesis H_1: $\theta_u \neq \theta_v$ for some groups u and v. There is a simple procedure for determining which pairs of groups are different. We begin by obtaining the differences $|\bar{R}_u - \bar{R}_v|$ for all pairs of groups. When the sample size is large, these differences are approximately normally distributed. However, since there are a large number of differences and because the differences are not independent, the comparison procedure must be adjusted appropriately. Suppose the hypothesis of no difference among k groups was tested and rejected at the α level of significance. We can test the significance of individual pairs of differences by using the following inequality. If

$$|\bar{R}_u - \bar{R}_v| \geq z_{\alpha/k(k-1)} \sqrt{\frac{N(N+1)}{12}\left(\frac{1}{n_u} + \frac{1}{n_v}\right)} \tag{8.6}$$

then we may reject the hypothesis H_0: $\theta_u = \theta_v$, and conclude that $\theta_u \neq \theta_v$. The value of $z_{\alpha/k(k-1)}$ is the abscissa value from the unit normal distribution above which lies $\alpha/k(k-1)$ percent of the distribution. The values of z can be obtained from Appendix Table A.

Because it is often necessary to obtain values based upon extremely small probabilities, especially when k is large, Appendix Table A_{II} may be used in place of Appendix Table A. This is a table of the standard normal distribution which has been arranged so that values used in multiple comparisons may be obtained easily. The table is arranged on the basis of the number of comparisons which can be made. The tabled values are the values of z associated with various values of α. The row entries ($\#c$) are the number of comparisons. When there are k groups, there are $k(k-1)/2$ comparisons possible.

Example 8.3c In the large-sample example in this section, we rejected H_0 and concluded that the medians were not equal. Since there are $k = 3$ groups, there are $3(3-1)/2 = 3$ comparisons possible. If we take the differences between the average rankings, we have

$$|\bar{R}_1 - \bar{R}_2| = |4.17 - 10.83| = 6.66$$

$$|\bar{R}_1 - \bar{R}_3| = |4.17 - 13.50| = 9.33$$

$$|\bar{R}_2 - \bar{R}_3| = |10.83 - 13.50| = 2.67$$

To find which of these comparisons is significant, we can apply the multiple-comparison test described in this section. It is necessary to find the critical value of z. Since we chose $\alpha = .05$ in the original analysis, the same level shall be used here, and since the number of comparisons is $\#c = k(k-1)/2 = 3(3-1)/2 = 3$, we may find the critical value of z from Appendix Table A_{II}; that value is $z = 2.394$. [This is the same value we would obtain from Appendix Table A: $z_{\alpha/k(k-1)} = z_{.05/3(3-1)} = z_{.0083} \approx 2.39$.] The critical difference is then found by using Eq. (8.6):

$$z_{\alpha/k(k-1)}\sqrt{\frac{N(N+1)}{12}\left(\frac{1}{n_u}+\frac{1}{n_v}\right)} = 2.394\sqrt{\frac{18(18+1)}{12}\left(\frac{1}{6}+\frac{1}{6}\right)} \tag{8.6}$$

$$= 2.394\sqrt{9.5}$$

$$= 7.38$$

Since only the difference between groups 1 and 3 (the irrelevant cue first versus both cues) exceeds the critical value 7.38, only that comparison was significant and it may be concluded that these medians are different.

It should be carefully noted that, in the application of Eq. (8.6) to the multiple comparisons in the above example, only a single critical difference was calculated. This was possible because each of the k groups was equal in size. Had the sample sizes been unequal, each of the observed differences would have to be compared against different critical differences.

COMPARISONS OF TREATMENTS VERSUS CONTROL. Sometimes a researcher includes a control group or standard group as one of the k groups. An example would be when a researcher wishes to assess the effects of various drugs on behavior. Although a major interest may be on whether the groups are different on the measured variable, the primary concern may be whether there is a difference between the behavior under administration of *any* of the drugs and behavior when no drug (or a placebo) is administered. In this case the researcher would still apply the Kruskal-Wallis one-way analysis of variance by ranks if the assumptions for its use were appropriate. However, if H_0 is rejected, the researcher is concerned about whether any of the drug groups differ from the control group. That is, if θ_c is the median for the control group, and θ_u is the median for the uth group, the researcher would like to test H_0: $\theta_c = \theta_u$ against H_1: $\theta_c \neq \theta_u$ (or perhaps H_1: $\theta_c > \theta_u$). Since we are not interested in comparing all groups, the multiple-comparison method given by Eq. (8.6) must be adjusted to account for the smaller number of comparisons. When there are k groups in the overall test, there will be $k - 1$ comparisons with a control; thus $\#c = k - 1$. The appropriate relations for the multiple comparisons in this case are the following:

To test H_1: $\theta_c \neq \theta_u$,

$$|\bar{R}_c - \bar{R}_u| \geq z_{\alpha/2(k-1)}\sqrt{\frac{N(N+1)}{12}\left(\frac{1}{n_c}+\frac{1}{n_u}\right)} \tag{8.7}$$

To test H_1: $\theta_c > \theta_u$,

$$\bar{R}_c - \bar{R}_u > z_{\alpha/(k-1)}\sqrt{\frac{N(N+1)}{12}\left(\frac{1}{n_c}+\frac{1}{n_u}\right)} \tag{8.8}$$

The critical values of z may be found by using Appendix Table A or Appendix Table A_{II} with $\#c = k - 1$. [*Note*: If the sample sizes for *all* groups are equal, a better approximation is obtained if the z values in Eqs. (8.7) and (8.8) are replaced by $q(\alpha, \#c)$ and Appendix Table A_{III} is used. (See Sec. 7.2.4 on the use of that table.)]

8.3.4 Summary of Procedure

These are the steps in the use of the Kruskal-Wallis one-way analysis of variance by ranks:

1. Rank all of the observations for the k groups in a single series, assigning ranks from 1 to N. (Tied observations are assigned the value of the average of the tied ranks.)
2. Determine the values R_j (the sum of the ranks) and $\bar{R}_j$ (the average of the ranks) for each of the k groups of ranks.
3. If a large proportion of the observations are tied, compute the value of KW by using Eq. (8.5); otherwise, use Eq. (8.3).
4. The method for determining the significance of the observed value of KW depends on the number of groups (k) and on the sizes of the groups (n_j):
   (*a*) If $k = 3$ and if $n_1, n_2, n_3 \leq 5$, Appendix Table O should be used to determine, under the assumption that H_0 is true, the associated probability of a KW as large as that observed.
   (*b*) In other cases, the significance of a value as large as the observed value of KW may be assessed by reference to Appendix Table C, with $df = k - 1$.
5. If the probability associated with the observed value of KW is equal to or less than the previously set level of significance α, reject H_0 in favor of H_1.
6. If H_0 is rejected, the method of multiple comparisons [Eq. (8.6)] may be used to determine which differences are significant. If the test involves a treatment versus control comparison, the comparison method given by Eqs. (8.7) or (8.8) should be used.

8.3.5 Power-Efficiency

Compared with the most powerful parametric test, the F test, and under conditions where the assumptions associated with the statistical model of the parametric analysis of variance are met, the Kruskal-Wallis test has asymptotic efficiency of $3/\pi = 95.5$ percent.

The Kruskal-Wallis test is more efficient than the extension of the median test because it utilizes more of the information in the observations, converting the scores into ranks rather than simply dichotomizing them as above or below the median.

8.3.6 References

The reader will find discussions of the one-way analysis of variance by ranks in Kruskal and Wallis (1952) and in Kruskal (1952). Other useful discussions may be found in Lehmann (1975) and Hettmansperger (1984).

8.4 THE JONCKHEERE TEST FOR ORDERED ALTERNATIVES

8.4.1 Function

The Kruskal-Wallis one-way analysis of variance by ranks tests the hypothesis that k independent groups or samples are the same against the alternative hypothesis that one or more of the groups differ from the others. However, in some experimental situations, the researcher may wish to entertain a more specific alternative hypothesis. For example, in an experiment on the effect of various dosages of drugs on performance in learning tasks, the researcher may wish to test the hypothesis of "no difference" against the hypothesis that increased dosages will result in increased impairment in performance. In this case the alternative hypothesis associated with the Kruskal-Wallis one-way analysis of variance by ranks, although valid, is too general. The *Jonckheere test for ordered alternatives* which is presented in this section tests the hypothesis that the samples (or groups) are ordered in a specific *a priori* sequence. To specify the null hypothesis and its alternative more explicitly, let θ_j be the population median for the jth group or sample. Then we may write the null hypothesis that the medians are the same as H_0: $\theta_1 = \theta_2 = \cdots = \theta_k$; and the alternative hypothesis may be written as H_1: $\theta_1 \leq \theta_2 \leq \cdots \leq \theta_k$, that is, the medians are ordered in magnitude. If the alternative hypothesis is true, at least one of the differences is a strict inequality ($<$). It is important to note that in order to ensure proper use of the test, the researcher must be able to specify the order of the groups or measures *a priori*. That is to say, one cannot look at the k medians and, on that basis, specify the alternative hypothesis. The ordering must be specified *before* the data are collected.

To apply the Jonckheere test, the data for the k independent samples or groups must be on at least an ordinal scale, and under the null hypothesis it is assumed that each sample is from the same population. We shall assume that there are N cases or observations of which there are n_j data in the jth group.

8.4.2 Rationale and Method

To apply the Jonckheere test for ordered alternatives, the researcher must first specify the *a priori* ordering of groups. The data are then cast into a two-way table with each column representing each successive sample or group arranged in the hypothesized order of medians. That is, the groups are ordered with the first group being the one with the smallest hypothesized median and group k being the group with the largest hypothesized median. Thus the data would be arranged in the following manner:

Group			
1	2	...	k
X_{11}	X_{12}	...	X_{1k}
X_{21}	X_{22}	...	X_{2k}
⋮			⋮
$X_{n_1 1}$	⋮		
		...	$X_{n_k k}$
	$X_{n_2 2}$		

The Jonckheere test involves counting the number of times an observation in the ith group or sample is preceded by an observation in the jth group or sample. Although the counting procedure appears to be rather tedious, it is actually fairly straightforward if the computational procedures are set up systematically.

First, we define the statistic, sometimes called the Mann-Whitney count,

$$U_{ij} = \sum_{h=1}^{n_i} \#(X_{hi}, j) \tag{8.9}$$

where $\#(X_{hi}, j)$ is the number of times the datum X_{hi} precedes (is smaller than) a datum in the sample j, where $i < j$. The Jonckheere test statistic J is then the total number of these counts:

$$J = \sum_{i<j}^{k} U_{ij} = \sum_{i=1}^{k-1} \sum_{j=i+1}^{k} U_{ij} \tag{8.10}$$

The sampling distribution of J has been tabled for small-sample sizes and is given in Appendix Table P. Entries in that table give the probabilities associated with values of J as large or larger than the tabled values for various values of J, the n_j's, and significance probability α. The reader should note that the table has two distinct parts. In the first part, the distribution of J for $k = 3$ and n_j's less than 9 are tabled, and in the second part, the distribution of J for $k = 4, 5, 6$ with equal n_j's up to 6 is tabled. If the observed value of J is greater than the tabled value for the chosen significance level, then the hypothesis H_0 may be rejected in favor of the alternative hypothesis H_1. For example, consider an example in which there are $k = 3$ groups and $n_1 = 3$, $n_2 = 4$, and $n_3 = 4$. A significance level of $\alpha = .05$ was chosen. The calculated value of the Jonckheere statistic was $J = 26$. Reference to Appendix Table P shows that the probability of observing a value of $J \geq 26$ exceeds .10; therefore we could not reject the hypothesis H_0 that the medians for the three groups are equal.

As the sample size becomes large, the sampling distribution of J is approximately normal, with mean

$$\mu_J = \frac{N^2 - \sum_{j=1}^{k} n_j^2}{4} \tag{8.11}$$

and variance

$$\sigma_J^2 = \frac{1}{72}\left[N^2(2N + 3) - \sum_{j=1}^{k} n_j^2(2n_j + 3)\right] \tag{8.12}$$

Thus the statistic

$$J^* = \frac{J - \mu_J}{\sigma_J} \tag{8.13}$$

is approximately normally distributed with mean zero and standard deviation one. Therefore, Appendix Table A may be used to test hypotheses about J^* and, hence, J. Of course, since the alternatives are ordered, the test is considered to be a one-tailed test.

Example 8.4 When sucrose and NaCl (salt) are mixed, a mutual masking of the judged sweetness and saltiness of the mixtures has been reported. There are several factors which affect the amount of masking. One is the type of masking compound used (e.g., quinine) and another is the concentration of the compound used. A third factor is the relative proportion of test stimuli to neutral or background stimuli. Experiments involving judgments of taste are often psychophysical tasks involving many trials, some with the relevant stimuli (signal trials) and the rest with the stimulus and the mixture (signal plus noise trials). In an experiment designed to assess the effect of the relative proportion of pure and mixed stimuli on judgments, Kroeze[7] varied the relative numbers of pure and mixed stimuli in a taste experiment. Such frequency effects in other behavioral areas have been reported and have been consistent with an explanation derived from Helson's adaptation level theory.[8] In a series of four independent samples, the physical intensity (= concentration) of the NaCl was held constant at .32 mole/l; in the test stimuli, the sucrose concentration was also held constant at .32 mole/l. Across the groups, the relative frequency [NaCl/(NaCl + sucrose)] of test trials was varied. The individual saltiness judgments for the various ratios are given in Table 8.10. Kroeze hypothesized that the judged saltiness would increase as the relative proportion of NaCl test trials decreased.

i. *Null hypothesis.* H_0: the relative mixtures of NaCl trials and NaCl + sucrose trials has no effect on saltiness judgment. H_1: subjects' judgments of saltiness is inversely related to the proportion of NaCl test trials in the experiment.

---

[7] Kroeze, J. H. A. (1982). The influence of relative frequencies of pure and mixed stimuli on mixture suppression in taste. *Perception & Psychophysics*, **31**, 276–278.

[8] Helson, H. (1964). *Adaptation-level theory*. New York: Harper & Row.

TABLE 8.10
Individual saltiness judgments of the mixture stimuli as a function of the percentage of pure-NaCl saltiness

Percentage of pure-NaCl stimuli			
80	**50**	**17**	**10**
8.82	13.53	19.23	73.51
11.27	28.42	67.83	85.25
15.78	48.11	73.68	85.82
17.39	48.64	75.22	88.88
24.99	51.40	77.71	90.33
39.05	59.91	83.67	118.11
47.54	67.98	86.83	
48.85	79.13	93.25	
71.66	103.05		
72.77			
90.38			
103.13			

Note: Each column represents a separate and independent sample of observations. Data have been arranged in increasing order within each group to facilitate computation of the U_{ij}. If the computer routine is used, ordering of data within each sample is not necessary.

ii. *Statistical test.* Because the experimenter hypothesized an ordering for the saltiness judgments, a test for ordered alternatives is appropriate. Since the test involves independent groups (a different group of subjects was used for each relative mixture), the Jonckheere test for ordered alternatives is appropriate.

iii. *Significance level.* Let $\alpha = .05$. The number of subjects is $n_1 = 12, n_2 = 9, n_3 = 8, n_4 = 6$ in the four groups.

iv. *Sampling distribution.* Because the samples are of unequal size and the number of groups is greater than three, the large-sample size approximation to the sampling distribution of the Jonckheere statistic will be used; that is, the statistic J^* defined in Eq. (8.13) will be calculated and its significance probability determined by using Appendix Table A.

v. *Rejection region.* The region of rejection consists of all values of J^* which are larger than 1.645, the value of the standard normal distribution associated with $\alpha = .05$.

vi. *Decision.* With the use of the data in Table 8.10, the U_{ij} statistics were computed and are summarized in Table 8.11. For example, consider the datum 47.54 in group 1. It precedes seven data in group 2 (48.11, 48.64, 51.40, 59.91, 79.13, 67.98, 103.05), seven data in group 3 (67.83, 73.68, 75.22, 77.71, 83.67, 86.83, 93.25), and all six data in group 4. The U_{ij} are the column sums of the precedence counts in Table 8.11. Thus, the value of the Jonckheere statistic for these data is

$$J = 66 + 73 + 62 + 52 + 48 + 36$$
$$= 337$$

TABLE 8.11
Precedence counts $\#(X_{hi}, j)$ for data in Table 8.10

				Percentage of pure-NaCl stimuli						
				80			**50**		**17**	**10**
i	**1**	**1**	**1**		**2**	**2**		**3**		
j	**2**	**3**	**4**		**3**	**4**		**4**		
	9	8	6	8.82	8	6	13.53	6	19.23	73.51
	9	8	6	11.27	7	6	28.42	6	67.83	85.25
	8	8	6	15.78	7	6	48.11	5	73.68	85.82
	8	8	6	17.39	7	6	48.64	5	75.22	88.88
	8	7	6	24.99	7	6	51.40	5	77.71	90.33
	7	7	6	39.05	7	6	59.91	5	83.67	118.11
	7	7	6	47.54	6	6	67.98	3	86.83	
	5	7	6	48.85	3	5	79.13	1	93.25	
	2	6	6	71.66	0	1	103.05			
	2	6	6	72.77						
	1	1	1	90.38						
	0	0	1	103.13						
U_{ij}	66	73	62		52	48		36		

It is necessary to calculate the mean and variance of the statistic J with Eqs. (8.11) and (8.12):

$$\mu_J = \frac{N^2 - \sum_{j=1}^{k} n_j^2}{4} \tag{8.11}$$

$$= \frac{35^2 - 12^2 - 9^2 - 8^2 - 6^2}{4}$$

$$= 225$$

and
$$\sigma_J^2 = \frac{1}{72}\left[N^2(2N+3) - \sum_{j=1}^{k} n_j^2(2n_j+3)\right] \tag{8.12}$$

$$= \tfrac{1}{72}\{35^2(70+3) - [12^2(24+3) + 9^2(18+3) + 8^2(16+3) + 6^2(12+3)]\}$$

$$= 1140$$

With these values we may calculate J^*:

$$J^* = \frac{J - \mu_J}{\sigma_J} \tag{8.13}$$

$$= \frac{337 - 225}{33.76}$$

$$= 3.32$$

Since the observed value of J^* exceeds the critical value of 1.645, we may reject the hypothesis of equal medians for the four groups and conclude that they are increasing in magnitude. (It should be noted that rejection of H_0 implies that at least one median is greater than one earlier in the sequence.)

TIED OBSERVATIONS. When ties occur between two or more scores when determining the precedence counts [Eq. (8.9)], the count should be increased by $\frac{1}{2}$ (rather than 1) for each tie. As with the Kruskal-Wallis test, the variance of J [Eq. (8.12)] is affected by ties, but unless the number of ties is great or there are many data tied at a single value, the effect on the sampling distribution of J^* is negligible.

8.4.3 Summary of Procedure

These are the steps in the use of the Jonckheere test for ordered alternatives:

1. Cast the scores into a two-way table in which the k columns represent the samples or groups arranged in their *a priori* order from smallest hypothesized median to the largest hypothesized median.
2. Calculate the precedence counts and Mann-Whitney counts (the U_{ij}) by using Eq. (8.9).
3. Determine the Jonckheere test statistic J which is the sum of the counts determined in step 2.
4. The method for determining the significance of the observed value of J depends upon the number of groups (k), and on the sizes of the groups or samples (n_j):
   (*a*) If $k = 3$ and if n_1, n_2, and $n_3 \leq 8$, Appendix Table P should be used to determine, under the assumption that H_0 is true, the associated probability of J being as large as the value observed.
   (*b*) If $k = 4$, 5, or 6, and the sample sizes (n_j's) are equal and less than seven, Appendix Table P should be used to determine, under the assumption that H_0 is true, the associated probability of J being as large as that observed.
   (*c*) If either the number of groups or the number of observations in a group is too large to use Appendix Table P, the statistic J^* should be calculated with Eq. (8.13), and the probability associated with its value determined with the use of Appendix Table A.

   If the value of J (or J^*) is large enough that one may reject H_0, the researcher may apply the multiple comparison techniques of Sec. 8.3.3. However, in this case, the comparisons are one-tailed and the value of z must be adjusted accordingly.
5. To facilitate the computation of J and J^*, the reader may wish to use a computer program such as the one in the Appendix. In the example in this section the computations were worked out in detail. Those results may be checked by using the sample program which includes the data as an example.

8.4.4 Power-Efficiency

The asymptotic efficiency of the Jonckheere test is $3/\pi = 95.5$ percent when compared against an appropriate t (or F) test for ordered alternatives. Thus, when compared with the appropriate parametric test for normally distributed data, the efficiency of the Jonckheere test is the same as that of the Kruskal-Wallis test.

8.4.5 References

The Jonckheere test for ordered alternatives is discussed by Jonckheere (1954), Lehmann (1975), and Terpstra (1952). Discussion of the relative efficiency of the Jonckheere test may be found in Puri (1975). Potter and Strum (1981) have discussed the rapidity with which the power of the Jonckheere test increases. Formulas for the correction of the variance when there are ties may be found in Lehmann (1975).

8.5 DISCUSSION

Four nonparametric statistical tests for analyzing data from k independent groups or samples were presented in this chapter.

The first of these, the chi-square test for k independent samples, is useful when the data are in frequencies and when measurement of the variables under study is in a nominal or categorical scale. The chi-square test could also be used when the data are in discrete categories in an ordinal scale; however, some of the other methods discussed in this chapter may be more appropriate in such cases. The chi-square test tests whether the proportions or frequencies in the various categories are independent of the condition (sample or group) under which they were observed, i.e., it tests the null hypothesis that the k samples have come from the same population or from identical populations with respect to the proportion of observations in the various categories.

The second test presented, the extension of the median test, requires at least ordinal measurement of the variable under study in order for proper interpretation to be made of the results of the analysis. It tests whether k independent groups or samples could have been drawn from populations having identical medians.

The Kruskal-Wallis one-way analysis of variance by ranks, the third test discussed, requires at least ordinal measurement of the variable. It tests whether k independent samples or groups could have been drawn from the same population or identical populations with the same continuous (but unknown) distribution of responses.

The fourth test discussed, the Jonckheere test for ordered alternatives, requires that the variables be measured on an ordinal scale. It tests the hypothesis that k independent samples or groups could have been drawn from the same population or identical populations with the same continuous (but unknown) distribution against the alternative hypothesis that the medians of the distributions are ordered in magnitude according to some *a priori* hypothesis.

We have no choice among these tests if the data are in frequencies rather than scores, i.e., if we have enumeration data or if the measurement is not stronger than nominal or categorical. The chi-square test for k independent samples is the best test among those presented in this chapter for such data.

The extension of the median test, the Kruskal-Wallis test, and the Jonckheere test may each be applied to the same data, i.e., they each make similar assumptions under H_0—that the variables come from populations having identical continuous distributions. When the data are such that either the median or the Kruskal-Wallis test might be used, the Kruskal-Wallis test will be found to be more efficient because it uses more of the information available in the observations. It converts the scores to ranks, whereas the extension of the median test converts the scores simply to either pluses (+'s) or minuses (−'s) depending upon whether the data are above or below the median. Thus the Kruskal-Wallis test preserves the magnitude of the observed data more fully than does the extension of the median test. For this reason it is usually more sensitive to differences among the k samples or groups. However, as noted in the discussion of the median test in Chap. 6, there may be situations involving ordered data for which the median test is the only alternative. This would occur when some of the values of the measured variable are too extreme to be coded and ranked accurately. In such a case, the median test could be applied but the ranks cannot be determined in order to apply the Kruskal-Wallis or the Jonckheere tests.

If there is an *a priori* ordering to the population medians of the groups, the Jonckheere test will be more powerful than the Kruskal-Wallis test. This is because it is more specific to the hypothesis being tested than the Kruskal-Wallis test.

One characteristic of the four tests presented in this chapter is that the test statistic, if significant, allows us to conclude that there are differences among the k groups. However, none of the tests tell us what the differences are. Fortunately, there are procedures which can help the researcher to locate the differences. For the chi-square test and the extension of the median test, the degrees of freedom may be partitioned to help locate the differences; in addition, analysis of residuals can provide further details about just where the significant differences are in the table. In the case of the Kruskal-Wallis and the Jonckheere tests, we can use multiple-comparison techniques to help determine which group differences are significant. Although the partitioning and multiple-comparison techniques are powerful tools for isolating effects, the researcher must be careful to apply these procedures only to data for which the overall test is significant.

There are several other nonparametric tests for differences among k independent samples or groups. One of these is the k-sample test of slippage (Mosteller, 1948; Mosteller and Tukey, 1950). Chacko (1963) and Puri (1965) have proposed tests that are generalizations of the Jonckheere test. Perhaps the most useful of these tests is the *umbrella* test (Mack and Wolfe, 1981) which tests the hypothesis that the medians, according to some *a priori* assumptions, first increase to a maximum and then decrease. That is, it tests the hypothesis H_0: $\theta_1 = \theta_2 = \cdots = \theta_k$ against the hypothesis H_1: $\theta_1 \leq \theta_2 \leq \cdots \leq \theta_h \geq \cdots \geq \theta_{k-1} \geq \theta_k$ for some predetermined group h. This test is relatively simple in that it is like performing *two* Jonckheere tests—one for one set of inequalities and one for the other set of inequalities.

CHAPTER 9

MEASURES OF ASSOCIATION AND THEIR TESTS OF SIGNIFICANCE

In research in the behavioral sciences, we frequently wish to know whether two sets of scores are related and if they are, the degree of their relation. Establishing that a correlation exists between two variables may be the ultimate aim of a research study, as in some studies of personality dynamics, person perception, intragroup similarity, etc. Or establishing a correlation may be but one step in a study having other ends, as in the case when we use measures of correlation to test the reliability of our observations.

This chapter is devoted to the presentation of nonparametric measures of correlation and statistical tests which determine the probability associated with the occurrence of a correlation as large as the one observed in the sample under the null hypothesis that the variables are independent or unrelated in the population. That is, in addition to presenting measures of association, we shall present statistical tests which determine the "significance" of the observed association. The problem of measuring *degree* of association between two sets of scores is more general in character than that of testing for the *existence* of some degree of association in some population. It is, of course, of some interest to be able to state the degree of association between two sets of scores obtained from a given group of subjects. But it is perhaps of greater interest to be able to say whether or not some observed association in a *sample* of scores indicates that the variables under study are associated in the *population* from which the sample was drawn. The observed correlation itself represents an estimate of the degree of association. Tests of significance of that coefficient determine, at a stated level of confidence, the probability that random samples from a population in which there was no association between the variables would yield a correlation as large as (or larger than) the one obtained.

In the parametric case, the usual measure of correlation is the Pearson product-moment correlation coefficient r. This statistic requires variables which represent measurement in at least an equal-interval scale for proper interpretation of the statistic. If we wish to test the significance of an observed value or r, we must not only meet the measurement requirement but also assume that the observations are sampled from a bivariate normal distribution. Moreover, the Pearson product-moment correlation coefficient measures the degree to which there is a linear functional relation between the variables.

If, for a given set of data, the assumptions associated with the Pearson product-moment correlation coefficient r are not tenable or are unrealistic, then one of the nonparametric correlation coefficients and associated significance tests presented in this chapter may be used. Nonparametric measures of correlation are available for both categorical and ordered data. The tests make no or few assumptions about the population distribution from which the scores were drawn. Some assume that the variables have underlying continuity, whereas others do not even make this assumption. Some test for monotonic (but not necessarily linear) relations between the variables, whereas others measure association of any form. Moreover, the researcher will find that, especially with small samples, the computation of nonparametric measures of association and tests of significance is no harder and often is easier than the computation of the Pearson r.

The uses and limitations of each measure will be discussed as the measure is presented. A discussion comparing the merits and uses of the various measures will be offered at the end of the chapter.

9.1 THE CRAMÉR COEFFICIENT C

9.1.1 Function

The *Cramér coefficient C* is a measure of the degree of association or relation between two sets of attributes or variables. It is uniquely useful when we have only categorical (nominal scale) information about one or both sets of attributes or variables. That is, it may be used when the information about the attributes consists of an unordered series of categories.

To use the Cramér coefficient, it is not necessary to assume underlying continuity for the various categories used to measure either or both sets of attributes. In fact, we do not even need to be able to order the categories in any particular way. The Cramér coefficient, as computed from a contingency table, will have the same value regardless of how the categories are arranged in the rows and columns.

9.1.2 Method

We begin by assuming that we have data on two sets of nonordered categorical variables. For convenience, we shall denote these variables as A and B. To compute the Cramér coefficient between scores on two sets of categorical variables A, with categories $A_1, A_2, \ldots, A_k$, and B, with categories $B_1, B_2, \ldots, B_r$, we arrange the frequencies into the following contingency table.

	A_1	A_2	$\cdots$	A_k	Total
B_1	n_{11}	n_{12}	$\cdots$	n_{1k}	R_1
B_2	n_{21}	n_{22}	$\cdots$	n_{2k}	R_2
$\vdots$	$\vdots$	$\vdots$		$\vdots$	$\vdots$
B_r	n_{r1}	n_{r2}	$\cdots$	n_{rk}	R_r
Total	C_1	C_2	$\cdots$	C_k	N

The data may consist of any number of categories. That is, one may compute a Cramér coefficient for data from a 2×2 table, a 2×5 table, a 4×4 table, a 3×7 table, or any $r \times k$ table.

In such a table, we may enter expected frequencies for each cell (the E_{ij}'s) by determining what frequencies would be expected to occur if there were no association between the two variables, that is, the frequencies expected in each cell if the variables were independent of unrelated. The larger the discrepancy between these expected cell values and the observed cell values, the higher is the degree of association between the two variables and, thus, the larger is the value of the Cramér coefficient.

The degree of association between two sets of attributes as measured by the Cramér coefficient, whether orderable or not and irrespective of the nature of the variable (it may be either continuous or discrete) or of the underlying distribution of the attribute (the population distribution may be normal or any other shape), may be found from a contingency table of frequencies of observations by

$$C = \sqrt{\frac{X^2}{N(L-1)}} \tag{9.1}$$

where

$$X^2 = \sum_{i=1}^{r} \sum_{j=1}^{k} \frac{(n_{ij} - E_{ij})^2}{E_{ij}} \tag{6.2}$$

or

$$X^2 = \sum_{i=1}^{r} \sum_{j=1}^{k} \frac{n_{ij}^2}{E_{ij}} - N \tag{6.2a}$$

is computed by the method presented earlier (in Sec. 6.2) and L is the *minimum* of the number of rows or columns in the contingency table. In other words, in order to compute C, one first computes the value of X^2 with Eq. (6.2) and then inserts that value into Eq. (9.1) to obtain C. It should be noted that, like the Pearson product-moment correlation, the Cramér coefficient has a maximum value of 1, and C will be equal to 0 when the variables or attributes are independent. Unlike the Pearson product-moment correlation, the Cramér coefficient cannot be negative. This is to be expected, since the statistic measures the relation between categorical variables which have no inherent order to them.

Example 9.1*a* [1] As part of a study concerning the process by which financial accounting standards are modified, Hussein[2] developed a survey questionnaire which was to be sent to members of the Financial Accounting Standards Board (FASB) advisory council and to members of various committees which specialize in financial accounting standards in FASB's sponsoring organizations. The FASB is the organization by which changes in accounting standards and procedures must be approved. The survey, the details of which are not relevant to this example, was designed to assess the informational, economic, organizational, and cognitive factors involved in the process of setting the standards. In survey research, it is rare for the response rate to mailed surveys to be large. However, in order for a survey of the various groups to be meaningful, the response rate from the various organizations should be similar. If it is not, then the responses (or nonresponses) from one group may yield a biased view of the overall process.

To determine whether the initial response rate was associated with organization, i.e., varied between the various sponsoring organizations, data concerning response rate were analyzed. There were six organizations or groups receiving questionnaires ($k = 6$), and there were three possible dispositions for each questionnaire—received and completed, declined, and no response ($r = 3$). These data are summarized in Table 9.1.

To calculate the Cramér coefficient C it is necessary to first calculate the chi-square statistic X^2. A first step in calculating X^2 is to find the expected values, the E_{ij}'s, for each

---

[1] In testing a measure of association for significance, we follow the same six steps which we have followed for all other statistical tests throughout this book. These steps are: (i) The null hypothesis H_0 is that the two variables are unrelated or independent in the population, whereas H_1 is that they are related or associated in the population. (ii) The statistical test is the significance test which is appropriate for the chosen measure of association. (iii) The level of significance is specified in advance, and may be any small probability, for example, $\alpha = .05$ or $\alpha = .01$, etc., while N is the number of cases for which there are scores on both variables. (iv) The sampling distribution is the theoretical distribution of the statistic used to test H_0, exact probabilities or critical values which are given in tables used to test the statistic for significance. (v) The rejection region consists of all values of the measure of association which are so extreme that the probability associated with their occurrence under H_0 is equal to or less than α (and a one-tailed region of rejection is used when the *sign* of the association is predicted in H_1). (vi) The decision consists of determining the observed value of the measure of association and then determining the probability, under the assumption that H_0 is true, of such an extreme value; if and only if that probability is equal to or less than α, the decision is to reject H_0 in favor of H_1.

Because the same or similar sets of data are repeatedly used for illustrative material in the discussions of the various measures of association in order to highlight the differences and similarities among these measures, the constant repetition of the six steps of statistical inference in the examples would lead to unnecessary redundancy. Therefore we have chosen not to include these six steps in the presentation of the examples in this chapter. We mention here that they might well have been included to point out to the reader that the decision-making procedure used in testing the significance of a measure of association is identical to the decision-making procedure used in other sorts of statistical tests.

[2] Hussein, M. E. (1981). The innovative process in financial accounting standards. *Accounting, Organizations, and Society*, **6**, 27–37.

TABLE 9.1
Responses to the survey questionnaire

Survey disposition	Organization						
	AAA	AICPA	FAF	FASB	FEI	NAA	Total
Completed	8	8	3	11	17	2	49
	7.49	*7.15*	*6.46*	*10.89*	*11.91*	*5.10*	
Declined	2	5	1	2	0	13	23
	3.51	*3.35*	*3.04*	*5.11*	*5.59*	*2.40*	
No response	12	8	15	19	18	0	72
	11.00	*10.50*	*9.50*	*16.00*	*17.50*	*7.50*	
Total	22	21	19	32	35	15	144

cell in the table. These are given in italics in Table 9.1. By using Eq. (6.2), we find the value of the chi-square statistic:

$$X^2 = \sum_{i=1}^{r} \sum_{j=1}^{k} \frac{(n_{ij} - E_{ij})^2}{E_{ij}} \tag{6.2}$$

$$= \frac{(8 - 7.49)^2}{7.49} + \frac{(8 - 7.15)^2}{7{:}15} + \cdots + \frac{(0 - 7.50)^2}{7.50}$$

$$= 75.25$$

Next, we use Eq. (9.1) to calculate C:

$$C = \sqrt{\frac{X^2}{N(L-1)}} \tag{9.1}$$

$$= \sqrt{\frac{75.25}{144(3-1)}}$$

$$= \sqrt{.2613}$$

$$= .51$$

Thus, we find that there is a moderate degree of association between survey response disposition and the organization to which the recipient belongs.

9.1.3 Testing the Significance of the Cramér Coefficient

The scores or observations we deal with in research are frequently from individuals in whom we are interested because they constitute a random sample from a population in which we are interested. When we observe a correlation between two sets of attributes in the sample, we may wish to determine whether it is plausible for us to conclude that they are associated in the population that is represented by the sample.

If a group of subjects constitutes a random sample from some population, we may determine whether the association that exists between two sets of scores from that sample indicates that an association exists in the population by testing the association for "significance." In testing the significance of a measure of association, we are testing the null hypothesis that there is no correlation in the population, i.e., that the observed value of the measure of association in the sample could have arisen by chance in a random sample from a population in which the two variables are independent, i.e., uncorrelated. The alternative hypothesis is that the variables are not independent.

To test the null hypothesis, we usually ascertain the null sampling distribution of the statistic (in this case the measure of association) under the assumption that H_0 is true. We then use an appropriate statistical test to determine whether the observed value of that statistic can reasonably be thought to have arisen under H_0, referring to some predetermined level of significance. If the probability associated with the occurrence under H_0 of a value as large as the observed value of the statistic is equal to or less than our predetermined level of significance, that is, if $p \leq \alpha$, then we may reject H_0 and conclude that the observed association in our sample is not a result of chance deviation from independence in the population but rather represents a genuine relation between the variables in the population. However, if the statistical test reveals that it is likely that our observed value might have arisen under H_0, that is, if $p > \alpha$, then our data do not permit us to conclude that there is a relation between the variables in the population from which the sample was drawn; that is, we cannot conclude that the variables are not independent in the population. This method of testing hypotheses should by now be thoroughly familiar to the reader. A fuller discussion of the method is given in Chap. 2, and illustrations of its use occur throughout this book.

Now the reader may know that the significance of the Pearson product-moment correlation coefficient r may be tested by exactly the method described above. Reading further in this chapter, one will discover that the significance of the various nonparametric measures of association is tested by just such a method. As it happens, however, the Cramér coefficient is a special case. One reason that we do not refer to the sampling distribution of C in order to test an observed C for significance is that the mathematical complexities of such a procedure are considerable. However, a better reason is that, in the course of computing the value of C, we compute a statistic which itself provides a simple and adequate indication of the significance of C. This statistic is, of course, X^2 which is distributed as χ^2 when the sample size is large. We may test whether an observed C differs significantly from zero simply by determining the significance of the X^2 statistic for the associated contingency table because C^2 is a linear function of X^2. Since we know the sampling distribution of X^2, we know that of C^2 and, hence, that of C.

For any $r \times k$ contingency table, we may determine the significance of the degree of association (the significance of C) by ascertaining the probability associated with the occurrence when H_0 is true of values as large as the observed value of X^2, with $df = (r - 1)(k - 1)$. If that probability is equal to or less than α, the null hypothesis may be rejected at that level of significance. Appendix Table C gives the probability associated with the occurrence under H_0 of values as large as an observed X^2. If the X^2 for the sample statistic is significant, then we may conclude that in the population the association between the two sets of attributes is not zero, that is, that the attributes or variables are not independent.

Example 9.1*b* We have shown in the last example that the relation between organization membership and survey response disposition is .51 as measured by the Cramér coefficient C. In the course of calculating C, we determined that $X^2 = 75.25$. Now if we consider the individuals to whom questionnaires were sent to be a random sample from the population of individuals responsible for the process of setting standards, that is, a population of people meeting the selection criteria of the study, we may test whether the organization membership is associated with response disposition by testing $X^2 = 75.25$ for significance. By referring to Appendix Table C, we may determine that $X^2 \geq 75.25$ with $df = (r - 1)(k - 1) = (3 - 1)(6 - 1) = 10$ has probability of occurrence when H_0 is true of less than .001. Thus we may reject H_0 at the $\alpha = .001$ level of significance, and conclude that the response disposition to the survey varies among the various organizations surveyed. That is, we conclude that since C is significantly different from zero, the association in the population is greater than zero.

9.1.4 Summary of Procedure

There are the steps in the use of the Cramér coefficient:

1. Arrange the observed frequencies in an $r \times k$ contingency table, like Table 9.1, where r is the number of categories on which one variable is scored and k is the number of categories on which the other variable is scored.
2. Determine the expected frequency under H_0 for each cell by multiplying the two marginal totals common to that cell and then dividing this product by N, the total number of cases. That is, for each cell in the contingency table calculate $E_{ij} = R_i C_j / N$. If more than about 20 percent of the cells have expected frequencies less than 5 or if any cells have an expected frequency less than 1, combine categories (either rows or columns) to increase the expected frequencies which are deficient (see Sec. 6.2.6).
3. By using Eq. (6.2) or (6.2*a*), compute the value of X^2 for the data.
4. Use this value of X^2 to compute the value of C with Eq. (9.1).
5. To test whether the observed value of C indicates that there is a significant association between the two variables in the population sampled, determine the associated probability under H_0 of a value as large as the observed X^2 with $df = (r - 1)(k - 1)$ by referring to Appendix Table C. If that probability is equal to or less than α, reject H_0 in favor of H_1.

9.1.5 Limitations of the Cramér Coefficient

The wide applicability and relative ease of computation of C may seem to make it an ideal measure of association. Although it is extremely useful, there are some limitations or deficiencies of the statistic with which the researcher should be familiar.

In general, we may say that it is desirable for an index of correlation to show at least the following characteristics: (1) When the variables are independent and there is a complete lack of association between the variables, the value of the index should be zero; and (2) when the variables show complete dependence upon each other, that is, when they are perfectly correlated, the statistic should be equal to unity or 1. The Cramer coefficient has the first characteristic—it equals zero when there is no association between the variables in the sample. Of course, when there is no association between the variables in the population, we will generally observe a sample value of C greater (but not significantly greater) than 0. However, when it is equal to unity, there may not be "perfect" correlation between the variables. This is the first limitation of C.

When $C = 1$, it does indicate that the variables are perfectly correlated when the associated contingency table is square, that is, when $r = k$. In that case, each row and each column will have only a *single* cell in which there are nonzero frequencies. However, if the contingency table is not square, it is still possible for C to equal unity. However, in this case there is perfect association between the variables in only *one direction*. To understand this situation, suppose $r < k$. Then, if $C = 1$, there will be only one nonzero entry in each *column*, but there must be some *rows* with more than one nonzero entry. (Actually, there will be $k - r$ "extra" cells with nonzero frequencies.) Thus, in this situation, there is perfect association from the *column* variable to the row variable, but there is *not* perfect association from the *row* variable to the column variable. The converse relation holds when $C = 1$ and $r > k$. One might consider $C = 1$ for a nonsquare contingency table as representing an "asymmetrical" perfect relation—it is perfect in one direction but not the other.

A second limitation of C is that the data must be amenable to the use of the X^2 statistic in order that its significance may be properly interpreted. The reader will recall that the significance of the chi-square test of independence assumes that the expected values are large. In practice, the rule of thumb concerning expected values is that the test may be appropriately applied only if fewer than about 20 percent of the cells in the contingency table have expected frequencies less than 5 and no cell has an expected frequency of less than 1.

A third limitation of C is that it is not directly comparable to any other measure of correlation, e.g., the Pearson r (except when the contingency table is 2×2, the Spearman r_s, or the Kendall T. These measures apply to ordered variables whereas the Cramér coefficient is appropriate for use with categorical (nominally scaled) variables. Although the Cramér coefficient is generally not appropriate for use with ordered variables, it could be employed to assess the degree of nonmonotonic association between two ordered variables.

Finally, readers accustomed to thinking of r^2 (the squared Pearson product-moment correlation) as a proportion of variance accounted for by the relation between two variables should be cautioned against such an interpretation of C or C^2. Although one can interpret larger values of C as indicating a greater degree of relation than indicated by smaller values, differences in magnitude have no direct interpretation.

In spite of these limitations, the Cramér coefficient is an extremely useful measure of association because of its wide applicability. The Cramér coefficient makes no assumptions about the shape of the population distributions of the variables from which it is computed, it does not require underlying continuity in the variables, and it requires only categorical measurement of the variables. Because of this freedom from assumptions, C may often be used to indicate the degree of relation between two sets of variables to which none of the other measures of association which we shall present is applicable.

Another *advantage* of the Cramér coefficient is that it enables the researcher to compare contingency tables of different sizes and, more importantly, tables based on different sample sizes. Although the X^2 statistic does measure the independence of two variables, it is sensitive to the size of the sample. The Cramér coefficient makes comparison of the relations obtained in different contingency tables easier.

9.1.6 Power

Because of its nature and its limitations, we should not expect the Cramér coefficient to be very powerful in detecting a relation in the population. However, its ease of computation and its complete freedom from restrictive assumptions recommend its use where other measures of correlation may be inapplicable. Because C is a function of the chi-square statistic X^2, its limiting power distribution, like that of X^2, tends to 1 as N becomes large (Cochran, 1952).

9.1.7 References

For other discussions of the Cramér coefficient, the reader is referred to Kendall (1975) and McNemar (1969).

9.2 THE PHI COEFFICIENT FOR 2 × 2 TABLES: r_ϕ

9.2.1 Function

The *phi coefficient* r_ϕ is a measure of the extent of association or relation between two sets of attributes measured on nominal scale, each of which may take on only two values. It is, in fact, identical in value to the Cramér coefficient presented in Sec. 9.1.[3] It will be assumed that the reader has read that section; thus, the presentation here will be brief.

---

[3] In some other references, the phi coefficient r_ϕ is defined for *all* contingency tables. It is discussed here in the context of 2 × 2 tables only because of the superiority of the Cramér coefficient C for other tables. One disadvantage of r_ϕ as an index of association for larger tables is that it is not equal to unity when there is perfect association in nonsquare frequency tables (see Sec. 9.1.5).

9.2.2 Method

To calculate the phi coefficient, it is convenient to arrange the data in a 2×2 table. Since the data are dichotomous, we shall assume that the data are coded 0 and 1 for each variable, although any binary value assignments could be used:

	Variable X		
Variable Y	**0**	**1**	Total
1	A	B	$A + B$
0	C	D	$C + D$
Total	$A + C$	$B + D$	N

Since this contingency table is much simpler than the general contingency table described in the previous section, we have replaced the cell frequencies n_{ij} with A, B, C, and D. The phi coefficient for a 2×2 table is defined as

$$r_\phi = \frac{|AD - BC|}{\sqrt{(A + B)(C + D)(A + C)(B + D)}} \tag{9.2}$$

which can range from zero to one. The phi coefficient is related to the X^2 statistic which is used to test independence of categorical (nominally scaled) variables. Therefore the significance of the phi coefficient may be tested by using the X^2 statistic presented in Sec. 6.2:

$$X^2 = \frac{N(|AD - BC| - N/2)^2}{(A + B)(C + D)(A + C)(B + D)} \tag{6.3}$$

which, as we saw in that section, is distributed as χ^2 with $df = 1$. This statistic tests the hypothesis H_0 that the phi coefficient in the population from which the variables were sampled is zero (i.e., that the variables are independent) against the hypothesis H_1 that the variables are related.

It should be noted that if the sample size is small, the significance of r_ϕ can be tested with the Fisher exact test (Sec. 6.1).

Example 9.2 In an experiment involving the effects of media-transmitted behavior on individual preferences, an experiment was designed in which an audience would show approval (by applause) of a speaker's presentation in a large group discussion.[4] The topic of discussion was whether members of radical political parties should or should not be refused public employment. There were two speakers, one on each side of the issue. There were two conditions—in one, the audience showed strong approval of one argument (pro)

[4] Stocker-Kreichgauer, G., and von Rosenstiel, L. (1982). Attitude change as a function of the observation of vicarious reinforcement and friendliness/hostility in a debate. In B. Brandstatter, J. H. Davis, and G. Stocker-Kreichgauer (eds.), *Group decision making*. New York: Academic Press, pp. 241–255.

TABLE 9.2
Number of people changing preference towards speaker (pro) or speaker (con)

Audience supports speaker	Change in preference toward Pro	Con	Total
Con	21	37	58
Pro	26	14	40
Total	47	51	98

and in the other, the audience showed strong approval of the other argument (con). Subjects who viewed the debate and the audience reactions were asked to indicate their own preference for one of the two speakers. The researchers hypothesized that the audience's approval would affect the subject's preference; specifically, the applauded speaker would be more favored and the nonapplauded speaker would become less favored. Subjects rated their own position on the issue before and after the debate. The data consisted of the change in these ratings. The magnitude of the change was ignored, and only the *direction* of the change was coded. The data for the experiment are summarized in Table 9.2.

The researchers wished to determine the strength of the relation between the audience behavior and the change in preference by observers. Since the data are dichotomous and only categorical, the phi coefficient is the appropriate index. By using the data in Table 9.2, the value of r_ϕ may be determined with Eq. (9.2):

$$r_\phi = \frac{|AD - BC|}{\sqrt{(A + B)(C + D)(A + C)(B + D)}} \tag{9.2}$$

$$= \frac{|(21)(14) - (37)(26)|}{\sqrt{(21 + 37)(26 + 14)(21 + 26)(37 + 14)}}$$

$$= .28$$

Thus there is a moderate relation between subjects' preference changes and audience approval. To determine whether this relation is significant, the X^2 test for 2×2 contingency tables [Eq. (6.3)] is used:

$$X^2 = \frac{N(|AD - BC| - N/2)^2}{(A + B)(C + D)(A + C)(B + D)} \tag{6.3}$$

$$= \frac{98[|(21)(14) - (37)(26)| - 98/2]^2}{(21 + 37)(26 + 14)(21 + 26)(37 + 14)}$$

$$= 6.75$$

Since the statistic X^2 is distributed as χ^2 with $df = 1$, we may determine its significance and, hence, the significance of r_ϕ by reference to Appendix Table C. Reference to that table shows that $X^2 \geq 6.75$ with $df = 1$ has probability of occurrence when H_0 is true of less than .01. Thus we may reject H_0 at the $\alpha = .01$ level of significance and conclude that audience reaction has an effect upon preference for speakers (and arguments) in debates and that the relation between preference changes and audience approval is not zero.

9.2.3 Summary of Procedure

These are the steps in the use of the phi coefficient:

1. Arrange the observed frequencies in a 2×2 contingency table.
2. Use the frequencies in the 2×2 table to calculate the phi coefficient r_ϕ with Eq. (9.2).
3. To test whether the observed value of r_ϕ indicates that there is a significant association between the two variables in the population sampled, determine the associated chi-square statistic X^2 by using Eq. (6.3). Then determine the probability under H_0 of obtaining a value as large as the observed X^2 with $df = 1$ by referring to Appendix Table C. If that probability is equal to or less than α, reject H_0 in favor of H_1.

9.2.4 Power-Efficiency

Since the test for the phi coefficient is similar to the test for the Cramér coefficient (they are both based on the χ^2 distribution), the reader should refer to the discussion of power in Sec. 9.1.6. However, the reader should be aware that, if the variables are ordered, the sacrifice of information to form the 2×2 table and calculate the phi coefficient is quite large. For ordered variables, the researcher should use one of the methods discussed in subsequent sections of this chapter.

9.2.5 References

The reader is referred to the references in the previous section and Sec. 6.2.

9.3 THE SPEARMAN RANK-ORDER CORRELATION COEFFICIENT r_s

9.3.1 Function

Of all the statistics based on ranks, the *Spearman rank-order correlation coefficient* r_s was the earliest to be developed and is perhaps the best known today. It is a measure of association between two variables which requires that both variables be measured in at least an ordinal scale so that the objects or individuals under study may be ranked in two ordered series.

9.3.2 Rationale

Suppose N individuals are ranked on each of two variables. For example, we might arrange a group of students in the order of their scores on a college entrance test and again in the order of their grade point average at the end of the freshman year. If the students' *rankings* on the entrance test are denoted as $X_1, X_2, \ldots, X_N$ and the *rankings* on grade point average are represented by $Y_1, Y_2, \ldots, Y_N$, we may use a measure of rank-order correlation to determine the relation between the X's and the Y's.

We can see that the correlation between the entrance examination ranks and the grade point average ranks would be perfect if and only if $X_i = Y_i$ for all i's, that is, if each person had the same ranking on both variables. Therefore, it would seem logical to use the various differences

$$d_i = X_i - Y_i$$

as an indication of the disparity between the two sets of rankings. Suppose Mary McCord received the top score on the entrance examination but placed fifth in her class on grade point average. Her d would be $1 - 5 = -4$. John Stanislowski, on the other hand, placed tenth on the entrance examination but leads the class in grade point average; for him $d = 10 - 1 = 9$. The magnitude of these various d_i's gives us an idea of how close is the relation between entrance examination scores and academic standing. If the relation between the two sets of ranks were perfect, every d would be zero. The larger the d_i's, the less perfect is the association between the two variables.

In computing a correlation coefficient it would be awkward or inconvenient to use the d_i's directly. One difficulty is that the negative d_i's would cancel out the positive ones when we tried to determine the total magnitude of the discrepancy between the rankings, even though it is the *magnitude* rather than the sign of the discrepancy which is an index of the disparity of the rankings. However, if d_i^2 is employed rather than d_i, this difficulty is circumvented. It is clear that the larger the various d_i's, the larger will be the value of Σd_i^2, which is the sum of the squared differences for the N pairs of data.

The derivation of the computing formula for r_s is fairly simple. It is done by simplifying the formula for the Pearson product-moment correlation coefficient r when the data are comprised of ranks. We shall give two alternative expressions for r_s. One of these alternative forms is useful in the computation of the coefficient and the other will be used later when we find it necessary to correct the coefficient when tied scores are present in the data. If $x = X - \bar{X}$, where $\bar{X}$ is the mean of the *scores* on the X variable, and if $y = Y - \bar{Y}$, where $\bar{Y}$ is the mean of the *scores* on the Y variable, then a general expression for the Pearson product-moment correlation coefficient is

$$r = \frac{\Sigma xy}{\sqrt{\Sigma x^2 \Sigma y^2}} \tag{9.3}$$

in which the sums are over the N values in the sample.[5] Now when the X's and Y's are *ranks*, $r = r_s$. Knowing that the data are rankings, we can simplify Eq.

[5] In this section we shall use the abbreviated form of the summation operator Σ, in which we shall omit the index for the summation as well as the subscript for the indexed variable. The context should make clear over what variables and over what range the sum is to be taken. In this case the summation is over all N variables.

(9.3) to yield the following expressions for the Spearman rank-order correlation coefficient:

$$r_s = \frac{\Sigma x^2 + \Sigma y^2 - \Sigma d^2}{2\sqrt{\Sigma x^2 \Sigma y^2}} \tag{9.4}$$

and

$$r_s = 1 - \frac{6 \sum_{i=1}^{N} d_i^2}{N^3 - N} \tag{9.5}$$

Recall that $d_i = X_i - Y_i$, the difference in ranks on the two variables. The simplification of Eq. (9.4) to the form given in Eq. (9.5) is possible by noting that when the data are in ranks and there are no ties in the data, $\Sigma x^2 = \Sigma y^2 = (N^3 - N)/12$. It should be noted that if there are ties, the use of either Eq. (9.3) or (9.4) will yield the correct value of r_s; a correction for ties for Eq. (9.5) will be given later.

9.3.3 Method

To compute r_s, make a list of the N subjects or observations. Next to each subject's entry, enter the ranking for the X variable and the ranking for the Y variable. Assign a rank of 1 to the smallest X and a rank of N to the largest X, etc. Determine next the values of d_i, which is the difference between the X and Y rankings for the ith observation. Square each d_i, and then sum all values of d_i^2 to obtain Σd_i^2. Then enter this value and the value N (the number of observations or subjects) directly into Eq. (9.5).

Example 9.3a As part of a study of the effect of group pressures for conformity upon an individual in a situation involving monetary risk, two researchers[6] administered the F scale, a measure of authoritarianism, and a scale designed to measure social status strivings[7] to 12 students. Information about the correlation between the scores on authoritarianism and those on social status strivings was desired. (Social status strivings were indicated by agreement with such statements as, "People shouldn't marry below their social level," "For a date, attending a horse show is better than going to a baseball game," and "It is worthwhile to trace back your family tree.") Table 9.3 gives each of the 12 students' scores on the two scales.

To compute the Spearman rank-order correlation between these two sets of scores, it is necessary to rank-order them in two series. The ranks of the scores given in Table 9.3 are shown in Table 9.4, which also shows the various values of d_i and d_i^2. Thus, for example, Table 9.4 shows that the student (subject J) who showed the most authoritarianism (on the F scale) also showed the most extreme social status strivings, and thus was assigned a rank of 12 on both variables. The reader will observe that no subject's rank on one variable was more than three ranks distant from the rank on the other variable, i.e., the largest d_i is 3.

---

[6] Siegel, S., and Fagan, J. The Asch effect under conditions of risk. (Unpublished study.) The data reported here are from a pilot study.

[7] Siegel, A. E., and Siegel, S. An experimental test of some hypotheses in reference group theory. (Unpublished study.)

TABLE 9.3
Scores on authoritarianism and social status strivings

Subject	Score: Authoritarianism	Score: Social status strivings
A	82	42
B	98	46
C	87	39
D	40	37
E	116	65
F	113	88
G	111	86
H	83	56
I	85	62
J	126	92
K	106	54
L	117	81

From the data shown in Table 9.4, we may compute the value of r_s by applying Eq. (9.5) to these data:

$$r_s = 1 - \frac{6 \sum_{i=1}^{N} d_i^2}{N^3 - N} \tag{9.5}$$

$$= 1 - \frac{6(52)}{(12)^3 - 12}$$

$$= .82$$

We observe that for these 12 students the correlation between authoritarianism and social status is $r_s = .82$.

TABLE 9.4
Ranks on authoritarianism and social status strivings

Subject	Rank: Authoritarianism	Rank: Social status strivings	d_i	d_i^2
A	2	3	−1	1
B	6	4	2	4
C	5	2	3	9
D	1	1	0	0
E	10	8	2	4
F	9	11	−2	4
G	8	10	−2	4
H	3	6	−3	9
I	4	7	−3	9
J	12	12	0	0
K	7	5	2	4
L	11	9	2	4
				$\Sigma d_i^2 = 52$

9.3.4 Tied Observations

Occasionally two or more subjects will receive the same score on the same variable. When tied scores occur, each of them is assigned the average of the ranks that would have been assigned had no ties occurred, which is our usual procedure for assigning ranks to tied observations.

If the proportion of tied observations is not large, their effect on r_s is negligible, and Eq. (9.5) may still be used for computation. However, if the proportion of ties is large, then a correction factor must be incorporated into the computation of r_s.

The effect of tied ranks in the X variable is to reduce the sum of squares (Σx^2) below the value of $(N^3 - N)/12$, that is, when there are ties,

$$\Sigma x^2 < \frac{N^3 - N}{12}$$

Therefore, it is necessary to correct the sum of squares, taking ties into account. (Tied ranks have no effect on the mean or Σx which is always $= 0$.) The correction factor is

$$T_x = \sum_{i=1}^{g} (t_i^3 - t_i) \tag{9.6}$$

where g is the number of groupings of different tied ranks and t_i is the number of tied ranks in the ith grouping. When the sum of squares is corrected for ties, it becomes

$$\Sigma x^2 = \frac{N^3 - N - T_x}{12}$$

Ties occurring in the Y variable require correction in the same manner, and the correction factor is denoted T_y. When a considerable number of ties are present, one of the following equations may be used to calculate r_s:

$$r_s = \frac{\Sigma x^2 + \Sigma y^2 - \Sigma d^2}{2\sqrt{\Sigma x^2 \Sigma y^2}} \tag{9.4}$$

or

$$r_s = \frac{(N^3 - N) - 6\Sigma d^2 - (T_x + T_y)/2}{\sqrt{(N^3 - N)^2 - (T_x + T_y)(N^3 - N) + T_x T_y}} \tag{9.7}$$

Example 9.3*b* **With ties.** In the study cited in the previous example, each student was individually observed in the group pressure situation developed by Asch.[8] In this situation, a group of subjects is asked individually to state which of a set of alternative lines is the same length as a standard line. All but one of the subjects are confederates of the experimenter, and on certain trials they unanimously choose an incorrect match. The naive subject, who is seated so that he or she is the last person asked to report his or her judgment, has the choice of standing alone in selecting the true match (which is unmistakable to people in

[8] Asch, S. E. (1952). *Social psychology*. New York: Prentice-Hall, pp. 451–476.

TABLE 9.5
Original scores and ranks on yielding and social status strivings

	Number of yieldings		Social status strivings			
Subject	**Data**	**Rank**	**Data**	**Rank**	d_i	d_i^2
A	0	1.5	42	3	−1.5	2.25
B	0	1.5	46	4	−2.5	6.25
C	1	3.5	39	2	1.5	2.25
D	1	3.5	37	1	2.5	6.25
E	3	5	65	8	−3.0	9.00
F	4	6	88	11	−5.0	25.00
G	5	7	86	10	−3.0	9.00
H	6	8	56	6	2.0	4.00
I	7	9	62	7	2.0	4.00
J	8	10.5	92	12	−1.5	2.25
K	8	10.5	54	5	−5.5	30.25
L	12	12	81	9	3.0	9.00
					$\Sigma d_i^2 =$	109.50

situations where no contradictory group pressures are involved) or "yielding" to group pressures by stating that the incorrect line is the match.

The modification which Siegel and Fagan introduced into this experiment was to agree to pay each subject 50 cents for every correct judgment and to penalize the subject 50 cents for every incorrect one. The subjects were given 2 dollars at the beginning of the experiment, and they understood that they could keep all money in their possession at the end of the session. So far as the naive subject knew, this agreement had been made with all members of the group making the judgments. Each naive subject participated in 12 "crucial" trials, i.e., in 12 trials in which the confederates unanimously chose the wrong line as the match. Thus each naive subject could "yield" as often as 12 times.

As part of the study, the experimenters wanted to know whether yielding in this situation is correlated with social status strivings, as measured by the scale described in the previous example. This was determined by computing the Spearman rank-order correlation between the scores of each of the 12 naive subjects on the social-status-strivings scale and the number of times that each yielded to the group pressures. The data on these two variables are presented in Table 9.5. Observe that two of the naive subjects did not yield at all (subjects *A* and *B*), whereas only one (subject *L*) yielded on every crucial trial. The rankings for the original scores listed in Table 9.5 are given in separate columns in that table. Observe that for these data, there are three groups of tied observations on the *X* variable (number of yieldings). When there are ties, the rank assigned as the *average of the ranks* which would have been assigned if the values had differed slightly.[9] Two subjects tied at 0; both were

[9] In this section it is assumed that the reader knows how to perform rankings of data when there are ties in the observations. The procedure for scoring tied ranks is discussed in detail in Sec. 5.3.2.

given ranks of 1.5. Two tied at 1; both were given ranks of 3.5. Two tied at 8; both were given ranks of 10.5.

Because of the relatively large proportion of tied observations in the X variable, Eq. (9.7) should be used to compute the value of r_s. To use that equation, we must first determine the value of Σx^2 and Σy^2 corrected for ties, that is, we must find T_x and T_y.

Now with $g = 3$ groups of tied observations on the X variable, where $t_i = 2$ in each set, we have

$$T_x = (2^3 - 2) + (2^3 - 2) + (2^3 - 2)$$
$$= 18$$

and

$$\Sigma x^2 = \frac{N^3 - N - T_x}{12}$$
$$= \frac{12^3 - 12 - 18}{12}$$
$$= 141.5$$

That is, corrected for ties, $\Sigma x^2 = 141.5$. We find Σy^2 by a comparable method. However, since there are no ties in the Y scores (the scores on social strivings) in these data, $T_y = 0$ and

$$\Sigma y^2 = \frac{N^3 - N - T_y}{12}$$
$$= \frac{12^3 - 12 - 0}{12}$$
$$= 143$$

Thus, corrected for ties, $\Sigma x^2 - 141.5$ and $\Sigma y^2 = 143$. From the addition shown in Table 9.5, we know that $\Sigma d^2 = 109.5$. Substituting these values into Eq. (9.7), we have

$$r_s = \frac{(N^3 - N) - 6\Sigma d^2 - (T_x + T_y)/2}{\sqrt{(N^3 - N)^2 - (T_x + T_y)(N^3 - N) + T_x T_y}} \qquad (9.7)$$
$$= \frac{1716 - 6(109.5) - 18/2}{\sqrt{1716^2 - (18)(1716) + 0}}$$
$$= \frac{1050}{1706.976}$$
$$= .615$$

Corrected for ties, the correlation between amount of yielding and degree of social status strivings is $r_s = .615$. If we had computed r_s with Eq. (9.5), i.e., if we had not corrected for ties, we would have found $r_s = .617$. This illustrates the relatively small effect of ties upon the value of the Spearman rank-order correlation coefficient when there are few groups of ties or the number of ties within a group of ties is small. Notice, however, that the effect of ties in the rankings is to inflate the value of the (uncorrected) correlation r_s. For this reason, the correction should be used where there is a large proportion of ties in either or both of the X and Y variables or the number of ties in a grouping of ties is large.

9.3.5 Testing the Significance of r_s

If the subjects whose scores are used in computing r_s are drawn randomly from some population, we may use those scores to determine whether the two variables are associated in the population. That is, we may test the null hypothesis that the two variables under study are *not* associated (i.e., are independent) in the population and the observed value of r_s differs from zero only by chance. Thus, we may test the hypothesis H_0: there is no association between X and Y, against the hypothesis H_1: there is association between X and Y (a two-tailed test) or H_1: there is positive (or negative) association between X and Y (a one-tailed test). It should be noted that we have not specified the two hypotheses as H_0: $\rho_s = 0$ against H_1: $\rho_s \neq 0$ because, unlike the case in which the variables are normally distributed, $\rho_s = 0$ does not necessarily mean that the variables are independent, whereas if they are independent, then $\rho_s = 0$. As a result, we should be careful in interpreting the significance of r_s.

SMALL SAMPLES. Suppose that the null hypothesis is true. That is, suppose that there is no relation in the population between the X and Y variables. Now if a sample of X and Y scores is drawn randomly from that population, for a given rank order of the Y scores any rank order of the X scores is just as likely as any other rank order of the X scores; and for any given order of the X scores, all possible orders of the Y scores are equally likely. For the N subjects, there are $N!$ possible rankings of X scores which may occur in association with any given ranking of Y scores. Since these are equally likely, the probability of occurrence of any particular ranking of the X scores with a given ranking of the Y scores is $1/N!$.

For each of the possible rankings of Y there will be associated a value of r_s. When H_0 is true, the probability of the occurrence of any particular r_s is thus proportional to the number of permutations giving rise to that value.

By using Eq. 9.5, the computational formula for r_s, we find that, for $N = 2$, only two values of r_s are possible: $+1$ and -1. Each of these has probability of occurrence under H_0 of $\frac{1}{2}$.

For $N = 3$, the possible values of r_s are -1, $-\frac{1}{2}$, $+\frac{1}{2}$, and $+1$. When H_0 is true, the respective probabilities are $\frac{1}{6}$, $\frac{1}{3}$, $\frac{1}{3}$, and $\frac{1}{6}$.

Appendix Table Q gives critical values of r_s which have been arrived at by a similar method of generating all possible rankings. For N from 4 to 50, the table gives critical values of the Spearman rank-order correlation r_s under H_0 for several values of α between .25 and .0005. The table is one-tailed, i.e., the stated probabilities apply when the observed value of r_s is in the predicted direction, either positive or negative. If an observed value of r_s equals or exceeds a particular tabled value, that observed value is significant (for a one-tailed test) at the level indicated. For a two-tailed test in which the alternative hypothesis H_1 is that the two variables are related but we make no assumption about the direction of relation between them, the probabilities in Appendix Table Q should be doubled. For convenience, the two-tailed probabilities are noted in the table.

Example 9.3c We have already found that for $N = 12$ the Spearman rank-order correlation between authoritarianism and social status strivings is $r_s = .82$. Appendix Table Q shows that a value as large as this is significant at the $p < .001$ level (one-tailed test). Thus we could reject H_0 at the $\alpha = .001$ level, concluding that, in the population of students from which the sample was drawn, authoritarianism and social status strivings are not independent.

We also have seen that the relation between social status strivings and amount of yielding to group pressures is $r_s = .62$ in our group of 12 subjects. By referring to Appendix Table Q, we can determine that $r_s \geq .62$ has probability of occurrence when H_0 is true between $p = .025$ and $p = .01$ (one-tailed test). Thus we could conclude, at the $\alpha = .025$ level, that these two variables are not independent in the population from which the sample was drawn.

LARGE SAMPLES. When N is larger than about 20 to 25, the significance of an obtained r_s under the null hypothesis also may be tested by the statistic

$$z = r_s\sqrt{N - 1} \qquad (9.8)^{10}$$

For large N, the value defined by Eq. (9.8) is approximately normally distributed with mean 0 and standard deviation 1. Thus the associated probability when H_0 is true of any value as extreme as an observed value of r_s may be determined by computing the z associated with that value by using Eq. (9.8), and then determining the significance of the z by referring to Appendix Table A. Although the large-sample test could be employed when N is as small as 20, the use of Appendix Table Q is preferred for $N \leq 50$.

Example 9.3d We have already determined that the relation between social status strivings and amount of yielding to group pressure is $r_s = .62$ for $N = 12$. Although N is small, we will use the large sample approximation for testing this r_s for significance as an example:

$$\begin{aligned} z &= r_s\sqrt{N - 1} \qquad (9.8) \\ &= .62\sqrt{12 - 1} \\ &= 2.05 \end{aligned}$$

Appendix Table A shows that a z as large as 2.05 is significant at the .05 level but not at the .01 level for a one-tailed test. This is essentially the same result we obtained previously by using Appendix Table Q. In that case we could reject H_0 at $\alpha = .025$, concluding that social status strivings and amount of yielding are associated in the population of which the 12 students were a sample.

---

[10] Some statisticians recommend the slightly better statistic

$$t = r_s\sqrt{\frac{N - 2}{1 - r_s^2}}$$

which is approximately distributed as Student's t with $df = N - 2$ (Appendix B). Because of the availability of Appendix Table Q which tables the exact upper-tail probabilities of the sampling distribution of r_s for $N \leq 50$, we have opted for the simpler expression in Eq. (9.8). In actual practice and with large N, the advantage of t over z is small.

9.3.6 Summary of Procedure

These are the steps in the use of the Spearman rank-order correlation coefficient:

1. Rank the subjects (observations) on the X variable from 1 to N. Rank the observations on the Y variable from 1 to N. For tied X's (or Y's) assign each the average value of the associated ranks.
2. List the N subjects. Put each subject's rank on the X variable and Y variable next to the entry.
3. Determine the value of d_i for each subject by subtracting the Y rank from the corresponding X rank. Square this value to determine d_i^2. Sum the d_i^2's for the N cases to determine Σd_i^2.
4. If the proportion of ties in either the X or the Y observations is large, use Eq. (9.7) to compute r_s.[11] In other cases, use Eq. (9.5).
5. If the subjects constitute a random sample from some population, one may test whether the observed value of r_s indicates an association between the X and the Y variables in the population. The hypotheses are H_0: there is no association between X and Y, and H_1: there is association between X and Y. The method for doing this depends upon the sample size N:
   (*a*) For N from 4 to 50, critical values of r_s between the .25 and .0005 levels of significance (one-tailed) are given in Appendix Table Q. For a two-tailed test, the corresponding significance probabilities are doubled.
   (*b*) For $N > 50$, the probability associated with a value as large as the observed value of r_s may be approximated by computing the z associated with that value by using Eq. (9.8) and then determining the significance of that value of z by referring to Appendix Table A.
6. If the value of r_s (or z) exceeds the critical value, reject H_0 in favor of H_1.

9.3.7 Relative Efficiency

The efficiency of the Spearman rank-order correlation coefficient when compared with the most powerful parametric correlation—the Pearson product-moment correlation coefficient r—is about 91 percent. That is, when r_s is used with a sample to test for the existence of association in a population for which the assumptions and requirements underlying the Pearson r are met, i.e., when the population has a bivariate normal distribution, then r_s is 91 percent as efficient as r in rejecting H_0. If a correlation between X and Y exists in that population, with 100 cases r_s will reveal that correlation with the same significance which r attains with 91 cases.

9.3.8 References

For other discussions of the Spearman rank-order correlation coefficient, the reader should consult McNemar (1969) or Gibbons (1985).

[11] Equation (9.3) could be used to compute r_s whether or not there are ties, but its use may be more cumbersome. However, many calculators facilitate the (correct) computation of r_s using Eq. (9.3) whether or not there are ties. The choice of formula is up to the user.

9.4 THE KENDALL RANK-ORDER CORRELATION COEFFICIENT T

9.4.1 Function

The *Kendall rank-order correlation coefficient* T is suitable as a measure of correlation with the same sort of data for which r_s is useful.[12] That is, if at least ordinal measurement of both X and Y variables has been achieved, so that every subject can be assigned a rank on both X and Y, then T_{xy} (or simply T if the context is clear) will give a measure of the degree of association or correlation between the two sets of ranks. The sampling distribution of T under the null hypothesis of independence is known and, therefore, T, like r_s, may be used in tests of significance.

One advantage of T over r_s is that T can be generalized to a partial correlation coefficient. This partial coefficient will be presented in the next section. Coefficient T also is particularly well-suited for assessing the agreement among multiple judges, which will be discussed in Secs. 9.6 and 9.7.

9.4.2 Rationale

Suppose we ask judge X and judge Y to rank four objects. For example, we might ask them to rank four essays in order of quality of expository style. We represent the four papers as a, b, c, and d. The obtained rankings are:

Essay:	*a*	*b*	*c*	*d*
Judge X:	3	4	2	1
Judge Y:	3	1	4	2

If we rearrange the order of the essays so that judge X's ranks appear in natural[13] order (i.e., $1, 2, \ldots, N$), we get

Essay:	*d*	*c*	*a*	*b*
Judge X:	1	2	3	4
Judge Y:	2	4	3	1

We are now in a position to determine the degree of correspondence between the judgments X and Y. Judge X's rankings being in their natural order, we proceed to determine how many pairs of ranks in judge Y's set are in their correct (natural) order with respect to those of judge X. We shall count the number of agreements in ordering *and* the number of disagreements in the observed ordering of ranks.

---

[12] Some authors refer to the coefficient discussed in this section as Kendall's τ (tau). However, we shall distinguish between T, a statistic based on a sample, and τ, the population parameter.

[13] By *natural order* we mean the order in which the observed values of the variable may be placed. It should be noted that placement of one variable in natural order is necessary only to make the computation of the rank-order statistic easier. Moreover, it does not matter which variable is placed in order—the researcher may place either in natural order—the value of the resulting rank-order statistic is unaffected.

Consider first all possible *pairs* of ranks in which judge Y's rank is 2 (the first rank in his set) is a member and the other member is a "later" rank (to the right). The first pair (2 – 4) has the correct order—2 precedes 4. Since the order is "natural," we assign a score of +1 to this pair. Ranks 2 and 3 constitute the second pair (2 – 3). This pair is also in the correct order, so it also is assigned a score of +1. Now the third pair (2 – 1) consists of ranks 2 and 1. These ranks are not in natural order—2 precedes 1. Therefore we assign this pair a score of –1. For all pairs that include rank 2, we total the scores:

$$(+1) + (+1) + (-1) = +1$$

Now consider all possible pairs of ranks that include rank 4 (which is the rank second from the left in judge Y's set). The pairs are (4 – 3) and (4 – 1); since both of these pairs are not in the natural order, a score of –1 is assigned to each. The total of these scores is

$$(-1) + (-1) = -2$$

When we consider rank 3 and succeeding ranks, there is only the pair (3 – 1). The two members of this pair are in the wrong order; therefore this pair receives a score of –1.

The total of all of the scores we have assigned is

$$(+1) + (-2) + (-1) = -2$$

This sum is the number of agreements in ordering among the ranks less the number of disagreements in ordering among the ranks.

Now what is the *maximum possible* total we could have obtained for the scores assigned to all the pairs in judge Y's ranking? The maximum possible total would have occurred if the rankings of judges X and Y had agreed perfectly, for then, when the rankings of judge X were arranged in their natural order, every pair of judge Y's ranks would also be in the correct order and, thus, every pair would receive a score of +1. The maximum possible total, the one which would occur in the case of perfect agreement between X and Y, would be the combination of four objects taken two at a time or

$$\binom{4}{2} = 6$$

which is the number of different pairs which may be made of four objects.

The degree of relation between the two sets of ranks is indicated by the ratio of the actual total of +1s and –1s to the maximum possible total which is the number of possible pairs. The Kendall rank-order correlation coefficient is that ratio:

$$T = \frac{\#\text{ agreements} - \#\text{ disagreements}}{\text{total number of pairs}} = \frac{-2}{6} = -.33$$

That is, $T = -.33$ is a measure of the agreement between the ranks assigned to the essays by judge X and those assigned by judge Y.

One may think of T as a function of the minimum number of inversions or interchanges between neighboring ranks which is required to transform one ranking into another. That is, T is a sort of coefficient of disarray.

9.4.3 Method

We have seen that

$$T = \frac{\#\text{ agreements} - \#\text{ disagreements}}{\text{total number of pairs}}$$

In general, the maximum possible total will be $\binom{N}{2}$, which can be expressed as $N(N-1)/2$. This last expression may be the denominator of the formula for T. For the numerator, let us denote the observed sum of the $+1$ scores (agreements) and -1 scores (disagreements) for all pairs as S. Then

$$T = \frac{2S}{N(N-1)} \tag{9.9}$$

where N is the number of objects or individuals ranked on both X and Y.

As we shall see, the calculation of S may be shortened considerably from the method described above when we discussed of the logic of the measure.

When the ranks of judge X were in the natural order, the corresponding ranks of judge Y were in this order:

Judge Y: 2 4 3 1

We can determine S by starting with the first number on the left and counting the number of ranks to its right that are *larger*—these are the agreements in order. We subtract from this the number of ranks to its right that are *smaller*—these are the disagreements in order. If we do this for all ranks and then sum the results, we obtain S. This procedure is outlined below:

Judge Y:	2	4	3	1	Total
	2→	+	+	−	+1
		4→	−	−	−2
			3→	−	−1
				1→	0
			Grand total =		−2

Thus the total number of agreements in ordering minus the number of disagreements in ordering is $S = -2$. Knowing S, we may use Eq. (9.9) to compute the value of T for the ranks assigned by the two judges:

$$T = \frac{2S}{N(N-1)} \tag{9.9}$$

$$= \frac{2(-2)}{(4)(4-1)}$$

$$= -.33$$

Example 9.4*a* In the last section we computed the Spearman r_s for 12 students' scores on authoritarianism and on social status strivings. The scores of the 12 students are presented in Table 9.3 and the ranks of these scores are presented in Table 9.4. We may compute the value of Kendall's T for the same data.

The two sets of ranks to be correlated (shown in Table 9.4) are these:

Subject:	*A*	*B*	*C*	*D*	*E*	*F*	*G*	*H*	*I*	*J*	*K*	*L*
Status strivings rank:	3	4	2	1	8	11	10	6	7	12	5	9
Authoritarianism rank:	2	6	5	1	10	9	8	3	4	12	7	11

To compute T, we shall rearrange the order of the subjects so that the rankings on social status strivings are in the natural order:

Subject:	*D*	*C*	*A*	*B*	*K*	*H*	*I*	*E*	*L*	*G*	*F*	*J*	
Status strivings rank:	1	2	3	4	5	6	7	8	9	10	11	12	
Authoritarianism rank:	1	5	2	6	7	3	4	10	11	8	9	12	Total
	1→	+	+	+	+	+	+	+	+	+	+	+	+11
		5→	−	+	+	−	−	+	+	+	+	+	+4
			2→	+	+	+	+	+	+	+	+	+	+9
				6→	+	−	−	+	+	+	+	+	+4
					7→	−	−	+	+	+	+	+	+3
						3→	+	+	+	+	+	+	+6
							4→	+	+	+	+	+	+5
								10→	+	−	−	+	0
									11→	−	−	+	−1
										8→	+	+	+2
											9→	+	+1
												12→	0
												Grand total =	+44

Having arranged the ranks on variable X in their natural order, we determine the value of S for the corresponding order of ranks on the variable Y:

$$\begin{aligned} S &= (11-0) + (7-3) + (9-0) + (6-2) + (5-2) + (6-0) \\ &\quad + (5-0) + (2-2) + (1-2) + (2-0) + (1-0) \\ &= 44 \end{aligned}$$

The authoritarianism rank farthest to the left is 1. This rank has 11 ranks that are larger to its right and 0 ranks that are smaller, so its contribution of S is $11 - 0 = 11$. The next rank is 5. It has seven ranks to its right that are larger and three to its right that are smaller, so that its contribution to S is $(7 - 3) = 4$. By proceeding in this way, we obtain the various values shown above, which we have summed to yield $S = 44$. Note that the individual sums are given in the last column above. Knowing that $S = 44$ and $N = 12$, we may use Eq. (9.9) to compute T:

$$T = \frac{2S}{N(N-1)} \tag{9.9}$$

$$= \frac{2(44)}{(12)(12-1)}$$

$$= .67$$

The value $T = .67$ represents the degree of relation between authoritarianism and social status strivings shown by the 12 students.

9.4.4 Tied Observations

When two or more observations on either the X or the Y variable are tied, we turn to our usual procedure in ranking tied scores—the tied observations are given the average of the ranks they would have received had there been no ties.

The effect of ties is to change the denominator of our equation for T. In the case of ties, T becomes

$$T = \frac{2S}{\sqrt{N(N-1) - T_x}\sqrt{N(N-1) - T_y}} \tag{9.10}$$

where $T_x = \Sigma t(t - 1)$, t being the number of tied observations in each group of ties on the X variable

$T_y = \Sigma t(t - 1)$, t being the number of tied observations in each group of ties on the Y variable

The determination of the values of t was discussed in Sec. 9.3.4. [The reader is cautioned that T_x and T_y are different from the seemingly similar statistics defined by Eq. (9.6).] The computations required by Eq. (9.10) are illustrated in the following example.

Example 9.4*b* **With ties.** Again we shall repeat an example which was first presented in the discussion of the Spearman r_s. We correlated the scores of 12 subjects on a scale measuring social status strivings with the number of times that each yielded to group pressures in judging the length of lines. The data for this study are presented in Table 9.5 and the corresponding ranks are also in that table.

The two sets of ranks to be correlated (first presented in Table 9.5) are:

Subject:	*A*	*B*	*C*	*D*	*E*	*F*	*G*	*H*	*I*	*J*	*K*	*L*
Status strivings rank:	3	4	2	1	8	11	10	6	7	12	5	9
Yielding rank:	1.5	1.5	3.5	3.5	5	6	7	8	9	10.5	10.5	12

As usual, we first rearrange the order of the subjects, so that the ranks on the variable X occur in natural order:

Subject:	D	C	A	B	K	H	I	E	L	G	F	J	
Status strivings rank:	1	2	3	4	5	6	7	8	9	10	11	12	
Yielding rank:	3.5	3.5	1.5	1.5	10.5	8	9	5	12	7	6	10.5	Total
	3.5→	0	−	−	+	+	+	+	+	+	+	+	6
		3.5→	−	−	+	+	+	+	+	+	+	+	6
			1.5→	0	+	+	+	+	+	+	+	+	8
				1.5→	+	+	+	+	+	+	+	+	8
					10.5→	−	−	−	+	−	−	0	−4
						8→	+	−	+	−	−	+	0
							9→	−	+	−	−	+	−1
								5→	+	+	+	+	4
									12→	−	−	−	−3
										7→	−	+	0
											6→	+	1
												10.5→	0
												Grand total =	25

We then compute the value of S in the usual way:

$$S = (8-2)+(8-2)+(8-0)+(8-0)+(1-5)+(3-3)$$
$$+(2-3)+(4-0)+(0-3)+(1-1)+(1-0)$$
$$= 25$$

It should be noted that, when there are tied observations, the ranks will be tied and neither rank in a comparison pair precedes the other, so a value of 0 is assigned in the computation of S.

Having determined that $S = 25$, we now determine the values of T_x and T_y. There are no ties among the scores on social status strivings, i.e., in the X ranks, and thus $T_x = 0$.

On the Y variable (yielding), there are three sets of tied ranks. Two subjects are tied at rank 1.5, two are tied at 3.5, and two are tied at 10.5. In each of these cases, $T = 2$, the number of tied observations. Thus T_y may be computed:

$$T_y = \Sigma t(t-1)$$
$$= 2(2-1)+2(2-1)+2(2-1)$$
$$= 6$$

With $T_x = 0$, $T_y = 6$, $S = 25$, and $N = 12$, we may determine the value of T by using Eq. (9.10):

$$T = \frac{2S}{\sqrt{N(N-1)-T_x}\sqrt{N(N-1)-T_y}} \tag{9.10}$$

$$T = \frac{2(25)}{\sqrt{(12)(12-1)-0}\sqrt{(12)(12-1)-6}}$$

$$= .39$$

If we had not corrected the above coefficient for ties, i.e., if we had used Eq. (9.9) in computing T, we would have found $T = .38$. Observe that the effect of correcting for ties is relatively small unless the proportion of tied ranks is large or the number of ties in a group of ties is large.

9.4.5 Comparison of T and r_s

In two cases we have computed both T and r_s for the same data. The reader will have noted that the numerical values of T and r_s are not identical when both are computed from the same pairs of rankings. For the relation between authoritarianism and social status strivings, $r_s = .82$ whereas $T = .67$. For the relation between social status strivings and number of yieldings to group pressures, $r_s = .62$ and $T = .39$.

These examples illustrate the fact that T and r_s have different underlying scales, and numerically they are not directly comparable to each other. That is, if we measure the degree of correlation between the variables A and B by using r_s, and then do the same for A and C by using T, we cannot then say whether A is more closely related to B or to C because we have used noncomparable measures of correlation. It should be noted, however, that there is a relation between the two measures which is best expressed in the following inequality:

$$-1 \leq 3T - 2r_s \leq 1$$

There are also differences in the interpretation of the two measures. The Spearman rank-order correlation coefficient r_s is the same as a Pearson product-moment correlation coefficient computed between variables the values of which consist of ranks. On the other hand, the Kendall rank-order correlation coefficient has a different interpretation. It is the *difference* between the probability that, in the observed data, X and Y are in the same order and the probability that the X and Y data are in different orders. T_{xy} is the difference in the relative frequencies in the sample, and τ_{xy} is the difference between the probabilities in the population.

However, both coefficients utilize the same amount of information in the data, and thus both have the same sensitivity to detect the existence of association in the population. That is, the sampling distributions of T and r_s are such that for a given set of data both will lead to rejection of the null hypothesis (that the variables are unrelated in the population) at the same level of significance. However, it should be remembered that the measures are different and measure association in different ways. This should become clearer after the discussion of testing the significance of τ.

9.4.6 Testing the Significance of T

If a random sample is drawn from some population in which X and Y are unrelated and the members of the sample are ranked on X and Y, then for any given order of the X ranks all possible orders of the Y ranks are equally likely. That is, for a given order of the X ranks, any one of the possible orders of the Y ranks is just as likely to occur as any other possible order of the Y ranks. Suppose we order the X ranks in natural order, that is, 1, 2, 3, . . . , N. For that order of the X ranks all of the $N!$ possible orders of the Y ranks are equally

TABLE 9.6
Probabilities of T under H_0 for $N = 4$

Value of T	Frequency of occurrence under H_0	Probability of occurrence under H_0
-1.0	1	$\frac{1}{24}$
$-.67$	3	$\frac{3}{24}$
$-.33$	5	$\frac{5}{24}$
0	6	$\frac{6}{24}$
.33	5	$\frac{5}{24}$
.67	3	$\frac{3}{24}$
1.0	1	$\frac{1}{24}$

probable under H_0. Therefore any particular order of the Y ranks has probability of occurrence when H_0 is true of $1/N!$.

For each of the $N!$ possible rankings of Y, there will be associated a value of T. These possible values of T will range from $+1$ to -1, and they can be cast in a frequency distribution. For instance, for $N = 4$ there are $4! = 24$ possible arrangements of the Y ranks, and each has an associated value of T. Their frequency of occurrence when X and Y are independent is shown in Table 9.6. We could compute similar tables of probabilities for other values of N, but, of course, as N increases this method becomes increasingly tedious.

Fortunately, for $N > 10$, the sampling distribution of T may be approximated by the normal distribution. Therefore, for large N, we may use a table of the normal distribution (Appendix Table A) to determine the probability associated with the occurrence of any value as extreme as an observed value of T when H_0 is true.

However, when N is 10 or less, Appendix Table R_I may be used to determine the exact probability associated with the occurrence (one-tailed) under H_0 of any value as extreme as an observed T. For such small samples, the significance of an observed relation between two samples of ranks may be determined by simply finding the value of T and then referring to Appendix Table R_I to determine the probability (one-tailed) associated with that value. If the tabled $p \leq \alpha$, H_0 may be rejected. For example, suppose $N = 8$ and $T = .357$. Appendix Table R_I shows that $T \geq .357$ for $N = 8$ has probability of occurrence under H_0 of $p = .138$.

When the sample size is between 11 and 30, Appendix Table R_{II} may be used. That table gives critical values of Kendall's T for selected significance levels. When N is larger than 10, T is approximately normally distributed with

$$\text{Mean} = \mu_T = 0$$

and

$$\text{Variance} = \sigma_T^2 = \frac{2(2N+5)}{9N(N-1)}$$

That is,

$$z = \frac{T - \mu_T}{\sigma_T} = \frac{3T\sqrt{N(N-1)}}{\sqrt{2(2N+5)}} \tag{9.11}$$

is approximately normally distributed with 0 mean and variance 1. Thus the probability associated with the occurrence when H_0 is true of any value as extreme as an observed T may be determined by computing the values of z as defined by Eq. (9.11) and then determining the significance of that z by reference to Appendix Table A.

Example 9.4*c* **For $N > 10$.** We have already determined that among 12 students the correlation between authoritarianism and social status strivings is $T = .67$. If we consider these 12 students to be a random sample from some population, we may test the hypothesis that these two variables are independent in that population by referring to Appendix Table R_{II}. Reference to that table shows that the probability of obtaining a sample value of $T \geq .67$ when H_0 is true is less than .005.

Since $N > 10$, we could also use the normal approximation to the sampling distribution of T by using Eq. (9.11):

$$z = \frac{3T\sqrt{N(N-1)}}{\sqrt{2(2N+5)}} \tag{9.11}$$

$$z = \frac{(3)(.67)\sqrt{(12)(12-1)}}{\sqrt{2[2(12)+5]}}$$

$$= 3.03$$

By referring to Appendix Table A, we see that $z \geq 3.03$ has probability of occurrence when H_0 is true of $p = .0012$. Thus we could reject H_0 at the $\alpha = .0012$ level of significance and conclude that the two variables are not independent in the population from which this sample was drawn. This, of course, is consistent with the result obtained by use of Appendix Table R_{II}.

We have already mentioned that T and r_s have similar ability to reject H_0. That is, even though T and r_s are numerically different for the same set of data, their null sampling distributions are such that with the same data H_0 would be rejected at the approximately same level of significance by the significance tests associated with both measures. However, in the non-null case (when H_1 is true), they are sensitive to different aspects of the dependency between the variables.

In the present case, $T = .67$. Associated with this value is $z = 3.03$, which permits us to reject H_0 at $\alpha = .0012$. When the Spearman rank-order correlation coefficient was computed from the same data, we found $r_s = .82$. When we apply to that value the significance test for r_s [Eq. (9.8)], we find that $z = 2.72$. Appendix Table A shows that $z \geq 2.72$ has probability of occurrence when H_0 is true of slightly more than .003. Thus T and r_s for the same set of data have significance tests which reject H_0 at essentially the same level of significance.

9.4.7 Summary of Procedure

These are the steps in the use of the Kendall rank-order correlation coefficient T:

1. Rank the observations on the X variable from 1 to N. Rank the observations on the Y variable from 1 to N.

2. Arrange the list of N subjects so that the ranks of the subjects on variable X are in their natural order, that is, $1, 2, 3, \ldots, N$.
3. Observe the Y ranks in the order in which they occur when the X ranks are in natural order. Determine the value of S, the number of agreements in order minus the number of disagreements in order, for the observed order of the Y ranks.
4. If there are no ties among either the X or the Y observations, use Eq. (9.9) to compute the value of T. If there are ties, use Eq. (9.10).
5. If the N subjects constitute a random sample from some population, one may test the hypothesis that the variables X and Y are independent in that population. The method for doing so depends on the size of N:
   (*a*) For $N \leq 10$, Appendix Table R_I gives the associated probability (one-tailed) of a value as large as an observed T.
   (*b*) For $N > 10$, but less than 30, Appendix Table R_{II} gives the associated probability (one-tailed) of a value as large as an observed T.
   (*c*) For $N > 30$ (or for intermediate significance levels for $10 < N \leq 30$) compute the value of z associated with T by using Eq. (9.11). Appendix Table A may then be used to determine the associated probability of a value as large as the observed z and, hence, T.
6. If the probability yielded by the appropriate method is equal to or less than α, H_0 may be rejected in favor of H_1.

9.4.8 Efficiency

The Spearman r_s and the Kendall T are similar in their ability to reject H_0, inasmuch as they make similar use of the information in the data.

When used on data to which the Pearson product-moment correlation coefficient r is properly applicable, both T and r_s have efficiency of 91 percent. That is, T is approximately as sensitive a test of independence of two variables in a bivariate normal population with a sample of 100 cases as the Pearson r with 91 cases (Moran, 1951).

9.4.9 References

The reader will find other useful discussions of the Kendall τ in Kendall (1975) and Everitt (1977).

9.5 THE KENDALL PARTIAL RANK-ORDER CORRELATION COEFFICIENT $T_{xy.z}$

9.5.1 Function

When correlation is observed between two variables, there is always the possibility that the correlation is due to the association between each of the two variables and a third variable. For example, among a group of elementary school children of diverse ages, one might find a high correlation between size of vocabulary and height. This correlation may not reflect any genuine or direct relation between these two variables but rather may result from the fact that both vocabulary size and height are associated with a third variable, age.

Statistically, this problem may be attacked by methods of *partial correlation*. In partial correlation, the effects of variation in a third variable upon the relation between the X and Y variables are eliminated. In other words, the correlation between X and Y is found with the third variable Z kept constant.

In designing an experiment, one has the alternative of either introducing experimental controls to eliminate the influence of a third variable or using statistical methods to eliminate its influence. For example, one may wish to study the relation between memorization ability and the ability to solve certain kinds of problems. Both of these skills may be related to intelligence; therefore, to determine their direct relation to each other the influence of differences in intelligence must be controlled. To effect *experimental* control, we might choose subjects with equal intelligence. But if experimental controls are not feasible, then *statistical* controls can be applied. By the technique of partial correlation we could hold constant the effect of intelligence on the relation between memorization ability and ability to solve problems and, thereby, determine the extent of the direct or uncontaminated relation between these two skills.

In this section we shall present a method of statistical control which may be used with the Kendall rank-order correlation τ. To use this nonparametric method of partial correlation, we must have data which are measured in at least an ordinal scale. No assumptions about the shape of the population distribution of scores need be made.

9.5.2 Rationale

Suppose we obtain ranks of four subjects on three variables X, Y, and Z. We shall determine the correlation between X and Y when Z is partialed out, i.e., held constant. The ranks are

Subject:	*a*	*b*	*c*	*d*
Rank on Z:	1	2	3	4
Rank on X:	3	1	2	4
Rank on Y:	2	1	3	4

Now if we consider the possible pairs of ranks on any variable, we know that for these subjects there are $\binom{4}{2}$ possible pairs—four things taken two at a time. Having arranged the ranks on Z in natural order, let us examine every possible pair in the X ranks, the Y ranks, and the Z ranks. We shall assign a + to each of those pairs in which the variable with the lower rank precedes the variable with the higher rank, and a $-$ to each pair in which the variable with the higher rank precedes the lower:

	Pair					
Ranking	(a, b)	(a, c)	(a, d)	(b, c)	(b, d)	(c, d)
Z	+	+	+	+	+	+
X	$-$	$-$	+	+	+	+
Y	$-$	+	+	+	+	+

First, note that since the variable Z is in natural order, all of its precedence pairs are coded as +. Next, note that for variable X the score for the (a, b) pair is coded as a $-$ because the ranks for a and b, 3 and 1 respectively, occur in the "wrong" order—the variable with the higher rank precedes the lower. For variable X, the score for the pair (a, c) is also coded as a $-$ because the a rank 3 is higher than the c rank 2. For variable Y, the pair (a, c) receives a + because the a rank 2 is lower than the c rank 3.

We may summarize the information we have obtained by casting it in a 2×2 table, Table 9.7. Consider first the three signs under (a, b) above. For that set of paired ranks, both X and Y are assigned a $-$, whereas Z is assigned a +. Thus we may say that both X and Y "disagree" with Z. We summarize that information by casting pair (a, b) in cell D of Table 9.7. Consider next the pair (a, c). Here the Y sign agrees with the Z sign, but the X sign disagrees with the Z sign. Therefore pair (a, c) is assigned to cell C in Table 9.7. In each of the remaining pairs, both the Y and X signs agree with the Z sign; thus these four pairs are cast in cell A of Table 9.7.

In general, for three sets of rankings of N objects, we can use the method illustrated above to derive the sort of table for which Table 9.8 is a model. The *Kendall partial rank-order correlation coefficient* $T_{xy.z}$ (*read*: the correlation between X and Y with Z held constant) is computed from such a table. It is defined as

$$T_{xy.z} = \frac{AD - BC}{\sqrt{(A + B)(C + D)(A + C)(B + D)}} \tag{9.12}$$

TABLE 9.7
X and Y orders scored for matches with Z ordering

X pair \ Y pair	Sign agrees with the Z sign	Sign disagrees with the Z sign	Total
Sign agrees with the Z sign	A 4	B 0	4
Sign disagrees with the Z sign	C 1	D 1	2
Total	5	1	6

TABLE 9.8
Form for casting data for computation of $T_{xy.z}$ by Eq. (9.12)

Y pair / *X* pair	Sign agrees with the *Z* sign	Sign disagrees with the *Z* sign	Total
Sign agrees with the *Z* sign	A	B	$A + B$
Sign disagrees with the *Z* sign	C	D	$C + D$
Total	$A + C$	$B + D$	$\binom{N}{2}$

In the case of the four objects we have been considering, i.e., in the case of the data shown in Table 9.7,

$$T_{xy.z} = \frac{(4)(1) - (0)(1)}{\sqrt{(4)(2)(5)(1)}}$$

$$= .63$$

Thus, the correlation between X and Y with the effect of Z held constant is expressed by $T_{xy.z} = .63$. If we had computed the correlation between X and Y without considering the effect of Z, we would have found $T_{xy} = .67$. This suggests that the relations between X and Z and between Y and Z are only slightly influencing the observed relation between X and Y. However, this kind of inference must be made with reservation unless there are relevant *a priori* grounds for expecting whatever effect is observed. The reader will note that Eq. (9.12) is similar to the phi coefficient r_ϕ presented in Sec. 9.2. This similarity suggests that $T_{xy.z}$ measures the extent to which X and Y agree *independently* of their agreement with Z.

9.5.3 Method

Although the method shown for computing $T_{xy.z}$ is useful in revealing the nature of the partial correlation coefficient, as N gets larger this method becomes more tedious because of the rapid increase in the value of $\binom{N}{2}$, the number of pairs of the N observations. Fortunately, a simple computational form for $T_{xy.z}$ has been developed.

Kendall has shown that

$$T_{xy.z} = \frac{T_{xy} - T_{xz}T_{yz}}{\sqrt{(1 - T_{xz}^2)(1 - T_{yz}^2)}} \qquad (9.13)^{14}$$

Equation (9.13) is computationally easier than Eq. (9.12). To use it, one first must find the correlations (the T's between X and Y, X and Z, and Y and Z). Having obtained these values, one may use Eq. (9.13) to find $T_{xy.z}$.

[14] This formula is directly comparable to that used for finding the product-moment partial correlation. However, Kendall (1975) and others have noted that this similarity in form should be construed as coincidental.

For the X, Y, and Z ranks we have been considering $T_{xy} = .67$, $T_{xz} = .33$, and $T_{yz} = .67$. Inserting these values into Eq. (9.13), we have

$$T_{xy.z} = \frac{.67 - (.33)(.67)}{\sqrt{[1 - (.33)^2][1 - (.67)^2]}}$$

$$= .63$$

By using Eq. (9.13), we arrive at the same value for $T_{xy.z}$ which we already found with Eq. (9.12).

Example 9.5*a* We have already seen that in the data collected by Siegel and Fagan the correlation between scores on authoritarianism and scores on social status strivings is $T = .67$. However, we have also observed that there is a correlation between social status strivings and amount of conformity (yielding) to group pressures—$T = .39$. That may make us wonder whether the former correlation simply represents the operation of a third variable, namely, conformity to group pressures. That is, it may be that the subjects' need to conform affects their responses to both the authoritarianism scale and the social status strivings scale, and thus the correlation between the scores on these two scales may be due to an association between each of these variables and need to conform. We may check whether this is true by computing the partial correlation between authoritarianism and social status strivings, partialing out the effect of need to conform, as indicated by amount of yielding in the Asch situation.

The scores for the 12 subjects on each of the three variables are shown in Tables 9.3 and 9.5. The three sets of ranks are combined in Table 9.9. Observe that the variable the effect of which we wish to partial out—conformity—is the Z variable.

We have already determined that the correlation between social status strivings (the X variable) and authoritarianism (the Y variable) is $T_{xy} = .67$. We have also already determined that the correlation between social status strivings and conformity (the Z variable)

TABLE 9.9
Ranks on social status strivings, authoritarianism, and conformity

Subject	Social status strivings X	Authoritarianism Y	Conformity (yielding) Z
A	3	2	1.5
B	4	6	1.5
C	2	5	3.5
D	1	1	3.5
E	8	10	5
F	11	9	6
G	10	8	7
H	6	3	8
I	7	4	9
J	12	12	10.5
K	5	7	10.5
L	9	11	12

is $T_{xz} = .39$ (this value is corrected for ties). From the data presented in Table 9.9, we may readily determine, by using Eq. (9.10), that the correlation between authoritarianism and conformity is $T_{yz} = .36$ (this value is corrected for ties). With this information, we may determine the value of $T_{xy.z}$ by using Eq. (9.13):

$$T_{xy.z} = \frac{T_{xy} - T_{xz}T_{yz}}{\sqrt{(1 - T_{xz}^2)(1 - T_{yz}^2)}} \tag{9.13}$$

$$= \frac{.67 - (.39)(.36)}{\sqrt{[1 - (.39)^2][1 - (.36)^2]}}$$

$$= .62$$

We have determined that, when conformity is partialed out or controlled statistically, the correlation between social status strivings and authoritarianism is $T_{xy.z} = .62$. Since this value is not much smaller than $T_{xy} = .67$, we may conclude that the relation between social status strivings and authoritarianism (as measured by these scales) is relatively independent of the influence of conformity (as measured in terms of amount of yielding to group pressures.)

9.5.4 Testing the Significance of $T_{xy.z}$

If a random sample is drawn from some population in which X and Y are unrelated when the variable Z is controlled, then all possible rank orderings are equally likely. However, unlike the Kendall rank-order correlation coefficient T_{xy}, in which for every ordering of X there are $N!$ possible orderings of Y, the number of possible orderings which must be considered when calculating distribution of the Kendall partial rank-order correlation coefficient is $(N!)^2$. Under the assumption that each of the orderings is equally likely when there is no relation between the variables, it is possible to compute the distribution of $T_{xy.z}$. Because the computations are extremely laborious even for small samples, we must resort to tables of the sampling distribution. Appendix Table S gives critical values of $T_{xy.z}$ for all $N < 20$ and for selected values of N greater than 20.

Appendix Table S may be used to determine the exact probability associated with the occurrence (one-tailed) under H_0 of any value as extreme as an observed $T_{xy.z}$. In testing hypotheses about the Kendall rank-order correlation $\tau_{xy.z}$, the null hypothesis is H_0: $\tau_{xy.z} = 0$, or "X and Y are independent for fixed Z."

The alternative hypothesis might be that $\tau_{xy.z} > 0$ (a one-tailed test) or, more commonly, the alternative hypothesis is H_1: $\tau_{xy.z} \neq 0$, or "X and Y are not independent for fixed Z," which is a two-tailed test.

For example, suppose we have chosen $\alpha = .05$ and that $N = 11$, and we calculated the Kendall partial rank-order correlation to be $T_{xy.z} = .48$. We wish to test the hypothesis that X and Y are independent for fixed Z (or, equivalently, when we hold Z constant) against the hypothesis that X and Y are not independent for fixed Z. Entering Table S with $N = 11$ and $\alpha/2 = .025$ (because we want a two-tailed test), we find that the critical value is .453. Since the observed value of $T_{xy.z} = .48$ exceeds the critical value .453, we may reject at the $\alpha = .05$ level of significance the hypothesis that X and Y are independent for fixed values of the variables Z.

For large values of N, the distribution of $T_{xy.z}$ is complicated but does approximate a normal distribution. An approximation to the variance is

$$\sigma^2_{T_{xy.z}} = \frac{2(2N+5)}{9N(N-1)} \tag{9.14}$$

which is the same as the variance of T_{xy} given in Sec. 9.4.6. Therefore, when N is large, we can test the hypothesis H_0: $\tau_{xy.z} = 0$ by calculating

$$z = \frac{3T_{xy.z}\sqrt{N(N-1)}}{\sqrt{2(2N+5)}} \tag{9.15}$$

which is approximately normally distributed with mean 0 and standard deviation 1. Thus the probability associated with the occurrence of a value as extreme as an observed value of $T_{xy.z}$ when H_0 is true may be determined by using Eq. (9.15) and referring to Appendix Table A to determine the significance of that z.

Example 9.5*b* In the experiment conducted by Siegel and Fagan, the correlation between social status strivings and conformity was $T_{xz} = .39$. However, each of these variables is correlated with authoritarianism scores ($T_{xy} = .67$ and $T_{zy} = .36$ respectively). We would like to know if this correlation is mediated by the joint relation of each variable with authoritarianism. That is, for fixed levels of authoritarianism are social status strivings and conformity independent? To determine this, we need to calculate the partial correlation between social status strivings and conformity when authoritarianism is held constant, which may be found by using Eq. (9.13):

$$T_{xz.y} = \frac{T_{xz} - T_{xy}T_{zy}}{\sqrt{(1-T^2_{xy})(1-T^2_{zy})}} \tag{9.13}$$

$$= \frac{.39 - (.67)(.36)}{\sqrt{(1-.67^2)(1-.36^2)}}$$

$$= .21$$

To test the hypothesis about the conditional independence of X and Z, we may refer to Appendix Table S to determine the probability of obtaining a value $T_{xz.y} \geq .21$ when the rankings of the variables are independent. Entering that table for $N = 12$, we find that $.20 \leq p \leq .40$. Therefore, we may not reject the hypothesis that social status strivings and conformity are independent for fixed levels of authoritarianism.

It should be noted that the test of the null hypothesis that the two variables are independent for fixed levels of a third variable is based on the assumption that all rankings of the three variables are equally likely. In some applications, it may be appropriate to test the same hypothesis but not to assume that all rankings due to the third variable are equally likely; that is, one may not wish to assume that τ_{xz} and τ_{yz} are zero. It appears that the significance test given here is relatively robust in such cases.

9.5.5 A Caution about Partial Correlation Coefficients

The reader should be aware that partial correlation coefficients should be calculated and interpreted with extreme care. If a researcher wants to analyze the effect that one variable has upon the relation between two other variables—either to show that the observed dependence between the two variables is mediated by a third variable ($\tau_{xy.z} \approx 0$) or that a third variable has little effect upon the relation between two variables ($\tau_{xy.z} \approx \tau_{xy}$)—the rationale for analyzing the effect of the third variable should be based upon some *a priori* notions about what relations ought to obtain. There is considerable risk involved in the strategy of simply calculating all possible partial correlations and testing their significance, because, as the number of variables increases, the possibility of obtaining spurious differences increases owing to the large number of tests conducted.

9.5.6 Summary of Procedure

These are the steps in the use of the Kendall partial rank-order correlation coefficient $T_{xy.z}$:

1. Let X and Y be the two variables the relation of which is to be determined, and let Z be the variable the effect of which on X and Y is to be partialed out or held constant.
2. Rank the observations on the X variable from 1 to N. Do the same for the observations on the Y and Z variables.
3. With either Eq. (9.9) (if there are no tied ranks) or Eq. (9.10) (if there are ties), determine the observed values of T_{xy}, T_{xz}, and T_{yx}.
4. With the use of those values, compute the value of $T_{xy.z}$, using Eq. (9.13).
5. To test the significance of $T_{xy.z}$, that is, to test the hypothesis that the variables X and Y are independent for fixed levels of the variable Z, the obtained value of $T_{xy.z}$ is compared to critical values of the statistic given in Appendix Table S. For large values of N, the significance of $T_{xy.z}$ may be determined by calculating z with Eq. (9.15) and finding the associated probability of a value as large as the observed z and, hence, the partial rank-order correlation $T_{xy.z}$. In testing the hypothesis that the two variables are independent given fixed levels of a third variable, the alternative hypothesis is usually that the two variables are *not* independent; in that case, the significance test is two-tailed.

9.5.7 Efficiency

Little is known about the efficiency of the tests based upon the Kendall partial rank-order correlation coefficient. Although it is known that the test of H_0: $\tau_{xy.z} = 0$ assumes that all rankings on the three variables are equally likely, the test appears to be relatively robust with respect to violations of these assumptions concerning τ_{xz} and τ_{yz}.

9.5.8 References

The reader may find other discussions of this statistic in Kendall (1975) and in Moran (1951). For discussions concerning tests of significance of the Kendall partial rank-order correlation coefficient, the reader is referred to Johnson (1979), Maghsoodloo (1975), and Maghsoodloo and Pallos (1981).

9.6 THE KENDALL COEFFICIENT OF CONCORDANCE W

9.6.1 Function

In the previous sections of this chapter, we have been concerned with measures of the correlation between *two* sets of rankings of N objects or individuals. In this section and the next we shall consider two measures of the relation among *several* rankings of N objects or individuals.

When we have k sets of rankings, we may determine the association among them by using the *Kendall coefficient of concordance W*. Whereas Spearman's r_s and Kendall's T express the degree of association between two variables measured in, or transformed to, ranks, W expresses the degree of association among k such variables, that is, the association between k sets of rankings. Such a measure may be particularly useful in studies of interjudge or intertest reliability and also has applications in studies of clusters of variables.

9.6.2 Rationale

As a solution to the problem of ascertaining the overall agreement among k sets of rankings, it might seem reasonable to find the Spearman rank-order correlations (the r_s's) or the Kendall rank-order correlation coefficients (the T's) between all possible pairs of the rankings, and then compute the average of these coefficients to determine the overall association. If we used such a procedure, we would need to compute $\binom{k}{2}$ rank-order correlation coefficients. Unless k were very small, such a procedure would be extremely tedious.

The computation of W is much simpler; moreover, it bears a linear relation to the average r_s taken over all groups. If we denote the average value of the Spearman rank-order correlation coefficients between the $\binom{k}{2}$ possible pairs of rankings as ave(r_s), then it may be shown that

$$\text{ave}(r_s) = \frac{kW - 1}{k - 1} \tag{9.16}$$

Another approach would be to imagine how our data would look if there were no agreement among the several sets of rankings, and then to imagine how it would look if there were perfect agreement among the several sets of rankings. The coefficient of concordance would then be an index of the divergence of the

TABLE 9.10
Ranks assigned to six job applicants by three company executives (artificial data)

	Applicant					
Raters	*a*	*b*	*c*	*d*	*e*	*f*
Executive *X*	1	6	3	2	5	4
Executive *Y*	1	5	6	4	2	3
Executive *Z*	6	3	2	5	4	1
R_i	8	14	11	11	11	8
$\bar{R}_i$	2.67	4.67	3.67	3.67	3.67	2.67

actual agreement shown in the data from the maximum possible or perfect agreement. Very roughly speaking, W is just such a coefficient.

Suppose three company executives are asked to interview six job applicants and rank them in order of judged suitability for a job opening. The three independent sets of ranks given by the executives X, Y, and Z to applicants a through f might be those shown in Table 9.10. The last two rows of Table 9.10 give the sums of the ranks (labeled R_i) and the average rank ($\bar{R}_i$) assigned to each applicant.

Now if the three ($k = 3$) executives had been in *perfect* agreement about the applicants, i.e., if they had each ranked the six applicants in the same order, then one applicant would have received three ranks of 1, and the corresponding sum of ranks R_i would be $1 + 1 + 1 = 3 = k$. The applicant whom all executives designated as the runner-up would have

$$R_i = 2 + 2 + 2 = 6 = 2k$$

The least promising applicant among the six would have

$$R_i = 6 + 6 + 6 = 18 = 6k = Nk$$

In fact, with perfect agreement among the executives, the various sums of ranks R_i would be 3, 6, 9, 12, 15, 18, though not necessarily in that order. In general, when there is perfect agreement among k sets of rankings, we get, for the R_i, the series $k, 2k, 3k, \ldots, Nk$ and the average ranks would be $1, 2, 3, \ldots, N$.

On the other hand, if there had been random agreement among the three executives, then the various R_i's would be approximately equal.

From this example, it should be clear that the degree of agreement among the k judges is reflected by the degree of variation among the N sums of ranks. W, the coefficient of concordance, is a function of that degree of variance.

9.6.3 Method

To compute W, the data are first arranged into a $k \times N$ table with each row representing the ranks assigned by a particular judge to the N objects. Next, we find the sum of ranks R_i in each column of the table and divide each by k to find the average rank $\bar{R}_i$. Then we sum the $\bar{R}_i$ and divide that sum by k to obtain the mean value of the $\bar{R}_i$'s. Each of the $\bar{R}_i$ may then be expressed as a deviation from the grand mean. We have argued above that the larger these deviations, the greater the degree of association among the k sets of ranks. So the sum of squares of these deviations is found. Knowing these values, we may compute the value of W:

$$W = \frac{\sum_{i=1}^{N} (\bar{R}_i - \bar{R})^2}{N(N^2 - 1)/12} \tag{9.17a}$$

where k = number of sets of rankings, e.g., the number of judges
N = number of objects (or individuals) being ranked
$\bar{R}_i$ = average of the ranks assigned to the ith object or subject
$\bar{R}$ = the average (or grand mean) of the ranks assigned across all objects or subjects
$N(N^2 - 1)/12$ = maximum possible sum of the squared deviations, i.e., the numerator which would occur if there were perfect agreement among the k rankings, and the average rankings were 1, 2, . . . , N

For the data shown in Table 9.10, the rank totals are 8, 14, 11, 11, 11, and 8, and the average rankings are 2.67, 4.67, 3.67, 3.67, 3.67, and 2.67 respectively. The grand mean of these averages is 3.5.

To obtain the numerator of W in Eq. (9.17a), we square the deviation of each average rank $\bar{R}_i$ from the mean value and then sum those squares:

$$\begin{aligned}\sum_{i=1}^{N} (\bar{R}_i - \bar{R})^2 &= (2.67 - 3.5)^2 + (4.67 - 3.5)^2 + (3.67 - 3.5)^2 \\ &\quad + (3.67 - 3.5)^2 + (3.67 - 3.5)^2 + (2.67 - 3.5)^2 \\ &= 2.833\end{aligned}$$

Having obtained the numerator, we may find the value of W for the data in Table 9.10 by using Eq. (9.17a):

$$\begin{aligned}W &= \frac{2.833}{6(6^2 - 1)/12} \\ &= .16\end{aligned}$$

$W = .16$ expresses the degree of agreement among the three executives in ranking the six job applicants.

Although Eq. (9.17a) shows the "intuitive" rationale for the statistic W, a somewhat simpler formula may be used. Since the values of the data are known in advance when they are in the form of rankings, the value $\bar{R}$, the grand mean of all of the rankings, is known in advance as well. Since the sum of N ranks is $N(N + 1)/2$, the mean is therefore $(N + 1)/2$. By using this value, Eq. (9.17a) may be simplified:

$$W = \frac{12\Sigma\bar{R}_i^2 - 3N(N + 1)^2}{N(N^2 - 1)} \tag{9.17b}$$

or we may simplify further by using the rank totals R_i rather than the mean ranks $\bar{R}_i$:

$$W = \frac{12\Sigma R_i^2 - 3k^2N(N+1)^2}{k^2N(N^2-1)} \tag{9.17c}$$

where ΣR_i^2 is the sum of the squared sums of ranks for each of the N objects or individuals being ranked. For the data in Table 9.10,

$$\begin{aligned}\Sigma R_i^2 &= 8^2 + 14^2 + 11^2 + 11^2 + 11^2 + 8^2 \\ &= 687\end{aligned}$$

By using this value, and substituting into Eq. (9.17c), we find

$$\begin{aligned}W &= \frac{12(687) - 3(3^2)(6)(6+1)^2}{3^2(6)(6^2-1)} \\ &= .16\end{aligned}$$

Of course, this value is the same as that obtained by the equivalent expression, Eq. (9.17a). The choice of computational formula is up to the user. Equation (9.17c) is easier for quick computation. Many calculators can determine the sum of squared deviations directly, so Eq. (9.17a) may be appropriate in that case.

For the same data, we might have found ave(r_s) by either of two methods. One way would be to find the three rank-order correlations $r_{s_{xy}}$, $r_{s_{xz}}$, and $r_{s_{yz}}$. Then these three values could be averaged. For the data in Table 9.10, $r_{s_{xy}} = .31$, $r_{s_{yz}} = -.54$, and $r_{s_{yz}} = -.54$. The average of these values is

$$\begin{aligned}\text{ave}(r_s) &= \frac{.31 + (-.54) + (-.54)}{3} \\ &= -.26\end{aligned}$$

Another way to find ave(r_s) would be to use Eq. (9.16):

$$\text{ave}(r_s) = \frac{kW - 1}{k - 1} \tag{9.16}$$

$$\begin{aligned}&= \frac{3(.16) - 1}{3 - 1} \\ &= -.26\end{aligned}$$

Both methods yield the same value, ave(r_s) $= -.26$. As shown above, this value is a linear function of the value of W.

One difference between using W and ave(r_s) to express agreement among k rankings is that ave(r_s) may take values between $-1/(k-1)$ and $+1$, whereas W varies between 0 and $+1$, regardless of the number of sets of rankings. The reason that W cannot be negative is that when more than two sets or ranks are involved, the rankings cannot all disagree completely. For example, if judge X and judge Y are in disagreement, and judge X is also in disagreement with judge Z, then judges Y and Z must agree. That is, when more than two judges are involved, agreement and disagreement are not symmetrical opposites. A group of k judges may all agree, but they cannot all disagree completely. Therefore W must be zero or positive. Also, as noted in the rationale for W, the numerator is an index of the variability of the rankings. When there is no consensus among the raters, the variability of rankings will be zero, i.e., the average rank will be the same for all objects ranked.

Since the range of ave(r_s) depends upon the number of raters, the lower limit of $-1/(k-1)$ is not directly comparable across data sets. In the example above, the first two raters (X and Y) disagreed ($r_s = -1$), rater Z also disagreed perfectly with rater X ($r_s = -1$), and, of necessity, Y and Z must agree ($r_s = 1$). In this case, ave(r_s) $= -\frac{1}{3}$. The minimum possible ave(r_s) for $k = 3$ raters is $-\frac{1}{2}$.

The reader should notice that W bears a linear relation to r_s but seems to bear no orderly relation to Kendall's T. This reveals one of the advantages which r_s has over T; however, as we shall see in Sec. 9.7, there is a corresponding concordance index for T.

9.6.4 Tied Observations

When tied observations occur, the observations are each assigned the average of the ranks that would have been assigned had no ties occurred, which is our usual procedure in ranking tied scores.

The effect of tied ranks is to reduce the value of W as found by Eq. (9.17) (in any of its forms). If the proportion of tied ranks is small, that effect is negligible, and thus Eq. (9.17) could still be used. However, if the proportion of ties is large or the researcher would like a more precise estimate, a correction should be used. This correction will result in a slight increase in the value of W compared to the value which would have been obtained had no correction been made. The correction factor is the same as the one used with the Spearman rank-order correlation coefficient r_s:

$$T_j = \sum_{i=1}^{g_j} (t_i^3 - t_i)$$

where t_i is the number of tied ranks in the ith grouping of ties, and g_j is the number of groups of ties in the jth set of ranks. Thus, T_j is the correction factor required for the jth set of ranks.

With the correction for ties incorporated, the formula for the Kendall coefficient of concordance is

$$W = \frac{12\Sigma\bar{R}_i^2 - 3N(N+1)^2}{N(N^2-1) - (\Sigma T_j)/k} \tag{9.18a}$$

or

$$W = \frac{12\Sigma R_i^2 - 3k^2N(N+1)^2}{k^2N(N^2-1) - k\Sigma T_j} \tag{9.18b}$$

where ΣT_j directs one to sum the values of T_j for all of the k sets of rankings.

TABLE 9.11
Ratings of factors affecting the decision to attend a professional meeting

	Factors							
Raters	Airfare	Climate	Meet time	People	Program	Announ.	Present	Declining interest
1	2	7	3	5	4	6	1	8
2	6	5	7	3	4	2	1	8
3	1	6	4	5	2	7	3	8
4	5	6	7	1	2	4	3	8
5	1	8	6	5	2	4	3	7
6	2	7	5	1	3	6	4	8
7	2	7	1	4	3	6	5	8
8	1	4	7	2	3	6	5	8
9	1	7	3	6	2	4	5	8
10	1	6	7	3	2	4	5	8
11	4	5	1	3	2	7	6	8
12	1	4	6	7	2	5	3	8
13	1	5	2	3	4	6	7	8
14	1	6	5	2	3	4	7	8
15	1	7	2	4.5	3	4.5	6	8
16	1	6	5	2.5	2.5	7	4	8
17	1	7	6	4	3	5	2	8
18	3	7	5	6	1	4	2	8
19	1	6	2	4	5	7	3	8
20	1	6	5	3	4	7	2	8
21	1	7	6	2	3	5	4	8
22	1.5	8	1.5	4.5	3	6	4.5	7
R_i	39.5	137	96.5	80.5	62.5	116.5	85.5	174

Example 9.6*a* A professional and academic group, The Society for Cross-Cultural Research (SCCR), decided to conduct a survey of its membership concerning the choice of sites for its annual meeting.[15] To evaluate the interests of the society, a sample of the membership was asked to rate and rank those characteristics which could be used to describe factors affecting potential attendance at the meetings of the society. These factors include characteristics such as airfare, climate, and program content.

In addition to obtaining the average rank assigned to each of the factors affecting meeting attendance, it is desirable to know if the raters can be judged to have reached consensus. One way to measure consensus is to determine the degree of agreement among the raters in their judgments. The Kendall coefficient of concordance is a measure which would provide such an index. The ranks assigned to each of the $N = 8$ factors or attributes for each of the $k = 22$ respondents are given in Table 9.11. A rank of 1 meant that the characteristic would be important in deciding to attend the annual meetings, and a rank of 8 was assigned to the least important aspect.

To calculate the coefficient of concordance, it is first necessary to calculate the sum of ranks for each of the items which were ranked by the respondents. (Had the data not been

[15] Starr, B. J. (1982, Fall). A report from the SCCR Secretary-Treasurer. Society for Cross-Cultural Research: *SCCR Newsletter*, pp. 3 and 4.

collected as ranks, it would have been necessary to first transform the recorded data to ranks.) The sums of the ranks are given at the bottom of Table 9.11. The sum of squared ranks is

$$\begin{aligned}\Sigma R_i^2 &= 39.5^2 + 137^2 + 96.5^2 + 80.5^2 + 62.5^2 + 116.5^2 + 85.5^2 + 174^2 \\ &= 91186.5\end{aligned}$$

It should be noted that a check on the computations is possible here since ΣR_i should be equal to $kN(N + 1)/2$. Since the observed sum is 792, and $22(8)(9)/2 = 792$, we have partial check on the computations.

Next we observe that respondents 15, 16, and 22 have ties in their rankings. Therefore, it is necessary to find the correction terms (the T_j's) to calculate the value of W corrected for ties. For the 15th respondent, there is one group of ties of size 2; hence $g_{15} = 1$ and $t_1 = 2$; thus,

$$T_{15} = 2^3 - 2 = 6$$

Similarly, since respondent 16 had one group of ties of size 2, $T_{16} = 6$ as well. However, respondent 22 had two groups of ties, so

$$\begin{aligned}T_{22} &= (2^3 - 2) + (2^3 - 2) \\ &= 12\end{aligned}$$

With these results, and since $N = 8$ and $k = 22$, we may find the value of W by using Eq. (9.18):

$$W = \frac{12\Sigma R_i^2 - 3k^2N(N + 1)^2}{k^2N(N^2 - 1) - k\Sigma T_i} \tag{9.18b}$$

$$= \frac{12(91186.5) - 3(22^2)(8)(8 + 1)^2}{22^2(8)(8^2 - 1) - 22(6 + 6 + 12)}$$

$$= \frac{153342}{243408}$$

$$= .630$$

Thus we may conclude that there is good agreement among respondents in their rankings of important factors in the decision to attend meetings of the society. Also, we may conclude that cost of airfare and program content are judged as being most important (in that order), and declining interest in the area of cross-cultural work and climate are judged to be the least important factors in determining attendance at the annual meeting.

It was noted earlier that W is related the Spearman rank-order correlation coefficient. If we had calculated the value of r_s for each of the $\binom{22}{2} = 22(21)/2 = 231$ pairs of respondents, we would also have an index of agreement if we averaged the values. However, rather than calculate all such pairs, we may use Eq. (9.16):

$$\text{ave}(r_s) = \frac{kW - 1}{k - 1} \tag{9.16}$$

$$= \frac{22(.630) - 1}{22 - 1}$$

$$= .61$$

Thus the average interrespondent agreement concerning factors affecting attendance at meetings is .61.

Finally, it should be remarked that had we disregarded ties in the computation of W; that is, if we had used Eq. (9.17) instead of Eq. (9.18), we would have found $W = .6286$, which is somewhat smaller than the value obtained with the correction. The effect of ties is small in this case because the number of groups of tied ranks is small, and each group of ties contains no more than two ties.

9.6.5 Testing the Significance of W

As with several other nonparametric statistical techniques presented in this book, the method for testing the significance of the Kendall coefficient of concordance depends on the sample size—in this case, the number of objects being ranked.

SMALL SAMPLES. We may test the significance of any observed value of W by determining the probability associated with the occurrence when H_0 is true of a value as large as the observed value. If we obtain the sampling distribution of W for all permutations in the N ranks in all possible ways among the k rankings, we will have $(N!)^k$ sets of possible ranks. With these we may test the null hypothesis that the k sets of rankings are independent by taking from this distribution the probability associated with the occurrence under H_0 of a value as large as an observed W.

By this method the distribution of W under H_0 (the assumption that the rankings are independent) has been worked out and certain critical values have been tabled. Appendix Table T gives critical values of W for the $\alpha = .05$ and $\alpha = .01$ significance levels. This table is applicable for k from 3 to 20 and for N from 3 to 7. If an observed W is greater than or equal to that shown in Appendix Table T for a particular level of significance, then H_0 may be rejected at that level of significance. It should be recalled that as an index of concordance $0 \leq W \leq 1$, so that only one-tailed tests concerning W are appropriate.

For example, we saw that when $k = 3$ fictitious executives ranked $N = 6$ job applicants, their agreement was $W = .16$. Reference to Appendix Table T reveals that value of W is not significant at the $\alpha = .05$ level. For the concordance to have been significant at the $\alpha = .05$ level, the observed W would have to be .660 or larger.

LARGE SAMPLES. When N is larger than 7, Appendix Table T cannot be used to determine the significance of an observed W. However, the quantity

$$X^2 = k(N-1)W \tag{9.19}$$

is approximately distributed as chi square with $N - 1$ degrees of freedom. That is, the probability associated with the occurrence when H_0 is true of any value as large as an observed W may be determined by finding X^2 by using Eq. (9.19) and then determining the probability associated with as large a value of X^2 by referring to Appendix Table C.

If the value of X^2 computed from Eq. (9.19) equals or exceeds that shown in Appendix Table C for a particular level of significance and a particular value of $df = N - 1$, then the null hypothesis H_0 that the k rankings are unrelated (or independent) may be rejected at that level of significance.

Example 9.6b[16] In the study of factors affecting the decision to attend meetings of the Society for Cross-Cultural Research, $k = 22$ respondents rated $N = 8$ factors, and we found that $W = .630$. We may determine the significance of this concordance by applying Eq. (9.19):

$$X^2 = k(N - 1)W \tag{9.19}$$
$$= 22(8 - 1)(.630)$$
$$= 97.02$$

Referring to Appendix Table C, we find that $X^2 \geq 97.02$ with

$$df = N - 1 = 8 - 1 = 7$$

has probability of occurrence under H_0 of $p < .001$. We can conclude with considerable confidence that the agreement among the 22 respondents is higher than it would be by chance had their rankings been random or independent. The very low probability under H_0 associated with the observed value of W enables us to reject the null hypothesis that the respondents' ratings are unrelated to each other and conclude that there is good consensus among members concerning the factors which affect decisions to attend the meetings of the society.

9.6.6 Summary of Procedure

These are the steps in the use of W, the Kendall coefficient of concordance:

1. Let N be the number of entities or objects to be ranked, and let k be the number of judges assigning ranks. Cast the observed ranks in a $k \times N$ table.
2. For each object, determine R_i, the sum of the ranks assigned to that object by each of the k judges.
3. Determine the squared values of each of the sums (R_i^2).
4. If there are no ties or the proportion of tied ranks is small, compute the value of W with one of the forms of Eq. (9.17). If the proportion of ties among the N ranks is large, use Eq. (9.18) to determine the value of W.
5. The method for determining whether the observed value of W is significantly different from zero depends on the size of N, the number of objects ranked:
   (*a*) If $N \leq 7$, Appendix Table T gives critical values of W for significance levels $\alpha = .05$ and $\alpha = .01$.
   (*b*) If $N > 7$, Eq. (9.19) may be used to compute a value of X^2 which is approximately distributed as chi square, and the significance of which for $df = N - 1$ may be tested by reference to Appendix Table C.
6. If W is larger than the critical value found by using Appendix Table C or Appendix Table T, reject H_0 and conclude that the rankings are not independent.

---

[16] These data are also part of the SCCR survey reported earlier.

9.6.7 Interpretation of W

A high or significant value of W may be interpreted as meaning that the k observers or judges are applying essentially the same standard in ranking the N objects under study. Often their pooled ordering may be used as a "standard," especially when there is no relevant external criterion for ordering the objects.

It should be emphasized that a high or significant value of W does *not* mean that the orderings observed are *correct*. In fact, they may all be incorrect with respect to some external criterion. For example, the 22 respondents in the example agreed well in judging which factors were important in determining attendance at the annual meetings of the society; however, only time can tell if their judgments were sound. It is possible that a variety of judges can agree in ordering objects because all employ the "wrong" criterion. In this case, a high or significant W would simply show that all more or less agree in their use of a "wrong" criterion. To state the point another way, a high degree of agreement about an ordering does not necessarily mean that the order agreed upon is the "objective" one. In the behavioral sciences "objective" orderings and "consensual" orderings are often incorrectly thought to be synonymous.

Kendall suggests that the best estimate of the "true" ranking of the N objects is provided, when W is significant, by the order of the various sums of ranks R_i or, equivalently, the average rankings $\bar{R}_i$. If one accepts the criteria which the various judges have agreed upon (as evidenced by the magnitude and significance of W) in ranking the N entities, then the best estimate of the "true" ranking of those estimates is provided by the order of the sums (or averages) of ranks. This "best estimate" is associated, in a certain sense, with a least-squares estimate. Thus, in the employment example given earlier, our best estimate would be that either applicant a or f (see Table 9.10) should be hired for the job opening, for in each of their cases the sum of ranks are equal—$R_1 = R_6 = 8$—the lowest value observed. And our best estimate would be that, of the eight factors affecting attendance at meetings of SCCR, airfare is the most important factor and lack of interest is the least important factor.

Finally, it should be noted that the Kendall coefficient of concordance W is closely related to the Friedman statistic F_r discussed in Sec. 7.2. The careful reader will note that in discussing the Friedman two-way analysis of variance, the model was described as a set of k measures on each of N subjects. In our discussion of W, we described the model as involving a set of k judges ranking each of N objects. The two statistics are linearly related but, in our presentation, N and k are interchanged between the two statistics.

9.6.8 Efficiency

There is no direct parametric analog to W as interpreted as an index of agreement between a set of k rankings. However, as a test of equality of N rankings, we may appeal to its relation to the Friedman two-way analysis of variance. In that case, when the assumptions of the analysis of variance are satisfied, the efficiency of W is low when $N = 2$ ($2/\pi = .64$), but increases to .80 when $N = 5$ and to $3/\pi = .955$ when N is large. Thus, the efficiency of the test increases as the number of objects ranked increases.

9.6.9 References

Discussions of the Kendall coefficient of concordance are contained in Friedman (1940) and Kendall (1975). Other recent discussions may be found in Gibbons (1985).

9.7 THE KENDALL COEFFICIENT OF AGREEMENT *u* FOR PAIRED COMPARISONS OR RANKINGS

When we discussed the Kendall coefficient of concordance W, it was described as an index of the similarity of rank orderings produced by each of k judges. In this section, we shall discuss a similar measure, W_T, which is based upon the *Kendall coefficient of agreement u*. Sometimes, rather than ask a group of judges to rank a set of objects, we might present them with pairs of the objects, and ask each judge to indicate a preference for one of the two objects. A task in which we ask subjects to indicate preferences for one of a pair of objects is called *paired comparisons*.

In the method of paired comparisons, the preferences among the set of objects may be inconsistent. That is, if there are three objects to be compared, say, A, B, and C, the subject may prefer A to B, B to C, but prefer C to A. Had we asked the subject to rank the objects, it would be impossible since, when objects are ranked, the pairwise preferences must be consistent.[17] Although we might try very hard to avoid inconsistent preferences in a particular research study, it should be noted that they may occur more frequently than one might suppose. Consider the following example: We ask a school child to rank a group of fellow students from the one he or she would like most to play with to the one he or she would like least to play with. Such a task is difficult because we are asking the child to rank a group from first to last, which is not a "natural" behavior; moreover, it may not be possible because the preferences may not be transitive. However, if we would present the child with the names of two classmates, it should be possible, and certainly more natural, to indicate a preference for one person in each pair.

When data are gathered by the method of paired comparisons, it is possible to calculate the degree of agreement among individuals in their preferences. In this section, we shall discuss a coefficient of agreement u suitable for data from paired comparisons. In addition, we shall see that this coefficient is related to the average of the Kendall rank-order correlation coefficient T when the data are in ranks.

---

[17] Pairwise comparisons which are consistent are also *transitive*. See the discussion of ordinal scales in Sec. 3.3.2.

9.7.1 Rationale and Method

To calculate the coefficient of agreement, we need to look only at the preferences for each individual and then aggregate these into a single index. Suppose a person was asked to indicate preferences for $N = 4$ objects. To do this, we would need to present $\binom{4}{2} = (4)(3)/2 = 6$ pairs to the subject who would indicate a preference for one member of each pair. Each pair may be denoted (a, b), and the person expresses a preference $a > b$ or $b > a$. (Read $>$ as "is preferred to.") Thus, for the six pairs presented, suppose the preferences had been the following:

Pair	Preference
(a, b)	a
(a, c)	a
(a, d)	d
(b, c)	b
(b, d)	d
(c, d)	d

These preferences may be summarized in a preference matrix. A preference matrix is a table summarizing the number of times each object is preferred to (or ranked before) every other object. The table contains an entry for every pair in which the *row* variable is preferred to the *column* variable. The preference matrix for the preferences given above is the following:

Preference matrix

	a	b	c	d
a	—	1	1	—
b	—	—	1	—
c	—	—	—	—
d	1	1	1	—

If there are several judges or subjects performing the rankings, then their preferences are combined into the preference matrix. To illustrate the computation, we shall use the ranking example from Sec. 9.6.3. These data are summarized again in the top portion of Table 9.12. Next, we transform these ranking data into the preference table given in the bottom of Table 9.12. It should be remarked that, if there had been complete agreement among the three executives, exactly 15 cells of the table would have entries, and each entry would be equal to 3. [In general, if there is complete agreement among k judges making paired comparisons among N objects, then $N(N - 1)/2$ cells would have frequencies equal to k. The remaining $N(N - 1)/2$ cells would contain 0.] Kendall has proposed a coefficient of agreement

TABLE 9.12
Ranks assigned to six job applicants by three company executives (artificial data)

	Applicant					
Raters	*a*	*b*	*c*	*d*	*e*	*f*
Executive *X*	1	6	3	2	5	4
Executive *Y*	1	5	6	4	2	3
Executive *Z*	6	3	2	5	4	1

Preference matrix

	a	*b*	*c*	*d*	*e*	*f*
a	—	2	2	2	2	2
b	1	—	1	1	1	0
c	1	2	—	1	2	1
d	1	2	2	—	1	1
e	1	2	1	2	—	1
f	1	3	2	2	2	—

among the judges which is

$$u = \frac{2 \sum_{i=1}^{N} \sum_{j=1}^{N} \binom{a_{ij}}{2}}{\binom{k}{2}\binom{N}{2}} - 1 \qquad (9.20a)$$

where a_{ij} is the number of times that the object associated with row i is preferred to the object associated with row j. Although the calculation of u involves rather cumbersome and tedious computations, they can be done fairly directly. If we manipulate the combinatorial expressions and simplify, Eq. (9.20*a*) may be rewritten in the following form:

$$u = \frac{4 \sum_{i=}^{N} \sum_{j=1}^{N} a_{ij}(a_{ij} - 1)}{k(k-1)N(N-1)} - 1 \qquad (9.20b)$$

Again, by noting some relationships (primarily between cells in the upper half and lower half of the matrix), we can simplify the computational formula even further:

$$u = \frac{8(\Sigma a_{ij}^2 - k\Sigma a_{ij})}{k(k-1)N(N-1)} + 1 \qquad (9.20c)$$

where the summation is taken over the a_{ij}'s below *or* above the diagonal. If there are fewer nonzero entries (or smaller entries) on one side of the diagonal, that side may be chosen for convenience when applying Eq. (9.20*c*) to the calculation of the coefficient of agreement.

For the preference matrix given in Table 9.12, we have the following sums for the a_{ij}'s below the diagonal:

$$\Sigma a_{ij} = 1 + 1 + 1 + 1 + 1 + 2 + 2 + 2 + 3 + 2 + 1 + 2 + 2 + 2 + 2 = 25$$

and

$$\Sigma a_{ij}^2 = 1^2 + 1^2 + 1^2 + 1^2 + 1^2 + 2^2 + 2^2 + 2^2 + 3^2 + 2^2 + 1^2 + 2^2 + 2^2 + 2^2 + 2^2 = 47$$

With these values, we calculate u by using Eq. (9.20c):

$$u = \frac{8(\Sigma a_{ij}^2 - k\Sigma a_{ij})}{k(k-1)N(N-1)} + 1 \tag{9.20c}$$

$$= \frac{8[47 - 3(25)]}{(3)(2)(6)(5)} + 1$$

$$= \frac{8(-28)}{(6)(30)} + 1$$

$$= -.244$$

The reader may verify that this is the same value we would obtain had we applied Eq. (9.20c) to the entries above the diagonal or used either Eq. (9.20a) or (9.20b).

One useful aspect of this coefficient is that, if the paired comparisons for each subject are consistent, that is, a ranking of the N objects could be done, then *u is equal to the average T*. Alternatively, if we calculated the Kendall rank-order correlation for each pair of judges, then the average of all of the T's would be equal to u. In the example of the executives rating job applicants, $T_{xy} = .20$, $T_{yz} = -.467$, and $T_{xz} = -.467$; ave$(T) = (.20 - .467 - .467)/3 = -.244$, which is the value obtained by using Eq. (9.20).

As we noted in the discussion of the Kendall coefficient of concordance W, that index was a function of the average Spearman rank-order correlation coefficient. Like the statistic ave(r_s), u will be equal to one when there is complete agreement among the judges. However, although each value of T can range from -1 to $+1$, the average T cannot attain a minimum of -1. That is, because when there are more than two sets of rankings, they cannot all be in disagreement (or "reverse" rank order) with respect to each other. In fact, the minimum value of u is $-1/(k-1)$ when k is even and $-1/k$ when k is odd. To have an index of agreement similar to the Kendall coefficient of concordance, we can define W_T to be

$$W_T = \frac{(k-1)u + 1}{k} \quad \text{if } k \text{ is even} \tag{9.21a}$$

and

$$W_T = \frac{ku + 1}{k+1} \quad \text{if } k \text{ is odd} \tag{9.21b}$$

Thus, like W, W_T may vary from 0 to 1. For the example of the three executives,

$$W_T = \frac{3(-.244) + 1}{3 + 1}$$

$$= .067$$

which indicates that there is little agreement among the executives. As we would expect, the value is in accord with the value of the Kendall coefficient of concordance calculated in Sec. 9.5 where we found that $W = .16$.

Example 9.7.*a*. Multiattribute decision theory is applied to decision making by people in an effort to develop models of decision making which not only help psychologists better to understand the decision-making process but also to serve as an aid to improve the decision-making process when decisions are made under uncertainty. Multiattribute utility theory models the decision process as a linear model; that is, it assumes that decisions can be modeled as a weighted sum of the variables or factors involved in the decision. The weights applied to the factors are usually "importance" weights based upon the individual's subjective judgments of the importance of each factor in making a decision. In a study designed to assess the applicability of multiattribute utility models to decisions concerning land use,[18] subjects were asked to rate the importance of five general factors which describe the effect of particular land-use policies. The factors identified in the study were:

1. Multiple use, e.g., the location, access, and type of activities possible on the site.
2. Beauty, recreation, and wildlife, e.g., the potential support of wildlife populations, outdoor sports, and scenic areas.
3. Resource productivity, e.g., the potential for oil and gas, forest products, agriculture, and mining.
4. Income potential for the government, e.g., royalty income and maintenance costs.
5. Economic conditions, e.g., impact on local tax base, employment, and effect on vulnerable groups.

To determine the importance of each factor to each person in the study, subjects were given each of the five factors in pairs and asked to indicate which of the two they considered more important in assessing decisions concerning land use. Since there were five factors, 10 pairs of factors were judged by each subject. Because of the way in which the paired comparisons were made, it was possible for a subject to judge both members of a pair as equal in importance.

Although it is expected that in any assessment of the factors concerning land use people will express a wide variety of opinions, it is, nonetheless, desirable to determine the degree of consensus among people concerning the factors affecting land use. Since the data in this study are paired comparisons, the Kendall coefficient of agreement is an appropriate statistic for assessing the agreement among the raters.

In one condition in the study, $k = 10$ subjects or judges made paired comparisons among the $N = 5$ factors. Their choices are summarized in the preference matrix given in

---

[18] Sawyer, T. A., and Castellan, N. J., Jr. (1983). Preferences among predictions and the correlation between predicted and observed judgments.

TABLE 9.13
Preference matrix for 10 subjects in land-use study

	Multiple use	Beauty	Resources	Income	Economic condition
Multiple use	—	3	$4\frac{1}{2}$	$7\frac{1}{2}$	$2\frac{1}{2}$
Beauty	7	—	8	10	7
Resources	$5\frac{1}{2}$	2	—	6	$2\frac{1}{2}$
Income	$2\frac{1}{2}$	0	4	—	1
Economic conds.	$7\frac{1}{2}$	3	$7\frac{1}{2}$	9	—

Table 9.13. This preference matrix was formed by aggregating the preference matrices for each of the 10 subjects. (It should be noted that, when a subject is indifferent to the elements of a pair, a count of one-half is recorded in each of the corresponding cells in the matrix.) The coefficient of agreement was then calculated:

$$u = \frac{8(\Sigma a_{ij}^2 - k\Sigma a_{ij})}{k(k-1)N(N-1)} + 1 \tag{9.20c}$$

$$= \frac{8[(7^2 + 5.5^2 + \cdots + 9^2) - 10(7 + 5.5 + \cdots + 9)]}{(10)(10-1)(5)(5-1)} + 1$$

$$= \frac{8[(308) - 10(48)]}{(10)(9)(5)(4)} + 1$$

$$= .236$$

Thus we see that there is modest agreement among the subjects in their preferences for the factors. In the next section we shall determine whether this degree of agreement represents a significant departure from random agreement among the judges.

Although it might seem desirable to calculate W_T for these ratings, it must be remembered that it would be appropriate only if the ratings had been rankings. Since the ratings were paired comparisons, the concordance index W_T is not calculated for these data.

9.7.2 Testing the Significance of *u*

The statistic u can be thought of as an estimate of a population parameter υ, which represents the true degree of agreement in the population. In this case, the population consists of the objects being ranked. Unlike many other statistics discussed in this book, in testing hypotheses concerning the coefficient of agreement, there are two cases to consider since the sampling distribution of u depends upon whether the data are paired comparisons or rankings. We shall discuss each in turn. It must be emphasized at the outset that, in order to test hypotheses about υ properly, the researcher must know the nature of the data on which the coefficient of agreement was calculated.

TESTING SIGNIFICANCE WHEN THE DATA ARE PAIRED COMPARISONS. When the data used to calculate the coefficient of agreement are paired comparisons, we may test the null hypothesis H_0: $\upsilon = 0$ against the hypothesis H_1: $\upsilon \neq 0$.

That is, the null hypothesis is that there is no agreement among the raters, and the alternative is that the degree of agreement is greater than what one would expect had the paired comparisons been done at random. If the number of judges or rankers is small ($k \leq 6$) and the number of variables or factors being ranked is small ($N \leq 8$), then Appendix Table U may be used to test hypotheses concerning the agreement. For each value of k and N, the table lists the possible values of $u \geq 0$ together with the probability of obtaining a value of u equal to or greater than the tabled value. Suppose $k = 4$ judges rated a group of $N = 6$ objects by the method of paired comparisons. Suppose further that the observed value of u was .333. Referring to Appendix Table U we see that the probability of observing a value of $u \geq .333$ has probability of occurrence of .0037 had the judges alloted their preferences at random. In this case, it would be proper to conclude that there is significant agreement among the judges. For convenience, also included in Appendix Table U are the values of S which correspond to the summations in Eq. (9.20*c*):

$$S = \Sigma a_{ij}^2 - k\Sigma a_{ij}$$

In some cases, it may be more convenient to determine the significance of u by using S rather than u.

For other values of k and N, we may use a large-sample approximation to the sampling distribution. In this case the test statistic is

$$X^2 = \binom{N}{2}[1 + u(k-1)]$$

$$= \frac{N(N-1)[1 + u(k-1)]}{2} \tag{9.22}$$

which is asymptotically distributed as χ^2 with $\binom{N}{2} = N(N-1)/2$ degrees of freedom. The test is closely related to the chi-square goodness-of-fit test discussed in Sec. 4.2.

Example 9.7*b* In the decision-making example given earlier in this section, the value of the Kendall coefficient of agreement was $u = .236$. To test the hypothesis that there is agreement among the $k = 10$ subjects in rating the $N = 5$ factors affecting land use, we are unable to use Appendix Table U because the table is limited to $k \leq 6$. Therefore, we shall test the hypothesis H_0: $\upsilon = 0$ by using Eq. (9.22):

$$X^2 = \frac{N(N-1)[1 + u(k-1)]}{2} \tag{9.22}$$

$$= \frac{(5)(5-1)[1 + (.236)(10-1)]}{2}$$

$$= 10(1 + 2.124)$$

$$= 31.24$$

which is asymptotically distributed as χ^2 with $\binom{N}{2} = 5(5-1)/2 = 10$ degrees of freedom. Reference to Appendix Table C shows that we may reject the null hypothesis H_0: $v = 0$ at the $\alpha = .001$ level and conclude that there is strong agreement among the subjects in their ratings of the importance of land-use factors.

TESTING SIGNIFICANCE WHEN THE DATA ARE RANKS. When the data used to calculate the coefficient of agreement are based on ranks, the test of significance may be written in terms of $\bar{\tau}$, which is the population value for the average τ. Then the null hypothesis is H_0: $\bar{\tau} = 0$; the alternative hypothesis is that $\bar{\tau} \neq 0$. (Equivalently, we could consider the hypothesis that the population value of $W_\tau = 0$ against the hypothesis that the population value of $W_\tau \neq 0$.) The significance test is

$$X^2 = \frac{6(2N+5)\binom{N}{2}\binom{k}{2}}{(k-2)(2N^2+6N+7)}|u| + f$$

$$= \frac{3(2N+5)N(N-1)k(k-1)}{2(k-2)(2N^2+6N+7)}|u| + f \tag{9.23}$$

which is distributed approximately as χ^2 with f degrees of freedom:

$$f = \frac{2(2N+5)^3\binom{N}{2}\binom{k}{2}}{(k-2)^2(2N^2+6N+7)^2}$$

$$= \frac{(2N+5)^3N(N-1)k(k-1)}{2(k-2)^2(2N^2+6N+7)^2} \tag{9.24}$$

It should be noted that, in general, the degrees of freedom determined with Eq. (9.24) will not be an integer. For appropriate use of the approximation, it is sufficient to reduce f to the next smaller integer when entering a table of the χ^2 distribution such as that in Appendix Table C.

In the example of the three executives discussed earlier (see Table 9.12), we found that $u = -.244$. To test the hypothesis H_0: $\bar{\tau} = 0$, we first use Eq. (9.24) to find f, the degrees of freedom:

$$f = \frac{(2N+5)^3N(N-1)k(k-1)}{2(k-2)^2(2N^2+6N+7)^2} \tag{9.24}$$

$$= \frac{[(2)(6)+5]^3(6)(6-1)(3)(3-1)}{2(3-2)^2[(2)(6^2)+(6)(6)+7]^2}$$

$$= \frac{(17^3)(6)(5)(3)}{115^2}$$

$$= 33.43$$

Next, we use Eq. (9.23) to find the value of X^2:

$$X^2 = \frac{3(2N+5)N(N-1)k(k-1)}{2(k-2)(2N^2+6N+7)}|u| + f \tag{9.23}$$

$$= \frac{3[(2)(6)+5](6)(6-1)(3)(3-1)}{2(3-2)[(2)(6^2)+(6)(6)+7]}|-.244| + f$$

$$= \frac{(3)(17)(6)(5)(3)(2)}{2[(2)(36)+(6)(6)+7]}|-.244| + f$$

$$= \frac{(9180)|-.244|}{230} + 33.43$$

$$= 43.17$$

Reference to Appendix Table C with $f = 33$ degrees of freedom indicates that we cannot reject the hypothesis that the executives' rankings of applicants are unrelated (or independent) at the $\alpha = .05$ level. This result is consistent with that reported in Sec. 9.6.5.

9.7.3 Summary of Procedure

These are the steps in the determination of u, the Kendall coefficient of agreement:

1. Let N be the number of entities or objects to be rated (either by ranking or by paired comparisons) and let k be the number of judges who produce the ratings. Cast the data into an $N \times N$ preference matrix like that described in Sec. 9.7.1. If there are tied ranks, add $\frac{1}{2}$ to each cell ij and ji in which each of the ties occur. Denote the total frequency in the ijth cell as a_{ij}.
2. With the use of either the frequencies above *or* below the diagonal (whichever is convenient), calculate Σa_{ij}^2 and Σa_{ij} and determine the value of u with Eq. (9.20*c*).
3. The method for determining whether the observed value of u is significantly different from zero depends upon whether the data were obtained by paired comparisons or by rankings:
   (*a*) If the data were obtained by the method of paired comparisons, Appendix Table U gives upper-tail probabilities for u for $k \leq 6$ and $N \leq 8$. If the magnitude of k or N preclude the use of Appendix Table U, Eq. (9.22) may be used to compute a value of X^2 which is approximately distributed as χ^2, the significance of which for $df = N(N-1)/2$ may be determined by using Appendix Table C.
   (*b*) If the data were obtained by the method of rankings, Eq. (9.23) may be used to compute a value of X^2 which is approximately distributed as χ^2 with degrees of freedom given by Eq. (9.24). The significance of u may be obtained by using Appendix Table C. [If the degrees of freedom obtained with Eq. (9.24)

are not integral, reduce the value to the next lower integer before entering Appendix Table C.]

4. If the upper-tail probability obtained with Appendix Table U or Appendix Table C is less than or equal to the predetermined probability α, reject H_0 and conclude that the ratings (paired comparisons or rankings) are not independent.

9.7.4 The Correlation Between Several Judges and a Criterion Ranking T_C

One advantage of the Kendall coefficient of agreement u over the use of W, the Kendall coefficient of concordance, is that it is the *average* of the Kendall rank-order correlation among several judges. Another advantage is that it generalizes directly to the correlation between several judges and a criterion ranking. Suppose there were several clinical trainees who were asked to rank a group of patients in order of severity of pathology. The Spearman rank-order correlation coefficient r_s and the Kendall rank-order correlation coefficient T give an index of the relation between two rankers, and the Kendall coefficient of concordance W and Kendall coefficient of agreement u give an indication of the agreement (or concordance) *among* the rankers; however, these measures do not measure how close the rankings agree with some specified criterion. In this section we outline a procedure for calculating T_C, the correlation between k sets of rankings and a criterion ranking. It should be remarked at the outset that T_C is the *average* of the Kendall rank-order correlation coefficients between each ranker and the criterion ranking. However, we shall find that there is a relatively simple way to calculate the correlation T_C, and we may also perform a test for the significance of T_C.

THE CALCULATION OF T_C. The first step in computing T_C is to determine the criterion ranking for N objects. Use this ranking to construct a preference matrix in which the objects (variables) are listed in the criterion order. Next, for each of the k judges or rankers, enter the rankings into the preference matrix by using the method outlined in Sec. 9.7.1. Then, denoting the sum of the frequencies above the diagonal as $\Sigma^+ a_{ij}$ and those below the diagonal as $\Sigma^- a_{ij}$, we can calculate T_C, the correlation with a criterion ranking:

$$T_C = \frac{2(\Sigma^+ a_{ij} - \Sigma^- a_{ij})}{kN(N-1)} \tag{9.25}$$

Alternative, and often more convenient, computational forms for T_C are

$$T_C = \frac{4\Sigma^+ a_{ij}}{kN(N-1)} - 1 \tag{9.25a}$$

and

$$T_C = 1 - \frac{4\Sigma^- a_{ij}}{kN(N-1)} \tag{9.25b}$$

It should be noted that $\Sigma^+ a_{ij}$ is the number of agreements in rankings with the criterion taken across the rankers. Similarly, $\Sigma^- a_{ij}$ is the number of disagreements in order among the rankings.

TESTING THE SIGNIFICANCE OF T_C. Upper-tail probabilities for the sampling distribution of T_C are given in Appendix Table V for $k = 2$ and 3 and $2 \le N \le 5$. For other values, the sampling distribution of T_C is approximately normal. Therefore, to test the hypothesis H_0: $\tau_C = 0$ against the alternative hypothesis H_1: $\tau_C > 0$ we may use the statistic

$$z = \left[T_C \pm \frac{2}{kN(N-1)} \right] \frac{3\sqrt{kN(N-1)}}{\sqrt{2(2N+5)}} \tag{9.26}$$

which is approximately normally distributed with mean zero and standard deviation one. Appendix Table A may be used to estimate probabilities associated with values of T_C. In calculating z, $2/kN(N-1)$ is subtracted in the numerator if $T_C > 0$, otherwise the quantity is added (which would be the case if we were testing the hypothesis H_1: $\tau_C < 0$).

Example 9.7c[19] Suppose $k = 5$ judges have ranked $N = 5$ objects and we wish to determine the correlation between the judges' rankings and a criterion ranking. For convenience, the criterion ranking of the objects follows the order as their label codes, that is, *A*, *B*, *C*, *D*, *E*. The rankings assigned by the rankers to the objects are given in Table 9.14. The criterion ranking is used to label the rows and columns of the preference matrix in the lower portion of Table 9.14. By using the rankings, the data are then summarized in the preference table. For these data, we find that $\Sigma^+ a_{ij} = 37$, and $\Sigma^- a_{ij} = 13$.

To calculate T_C, we shall use Eq. (9.25*a*):

$$T_C = \frac{4\Sigma^+ a_{ij}}{kN(N-1)} - 1 \tag{9.25a}$$

$$= \frac{(4)(37)}{(5)(5)(4)} - 1$$

$$= .48$$

The reader may verify that the same values would be obtained had we used either Eq. (9.25) or (9.25*b*).

To test the hypothesis that the observed agreement between the rankings of the subjects and the criterion exceeds what one would expect if the rankings had been made randomly, we use Eq. (9.26) to test the hypothesis that the population value of $\tau_C = 0$ against

[19] These data are from an example given by Stilson and Campbell (1962).

TABLE 9.14
Ranking data for the computation of T_C, the correlation between several rankings and a criterion ranking*

	Patients				
Judge	*A*	*B*	*C*	*D*	*E*
I	1	2	3	4	5
II	2	1	4	3	5
III	4	1	3	2	5
IV	1	3	5	2	4
V	1	4	3	5	2

Preference matrix

	A	*B*	*C*	*D*	*E*
A	—	3	4	4	5
B	2	—	4	4	4
C	1	1	—	2	3
D	1	1	3	—	4
E	0	1	2	1	—

* Objects (patients) are listed in order of the criterion ranking.

the hypothesis that the population value of $\tau_C > 0$:

$$z = \left[T_C \pm \frac{2}{kN(N-1)} \right] \frac{3\sqrt{kN(N-1)}}{\sqrt{2(2N+5)}} \tag{9.26}$$

$$= (.48 - .02)\frac{3\sqrt{(5)(5)(5-1)}}{\sqrt{2[(2)(5)+5]}}$$

$$= 2.52$$

Reference to Appendix Table A reveals that the probability of obtaining a value of $z \geq 2.52$ is .0059 (one-tailed). Therefore we may conclude with a high degree of confidence that the raters as a group show strong agreement with the criterion ranking.

9.7.5 References

The coefficient of agreement is discussed by Kendall (1975) who also derived the sampling distribution of u when the data are based on paired comparisons. The sampling distribution of u when the data are based on ranks is also presented in Kendall's monograph; a useful discussion may be found in Ehrenberg (1952). For further information on u and on the correlation between a set of rankings and a criterion ranking T_C, the reader is referred to Hays (1960) and Stilson and Campbell (1962). Hays also discusses an index appropriate for assessing the agreement among several groups of judges. At this time, little is known about the power of the various indexes discussed in this section. Other approaches to the analysis of data derived from paired comparisons and rankings are discussed by Feigin and Cohen (1978).

9.8 NOMINALLY SCALED DATA AND THE KAPPA STATISTIC K

In the previous two sections we discussed two measures of agreement between a set of k raters or judges who have ranked or compared N objects (entities or subjects). Those measures, ave(r_s), the Kendall coefficient of concordance W, the Kendall coefficient of agreement u, and its corresponding concordance measure W_T, assumed that the objects could be ranked or, in the case of the Kendall coefficient of agreement, that paired comparisons could be made between the objects. In some situations, the objects may not be ordered but simply assigned into categories which may not have any inherent order to them. An example would be the case of a group of k psychologists who wish to assign each member of a group of N patients or clients into one of m diagnostic or treatment categories. The treatment categories are simply nominal classifications. Suppose each of the raters categorizes each patient independently of both the other patients and other raters. Given this situation, it would be possible for a given rater to assign each patient to the same category or to distribute the patients across the categories. What the researcher would like to know about the assignments is whether the raters agree with each other about the category membership of each patient. At one extreme, the raters could have complete agreement among each other, and at the other extreme, their assignments could show no agreement and appear to be random. (It should be noted that even if the raters assign patients to categories randomly, there would be some small agreement among them owing to chance assignments, especially if the number of raters k exceeded the number of categories m.)

The *kappa statistic* discussed in this section describes one of a number of measures of agreement which have been proposed for categorical variables. These measures are all similar; some are specialized to assess the agreement between only two raters or a single rater evaluating pairs of objects. Our choice is a statistic which is conceptually similar to our earlier measures of agreement and one which can apply to the assignments made by an arbitrary number of raters. The references will direct the reader to some of the other measures.

9.8.1 Rationale and Method

Consider a group of N objects or subjects, each of which is to be assigned to one of m categories. It is assumed that these categories are nominal. Each of a group of k raters assigns each object to a category. The data from the assignments can be cast into a $N \times m$ table:

	Category						
Object	**1**	**2**	$\cdots$	j	$\cdots$	m	
1	n_{11}	n_{12}	$\cdots$	n_{1j}	$\cdots$	n_{1m}	S_1
2	n_{21}						S_2
$\vdots$				$\vdots$			$\vdots$
i	n_{i1}		$\cdots$	n_{ij}	$\cdots$	n_{im}	S_i
$\vdots$				$\vdots$			$\vdots$
N	n_{N1}		$\cdots$	n_{Nj}	$\cdots$	n_{Nm}	S_N
	C_1	C_2	$\cdots$	C_j	$\cdots$	C_m	

where n_{ij} is the number of raters assigning the ith object to the jth category. Since each rater classifies each object, the sum of the frequencies in each row is equal to k. However, the number times that an object is assigned to a particular category will vary from category to category. We let C_j be the number of times that an object is assigned to the jth category, which is simply the column sum of frequencies:

$$C_j = \sum_{i=1}^{N} n_{ij}$$

Now, if the raters are in complete agreement concerning their assignments, one frequency in each row would be equal to k and the other frequencies would be equal to 0. If there is no consensus among the raters, the assignments would be random and the frequencies in each row would be proportional to the column totals. Of course, if the raters were to make assignments randomly, we would expect some agreement to occur purely by chance.

The kappa coefficient of agreement is the ratio of the proportion of times that the raters agree (corrected for chance agreement) to the maximum proportion of times that the raters could agree (corrected for chance agreement):[20]

$$K = \frac{P(A) - P(E)}{1 - P(E)} \tag{9.27}$$

where $P(A)$ is the proportion of times that the k raters agree and $P(E)$ is the proportion of times that we would expect the k raters to agree by chance. If there is complete agreement among the raters, then $K = 1$; whereas if there is no agreement (other than the agreement which would be expected to occur by chance) among the raters, then $K = 0$.

[20] It has been common in many textbooks and research reports to denote the kappa statistic by use of the greek letter κ. Also, many of the various "kappalike" statistics are also denoted with κ. In this book, we use κ to denote the parameter which is estimated by the kappa statistic K.

To find $P(E)$ we note that the proportion of objects assigned to the jth category is $p_j = C_j/Nk$. If the raters make their assignments at random, the expected proportion of agreement for each category would be p_j^2, and the total expected agreement across all categories would be

$$P(E) = \sum_{j=1}^{m} p_j^2 \tag{9.28}$$

The extent of the agreement among the raters concerning the ith subject is the proportion of the number of pairs for which there is agreement to the possible pairs of assignments. For the ith subject this is

$$S_i = \frac{\sum_{j=1}^{m} \binom{n_{ij}}{2}}{\binom{k}{2}} = \frac{1}{k(k-1)} \sum_{j=1}^{m} n_{ij}(n_{ij} - 1)$$

To obtain the total proportion of agreement, we find the average of these proportions across all objects rated:

$$P(A) = \frac{1}{N} \sum_{i=1}^{N} S_i = \left[\frac{1}{Nk(k-1)} \sum_{i=1}^{N} \sum_{j=1}^{m} n_{ij}^2 \right] - \frac{1}{k-1} \tag{9.29}$$

The values of $P(E)$ and $P(A)$ are then to be combined by using Eq. (9.27) to find the kappa statistic K.

Example 9.8*a*[21] It has been observed by researchers of animal behavior that the male stickleback fish changes color during the nesting and courtship cycle. When placed in a suitable environment, the male sticklebacks establish territories, build nests, and engage in courtship and aggression when stimulus fish are introduced into the environment. To analyze the relation between color and other behaviors during experimental study, it was necessary to code the fish in terms of their coloration. Since the fish must be observed from outside their environment, and because of variation in observational conditions, $k = 4$ trained raters evaluated the coloration of each fish. The colorations were divided into $m = 5$ categories. The first category was for those fish with minimal color development and the last category represented maximal color development and coloration, the other three categories involved varying degrees of coloration. In this study, a group of $N = 29$ fish was observed. The data are summarized in Table 9.15. Note that the raters were in complete agreement about the coloration of fish 1 and that they were divided in their ratings of fish 2. Examination of the rows of the table shows that there was complete agreement for some fish but low agreement about others.

[21] Rowland, W. J. (1984). The relationships among nuptial coloration, aggression, and courtship of male three-spined sticklebacks, *Gasterosteus aculeatus*. *Canadian Journal of Zoology*, **62**, 999–1004. Although the coloration changes with time (a continuous process), the colorations are distinct. An observer trained to identify the coloration could be completely unaware of the sequential aspects. Therefore, a categorical index of agreement is appropriate.

TABLE 9.15
Estimates of nuptial coloration of male sticklebacks*

	Coloration category					
Fish	**1**	**2**	**3**	**4**	**5**	S_i
1	—	—	—	—	4	$\frac{12}{12} = 1.$
2	2	—	2	—	—	$\frac{4}{12} = .333$
3	—	—	—	—	4	$\frac{12}{12} = 1.$
4	2	—	2	—	—	$\frac{4}{12} = .333$
5	—	—	—	1	3	$\frac{6}{12} = .50$
6	1	1	2	—	—	$\frac{2}{12} = .167$
7	3	—	1	—	—	$\frac{6}{12} = .50$
8	3	—	1	—	—	$\frac{6}{12} = .50$
9	—	—	2	2	—	$\frac{4}{12} = .333$
10	3	—	1	—	—	$\frac{6}{12} = .50$
11	—	—	—	—	4	$\frac{12}{12} = 1.$
12	4	—	—	—	—	$\frac{12}{12} = 1.$
13	4	—	—	—	—	$\frac{12}{12} = 1.$
14	4	—	—	—	—	$\frac{12}{12} = 1.$
15	—	—	3	1	—	$\frac{6}{12} = .50$
16	1	—	2	1	—	$\frac{2}{12} = .333$
17	—	—	—	2	2	$\frac{4}{12} = .333$
18	—	—	—	—	4	$\frac{12}{12} = 1.$
19	—	—	3	—	1	$\frac{6}{12} = .50$
20	—	1	3	—	—	$\frac{6}{12} = .50$
21	—	—	1	—	3	$\frac{6}{12} = .50$
22	—	—	3	1	—	$\frac{6}{12} = .50$
23	4	—	—	—	—	$\frac{12}{12} = 1.$
24	4	—	—	—	—	$\frac{12}{12} = 1.$
25	2	—	2	—	—	$\frac{4}{12} = .333$
26	1	—	3	—	—	$\frac{6}{12} = .50$
27	2	—	2	—	—	$\frac{4}{12} = .333$
28	2	—	2	—	—	$\frac{4}{12} = .333$
29	—	1	2	—	1	$\frac{2}{12} = .167$
C_j	42	3	37	8	26	
p_j	.362	.026	.319	.069	.224	

* Cell entries are the number of raters agreeing on that category. An empty cell indicates that the particular category was not chosen by any rater for that fish.

To assess the overall consensus among the raters, the kappa coefficient of agreement K will be computed. First, we find C_j, the number of times that a fish was assigned to the jth category. We sum the frequencies in each column to obtain the values given in the second to last row in the table. Each of these is divided by $Nk = (29)(4) = 116$ to obtain p_j, the proportion of observations assigned to category j. We find that $p_1 = C_1/Nk = \frac{42}{116} = .362$, etc. These values are given in the last row of the table. From those values we may determine the value of $P(E)$, the proportion of agreement which we would expect by chance:

$$P(E) = \sum_{j=1}^{m} p_j^2 \tag{9.28}$$

$$= .362^2 + .026^2 + .319^2 + .069^2 + .224^2$$

$$= .2884$$

Next we must find $P(A)$, the proportion of times that the raters agreed. One way is to determine the value of S_i for each fish and then average these values. The other way is to proceed to $P(A)$ directly by using the right side of Eq. (9.29). We shall illustrate both methods. The values of S_i are given in the table so that the reader may understand their computation.

$$S_1 = \frac{1}{k(k-1)} \sum_{j=1}^{m} n_{1j}(n_{1j} - 1)$$

$$= \frac{1}{(4)(3)} [0 + 0 + 0 + 0 + (4)(3)]$$

$$= \frac{12}{12}$$

$$= 1$$

$$S_2 = \frac{1}{(4)(3)} [(2)(1) + 0 + (2)(1) + 0 + 0]$$

$$= \frac{4}{12}$$

$$= .333$$

The reader should note that the value of S_i is a measure of agreement for the ith fish. Then, using these values, we find $P(A)$:

$$P(A) = \frac{1}{N} \sum_{i=1}^{N} S_i \tag{9.29}$$

$$= \frac{1 + .333 + 1 + .333 + .50 + \cdots + .333 + .167}{29}$$

$$= .5804$$

Alternatively, we could have bypassed computation of the S_i altogether by summing the squares of the cell frequencies:

$$P(A) = \left[\frac{1}{Nk(k-1)} \sum_{i=1}^{N} \sum_{j=1}^{m} n_{ij}^2\right] - \frac{1}{k-1} \tag{9.29}$$

$$= \frac{1}{(29(4)(3)} (4^2 + 2^2 + 2^2 + 4^2 \cdots + 1^2 + 2^2 + 1^2) - \frac{1}{4-1}$$

$$= \frac{318}{348} - \frac{1}{3}$$

$$= .5804$$

We may use these values of $P(E)$ and $P(A)$ to find K:

$$K = \frac{P(A) - P(E)}{1 - P(E)} \tag{9.27}$$

$$= \frac{.580 - .288}{1 - .288}$$

$$= .41$$

Thus we conclude that there is moderate agreement among the raters. Whether this value represents a significant difference from 0 will be addressed in the next section.

9.8.2 Testing the Significance of K

After determining the value of the kappa statistic K, one would usually want to determine whether the observed value was greater than the value which would be expected by chance. Note that, although we subtract a term from the proportion of agreements in ratings to correct for random agreement, such a correction subtracts only the *expected agreement* due to chance. Of course, chance agreement will not be a constant but will vary about some central or expected value. Although sampling distribution of K is complicated for small N, it has been found that, for large N, K is approximately normally distributed with mean 0 and variance

$$\text{var}(K) \approx \frac{2}{Nk(k-1)} \frac{P(E) - (2k-3)[P(E)]^2 + 2(k-2)\Sigma p_j^3}{[1 - P(E)]^2} \tag{9.30}$$

Therefore, we could use the statistic

$$z = \frac{K}{\sqrt{\text{var}(K)}} \tag{9.31}$$

to test the hypothesis is H_0: $\kappa = 0$ against the hypothesis H_1: $\kappa > 0$.

Example 9.8*b* For the coloration ratings given in the previous example, it was found that $K = .41$. To test H_0: $\kappa = 0$ against H_1: $\kappa > 0$, we must find the variance of K. The $\alpha = .01$ significance level is chosen. Recall that $N = 29$ (objects rated), $m = 5$ (rating categories), $k = 4$ (raters), and $P(E) = .288$. The only other information needed is Σp_j^3. Using the values of p_j given in Table 9.15, we have

$$\Sigma p_j^3 = .362^3 + .026^3 + .319^3 + .069^3 + .224^3 = .092$$

Then,

$$\text{var}(K) \approx \frac{2}{Nk(k-1)} \frac{P(E) - (2k-3)[P(E)]^2 + 2(k-2)\Sigma p_j^3}{[1 - P(E)]^2} \tag{9.30}$$

$$= \frac{2}{(29)(4)(3)} \frac{.288 - [(2)(4) - 3](.288^2) + (2)(4-2)(.092)}{(1 - .288)^2}$$

$$= \frac{2}{348}\left(\frac{.2413}{.5069}\right)$$

$$= .002736$$

Using this value for var(K), we may find z:

$$z = \frac{K}{\sqrt{\text{var}(K)}} \tag{9.31}$$

$$= \frac{.41}{\sqrt{.002736}}$$

$$= 7.84$$

This value exceeds the $\alpha = .01$ significance level (where $z = 2.32$). Therefore, the researcher may conclude that the raters exhibit significant agreement on their ratings.

9.8.3 Summary of Procedure

These are the steps in the determination of the kappa statistic K, the coefficient of agreement for nominally scaled data:

1. Let N be the number of objects (subjects or entities) to be rated, let m be the number of categories into which the objects are to be assigned, and let k be the number of raters or judges who produce the ratings. For each object, count the number of times that raters assign it to each category. Cast these frequencies into an $N \times m$ rating table like that described in Sec. 9.8.1. Note that the frequencies in each row of the table will sum to k, the number of raters.
2. For each category j find the number of times that any object is assigned to that category. This number is C_j. Next find p_j, the proportion of ratings assigned to the jth category. Then, by using Eq. (9.28), find $P(E)$, the expected proportion of agreement among raters had they been rating the objects at random.
3. Then, by using Eq. (9.29), find $P(A)$, the average proportion of agreement.
4. To find K, the coefficient of agreement, use the calculated values of $P(E)$ and $P(A)$ in Eq. (9.27).
5. Finally, to test the hypothesis H_0: $\kappa = 0$ against H_1: $\kappa > 0$, find the variance of K with Eq. (9.30) and find the corresponding z value with Eq. (9.31). If the obtained value of z exceeds the appropriate critical value of z in Appendix Table A, reject H_0.

9.8.4 A Note of Various Versions of the Kappa Statistic K

As noted earlier, there are various statistics which have been proposed to measure agreement for nominally scaled data. In many references these are denoted κ (kappa), regardless of the form of the statistic. These statistics are derived from the basic arguments made by Scott (1955) and Cohen (1960) for nominally scaled measures of agreement.[22] It is the form developed by Cohen (for the agreement

[22] Other kappalike statistics have been proposed for other purposes. Hammond, Householder, and Castellan (1970) describe a measure of dispersion (variability) for categorical data which is a function of the kappa statistic described in this section.

between two raters or for N pairs of ratings) which has motivated many generalizations. The form of the kappa statistic given in this section is a generalization of Cohen's statistic to k raters which is due to Fleiss (1971). However, because of some compelling arguments concerning the meaning of "chance" agreement, when $k = 2$, our kappa statistic K is the same as the earlier index proposed by Scott. The assumption made by Scott and Fleiss is that the p_j's are the same for all raters, i.e., the probability that an object is assigned to a particular category does not vary across raters. Although some researchers might take issue with this view, under the null hypothesis of no agreement the raters should be unable to distinguish one object from another. Fleiss argued that, "[S]uch an inability implies that the raters apply the overall rates of assignments, $\{p_j\}$, to each and every subject."

9.8.5 References

Basic references on K, the kappa statistic, and other indexes of agreement for nominally scaled data are the papers by Scott (1955), Cohen (1960), and Fleiss (1971). Cohen (1968) generalized his index to situations in which the categories are weighted by some objective or subjective function. Other generalizations can be found in Fleiss (1971) who included an index of agreement with a criterion (like T_C) and the work of Light (1971). Another useful discussion may be found in Bishop et al. (1975).

9.9 ORDERED VARIABLES AND THE GAMMA STATISTIC G

9.9.1 Function

We have discussed at some length measures useful in assessing the relation between two ordered variables. These measures included the Spearman rank-order correlation, r_s and the Kendall rank-order correlation T. Although these statistics are appropriate for use with variables that are rankings, they are less useful and less appropriate when there are many ties or in any situation in which it is meaningful to cast the data in the form of a contingency table. Many measures of association for ordered variables in contingency tables have been proposed. The index to be presented here is especially useful, relatively easy to compute, and closely related to other measures which we have discussed (in particular, Kendall's T). The *gamma statistic* G is appropriate for measuring the relation between two ordinally scaled variables. The gamma statistic was first discussed extensively by Goodman and Kruskal.

9.9.2 Rationale

The rationale of the gamma statistic is very similar to that of Kendall's T. Suppose we have two variables, A and B, which are both ordered variables. We shall assume that the variable A may take on the values $A_1, A_2, \ldots, A_k$. Moreover, we shall assume that the variables are ordered in magnitude by their subscripts, that is,

$A_1 < A_2 < \cdots < A_k$. Similarly, assume that the variable B is ordered in a similar fashion, $B_1 < B_2 < \cdots < B_r$. In the population from which the variables A and B are drawn, we define the population parameter γ to be function of the agreement in ordering of randomly selected *pairs of observations.* The reader should note that an observation consists of two data—an observation of the variable A and an observation of the variable B. The parameter γ is then the difference in the probability that within a pair of observations A and B are in the same order and the probability that within a pair of observations the A and B disagree in their ordering, provided there are no ties in the data. That is,

$$\gamma = \frac{P[A \,\&\, B \text{ agree in order}] - P[A \,\&\, B \text{ disagree in order}]}{1 - P[A \,\&\, B \text{ are tied}]}$$

$$= \frac{P[A \,\&\, B \text{ agree in order}] - P[A \,\&\, B \text{ disagree in order}]}{P[A \,\&\, B \text{ agree in order}] + P[A \,\&\, B \text{ disagree in order}]}$$

Since we seldom know the probabilities in the population, we must estimate them from the data; thus we must use the statistic G to estimate γ.

9.9.3 Method

To compute the gamma statistic G from two sets of ordinal variables, say $A_1, A_2, \ldots, A_k$ and $B_1, B_2, \ldots, B_r$, we arrange the frequencies in a contingency table:

	A_1	A_2	$\cdots$	A_k	Total
B_1	n_{11}	n_{12}	$\cdots$	n_{1k}	R_1
B_2	n_{21}	n_{22}	$\cdots$	n_{2k}	R_2
$\vdots$	$\vdots$	$\vdots$		$\vdots$	$\vdots$
B_r	n_{r1}	n_{r2}	$\cdots$	n_{rk}	R_r
Total	C_1	C_2	$\cdots$	C_k	N

The data may consist of any number of categories. That is, one may compute the gamma statistic for data from a 2×2 table, a 2×5 table, a 4×4 table, a 3×7 table, or any $r \times k$ table.

The gamma statistic G is defined as follows:

$$G = \frac{\#\text{ agreements} - \#\text{ disagreements}}{\#\text{ agreements} + \#\text{ disagreements}}$$

$$= \frac{\#(+) - \#(-)}{\#(+) + \#(-)} \tag{9.32}$$

where $\#(+)$ and $\#(-)$ denote the number of agreements and the number of disagreements, respectively, in the rankings. The reader should note the similarity between G and T discussed in Sec. 9.4.2. (If there are no tied observations, that is, if all frequencies in the contingency table are equal to 1 or 0, then $G = T$.) The interested reader should review Secs. 9.4.2 and 9.4.3 for details on computing the number of agreements and disagreements from the "raw" data. The expression given above is a perfectly good computational formula; however, an alternative approach can make the computation of G much simpler, especially if the data have been cast into a contingency table. We shall first give a "formal" approach to the computation; this will be followed by a heuristic approach that is extremely simple.

We first need a simple way to calculate the number of agreements and the number of disagreements in ordering for each observation when the data have been aggregated into a contingency table. We may do this as follows:

$$\#(+) = \#\text{ agreements}$$

$$= \sum_{i=1}^{r-1} \sum_{j=1}^{k-1} n_{ij} \sum_{p=i+1}^{r} \sum_{q=j+1}^{k} n_{pq} \tag{9.33a}$$

$$= \sum_{i,j} n_{ij} \mathbf{N}_{ij}^{+} \qquad i = 1, 2, \ldots, r-1 \quad j = 1, 2, \ldots, k-1 \tag{9.33b}$$

where $\mathbf{N}_{ij}^{+}$ is the *sum* of all of the frequencies *below and to the right* of the ijth cell.

$$\#(-) = \#\text{ disagreements}$$

$$= \sum_{i=1}^{r-1} \sum_{j=2}^{k} n_{ij} \sum_{p=i+1}^{r} \sum_{q=1}^{j-1} n_{pq} \tag{9.34a}$$

$$= \sum_{i,j} n_{ij} \mathbf{N}_{ij}^{-} \qquad i = 1, 2, \ldots, r-1 \quad j = 2, \ldots, k \tag{9.34b}$$

where $\mathbf{N}_{ij}^{-}$ is the *sum* of all of the frequencies *below and to the left* of the ijth cell in the contingency table. Graphically, we may depict the expressions as follows:

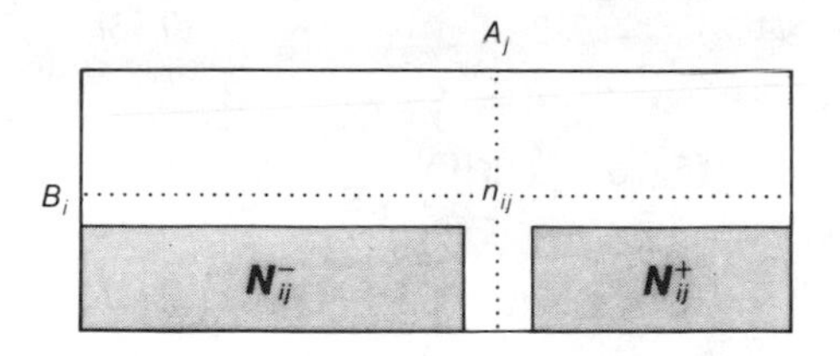

In this table, $\mathbf{N}_{ij}^{+}$ and $\mathbf{N}_{ij}^{-}$ are the sums of the frequencies in the corresponding portions of the table. With these sums, and weighting them by the frequency in the ijth cell, we count the agreements and disagreements for each pair of data in the entire table. (We have counted agreements and disagreements considering each pair only once.)

TABLE 9.16
Artificial data for the computation of the gamma statistic G

Variable B	Variable A A_1	A_2	A_3	A_4	Total
B_1	10	5	2	3	20
B_2	8	9	7	1	25
B_3	2	6	8	9	25
Total	20	20	17	13	70

As an illustration of the computation of the gamma statistic, consider the data in Table 9.16. Variable A may take on $k = 4$ values and variable B may take on $r = 3$ values. A total of $N = 70$ observations were taken and the data were cast into the contingency table. To calculate the number of agreements, $\#(+)$, and the number of disagreements, $\#(-)$, we must find various values of $\mathbf{N}_{ij}^{+}$ and N_{ij}^{-}:

$$\begin{aligned} \mathbf{N}_{11}^{+} &= 9 + 7 + 1 + 6 + 8 + 9 \\ &= 40 \end{aligned}$$

$$\begin{aligned} \mathbf{N}_{12}^{+} &= 7 + 1 + 8 + 9 \\ &= 25 \end{aligned}$$

$$\begin{aligned} \mathbf{N}_{12}^{-} &= 8 + 2 \\ &= 10 \end{aligned}$$

$$\begin{aligned} \mathbf{N}_{14}^{-} &= 8 + 9 + 7 + 2 + 6 + 8 \\ &= 40 \end{aligned}$$

With these values (and the other values of $\mathbf{N}_{ij}^{+}$ required), we compute

$$\begin{aligned} \#(+) &= \sum_{i,j} n_{ij}\mathbf{N}_{ij}^{+} \qquad i = 1, 2 \quad j = 1, 2, 3 \\ &= (10)(40) + (5)(25) + (2)(10) \\ &\quad + (8)(23) + (9)(17) + (7)(9) \\ &= 945 \end{aligned} \tag{9.33b}$$

and

$$\begin{aligned} \#(-) &= \sum_{i,j} n_{ij}\mathbf{N}_{ij}^{-} \qquad i = 1, 2 \quad j = 2, 3, 4 \\ &= (5)(10) + (2)(25) + (3)(40) \\ &\quad + (9)(2) + (7)(8) + (1)(16) \\ &= 310 \end{aligned} \tag{9.34b}$$

With these values we find

$$G = \frac{\#(+) - \#(-)}{\#(+) + \#(-)} \tag{9.32}$$

$$= \frac{945 - 310}{945 + 310}$$

$$= .51$$

Thus we may conclude that there is moderate agreement (or correlation) between the two variables.

The gamma statistic G is equal to 1 if the frequencies in the contingency table are concentrated on the diagonal from the upper left to the lower right of the contingency table. (Recall that the variables A and B are ordered by the magnitude of their subscripts.) $G = -1$ if the frequencies all lie on the diagonal from the upper right corner to the lower left corner of the contingency table. There are other cases for which $G = 1$. As long as there are no disagreements in the ordering of the variables, $G = 1$, that is, if $\#(-) = 0$. Similarly, if there are no agreements in the orderings $[\#(+) = 0]$, $G = -1$. For example, in each of the following tables $G = 1$:

	A_1	A_2	A_3
B_1	X	X	
B_2		X	X
B_3			X

	A_1	A_2	A_3
B_1	X		
B_2	X		
B_3	X	X	X

where X denotes any nonzero entry. If the variables A and B are independent, then $\gamma = 0$. However, except when the contingency table is 2×2, $\gamma = 0$ does not imply independence.

Example 9.9*a* There have been numerous studies in recent years concerning smoking behavior and the ability of individuals who so desire to stop smoking. One factor affecting many such studies is the variety of characteristics of the sample studied. In a recent study, a researcher examined the relation between the ability to stop smoking (cessation ability) and the number of years that a person had been smoking.[23] The subjects were all nurses who should be well aware of the benefits of smoking cessation. Moreover, because the subjects shared the same occupation, job stresses to continue smoking as well as health pressures to cease smoking should be similar.

The nurses in the study were all persons who had either stopped smoking or tried to stop smoking. Thus each was assigned to one of three categories—successful quitter, in-process quitter, and unsuccessful quitter. In addition, the subjects were categorized by the number of years that they had been smoking—from 1 to more than 25 years. The years of smoking were combined into seven categories. An important question is whether the success that one has in quitting is related to the number of years one has been smoking.

---

[23] Wagner, T. J. (1985). Smoking behavior of nurses in western New York. *Nursing Research*, **34**, 58–60.

TABLE 9.17
Cessation ability by length of time smoking

	Years of smoking							
	1	**2–4**	**5–9**	**10–14**	**15–19**	**20–25**	**>25**	Total
Successful quitter	13	29	26	22	9	8	8	115
In-process quitter	5	2	6	2	1	3	0	19
Unsuccessful quitter	1	9	16	14	21	16	29	106
Total	19	40	48	38	31	27	37	240

These data are summarized in Table 9.17 for the sample of $N = 240$ nurses. Since both variables are ordered, the gamma statistic G is an appropriate measure of association.

To calculate G, we need to calculate the number of agreements and disagreements in ordering of the variables in the table. Note that there are $r = 3$ rows in the table corresponding to the current smoking status. And there are $k = 7$ columns corresponding to the number of years that the subject had been smoking.

$$\#(+) = \sum_{i,j} n_{ij}\mathbf{N}_{ij}^{+} \qquad i = 1, 2 \quad j = 1, 2, \ldots, 6 \tag{9.33b}$$

$$= (13)(119) + (29)(108) + (26)(86) + \cdots + (1)(45) + (3)(29)$$

$$= 10{,}580$$

and

$$\#(-) = \sum_{i,j} n_{ij}\mathbf{N}_{ij}^{-} \qquad i = 1, 2 \quad j = 2, 3, \ldots, 7 \tag{9.34b}$$

$$= (29)(6) + (26)(17) + (22)(39) + \cdots + (3)(61) + (0)(77)$$

$$= 3690$$

Next, we compute the value of G:

$$G = \frac{\#(+) - \#(-)}{\#(+) + \#(-)} \tag{9.32}$$

$$= \frac{10{,}580 - 3690}{10{,}580 + 3690}$$

$$= .483$$

Thus for the smoking cessation data, there is a positive association between inability to stop smoking and the number of years a person has been smoking; that is, the longer a person has been smoking the less likely he or she will be successful in stopping the smoking habit.

9.9.4 Testing the Significance of G

To test the significance of G, we must resort to an approximation which requires large samples. If N is relatively large, the sampling distribution of G is approximately normal with mean γ. Although the expression for the variance is complicated, an upper limit for the variance can be written fairly simply:

$$\operatorname{var}(G) \leq \frac{N(1-G^2)}{\#(+) + \#(-)} \tag{9.35}$$

Therefore the quantity

$$z = (G - \gamma)\sqrt{\frac{\#(+) + \#(-)}{N(1-G^2)}} \tag{9.36}$$

is approximately normally distributed with mean 0 and standard deviation 1. Since the variance of G given by Eq. (9.35) is an upper limit, the test of significance by using Eq. (9.36) is conservative; that is, we may infer that the "true" significance level is *at least* that obtained by Eq. (9.36) using a table of the normal distribution (e.g., Appendix Table A).

Example 9.9*b* In the smoking cessation study, we found that $G = .483$. Although this association appears to be large, we would like to test the hypothesis H_0: $\gamma = 0$ against the hypothesis H_1: $\gamma \neq 0$. A two-tailed test is required because the researcher had no *a priori* hypothesis about the direction of association. We shall choose $\alpha = .01$ as the significance level. We first compute z:

$$\begin{aligned} z &= (G - \gamma)\sqrt{\frac{\#(+) + \#(-)}{N(1-G^2)}} \qquad (9.36) \\ &= (.483 - 0)\sqrt{\frac{10580 + 3690}{(240)(1 - .483^2)}} \\ &= (.483)(8.81) \\ &= 4.24 \end{aligned}$$

Since the value of z exceeds the critical value for $\alpha = .01$ ($z = 2.58$, two-tailed), we may reject the hypothesis that $\gamma = 0$ and conclude that the variables are not independent in the population.

9.9.5 Summary of Procedure

These are the steps in the calculation of the gamma statistic G:

1. Cast the N observed frequencies into an $r \times k$ contingency table, where r is the number of categories on which one variable is scored and k is the number of categories on which the other variable is scored. Since the variables are ordered, the column variable should be arranged in order of increasing magnitude across the columns; similarly the row variable should be arranged in order of increasing magnitude down the rows.
2. Use Eqs. (9.33*b*) and (9.34*b*) to calculate the number of agreements in ordering, $\#(+)$, and the number of disagreements in ordering, $\#(-)$. Enter these values into Eq. (9.32) to calculate G.

3. If N is moderate or large, test the hypothesis H_0: $\gamma = 0$ (or the hypothesis H_0: $\gamma = \gamma_0$ if appropriate) by using Eq. (9.36) to compute a normal deviate. Determine the significance probability with Appendix Table A. The obtained probability is a conservative estimate of the "true" significance probability.

9.9.6 References

The earlier references in this chapter are relevant to this section also. Thorough discussion of the gamma statistic may be found in a series of papers by Goodman and Kruskal (1954, 1959, 1963, 1972). Goodman and Kruskal (1963) give a more precise but computationally more complex estimate of the variance of G. Also of interest is the work of Somers (1980) who gives alternative expressions for the sampling variance of G. The paper by Goodman and Kruskal (1954) gives a rationale for a "partial gamma," which is similar to the Kendall partial rank-order correlation coefficient $T_{xy.z}$ discussed in Sec. 9.5.

9.10 ASYMMETRICAL ASSOCIATION AND THE LAMBDA STATISTIC L_B

9.10.1 Function and Rationale

In Sec. 9.1 the Cramér coefficient C was discussed as an index of association for an $r \times k$ table. Although that index is very useful, it has some limitations which were pointed out in Sec. 9.1.5. One of those limitations was that C does not measure the association which may exist differentially between the row and column variables; rather, it is an index of the degree of dependence (or nonindependence) between the two variables. The coefficient described in this section may be used when we would like to measure the association between one variable and another. An example would be when we have observed a sequence of behaviors and have coded some which are antecedents to a particular behavior and some which are consequents. Thus, the data consist of antecedent-consequent pairs. Of particular interest to a researcher might be the relation between the antecedents and the consequents (or the degree to which the consequents are related to the antecedents). In such situations the Cramér coefficient is not sensitive to the differences in dependency the researcher wishes to assess.

The *lambda statistic* L_B developed by Goodman and Kruskal is a suitable index of association when we wish to assess the relation between one variable and another. The lambda statistic makes few assumptions about the categories defining the original variables. It assumes that the data are only categorical or nominal, that is, the variables are not ordered. Since the lambda statistic is a measure of the asymmetric relation between the variables, there are two different indexes, one based on rows and one based on columns. In the example of sequential behavior described above, the researcher may be interested in how well variable A (an antecedent) "predicts" variable B (a consequent). However, the converse relation between the two variables may be of lesser (or no) interest. The statistic is designed to assess the relative decrease in the unpredictability of one variable (e.g., a consequent) when the other variable (e.g., an antecedent) is known; that is, it is a measure of the relative reduction in error in predicting one variable when another is known.

The rationale of the lambda statistic is relatively straightforward. Suppose that in the population, $P[\text{error}]$ is the probability of an error in predicting B, and $P[\text{error}|A]$ is the conditional probability of an error in predicting B when the variable A is known, the general form of the index may be written as

$$\lambda_B = \frac{P[\text{error}] - P[\text{error}|A]}{P[\text{error}]}$$

To calculate λ_B, we need to find the two probabilities $P[\text{error}]$ and $P[\text{error}|A]$. Intuitively, the best guess of $\boldsymbol{B}$ when the antecedent is unknown is to choose that B_i with the largest probability of occurrence. Similarly, if one knows the antecedent A_j, one would choose that consequent which had the largest probability of occurrence given A_j. However, we seldom know these probabilities. Therefore, they must be estimated and, hence, we estimate λ_B by using the statistic L_B.

9.10.2 Method

To compute the lambda statistic L_B from two sets of categorical variables, say $A_1, A_2, \ldots, A_k$, and $B_1, B_2, \ldots, B_r$, we arrange the frequencies in a contingency table:

	A_1	A_2	$\cdots$	A_k	Total
B_1	n_{11}	n_{12}	$\cdots$	n_{1k}	R_1
B_2	n_{21}	n_{22}	$\cdots$	n_{2k}	R_2
$\vdots$	$\vdots$	$\vdots$		$\vdots$	$\vdots$
B_r	n_{r1}	n_{r2}	$\cdots$	n_{rk}	R_r
Total	C_1	C_2	$\cdots$	C_k	N

The data may consist of any number of categories. That is, one may compute the lambda statistic for data from a 2×2 table, a 2×5 table, a 4×4 table, a 3×7 table, or any $r \times k$ table.

The lambda statistic L_B is calculated from a contingency table as follows:

$$L_B = \frac{\sum_{j=1}^{k} n_{Mj} - \max(R_i)}{N - \max(R_i)} \tag{9.37}$$

where n_{Mj} is the *largest* frequency in the jth column and $\max(R_i)$ is the *largest* row total.

To illustrate the computation of L_B, a set of artificial data are summarized in Table 9.18. The data consist of 60 antecedent-consequent pairs. For these data,

TABLE 9.18
Artificial data for computation of L_B

	Antecedent			
Consequent	A_1	A_2	A_3	Total
B_1	10	1	4	15
B_2	5	3	6	14
B_3	3	12	2	17
B_4	3	3	8	14
Total	21	19	20	60

the largest row total is 17, so $\max(R_i) = 17$. Next, we need to sum the largest frequencies in each column:

$$\sum_{j=1}^{k} n_{Mj} = 10 + 12 + 8 = 30$$

Then the value of the lambda statistic is

$$L_B = \frac{\sum_{j=1}^{k} n_{Mj} - \max(R_i)}{N - \max(R_i)} \tag{9.37}$$

$$= \frac{30 - 17}{60 - 17}$$

$$= .30$$

This value may be interpreted in the following manner. When we know the antecedent (variable A), there is a 30 percent reduction in error in predicting the value of variable B.

9.10.3 Testing the Significance of L_B

It is possible to test hypotheses concerning λ_B. However, the sampling distribution is relatively complicated and it is not possible to test the hypotheses that $\lambda_B = 0$ or $\lambda_B = 1$. We can test the hypothesis that reduction in error is a particular value, that is, we can test the hypothesis H_0: $\lambda_B = \lambda_{B0}$. When N is relatively large, L_B is approximately normally distributed with mean λ_{B0} and variance

$$\mathrm{var}(L_B) = \frac{\left(N - \sum_{j=1}^{k} n_{Mj}\right)\left(\sum_{j=1}^{k} n_{Mj} + \max(R_i) - 2\Sigma' n_{Mj}\right)}{[N - \max(R_i)]^3} \tag{9.38}$$

where $\Sigma' n_{Mj}$ is the sum of all of the *maximum* frequencies which happen to be in the row associated with $\max(R_i)$. If there is only one maximum in that row, then

$\Sigma' n_{Mj} = n_{Mj}$. As an illustration, in the example given above,

$$\mathrm{var}(L_B) = \frac{(60-30)[30+17-(2)(12)]}{(60-17)^3}$$
$$= .00868$$

Suppose we have as a null hypothesis H_0: $\lambda_{BO} = .10$, a significance level of $\alpha = .05$, and the data in Table 9.18. Then

$$z = \frac{.30 - .10}{\sqrt{.00868}}$$
$$= 2.15$$

Thus, we can reject the hypothesis H_0 that the value of λ_B is .10; that is, we may conclude that the decrease in error in predictability of B when A is known exceeds 10 percent.

9.10.4 Properties of L_B

Although λ_B shares some properties with the Cramér coefficient, it has distinct advantages because of its asymmetric properties. Some of the properties of λ_B are the following:

1. It may vary from 0 to 1. A value of zero means that variable A is of no value in predicting the variable B, whereas a value of 1 implies perfect predictability of variable B from variable A.
2. It is equal to 0 if and only if variable A is of no help in predicting the variable B.
3. It is equal to 1 only if there is complete predictability from variable A to B. That is, if $\lambda_B = 1$, then knowledge of the variable A will let one predict variable B *perfectly*. If $\lambda_B = 1$, then, for each value of the variable A, there is only *one* possible value for the variable B. Thus, if $L_B = 1$, then there is only one nonzero entry in each column of the contingency table.
4. If the variables A and B are independent, then $\lambda_B = 0$. However, $\lambda_B = 0$ does not imply that the variables A and B are independent.
5. The value of λ_B is unaffected by permutations of rows (or columns) of the contingency table. This reflects the fact that the statistic does not assume any ordering of the values of either of the variables.

It should be noted that, although there are many advantages to asymmetrical measures of association, one defect is that the measures are often confusing to the beginning researcher. Many of us are so accustomed to thinking about the usual (symmetrical) measures of association that it is difficult to interpret an asymmetrical index.

PREDICTING COLUMNS FROM ROWS: L_A. In our discussion of the lambda statistic, we have focused on L_B, which is used to measure the reduction in error of prediction of variable B when variable A is known. There is a corresponding index for assessing the reduction in error of prediction of variable A when variable B is known. Although we could interchange rows and columns and compute the lambda statistic with Eq. (9.37), it is usually more convenient to use an equation which does not require rearrangement of the entries in the frequency table:

$$L_A = \frac{\sum_{j=1}^{r} n_{iM} - \max(C_j)}{N - \max(C_j)} \tag{9.39}$$

where n_{iM} is the *largest* frequency in the ith row, and $\max(C_j)$ is the *largest* column total. Of course, the expression for the variance of L_A must be rewritten in a similar fashion:

$$\mathrm{var}(L_A) = \frac{\left(N - \sum_{i=1}^{r} n_{iM}\right)\left(\sum_{i=1}^{r} n_{iM} + \max(C_j) - 2\Sigma' n_{iM}\right)}{[N - \max(C_j)]^3} \tag{9.40}$$

where $\Sigma' n_{iM}$ is the sum of all of the *maximum* frequencies in the column associated with $\max(C_j)$. If there is only one maximum in that column, then $\Sigma' n_{iM} = n_{iM}$.

In general, $L_A \neq L_B$. The reader may verify as an exercise that for the data in Table 9.18, $L_A = .38$. In fact, it is possible for L_A (or L_B) to equal one (perfect predictability) while L_B (or L_A) can be quite small.

In Sec. 9.1.5 it was noted that, if the Cramér coefficient was equal to one and the contingency table was *not* square, then there was "perfect" association in only one direction. The lambda statistic L_B (or L_A) will be equal to one when $C = 1$. If the table is square, then if one index is equal to one, the other two will be equal to one also.

9.10.5 Summary of Procedure

These are the steps in the calculation of the lambda statistic L_B:

1. Cast the N observed frequencies into an $r \times k$ contingency table like Table 9.18, where r is the number of categories on which one variable is scored, and k is the number of categories on which the other variable is scored. Calculate the row and column marginal totals.
2. Determine the maximum frequency in each column of the contingency table (denoted n_{Mj}) and the maximum row total [denoted $\max(R_i)$]. Use these values to calculate the value of L_B by using Eq. (9.37).
3. To test the significance of L_B, use Eq. (9.38) to calculate the variance and use this value to calculate a z score. When N is large the significance of z (and, hence, L_B) may be determined with Appendix Table A. If the observed value of z exceeds the critical value, we may reject H_0: $\lambda_B = \lambda_{B0}$.

4. To calculate L_A and test hypotheses about λ_A, follow steps 1 through 3 by using Eqs. (9.39) and (9.40).

9.10.6 References

Discussions of the lambda statistic may be found in the series of papers by Goodman and Kruskal (1954, 1959, 1963, 1972). A general discussion of the application of L_B and L_A with emphasis on the analysis of sequential data may be found in Castellan (1979). The latter paper also discusses confidence intervals and tests for comparing two or more lambdas. All of the above references also discuss an index L_{AB}, which is a measure of the reduction in error of prediction from either the variable A or the variable B.

9.11 ASYMMETRICAL ASSOCIATION FOR ORDERED VARIABLES: SOMERS' d_{BA}

9.11.1 Function and Rationale

The gamma statistic discussed earlier in Sec. 9.10 is an appropriate index for measuring the association between ordered variables. As with the Cramér coefficient, which measured the association between two variables which are categorical, the gamma statistic is not sensitive to *differential* relation between two variables. When the variables are nominally scaled categorical variables, the lambda statistic is a suitable index of asymmetrical association between one variable and another. When the variables are ordered, there is sometimes a need to measure the degree of association between a particular variable and another. An example would be when one of the variables is designated as an independent variable and the other as a dependent variable. Another would be when we are studying sequences of behaviors—are antecedent behaviors related to consequent behaviors? *Somers'* Δ is an appropriate asymmetrical index of relation between one ordered variable and another ordered variable. Following the labeling in the previous section, suppose that variable A is an ordinally scaled variable for which $A_1 < A_2 < \cdots < A_k$, and which may be thought of as an independent variable. Furthermore, suppose that variable B is a ordinally scaled variable for which $B_1 < B_2 < \cdots < B_r$, and which may be thought of as a dependent variable. That is, we assume that A and B are ordered in magnitude by their subscripts. Then Δ_{BA} is an asymmetric index of association between the variables. If the roles of the two variables are reversed, then the index is denoted Δ_{AB}. In a sample, the corresponding statistics would be d_{BA} and d_{AB} respectively.

The parameter Δ_{BA} is the difference between the probability that within a pair of observations A an B are in the same order and the probability that within a pair of observations A and B disagree in their ordering, conditional upon *no* ties in variable A. An expression for this parameter is

$$\Delta_{BA} = \frac{P[A \;\&\; B \text{ agree in order}] - P[A \;\&\; B \text{ disagree in order}]}{P[\text{a pair of observations are not tied on } A]}$$

In a similar fashion,

$$\Delta_{AB} = \frac{P[A \,\&\, B \text{ agree in order}] - P[A \,\&\, B \text{ disagree in order}]}{P[\text{a pair of observations are not tied on } B]}$$

Since we seldom know the probabilities in the population, we must estimate them from the data; thus we must use the statistics d_{BA} and d_{AB} to estimate Δ_{BA} and Δ_{AB} respectively.

9.11.2 Method

To compute Somers' d from two sets of ordinal variables, say, $A_1, A_2, \ldots, A_k$ and $B_1, B_2, \ldots, B_r$, we arrange the frequencies in a contingency table:

	A_1	A_2	$\cdots$	A_k	Total
B_1	n_{11}	n_{12}	$\cdots$	n_{1k}	R_1
B_2	n_{21}	n_{22}	$\cdots$	n_{2k}	R_2
$\vdots$	$\vdots$	$\vdots$		$\vdots$	$\vdots$
B_r	n_{r1}	n_{r2}	$\cdots$	n_{rk}	R_r
Total	C_1	C_2	$\cdots$	C_k	N

The data may consist of any number of categories. That is, one may compute Somers' d statistic for data from a 2×2 table, a 2×5 table, or any $r \times k$ table.

As with the gamma statistic, we begin by computing the number of agreements and disagreements between pairs of variables; the difference between d and G is in the denominator since we must omit the ties on variable A. To compute d_{BA}, the equation is

$$d_{BA} = \frac{\#\text{ agreements} - \#\text{ disagreements}}{\#\text{ pairs not tied on variable } A}$$

$$= \frac{2[\#(+) - \#(-)]}{N^2 - \sum_{j=1}^{k} C_j^2} \tag{9.41}$$

where $\#(+)$ and $\#(-)$ are the number of agreements and disagreements in orderings respectively, as defined in Eqs. (9.33) and (9.34). The procedures for computing these counts from a contingency table are outlined in Sec. 9.3.3. N is the number of observations and C_j is the marginal frequency of the jth value of the variable A. Although the denominator may not appear to count the pairs and omit the ties on variable A, it does. If we counted each of the possible pairings of observations, there would be $\frac{1}{2}N^2$ pairings. (We include here the possibility of pairing an observation with itself but divide by 2 because we wish to count only unique pairings.) Then there are $\frac{1}{2}C_1^2$ pairings for first value of variable A, that is, A_1, $\frac{1}{2}C_2^2$ is the number of ties on A_2, etc. We subtract these ties from the total number of pairings.

If we wish to compute the asymmetrical index d_{AB}, the formula is

$$d_{AB} = \frac{\#\text{ agreements} - \#\text{ disagreements}}{\#\text{ pairs not tied on variable } B}$$

$$= \frac{2[\#(+) - \#(-)]}{N^2 - \sum_{i=1}^{r} R_i^2} \tag{9.42}$$

where R_i is the marginal frequency for the value B_i.

To illustrate the computation of d_{BA}, we shall calculate the statistic for the data in Table 9.16. The use of Somers' d_{BA} would be appropriate if we assume that variable A is an independent variable and that variable B is a dependent variable, and that we wish to assess the association from A to B. In Sec. 9.9.3 we found $\#(+) = 945$ and $\#(-) = 310$. By using these values and the column marginal totals from the table, we find

$$d_{BA} = \frac{2[\#(+) - \#(-)]}{N^2 - \sum_{j=1}^{k} C_j^2} \tag{9.41}$$

$$= \frac{2(945 - 310)}{70^2 - (20^2 + 20^2 + 17^2 + 13^2)}$$

$$= \frac{2(635)}{3642}$$

$$= .35$$

This value of d_{BA} indicates that there is a moderate asymmetric relation or association from variable A to variable B. (Note that we have not found d_{AB}. It will be left as an exercise for the reader.)

Example 9.11*a* With the development of bar-code scanners for use in supermarkets and many other stores, there has been a trend toward the omission of price markings on individual items. Retailers are keenly interested in not having to mark individual prices. Two of the most important reasons are (1) the labor savings resulting from not having to mark each item and (2) the ability to reprice items quickly in response to cost changes, special sales, etc. On the other hand, shoppers have become accustomed to having prices marked on individual items. Advantages of unit pricing which shoppers cite include the ability (1) to compare easily prices for different brands of a particular product; (2) to review the total cost of items in a market basket; and (3) to ensure correct charges in the checkout lane. If retailers want to move toward omisson of price markings, market specialists argue that public relations campaigns must be mounted to educate the public about the advantages of such omissions. To have an effective campaign, it is important to know current attitudes and what kind of shopper has the most resistance to omission of time pricing. In study of

TABLE 9.19
Attitude about item price omission for various education levels

	Education				
Attitude	**Less than high school**	**High school graduate**	**Some college**	**College graduate**	Total
Very bad to bad	22	39	19	8	88
No difference	6	8	6	14	34
Good to very good	5	16	12	10	43
Total	33	63	37	32	165

shoppers in a large midwestern city[24], attitudes toward item price omission were obtained and related to a number of demographic variables such as age, income, education, etc.

In a survey, the demographic variables can be thought of as independent variables and the response to an attitude question is the dependent variable. One of the demographic variables was education, and the researchers wanted to determine how education affected attitude. Since the variables education and attitude are both ordinal variables and because we are primarily interested in the effect of education on attitude, Somers' d_{BA} is an appropriate measure. Table 9.19 summarizes the responses from $N = 165$ women shoppers. To determine the association, Somers' d_{BA} will be calculated.

First we need to determine the number of agreements and disagreements in ordering for the two variables.

$$\#(+) = (22)(66) + (39)(42) + (19)(24) + \cdots + (8)(22) + (6)(10) = 4010$$

and

$$\#(-) = (39)(11) + (19)(35) + (8)(53) + \cdots + (6)(21) + (14)(33) = 2146$$

Next, we compute Somers' d_{BA}:

$$d_{BA} = \frac{2[\#(+) - \#(-)]}{N^2 - \sum_{j=1}^{k} C_j^2} \tag{9.41}$$

$$= \frac{2[4010 - 2146]}{165^2 - (33^2 + 63^2 + 37^2 + 32^2)}$$

$$= \frac{2(1864)}{19{,}774}$$

$$= .189$$

On the basis of this analysis we conclude that education has a small relation with attitude toward item price omission. The table shows a trend that women with more educa-

[24] Langrehr, F. W., and Langrehr, V. B. (1983). Consumer acceptance of item price removal: A survey study of Milwaukee shoppers. *Journal of Consumer Affairs*, **17**, 149–171.

tion have more positive attitudes toward item price omission and women with less education have more negative attitudes. Whether this trend will be significant will be discussed in Sec. 9.11.4.

9.11.3 The Interpretation of Somers' d_{BA}

Since Δ_{BA} "ignores" ties among the column variables, it is an index of the association between two pairs of observations which are in two different columns (i.e., untied on variable A). Consider two randomly selected observations, $(A - B)$ and $(A' - B')$, for which A and A' are different. Somer's Δ_{BA} is the difference in the probability that A and A' are in the same order as B and B' (with $B = B'$ counted as an agreement in order), minus the probability that A and A' are in a different order than B and B', all conditional upon $A \neq A'$.

The index $d_{BA} = 1$ if and only if $\#(-) = 0$ (there are no disagreements in order) *and* each row has at most one nonzero cell. The appearance of such contingency table would have the nonzero cells descending from upper left to lower right like a staircase. Similarly, $d_{BA} = -1$ if the nonzero cells ascend from lower left to upper right.

The index $d_{BA} = 0$ if the variables (in the sample) are independent; however, $d_{BA} = 0$ does not imply independence unless the contingency table is 2×2. The reader should note that in the population, if the variables A and B are independent, $\Delta_{BA} = 0$ while $\Delta_{BA} = 0$ does not imply independence.

If the researcher is focusing on d_{AB}, then corresponding arguments may be made; however, the role of rows and columns must be interchanged.

9.11.4 Testing the Significance of d_{BA}

Like many of the measures of association given in this chapter, the sampling distribution of d_{BA} is relatively complicated. However, there are some simplifications possible which can make testing significance easier.

Recall that, when we calculated the number of agreements $\#(+)$ and the number of disagreements $\#(-)$, we included only unique pairings of data in the counts. When calculating the variance of d_{BA} we shall need to count all of the agreements which occur with each datum. To do this we shall need some additional notation. When we described the computation of $\#(+)$ and $\#(-)$, we used the symbols $\mathbf{N}_{ij}^{+}$ and $\mathbf{N}_{ij}^{-}$ to denote the *sum* of the frequencies below and to the right and the *sum* of the frequencies below and to the left of the *ij*th cell respectively. To compute the variance of d_{BA} we shall need the frequencies above and to the left and above and to the right of the *ij*th cell. We shall denote these as $\mathbf{M}_{ij}^{+}$ and $\mathbf{M}_{ij}^{-}$ respectively. These two variables may be defined by using the following notation:

$$\mathbf{M}_{ij}^{+} = \sum_{p=1}^{i-1} \sum_{q=1}^{j-1} n_{pq} \tag{9.43}$$

$$\mathbf{M}_{ij}^{-} = \sum_{p=1}^{i-1} \sum_{q=j+1}^{k} n_{pq} \tag{9.44}$$

Graphically, we may depict the expressions as follows:

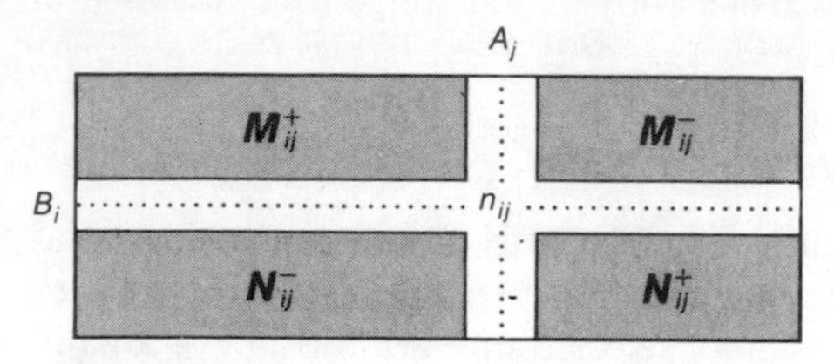

With the use of these sums, together with $\mathbf{N}_{ij}^+$ and $\mathbf{N}_{ij}^-$, and weighting them by the frequency in the ijth cell, we could count the agreements and disagreements for each pair of data in the entire table. (We have counted agreements and disagreements considering each object with every other object—each pair has been counted twice.) All of these terms are used to calculate the variance of d_{BA} under the hypothesis H_0: $\Delta_{BA} = 0$:

$$\operatorname{var}(d_{BA}) = \frac{4 \sum_{i=1}^{r} \sum_{j=1}^{k} n_{ij}(\mathbf{N}_{ij}^+ + \mathbf{M}_{ij}^+ - \mathbf{N}_{ij}^- - \mathbf{M}_{ij}^-)^2}{\left[N^2 - \sum_{j=1}^{k} C_j^2\right]^2} \tag{9.45}$$

If we make the assumption that the sampling has been from a population with a uniform distribution over all cells in the table, Eq. (9.45) simplifies to

$$\operatorname{var}(d_{BA}) = \frac{4(r^2 - 1)(k + 1)}{9Nr^2(k - 1)} \tag{9.46a}$$

Equation (9.46a) also appears to be a reasonable estimate of $\operatorname{var}(d_{BA})$ even when the sampling is not multinomial. Because of its ease of computation, Eq. (9.46a) could be used when the researcher can assume uniform multinomial sampling. In many cases the researcher does have some control over the sampling probabilities in at least the columns and could exert some additional control by choosing the B categories carefully; therefore the assumption of uniform multinomial sampling may be reasonable for those situations.

To test the hypothesis H_0: $\Delta_{BA} = 0$ against a one- or two-tailed alternative use the following statistic:

$$z = \frac{d_{BA}}{\sqrt{\operatorname{var}(d_{BA})}} \tag{9.47}$$

This value is approximately normally distributed with mean 0 and standard deviation 1. This significance of z and, hence, d_{BA} may be determined by reference to Appendix Table A.

If the researcher wants to test hypotheses about Δ_{AB}, then the variance $\operatorname{var}(d_{AB})$ would be computed with Eq. (9.45), except that the denominator would be replaced with

$$\left(N^2 - \sum_{i=1}^{r} R_i^2\right)^2$$

If the variance were to be estimated with Eq. (9.46*a*), the variables r and k would be interchanged:

$$\text{var}(d_{AB}) = \frac{4(k^2 - 1)(r + 1)}{9Nk^2(r - 1)} \tag{9.46b}$$

It should be noted that the variance given by Eq. (9.45) cannot be used to determine confidence intervals or to test hypotheses other than H_0: $\Delta_{BA} = 0$. The references at the end of this section give the variances for other situations.

Example 9.11*b* In the attitude survey in the previous example, we found that $d_{BA} = .189$. We cannot tell from the magnitude of d_{BA} alone whether the observed value is significantly different from 0. We shall test the hypothesis H_0: $\Delta_{BA} = 0$ against the hypothesis H_1: $\Delta_{BA} \neq 0$. A two-tailed test is used because the authors had no *a priori* notions about the relation between education and attitude. We begin by calculating var(d_{BA}):

$$\text{var}(d_{BA}) = \frac{4 \sum_{i=1}^{r} \sum_{j=1}^{k} n_{ij}(\mathbf{N}_{ij}^{+} + \mathbf{M}_{ij}^{+} - \mathbf{N}_{ij}^{-} - \mathbf{M}_{ij}^{-})^2}{\left(N^2 - \sum_{j=1}^{k} C_j^2\right)^2} \tag{9.45}$$

$$= \frac{4[(22)(66 - 0) + (39)(42 - 11) + \cdots + (12)(75 - 22) + (10)(100 - 0)]}{[165^2 - (33^2 + 63^2 + 37^2 + 32^2)]^2}$$

$$= \frac{4(389{,}112)}{19{,}774^2}$$

$$= .00398$$

Using this value for the variance, we may compute

$$z = \frac{d_{BA}}{\sqrt{\text{var}(d_{BA})}} \tag{9.47}$$

$$= \frac{.189}{\sqrt{.00398}}$$

$$= 3.00$$

Since this value exceeds the critical (two-tailed) value of z for $\alpha = .05$, we may reject the hypothesis that education has no relation to attitude. Note, however, that we have *not* tested whether there is association between education and attitude. We have considered only the asymmetric relation *from* education *to* attitude.

Finally, as a check on the approximation of var(d_{BA}) for uniform multinomial sampling, we shall calculate that estimate.

$$\text{var}(d_{BA}) = \frac{4(r^2 - 1)(k + 1)}{9Nr^2(k - 1)} \tag{9.46a}$$

$$= \frac{4(3^3 - 1)(4 + 1)}{9(165)(3^2)(4 - 1)}$$

$$= .00399$$

This value is very close to the value obtain by Eq. (9.45). Although the values were extremely close in this example, there is no assurance that they will always be so. Nonetheless, Monte Carlo studies by Somers have found that the difference is relatively small in many cases.

9.11.5 Summary of Procedure

These are the steps in the computation of Somers' d_{BA}.

1. Cast the N observed frequencies into an $r \times k$ contingency table, where r is the number of categories on which one variable is scored and k is the number of categories on which the other variable is scored. For the row variable, values should be tabled in order of increasing magnitude across the columns. Similarly, the row variable should be listed in increasing magnitude down the rows. Denote the column variable as A and the row variable as B.
2. Use Eqs. (9.33*b*) and (9.34*b*) to calculate the number of agreements in ordering, $\#(+)$, and the number of disagreements in ordering, $\#(-)$. Enter those values into Eq. (9.41) [or (9.42)] to determine d_{BA} (or d_{AB}).
3. If N is moderate or large, test the hypothesis H_0: $\Delta_{BA} = 0$ (or H_0: $\Delta_{AB} = 0$ if appropriate) by using Eq. (9.47) to compute a normal deviate z. Use Appendix Table A to determine the significance of z.

9.11.6 References

The asymmetrical index of association Δ_{BA} was proposed by Somers (1962) who also has considered alternative forms for its sampling distribution (1980). The references from the previous two sections, particularly those of Goodman and Kruskal (1963, 1972), are also relevant.

9.12 DISCUSSION

In this chapter we have presented many nonparametric techniques for measuring the degree of association between variables in a sample. For each of these, tests of the significance of the observed association were presented.

9.12.1 Association for Nominally Scaled Variables

Four of these techniques, the Cramér coefficient C, the phi coefficient r_ϕ, the kappa statistic K, and the lambda coefficient L_B are applicable when the data are categorical and lie in a nominal scale. That is, if the measurement is such that the classifications involved are unrelated within any set and, thus, cannot be meaningfully ordered, then these coefficients provide meaningful measures of the degree of association in the data.

The Cramér coefficient C is one of the simplest measures of association for categorical variables. Although it provides minimum information about the association between the variables, there may be no practical alternative. The phi coefficient r_ϕ is an index of association appropriate when there are two levels of each variable and the relation is summarized in a 2×2 table.

The kappa statistic K is a useful index when several raters have categorized each of a group of objects or subjects into nominal categories. K is an index of agreement among the raters.

The lambda coefficient L_B is an asymmetric index of association which is a measure of the predictability of one of the categorical variables when the value of the other variable is known. There are two measures: L_B, where the predictability of variable B from variable A is measured and L_A, where the predictability of variable A from variable B is measured. In general $L_B \neq L_A$. As a result, special care must be taken in interpreting the statistic.

9.12.2 Association for Ordinal-Scaled Variables

If the variables under study have been measured in at least an ordinal scale, one could still use one of the four categorical measures of association; however, one of the various measures of *rank* correlation will utilize the order information in the data and is, therefore, preferable.

If the data are at least ordinal, the two rank-order correlation coefficients, the Spearman r_s and the Kendall T, are appropriate. The Spearman r_s is somewhat easier to compute. The Kendall T has the additional advantage of being generalizable to a partial correlation coefficient $T_{xy.z}$.

The Kendall partial rank-order correlation coefficient $T_{xy.z}$ measures the degree of relation between two variables X and Y when a third variable Z (on which the association between X and Y might logically depend) is held constant. $T_{xy.z}$ is the nonparametric equivalent of the product-moment partial correlation coefficient. Under reasonable assumptions, hypotheses about the corresponding population parameter may be tested.

If there are several sets of rankings or orderings to be analyzed, there are two measures of concordance or agreement among the several sets of rankings which can be used. The Kendall coefficient of concordance W and the Kendall coefficient of agreement u measure the extent of association among several (k) sets of rankings of N entities. Each is useful in determining the agreement among several judges or the association among three or more variables. The Kendall coefficient of concordance W is linearly related to the Spearman r_s. The other index, the Kendall coefficient of agreement u, is linearly related to the Kendall T.

The Kendall coefficient of agreement can also be generalized to a measure of the concordance between several judges and a criterion ranking T_C. The coefficient of agreement may also be used to provide a standard method of ordering entities according to consensus when no objective order for the objects is available or known *a priori.*

The Kendall coefficient of agreement u also has the advantage of being an appropriate index of association when data have been gathered by the method of paired comparisons rather than rankings. For certain experimental designs, paired comparisons may be more appropriate data than rankings. The index can be used even if the comparisons are not consistent or transitive.

The Goodman and Kruskal gamma statistic G and Somers' d_{BA} are appropriate measures of association when the observations of two ordered variables are summarized in a contingency table or when the variables are rankings for which there are many ties. Somers' d_{BA} gives a measure of association when one of the two variables is of particular importance or there is a special distinction between the variables, for example, when one is a dependent variable and the other is an independent variable. Like the lambda statistic, Somers' d_{BA} is asymmetric and care must be taken in its interpretation.

There are many measures of association which have been developed for use with categorical and ordinal data. In this chapter it has not been possible to discuss them all. Our choices were motivated by a desire to provide coverage of those techniques we believe to be most useful to researchers. Some of these, such as the Cramér coefficient, the Spearman r_s, and Kendall T, are familiar to many researchers. Others, like the kappa statistic and the Kendall coefficient of agreement are less familiar. All of them should be useful when appropriately applied.

REFERENCES

Bailey, D. E. (1971). *Probability and statistics: models for research.* New York: J. Wiley.

Bishop, Y. M. M., Feinberg, S. E., and Holland, P. W. (1975). *Discrete multivariate analysis: theory and practice.* Cambridge, MA: MIT Press.

Bradley, J. V. (1968). *Distribution-free statistical tests.* Englewood Cliffs, NJ: Prentice-Hall.

Castellan, N. J., Jr. (1965). On the partitioning of contingency tables. *Psychological Bulletin,* **64,** 330–338.

———. (1979). The analysis of behavior sequences. In R. B. Cairns (ed.), *The analysis of social interactions: methods, issues, and illustrations.* Hillsdale, NJ: L. Erlbaum, pp. 81–116.

Chacko, V. J. (1963). Testing homogeneity against ordered alternatives. *Annals of Mathematical Statistics,* **34**, 945–956.

Cochran, W. G. (1950). The comparison of percentages in matched samples. *Biometrika,* **37**, 256–266.

———. (1952). The χ^2 test of goodness of fit. *Annals of Mathematical Statistics,* **23**, 315–345.

———. (1954). Some methods for strengthening the common χ^2 tests. *Biometrics,* **10**, 417–451.

Cohen, J. (1960). A coefficient of agreement for nominal scales. *Educational and Psychological Measurement,* **20,** 37–46.

———. (1968). Weighted kappa: Nominal scale agreement with provision for scaled disagreement or partial credit. *Psychological Bulletin,* **70**, 213–220.

Davidson, D., Suppes, P., and Siegel, S. (1957). *Decision making: an experimental approach.* Stanford, CA: Stanford University Press.

Delucchi, K. L. (1983). The use and misuse of chi-square: Lewis and Burke revisited. *Psychological Bulletin,* **94,** 166–176.

Dixon, W. J., and Massey, F. J. (1983). *Introduction to statistical analysis* (fourth edition). New York: McGraw-Hill.

Edwards, A. L. (1967). *Statistical methods* (second edition). New York: Holt, Rinehart and Winston.

Ehrenberg, A. S. C. (1952). On sampling from a population of rankers. *Biometrika,* **39**, 82–87.

Everitt, B. S. (1977). *The analysis of contingency tables.* London: Chapman and Hall.

Feigin, P. D. and Cohen, A. (1978). On a model for concordance between judges. *Journal Royal Statistical Society* (Series B), **40**, 203–221.

Fisher, R. A. (1973). *Statistical methods for research workers* (14th edition). New York: Hafner.

Fleiss, J. L. (1971). Measuring nominal scale agreement among many raters. *Psychological Bulletin,* **76,** 378–382.

Fligner, M. A., and Policello, G. E., III (1981). Robust rank procedures for the Behrens-Fisher problem. *Journal of the American Statistical Association*, **76**, 162–168.

Fraser, C. O. (1980). Measurement in psychology. *British Journal of Psychology*, **71**, 23–34.

Friedman, M. (1937). The use of ranks to avoid the assumption of normality implicit in the analysis of variance. *Journal of the American Statistical Association*, **32**, 675–701.

———. (1940). A comparison of alternative tests of significance for the problem of *m* rankings. *Annals of Mathematical Statistics*, **11**, 86–92.

Gibbons, J. D. (1976). *Nonparametric methods for quantitative analysis*. New York: Holt, Rinehart and Winston.

———. (1985). *Nonparametric statistical inference* (second edition, revised and expanded). New York: Marcel Dekker.

Goodman, L. A. (1954). Kolmogorov-Smirnov tests for psychological research. *Psychological Bulletin*, **51**, 160–168.

——— and Kruskal, W. H. (1954). Measures of association for cross classifications. *Journal of the American Statistical Association*, **49**, 732–764.

——— and ———. (1959). Measures of association for cross classifications. II: Further discussion and references. *Journal of the American Statistical Association*, **54**, 123–163.

——— and ———. (1963). Measures of association for cross classifications. III: Approximate sampling theory. *Journal of the American Statistical Association*, **58**, 310–364.

——— and ———. (1972). Measures of association for cross classifications. IV: Simplification of asymptotic variances. *Journal of the American Statistical Association*, **67**, 415–421.

Haberman, S. J. (1973). The analysis of residuals in cross-classified tables. *Biometrics*, **29**, 205–220.

Hammond, K. R., Householder, J. E., and Castellan, N. J., Jr. (1970). *Introduction to the statistical method* (second edition). New York: A. A. Knopf.

Hays, W. L. (1960). A note on average tau as a measure of concordance. *Journal of the American Statistical Association*, **55**, 331–341.

———. (1981). *Statistics* (third edition). New York: Holt, Rinehart and Winston.

Hettmansperger, T. P. (1984). *Statistical inference based on ranks*. New York: J. Wiley.

Hollander, M. (1967). Asymptotic efficiency of two nonparametric competitors of Wilcoxon's two sample test. *Journal of the American Statistical Association*, **62**, 939–949

——— and Wolfe, D. A. (1973). *Nonparametric statistical methods*. New York: J. Wiley.

Johnson, N. S. (1979). Nonnull properties of Kendall's partial rank correlation coefficient. *Biometrika*, **66**, 333–338.

Jonckheere, A. R. (1954). A distribution-free *k*-sample test against ordered alternatives. *Biometrika*, **41**, 133–145.

Kendall, M. G. (1970). *Rank correlation methods* (fourth edition). London: Griffin.

Kolmogorov, A. (1941). Confidence limits for an unknown distribution function. *Annals of Mathematical Statistics*, **12**, 461–463.

Kruskal, W. H. (1952). A nonparametric test for the several sample problem. *Annals of Mathematical Statistics*, **23**, 525–540.

——— and Wallis, W. A. (1952). Use of ranks in one-criterion variance analysis. *Journal of the American Statistical Association*, **47**, 583–621.

Lehmann, E. L. (1975). *Nonparametrics: statistical methods based on ranks*. San Francisco: Holden-Day.

Lewis, D., and Burke, C. J. (1949). The use and misuse of the chi-square test. *Psychological Bulletin*, **46**, 433–489.

Lienert, G. A., and Netter, P. (1987). Nonparametric analysis of treatment-response tables by bipredictive configural frequency analysis. *Methods of Information in Medicine*, **26**, 89–92.

Light, R. J. (1971). Measures of response agreement for qualitative data: some generalizations and alternatives. *Psychological Bulletin*, **76**, 365–377.

McNemar, Q. (1969). *Psychological statistics* (fourth edition). New York: J. Wiley.

Mack, G. A., and Wolfe, D. A. (1981). *k*-sample rank tests for umbrella alternatives. *Journal of the American Statistical Association*, **76**, 175–181.

Maghsoodloo, S. (1975). Estimates of the quantiles of Kendall's partial rank correlation coefficient. *Journal of Statistical Computing and Simulation*, **4**, 155–164.

——— and Pallos, L. L. (1981). Asymptotic behavior of Kendall's partial rank correlation coefficient and additional quantile estimates. *Journal of Statistical Computing and Simulation*, **13**, 41–48.

Mann, H. B., and Whitney, D. R. (1947). On a test of whether one of two random variables is stochastically larger than the other. *Annals of Mathematical Statistics*, **18**, 50–60.

Marascuilo, L. A., and McSweeney, M. (1977). *Nonparametric and distribution-free methods for the social sciences*. Monterey, CA: Brooks/Cole.

Mood, A. M. (1950). *Introduction to the theory of statistics*. New York: McGraw-Hill.

Moran, P. A. P. (1951). Partial and multiple rank correlation. *Biometrika*, **38**, 26–32.

Moses, L. E. (1952). Non-parametric statistics for psychological research. *Psychological Bulletin*, **49**, 122–143.

———. (1963). Rank tests of dispersion. *Annals of Mathematical Statistics*, **34**, 973–983.

Mosteller, F. (1948). A *k* sample slippage test for an extreme population. *Annals of Mathematical Statistics*, **19**, 58–65.

——— and Tukey, J. W. (1950). Significance levels for a *k*-sample slippage test. *Annals of Mathematical Statistics*, **21**, 120–123.

Page, E. B. (1963). Ordered hypotheses for multiple treatments: A significance test for linear ranks. *Journal of the American Statistical Association*, **58**, 216–230.

Page, E. S. (1955). A test for a change in a parameter occurring at an unknown point. *Biometrika*, **42**, 523–527.

Patil, K. D. (1975). Cochran's Q test: Exact distribution. *Journal of the American Statistical Association*, **70**, 186–189.

Pettitt, A. N. (1979). A non-parametric approach to the change-point problem. *Applied Statistics*, **28**, 126–135.

Pitman, E. J. G. (1937*a*). Significance tests which may be applied to samples from any populations. Supplement to *Journal of the Royal Statistical Society*, **4**, 119–130.

———. (1937*b*). Significance tests which may be applied to samples from any populations. II. The correlation coefficient test. Supplement to *Journal of the Royal Statistical Society*, **4**, 225–232.

———. (1937*c*). Significance tests which may be applied to samples from any populations. III. The analysis of variance test. *Biometrika*, **29**, 322–335.

Potter, R. W., and Strum, G. W. (1981). The power of Jonckheere's test. *Journal of the American Statistical Association*, **35**, 249–250.

Puri, M. L. (1965). Some distribution-free *k*-sample rank tests for homogeneity against ordered alternatives. *Communications Pure Applied Mathematics*, **18**, 51–63.

Randles, R. H., Fligner, M. A., Policello, G. E., III, and Wolfe, D. A. (1980). An asymptotically distribution-free test for symmetry versus asymmetry. *Journal of the American Statistical Association*, **75**, 168–172.

——— and Wolfe, D. A. (1979). *Introduction to the theory of nonparametric statistics*. New York: J. Wiley.

Scheffé, H. V. (1943). Statistical inference in the non-parametric case. *Annals of Mathematical Statistics*, **14**, 305–332..

Schorak, G. R. (1969). Testing and estimating ratios of scale parameters. *Journal of the American Statistical Association*, **64**, 999–1013.

Scott, W. A. (1955). Reliability of content analysis: The case of nominal scale coding. *Public Opinion Quarterly*, **19**, 321–325.

Shaffer, J. P. (1973). Defining and testing hypotheses in multidimensional contingency tables. *Psychological Bulletin*, **79**, 127–141.

Siegel, S., and Tukey, J. W. (1960). A nonparametric sum of ranks procedure for relative spread in unpaired samples. *Journal of the American Statistical Association*, **55**, 429–445. (Correction in *Journal of the American Statistical Association*, 1961, **56**, 1005.)

Smirnov, N. V. (1948). Table for estimating the goodness of fit of empirical distributions. *Annals of Mathematical Statistics*, **19**, 279–281.

Somers, R. H. (1962). A new asymmetric measure of association for ordinal variables. *American Sociological Review*, **27**, 799–811.

———. (1980). Simple approximations to null sampling variances: Goodman and Kruskal's gamma, Kendall's tau, and Somers's d_{yx}. *Sociological Methods and Research*, **9**, 115–126.

Stilson, D. W., and Campbell, V. N. (1962). A note on calculating tau and average tau and on the sampling distribution of average tau with a criterion ranking. *Journal of the American Statistical Association*, **57**, 567–571.

Swed, F. S., and Eisenhart, C. (1943). Tables for testing randomness of grouping in a sequence of alternatives. *Annals of Mathematical Statistics*, **14**, 83–86.

Terpstra, T. J. (1952). The asymptotic normality and consistency of Kendall's test against trend, when ties are present in one ranking. *Indagationes Mathematicae*, **14**, 327–333.

Townsend, J. T., and Ashby, F. G. (1984). Measurement scales and statistics: The misconception misconceived. *Psychological Bulletin*, **96**, 394–401.

Whitney, D. R. (1948). A comparison of the power of non-parametric tests and tests based on the normal distribution under non-normal alternatives. (Unpublished doctoral dissertation, Ohio State University.)

Wilcoxon, F. (1945). Individual comparisons by ranking methods. *Biometrics*, **1**, 80–83.

———. (1947). Probability tables for individual comparisons by ranking methods. *Biometrics*, **3**, 119–122.

———. (1949). *Some rapid approximate statistical procedures*. Stamford, CT: American Cyanamid.

Yates, F. (1934). Contingency tables involving small numbers and the χ^2 test. *Journal of the Royal Statistical Society Supplement*, **1**, 217–235.

APPENDIX I
TABLES

A. Probabilities associated with the upper tail of the normal distribution
A_{II}. Critical z values for $\#c$ multiple comparisons
A_{III}. Critical values $q(\alpha, \#c)$ for $\#c$ dependent multiple comparisons
B. Critical values of Student's t distribution
C. Critical values of the chi-square distribution
D. Table of probabilities associated with values as small as (or smaller than) observed values of k in the binomial test
E. The binomial distribution
F. Critical values of D in the Kolmogorov-Smirnov one-sample test
G. Critical values of r in the runs test
H. Critical values of T^+ for the Wilcoxon signed ranks test
I. Fisher exact text, probabilities for fourfold tables, $N \leqslant 15$
J. Lower- and upper-tail probabilities for W_x, the Wilcoxon-Mann-Whitney rank-sum statistic
K. Critical values of $\grave{U}$ for robust rank order test
L_I. Kolmogorov-Smirnov two-sample test (one-tailed)
L_{II}. Kolmogorov-Smirnov two-sample test (two-tailed)
L_{III}. Critical values of $D_{m,n}$ for Kolmogorov-Smirnov two-sample test (large samples: two-tailed test)
M. Critical values for the Friedman two-way analysis of variance by ranks statistic F_r
N. Critical values for Page's L statistic
O. Critical values for the Kruskal-Wallis one-way analysis of variance by ranks statistic KW
P. Critical values for the Jonckheere statistic J
Q. Critical values of r_s, the Spearman rank-order correlation coefficient
R_I. Upper-tail probabilities for T, the Kendall rank-order correlation coefficient ($N \leq 10$)
R_{II}. Critical values for T, the Kendall rank-order correlation coefficient
S. Critical values for $T_{xy.z}$, the Kendall partial rank-order correlation coefficient
T. Critical values for the Kendall coefficient of concordance W
U. Upper-tail probabilities of u, the Kendall coefficient of agreement when data are based upon paired comparisons
V. Upper-tail probabilities of T_C, the correlation of k rankings with a criterion ranking
W. Factorials
X. Binomial coefficients

APPENDIX I
TABLES

TABLE A

Probabilities associated with the upper tail of the normal distribution

The body of the table gives one-tailed probabilities under H_0 of z. The left-hand marginal column gives various values of z to one decimal place. The top row gives various values to the second decimal place. Thus, for example, the one-tailed p of $z \geq .11$ or $z \leq -.11$ is $p = .4562$.

z	.00	.01	.02	.03	.04	.05	.06	.07	.08	.09
.0	.5000	.4960	.4920	.4880	.4840	.4801	.4761	.4721	.4681	.4641
.1	.4602	.4562	.4522	.4483	.4443	.4404	.4364	.4325	.4286	.4247
.2	.4207	.4168	.4129	.4090	.4052	.4013	.3974	.3936	.3897	.3859
.3	.3821	.3783	.3745	.3707	.3669	.3632	.3594	.3557	.3520	.3483
.4	.3446	.3409	.3372	.3336	.3300	.3264	.3228	.3192	.3156	.3121
.5	.3085	.3050	.3015	.2981	.2946	.2912	.2877	.2843	.2810	.2776
.6	.2743	.2709	.2676	.2643	.2611	.2578	.2546	.2514	.2483	.2451
.7	.2420	.2389	.2358	.2327	.2296	.2266	.2236	.2206	.2177	.2148
.8	.2119	.2090	.2061	.2033	.2005	.1977	.1949	.1922	.1894	.1867
.9	.1841	.1814	.1788	.1762	.1736	.1711	.1685	.1660	.1635	.1611
1.0	.1587	.1562	.1539	.1515	.1492	.1469	.1446	.1423	.1401	.1379
1.1	.1357	.1335	.1314	.1292	.1271	.1251	.1230	.1210	.1190	.1170
1.2	.1151	.1131	.1112	.1093	.1075	.1056	.1038	.1020	.1003	.0985
1.3	.0968	.0951	.0934	.0918	.0901	.0885	.0869	.0853	.0838	.0823
1.4	.0808	.0793	.0778	.0764	.0749	.0735	.0721	.0708	.0694	.0681
1.5	.0668	.0655	.0643	.0630	.0618	.0606	.0594	.0582	.0571	.0559
1.6	.0548	.0537	.0526	.0516	.0505	.0495	.0485	.0475	.0465	.0455
1.7	.0446	.0436	.0427	.0418	.0409	.0401	.0392	.0384	.0375	.0367
1.8	.0359	.0351	.0344	.0336	.0329	.0322	.0314	.0307	.0301	.0294
1.9	.0287	.0281	.0274	.0268	.0262	.0256	.0250	.0244	.0239	.0233
2.0	.0228	.0222	.0217	.0212	.0207	.0202	.0197	.0192	.0188	.0183
2.1	.0179	.0174	.0170	.0166	.0162	.0158	.0154	.0150	.0146	.0143
2.2	.0139	.0136	.0132	.0129	.0125	.0122	.0119	.0116	.0113	.0110
2.3	.0107	.0104	.0102	.0099	.0096	.0094	.0091	.0089	.0087	.0084
2.4	.0082	.0080	.0078	.0075	.0073	.0071	.0069	.0068	.0066	.0064
2.5	.0062	.0060	.0059	.0057	.0055	.0054	.0052	.0051	.0049	.0048
2.6	.0047	.0045	.0044	.0043	.0041	.0040	.0039	.0038	.0037	.0036
2.7	.0035	.0034	.0033	.0032	.0031	.0030	.0029	.0028	.0027	.0026
2.8	.0026	.0025	.0024	.0023	.0023	.0022	.0021	.0021	.0020	.0019
2.9	.0019	.0018	.0018	.0017	.0016	.0016	.0015	.0015	.0014	.0014
3.0	.0013	.0013	.0013	.0012	.0012	.0011	.0011	.0011	.0010	.0010
3.1	.0010	.0009	.0009	.0009	.0008	.0008	.0008	.0008	.0007	.0007
3.2	.0007									
3.3	.0005									
3.4	.0003									
3.5	.00023									
3.6	.00016									
3.7	.00011									
3.8	.00007									
3.9	.00005									
4.0	.00003									

TABLE A (continued)

Selected significance levels for the normal distribution

Two-tailed α	.20	.10	.05	.02	.01	.002	.001	.0001	.00001
One-tailed α	.10	.05	.025	.01	.005	.001	.0005	.00005	.000005
z	1.282	1.645	1.960	2.326	2.576	3.090	3.291	3.891	4.417

TABLE A_{II}

Critical z values for #c multiple comparisons*

Entries in the table for a given #c and level of significance α is the point on the standard normal distribution such that the upper-tail probability is equal to $\frac{1}{2}\alpha/\#c$. For values of #c outside the range included in the table, z can be found by using Appendix Table A.

	α					
	Two-Tailed .30	.25	.20	.15	.10	.05
#c	One-tailed .15	.125	.10	.075	.05	.025
1	1.036	1.150	1.282	1.440	1.645	1.960
2	1.440	1.534	1.645	1.780	1.960	2.241
3	1.645	1.732	1.834	1.960	2.128	2.394
4	1.780	1.863	1.960	2.080	2.241	2.498
5	1.881	1.960	2.054	2.170	2.326	2.576
6	1.960	2.037	2.128	2.241	2.394	2.638
7	2.026	2.100	2.189	2.300	2.450	2.690
8	2.080	2.154	2.241	2.350	2.498	2.734
9	2.128	2.200	2.287	2.394	2.539	2.773
10	2.170	2.241	2.326	2.432	2.576	2.807
11	2.208	2.278	2.362	2.467	2.608	2.838
12	2.241	2.301	2.394	2.498	2.638	2.866
15	2.326	2.394	2.475	2.576	2.713	2.935
21	2.450	2.515	2.593	2.690	2.823	3.038
28	2.552	2.615	2.690	2.785	2.913	3.125

* #c is the number of comparisons.

TABLE A_{III}

Critical values $q(\alpha, \#c)$ for $\#c$ dependent multiple comparisons*†‡

Entries in the table for a given $\#c$ and level of significance α are critical values for the maximum absolute values of $\#c$ standard normal random variables with common correlation .5 for the two-tailed test, and critical values for the upper tail of $\#c$ standard normal random variables with common correlation .5 for the one-tailed test.

	Two-Tailed		One-Tailed	
#c α:	.05	.01	.05	.01
1	1.96	2.58	1.65	2.33
2	2.21	2.79	1.92	2.56
3	2.35	2.92	2.06	2.69
4	2.44	3.00	2.16	2.77
5	2.51	3.06	2.24	2.84
6	2.57	3.11	2.29	2.89
7	2.61	3.15	2.34	2.94
8	2.65	3.19	2.38	2.97
9	2.69	3.22	2.42	3.00
10	2.72	3.25	2.45	3.03
11	2.74	3.27	2.48	3.06
12	2.77	3.29	2.50	3.08
15	2.83	3.35	2.57	3.14
20	2.91	3.42	2.64	3.21

* $\#c$ is the number of comparisons.

† Two-tailed entries are adapted from Dunnett, C. W. (1964). New tables for multiple comparisons with a control. *Biometrics*, **20**, 482–491. (With the permission of the author and the editor of *Biometrics*.)

‡ One-tailed entries are adapted from Gupta, S. S. (1963). Probability integrals of multivariate normal and multivariate *t*. *Annals of Mathematical Statistics*, **34**, 792–828. (With the permission of the author and the publisher at *Annals of Mathematical Statistics*.)

TABLE B
Critical values of Student's *t* distribution*

df	Level of significance for one-tailed test					
	.10	.05	.025	.01	.005	.0005
	Level of significance for two-tailed test					
	.20	.10	.05	.02	.01	.001
1	3.078	6.314	12.706	31.821	63.657	636.619
2	1.886	2.920	4.303	6.965	9.925	31.598
3	1.638	2.353	3.182	4.541	5.841	12.941
4	1.533	2.132	2.776	3.747	4.604	8.610
5	1.476	2.015	2.571	3.365	4.032	6.859
6	1.440	1.943	2.447	3.143	3.707	5.959
7	1.415	1.895	2.365	2.998	3.499	5.405
8	1.397	1.860	2.306	2.896	3.355	5.041
9	1.383	1.833	2.262	2.821	3.250	4.781
10	1.372	1.812	2.228	2.764	3.169	4.587
11	1.363	1.796	2.201	2.718	3.106	4.437
12	1.356	1.782	2.179	2.681	3.055	4.318
13	1.350	1.771	2.160	2.650	3.012	4.221
14	1.345	1.761	2.145	2.624	2.977	4.140
15	1.341	1.753	2.131	2.602	2.947	4.073
16	1.337	1.746	2.120	2.583	2.921	4.015
17	1.333	1.740	2.110	2.567	2.898	3.965
18	1.330	1.734	2.101	2.552	2.878	3.922
19	1.328	1.729	2.093	2.539	2.861	3.883
20	1.325	1.725	2.086	2.528	2.845	3.850
21	1.323	1.721	2.080	2.518	2.831	3.819
22	1.321	1.717	2.074	2.508	2.819	3.792
23	1.319	1.714	2.069	2.500	2.807	3.767
24	1.318	1.711	2.064	2.492	2.797	3.745
25	1.316	1.708	2.060	2.485	2.787	3.725
26	1.315	1.706	2.056	2.479	2.779	3.707
27	1.314	1.703	2.052	2.473	2.771	3.690
28	1.313	1.701	2.048	2.467	2.763	3.674
29	1.311	1.699	2.045	2.462	2.756	3.659
30	1.310	1.697	2.042	2.457	2.750	3.646
40	1.303	1.684	2.021	2.423	2.704	3.551
60	1.296	1.671	2.000	2.390	2.660	3.460
120	1.289	1.658	1.980	2.358	2.617	3.373
∞	1.282	1.645	1.960	2.326	2.576	3.291

* Table B is abridged from Table III of Fisher and Yates: *Statistical tables for biological, agricultural, and medical research*, published by Longman Group UK Ltd., London (previously published by Oliver and Boyd Ltd., Edinburgh) and by permission of the authors and publishers.

TABLE C
Critical values of the chi-square distribution*

df	Probability under H_0 that $\chi^2 \geq X^2$													
	.99	.98	.95	.90	.80	.70	.50	.30	.20	.10	.05	.02	.01	.001
1	.00016	.00063	.0039	.016	.064	.15	.46	1.07	1.64	2.71	3.84	5.41	6.64	10.83
2	.02	.04	.10	.21	.45	.71	1.39	2.41	3.22	4.60	5.99	7.82	9.21	13.82
3	.12	.18	.35	.58	1.00	1.42	2.37	3.66	4.64	6.25	7.82	9.84	11.34	16.27
4	.30	.43	.71	1.06	1.65	2.20	3.36	4.88	5.99	7.78	9.49	11.67	13.28	18.46
5	.55	.75	1.14	1.61	2.34	3.00	4.35	6.06	7.29	9.24	11.07	13.39	15.09	20.52
6	.87	1.13	1.64	2.20	3.07	3.83	5.35	7.23	8.56	10.64	12.59	15.03	16.81	22.46
7	1.24	1.56	2.17	2.83	3.82	4.67	6.35	8.38	9.80	12.02	14.07	16.62	18.48	24.32
8	1.65	2.03	2.73	3.49	4.59	5.53	7.34	9.52	11.03	13.36	15.51	18.17	20.09	26.12
9	2.09	2.53	3.32	4.17	5.38	6.39	8.34	10.66	12.24	14.68	16.92	19.68	21.67	27.88
10	2.56	3.06	3.94	4.86	6.18	7.27	9.34	11.78	13.44	15.99	18.31	21.16	23.21	29.59
11	3.05	3.61	4.58	5.58	6.99	8.15	10.34	12.90	14.63	17.28	19.68	22.62	24.72	31.26
12	3.57	4.18	5.23	6.30	7.81	9.03	11.34	14.01	15.81	18.55	21.03	24.05	26.22	32.91
13	4.11	4.76	5.89	7.04	8.63	9.93	12.34	15.12	16.98	19.81	22.36	25.47	27.69	34.53
14	4.66	5.37	6.57	7.79	9.47	10.82	13.34	16.22	18.15	21.06	23.68	26.87	29.14	36.12
15	5.23	5.98	7.26	8.55	10.31	11.72	14.34	17.32	19.31	22.31	25.00	28.26	30.58	37.70
16	5.81	6.61	7.96	9.31	11.15	12.62	15.34	18.42	20.46	23.54	26.30	29.63	32.00	39.29
17	6.41	7.26	8.67	10.08	12.00	13.53	16.34	19.51	21.62	24.77	27.59	31.00	33.41	40.75
18	7.02	7.91	9.39	10.86	12.86	14.44	17.34	20.60	22.76	25.99	28.87	32.35	34.80	42.31
19	7.63	8.57	10.12	11.65	13.72	15.35	18.34	21.69	23.90	27.20	30.14	33.69	36.19	43.82
20	8.26	9.24	10.85	12.44	14.58	16.27	19.34	22.78	25.04	28.41	31.41	35.02	37.57	45.32
21	8.90	9.92	11.59	13.24	15.44	17.18	20.34	23.86	26.17	29.62	32.67	36.34	38.93	46.80
22	9.54	10.60	12.34	14.04	16.31	18.10	21.24	24.94	27.30	30.81	33.92	37.66	40.29	48.27
23	10.20	11.29	13.09	14.85	17.19	19.02	22.34	26.02	28.43	32.01	35.17	38.97	41.64	49.73
24	10.86	11.99	13.85	15.66	18.06	19.94	23.34	27.10	29.55	33.20	36.42	40.27	42.98	51.18
25	11.52	12.70	14.61	16.47	18.94	20.87	24.34	28.17	30.68	34.38	37.65	41.57	44.31	52.62
26	12.20	13.41	15.38	17.29	19.82	21.79	25.34	29.25	31.80	35.56	38.88	42.86	45.64	54.05
27	12.88	14.12	16.15	18.11	20.70	22.72	26.34	30.32	32.91	36.74	40.11	44.14	46.96	55.48
28	13.56	14.85	16.93	18.94	21.59	23.65	27.34	31.39	34.03	37.92	41.34	45.42	48.28	56.89
29	14.26	15.57	17.71	19.77	22.48	24.58	28.34	32.46	35.14	39.09	42.56	46.69	49.59	58.30
30	14.95	16.31	18.49	20.60	23.36	25.51	29.34	33.53	36.25	40.26	43.77	47.96	50.89	59.70

* Table C is abridged from Table IV of Fisher and Yates: *Statistical tables for biological, agricultural, and medical research*, published by Longman Group UK Ltd., London (previously published by Oliver and Boyd Ltd., Edinburgh) and by permission of the authors and publishers.

TABLE D

Table of probabilities associated with values as small as (or smaller than) observed values of k in the binomial test

Given in the body of the table are one-tailed probabilities under H_0 for the binomial test when $p = q = \frac{1}{2}$.

Entries are $P[Y \leq k]$. Note that entries may also be read as $P[Y \geq N - k]$

N \ k	0	1	2	3	4	5	6	7	8	9	10	11	12	13	14	15	16	17
4	062	312	688	938	1.0													
5	031	188	500	812	969	1.0												
6	016	109	344	656	891	984	1.0											
7	008	062	227	500	773	938	992	1.0										
8	004	035	145	363	637	855	965	996	1.0									
9	002	020	090	254	500	746	910	980	998	1.0								
10	001	011	055	172	377	623	828	945	989	999	1.0							
11		006	033	113	274	500	726	887	967	994	999+	1.0						
12		003	019	073	194	387	613	806	927	981	997	999+	1.0					
13		002	011	046	133	291	500	709	867	954	989	998	999+	1.0				
14		001	006	029	090	212	395	605	788	910	971	994	999	999+	1.0			
15			004	018	059	151	304	500	696	849	941	982	996	999+	999+	1.0		
16			002	011	038	105	227	402	598	773	895	962	989	998	999+	999+	1.0	
17			001	006	025	072	166	315	500	685	834	928	975	994	999	999+	999+	1.0
18			001	004	015	048	119	240	407	593	760	881	952	985	996	999	999+	999+
19				002	010	032	084	180	324	500	676	820	916	968	990	998	999+	999+
20				001	006	021	058	132	252	412	588	748	868	942	979	994	999	999+

Note: Decimal points omitted, and values less than .0005 are omitted.

TABLE D (continued)

	k																	
N	0	1	2	3	4	5	6	7	8	9	10	11	12	13	14	15	16	17
21				001	004	013	039	095	192	332	500	668	808	905	961	987	996	999
22					002	008	026	067	143	262	416	584	738	857	933	974	992	998
23					001	005	017	047	105	202	339	500	661	798	895	953	983	995
24					001	003	011	032	076	154	271	419	581	729	846	924	968	989
25						002	007	022	054	115	212	345	500	655	788	885	946	978
26						001	005	014	038	084	163	279	423	577	721	837	916	962
27						001	003	010	026	061	124	221	351	500	649	779	876	939
28							002	006	018	044	092	172	286	425	575	714	828	908
29							001	004	012	031	068	132	229	356	500	644	771	868
30							001	003	008	021	049	100	181	292	428	572	708	819
31								002	005	015	035	075	141	237	360	500	640	763
32								001	004	010	025	055	108	189	298	430	570	702
33								001	002	007	018	040	081	148	243	364	500	636
34									001	005	012	029	061	115	196	304	432	568
35									001	003	008	020	045	088	155	250	368	500

Note: Decimal points omitted, and values less than .0005 are omitted.

TABLE E
The binomial distribution*

$$P[Y=k] = \binom{N}{k} p^k (1-p)^{N-k}$$

Decimal point has been omitted. All entries should be read as *.nnnn*.
For values of $p \leq .5$ use top row for p and left column for k.
For values of $p > .5$ use bottom row for p and right column for k.

		p												
N	k	.01	.05	.10	.15	.20	.25	.30	1/3	.40	.45	.50		
2	0	9801	9025	8100	7225	6400	5625	4900	4444	3600	3025	2500	2	2
	1	198	950	1800	2550	3200	3750	4200	4444	4800	4950	5000	1	
	2	1	25	100	225	400	625	900	1111	1600	2025	2500	0	
3	0	9703	8574	7290	6141	5120	4219	3430	2963	2160	1664	1250	3	3
	1	294	1354	2430	3251	3840	4219	4410	4444	4320	4084	3750	2	
	2	3	71	270	574	960	1406	1890	2222	2880	3341	3750	1	
	3	0	1	10	34	80	156	270	370	640	911	1250	0	
4	0	9606	8145	6561	5220	4096	3164	2401	1975	1296	915	625	4	4
	1	388	1715	2916	3685	4096	4219	4116	3951	3456	2995	2500	3	
	2	6	135	486	975	1536	2109	2646	2963	3456	3675	3750	2	
	3	0	5	36	115	256	469	756	988	1536	2005	2500	1	
	4	0	0	1	5	16	39	81	123	256	410	625	0	
5	0	9510	7738	5905	4437	3277	2373	1681	1317	778	503	312	5	5
	1	480	2036	3280	3915	4096	3955	3602	3292	2592	2059	1562	4	
	2	10	214	729	1382	2048	2637	3087	3292	3456	3369	3125	3	
	3	0	11	81	244	512	879	1323	1646	2304	2757	3125	2	
	4	0	0	4	22	64	146	283	412	768	1128	1562	1	
	5	0	0	0	1	3	10	24	41	102	185	312	0	
6	0	9415	7351	5314	3771	2621	1780	1176	878	467	277	156	6	6
	1	571	2321	3543	3993	3932	3560	3025	2634	1866	1359	938	5	
	2	14	305	984	1762	2458	2966	3241	3292	3110	2780	2344	4	
	3	0	21	146	415	819	1318	1852	2195	2765	3032	3125	3	
	4	0	1	12	55	154	330	595	823	1382	1861	2344	2	
	5	0	0	1	4	15	44	102	165	369	609	938	1	
	6	0	0	0	0	1	2	7	14	41	83	156	0	
7	0	9321	6983	4783	3206	2097	1335	824	585	280	152	78	7	7
	1	659	2573	3720	3960	3670	3115	2471	2048	1306	872	547	6	
	2	20	406	1240	2097	2753	3115	3177	3073	2613	2140	1641	5	
	3	0	36	230	617	1147	1730	2269	2561	2903	2918	2734	4	
	4	0	2	26	109	287	577	972	1280	1935	2388	2734	3	
	5	0	0	2	12	43	115	250	384	774	1172	1641	2	
	6	0	0	0	1	4	13	36	64	172	320	547	1	
	7	0	0	0	0	0	1	2	5	16	37	78	0	
		.99	.95	.90	.85	.80	.75	.70	2/3	.60	.55	.50	k	N
		p												

TABLE E (continued)

		p												
N	k	.01	.05	.10	.15	.20	.25	.30	1/3	.40	.45	.50		
8	0	9227	6634	4305	2725	1678	1001	576	390	168	84	39	8	8
	1	746	2793	3826	3847	3355	2670	1977	1561	896	548	312	7	
	2	26	515	1488	2376	2936	3115	2965	2731	2090	1569	1094	6	
	3	1	54	331	839	1468	2076	2541	2731	2787	2568	2188	5	
	4	0	4	46	185	459	865	1361	1707	2322	2627	2734	4	
	5	0	0	4	26	92	231	467	683	1239	1719	2188	3	
	6	0	0	0	2	11	38	100	171	413	703	1094	2	
	7	0	0	0	0	1	4	12	24	79	164	312	1	
	8	0	0	0	0	0	0	1	2	7	17	39	0	
9	0	9135	6302	3874	2316	1342	751	404	260	101	46	20	9	9
	1	830	2985	3874	3679	3020	2253	1556	1171	605	339	176	8	
	2	34	629	1722	2597	3020	3003	2668	2341	1612	1110	703	7	
	3	1	77	446	1069	1762	2336	2668	2731	2508	2119	1641	6	
	4	0	6	74	283	661	1168	1715	2048	2508	2600	2461	5	
	5	0	0	8	50	165	389	735	1024	1672	2128	2461	4	
	6	0	0	1	6	28	87	210	341	743	1160	1641	3	
	7	0	0	0	0	3	12	39	73	212	407	703	2	
	8	0	0	0	0	0	1	4	9	35	83	176	1	
	9	0	0	0	0	0	0	0	1	3	8	20	0	
10	0	9044	5987	3487	1969	1074	563	282	173	60	25	10	10	10
	1	914	3151	3874	3474	2684	1877	1211	867	403	207	98	9	
	2	42	746	1937	2759	3020	2816	2335	1951	1209	763	439	8	
	3	1	105	574	1298	2013	2503	2668	2601	2150	1665	1172	7	
	4	0	10	112	401	881	1460	2001	2276	2508	2384	2051	6	
	5	0	1	15	85	264	584	1029	1366	2007	2340	2461	5	
	6	0	0	1	12	55	162	368	569	1115	1596	2051	4	
	7	0	0	0	1	8	31	90	163	425	746	1172	3	
	8	0	0	0	0	1	4	14	30	106	229	439	2	
	9	0	0	0	0	0	0	1	3	16	42	98	1	
	10	0	0	0	0	0	0	0	0	1	3	10	0	
15	0	8601	4633	2059	874	352	134	47	23	5	1	0	15	15
	1	1303	3658	3432	2312	1319	668	305	171	47	16	5	14	
	2	92	1348	2669	2856	2309	1559	916	599	219	90	32	13	
	3	4	307	1285	2184	2501	2252	1700	1299	634	318	139	12	
	4	0	49	428	1156	1876	2252	2186	1948	1268	780	417	11	
	5	0	6	105	449	1032	1651	2061	2143	1859	1404	916	10	
	6	0	0	19	132	430	917	1472	1786	2066	1914	1527	9	
	7	0	0	3	30	138	393	811	1148	1771	2013	1964	8	
	8	0	0	0	5	35	131	348	574	1181	1647	1964	7	
	9	0	0	0	1	7	34	116	223	612	1048	1527	6	
	10	0	0	0	0	1	7	30	67	245	515	916	5	
	11	0	0	0	0	0	1	6	15	74	191	417	4	
	12	0	0	0	0	0	0	1	3	16	52	139	3	
	13	0	0	0	0	0	0	0	0	3	10	32	2	
	14	0	0	0	0	0	0	0	0	0	1	5	1	
	15	0	0	0	0	0	0	0	0	0	0	0	0	
		.99	.95	.90	.85	.80	.75	.70	2/3	.60	.55	.50	k	N
		p												

TABLE E (continued)

N	k	.01	.05	.10	.15	.20	.25	.30	1/3	.40	.45	.50		
20	0	8179	3585	1216	388	115	32	8	3	0	0	0	20	20
	1	1652	3774	2702	1368	576	211	68	30	5	1	0	19	
	2	159	1887	2852	2293	1369	669	278	143	31	8	2	18	
	3	10	596	1901	2428	2054	1339	716	429	123	40	11	17	
	4	0	133	898	1821	2182	1897	1304	911	350	139	46	16	
	5	0	22	319	1028	1746	2023	1789	1457	746	365	148	15	
	6	0	3	89	454	1091	1686	1916	1821	1244	746	370	14	
	7	0	0	20	160	545	1124	1643	1821	1659	1221	739	13	
	8	0	0	4	46	222	609	1144	1480	1797	1623	1201	12	
	9	0	0	1	11	74	271	654	987	1597	1771	1602	11	
	10	0	0	0	2	20	99	308	543	1171	1593	1762	10	
	11	0	0	0	0	5	30	120	247	710	1185	1602	9	
	12	0	0	0	0	1	8	39	92	355	727	1201	8	
	13	0	0	0	0	0	2	10	28	146	366	739	7	
	14	0	0	0	0	0	0	2	7	49	150	370	6	
	15	0	0	0	0	0	0	0	1	13	49	148	5	
	16	0	0	0	0	0	0	0	0	3	13	46	4	
	17	0	0	0	0	0	0	0	0	0	2	11	3	
	18	0	0	0	0	0	0	0	0	0	0	2	2	
	19	0	0	0	0	0	0	0	0	0	0	0	1	
	20	0	0	0	0	0	0	0	0	0	0	0	0	
25	0	7778	2774	718	172	38	8	1	0	0	0	0	25	25
	1	1964	3650	1994	759	236	63	14	5	0	0	0	24	
	2	238	2305	2659	1607	708	251	74	30	4	1	0	23	
	3	18	930	2265	2174	1358	641	243	114	19	4	1	22	
	4	1	269	1384	2110	1867	1175	572	313	71	18	4	21	
	5	0	60	646	1564	1960	1645	1030	658	199	63	16	20	
	6	0	10	239	920	1633	1828	1472	1096	442	172	53	19	
	7	0	1	72	441	1108	1654	1712	1487	800	381	143	18	
	8	0	0	18	175	623	1241	1651	1673	1200	701	322	17	
	9	0	0	4	58	294	781	1336	1580	1511	1084	609	16	
	10	0	0	1	16	118	417	916	1264	1612	1419	974	15	
	11	0	0	0	4	40	189	536	862	1465	1583	1328	14	
	12	0	0	0	1	12	74	268	503	1140	1511	1550	13	
	13	0	0	0	0	3	25	115	251	760	1236	1550	12	
	14	0	0	0	0	1	7	42	108	434	867	1328	11	
	15	0	0	0	0	0	2	13	40	212	520	974	10	
	16	0	0	0	0	0	0	4	12	88	266	609	9	
	17	0	0	0	0	0	0	1	3	31	115	322	8	
	18	0	0	0	0	0	0	0	1	9	42	143	7	
	19	0	0	0	0	0	0	0	0	2	13	53	6	
	20	0	0	0	0	0	0	0	0	0	3	16	5	
	21	0	0	0	0	0	0	0	0	0	1	4	4	
	22	0	0	0	0	0	0	0	0	0	0	1	3	
	23	0	0	0	0	0	0	0	0	0	0	0	2	
	24	0	0	0	0	0	0	0	0	0	0	0	1	
	25	0	0	0	0	0	0	0	0	0	0	0	0	
		.99	.95	.90	.85	.80	.75	.70	2/3	.60	.55	.50	k	N

Top column header: p (.01–.50); bottom column header: p (.99–.50).

TABLE E (continued)

N	k	.01	.05	.10	.15	.20	.25	.30	1/3	.40	.45	.50		
		p												
30	0	7397	2146	424	76	12	2	0	0	0	0	0	30	30
	1	2242	3389	1413	404	93	18	3	1	0	0	0	29	
	2	328	2586	2277	1034	337	86	18	6	0	0	0	28	
	3	31	1270	2361	1703	785	269	72	26	3	0	0	27	
	4	2	451	1771	2028	1325	604	208	89	12	2	0	26	
	5	0	124	1023	1861	1723	1047	464	232	41	8	1	25	
	6	0	27	474	1368	1795	1455	829	484	115	29	6	24	
	7	0	5	180	828	1538	1662	1219	829	263	81	19	23	
	8	0	1	58	420	1106	1593	1501	1192	505	191	55	22	
	9	0	0	16	181	676	1298	1573	1457	823	382	133	21	
	10	0	0	4	67	355	909	1416	1530	1152	656	280	20	
	11	0	0	1	22	161	551	1103	1391	1396	976	509	19	
	12	0	0	0	6	64	291	749	1101	1474	1265	805	18	
	13	0	0	0	1	22	134	444	762	1360	1433	1115	17	
	14	0	0	0	0	7	54	231	463	1101	1424	1354	16	
	15	0	0	0	0	2	19	106	247	783	1242	1445	15	
	16	0	0	0	0	0	6	42	116	489	953	1354	14	
	17	0	0	0	0	0	2	15	48	269	642	1115	13	
	18	0	0	0	0	0	0	5	17	129	379	805	12	
	19	0	0	0	0	0	0	1	5	54	196	509	11	
	20	0	0	0	0	0	0	0	1	20	88	280	10	
	21	0	0	0	0	0	0	0	0	6	34	133	9	
	22	0	0	0	0	0	0	0	0	1	12	55	8	
	23	0	0	0	0	0	0	0	0	0	3	19	7	
	24	0	0	0	0	0	0	0	0	0	1	6	6	
	25	0	0	0	0	0	0	0	0	0	0	1	5	
	26	0	0	0	0	0	0	0	0	0	0	0	4	
	27	0	0	0	0	0	0	0	0	0	0	0	3	
	28	0	0	0	0	0	0	0	0	0	0	0	2	
	29	0	0	0	0	0	0	0	0	0	0	0	1	
	30	0	0	0	0	0	0	0	0	0	0	0	0	
		.99	.95	.90	.85	.80	.75	.70	2/3	.60	.55	.50	k	N
		p												

* Reprinted from Hammond, K. R., Householder, J. E., and Castellan, N. J., Jr. (1970). *Introduction to the statistical method* (second edition). New York: A. A. Knopf, with the permission of the authors and publisher.

TABLE F

Critical values of D in the Kolmogorov-Smirnov one-sample test*

Sample size (N)	Level of significance for D = maximum $\lvert F_0(X) - S_N(X)\rvert$				
	.20	.15	.10	.05	.01
1	.900	.925	.950	.975	.995
2	.684	.726	.776	.842	.929
3	.565	.597	.642	.708	.828
4	.494	.525	.564	.624	.733
5	.446	.474	.510	.565	.669
6	.410	.436	.470	.521	.618
7	.381	.405	.438	.486	.577
8	.358	.381	.411	.457	.543
9	.339	.360	.388	.432	.514
10	.322	.342	.368	.410	.490
11	.307	.326	.352	.391	.468
12	.295	.313	.338	.375	.450
13	.284	.302	.325	.361	.433
14	.274	.292	.314	.349	.418
15	.266	.283	.304	.338	.404
16	.258	.274	.295	.328	.392
17	.250	.266	.286	.318	.381
18	.244	.259	.278	.309	.371
19	.237	.252	.272	.301	.363
20	.231	.246	.264	.294	.356
25	.21	.22	.24	.27	.32
30	.19	.20	.22	.24	.29
35	.18	.19	.21	.23	.27
Over 35	$\frac{1.07}{\sqrt{N}}$	$\frac{1.14}{\sqrt{N}}$	$\frac{1.22}{\sqrt{N}}$	$\frac{1.36}{\sqrt{N}}$	$\frac{1.63}{\sqrt{N}}$

* Adapted from Massey, F. J., Jr. (1951). The Kolmogorov-Smirnov test for goodness of fit. *Journal of the American Statistical Association*, **46**, 70, with the kind permission of the author and publisher.

TABLE G
Critical values of r in the runs test*

Given in the tables are various critical values of r for values of m and n less than or equal to 20. For the one-sample runs test, any observed value of r which is less than or equal to the smaller value, or is greater than or equal to the larger value in a pair is significant at the $\alpha = .05$ level.

m \ n	2	3	4	5	6	7	8	9	10	11	12	13	14	15	16	17	18	19	20
2											2 –	2 –	2 –	2 –	2 –	2 –	2 –	2 –	2 –
3					2 –	2 –	2 –	2 –	2 –	2 –	2 –	2 –	2 –	3 –	3 –	3 –	3 –	3 –	3 –
4				2 9	2 9	2 –	3 –	3 –	3 –	3 –	3 –	3 –	3 –	3 –	4 –	4 –	4 –	4 –	4 –
5			2 9	2 10	3 10	3 11	3 11	3 –	3 –	4 –	4 –	4 –	4 –	4 –	4 –	4 –	5 –	5 –	5 –
6		2 –	2 9	3 10	3 11	3 12	3 12	4 13	4 13	4 13	4 13	5 –	5 –	5 –	5 –	5 –	5 –	6 –	6 –
7		2 –	2 –	3 11	3 12	3 13	4 13	4 14	5 14	5 14	5 14	5 15	5 15	6 15	6 –	6 –	6 –	6 –	6 –
8		2 –	3 –	3 11	3 12	4 13	4 14	5 14	5 15	5 15	6 16	6 16	6 16	6 16	6 17	7 17	7 17	7 17	7 17
9		2 –	3 –	3 –	4 13	4 14	5 14	5 15	5 16	6 16	6 16	6 17	7 17	7 18	7 18	7 18	8 18	8 18	8 18
10		2 –	3 –	3 –	4 13	5 14	5 15	5 16	6 16	6 17	7 17	7 18	7 18	7 18	8 19	8 19	8 19	8 20	9 20
11		2 –	3 –	4 –	4 13	5 14	5 15	6 16	6 17	7 17	7 18	7 19	8 19	8 19	8 20	9 20	9 20	9 21	9 21
12	2 –	2 –	3 –	4 –	4 13	5 14	6 16	6 16	7 17	7 18	7 19	8 19	8 20	8 20	9 21	9 21	9 21	10 22	10 22
13	2 –	2 –	3 –	4 –	5 –	5 15	6 16	6 17	7 18	7 19	8 19	8 20	9 20	9 21	9 21	10 22	10 22	10 23	10 23
14	2 –	2 –	3 –	4 –	5 –	5 15	6 16	7 17	7 18	8 19	8 20	9 20	9 21	9 22	10 22	10 23	10 23	11 23	11 24
15	2 –	3 –	3 –	4 –	5 –	6 15	6 16	7 18	7 18	8 19	8 20	9 21	9 22	10 22	10 23	11 23	11 24	11 24	12 25
16	2 –	3 –	4 –	4 –	5 –	6 –	6 17	7 18	8 19	8 20	9 21	9 21	10 22	10 23	11 23	11 24	11 25	12 25	12 25
17	2 –	3 –	4 –	4 –	5 –	6 –	7 17	7 18	8 19	9 20	9 21	10 22	10 23	11 23	11 24	11 25	12 25	12 26	13 26
18	2 –	3 –	4 –	5 –	5 –	6 –	7 17	8 18	8 19	9 20	9 21	10 22	10 23	11 24	11 25	12 25	12 26	13 26	13 27
19	2 –	3 –	4 –	5 –	6 –	6 –	7 17	8 18	8 20	9 21	10 22	10 23	11 23	11 24	12 25	12 26	13 26	13 27	13 27
20	2 –	3 –	4 –	5 –	6 –	6 –	7 17	8 18	9 20	9 21	10 22	10 23	11 24	12 25	12 25	13 26	13 27	13 27	14 28

* Adapted from Swed, and Eisenhart, C. (1943). Tables for testing randomness of grouping in a sequence of alternatives. *Annals of Mathematical Statistics*, **14**, 83–86, with the kind permission of the authors and publisher.

TABLE H
Critical values of T^+ for the Wilcoxon signed ranks test*

Table entries for a given N is $P[T^+ \geq c]$, the probability that T^+ is greater than or equal to the sum c.

	N						
c	3	4	5	6	7	8	9
3	.6250						
4	.3750						
5	.2500	.5625					
6	.1250	.4375					
7		.3125					
8		.1875	.5000				
9		.1250	.4063				
10		.0625	.3125				
11			.2188	.5000			
12			.1563	.4219			
13			.0938	.3438			
14			.0625	.2813	.5313		
15			.0313	.2188	.4688		
16				.1563	.4063		
17				.1094	.3438		
18				.0781	.2891	.5273	
19				.0469	.2344	.4727	
20				.0313	.1875	.4219	
21				.0156	.1484	.3711	
22					.1094	.3203	
23					.0781	.2734	.5000
24					.0547	.2305	.4551
25					.0391	.1914	.4102
26					.0234	.1563	.3672
27					.0156	.1250	.3262
28					.0078	.0977	.2852
29						.0742	.2480
30						.0547	.2129
31						.0391	.1797
32						.0273	.1504
33						.0195	.1250
34						.0117	.1016
35						.0078	.0820
36						.0039	.0645
37							.0488
38							.0371
39							.0273
40							.0195
41							.0137
42							.0098
43							.0059
44							.0039
45							.0020

TABLE H (continued)

	N					
c	10	11	12	13	14	15
28	.5000					
29	.4609					
30	.4229					
31	.3848					
32	.3477					
33	.3125	.5171				
34	.2783	.4829				
35	.2461	.4492				
36	.2158	.4155				
37	.1875	.3823				
38	.1611	.3501				
39	.1377	.3188	.5151			
40	.1162	.2886	.4849			
41	.0967	.2598	.4548			
42	.0801	.2324	.4250			
43	.0654	.2065	.3955			
44	.0527	.1826	.3667			
45	.0420	.1602	.3386			
46	.0322	.1392	.3110	.5000		
47	.0244	.1201	.2847	.4730		
48	.0186	.1030	.2593	.4463		
49	.0137	.0874	.2349	.4197		
50	.0098	.0737	.2119	.3934		
51	.0068	.0615	.1902	.3677		
52	.0049	.0508	.1697	.3424		
53	.0029	.0415	.1506	.3177	.5000	
54	.0020	.0337	.1331	.2939	.4758	
55	.0010	.0269	.1167	.2709	.4516	
56		.0210	.1018	.2487	.4276	
57		.0161	.0881	.2274	.4039	
58		.0122	.0757	.2072	.3804	
59		.0093	.0647	.1879	.3574	
60		.0068	.0549	.1698	.3349	.5110
61		.0049	.0461	.1527	.3129	.4890
62		.0034	.0386	.1367	.2915	.4670
63		.0024	.0320	.1219	.2708	.4452
64		.0015	.0261	.1082	.2508	.4235
65		.0010	.0212	.0955	.2316	.4020
66		.0005	.0171	.0839	.2131	.3808
67			.0134	.0732	.1955	.3599
68			.0105	.0636	.1788	.3394
69			.0081	.0549	.1629	.3193
70			.0061	.0471	.1479	.2997
71			.0046	.0402	.1338	.2807
72			.0034	.0341	.1206	.2622
73			.0024	.0287	.1083	.2444
74			.0017	.0239	.0969	.2271
75			.0012	.0199	.0863	.2106
76			.0007	.0164	.0765	.1947
77			.0005	.0133	.0676	.1796
78			.0002	.0107	.0594	.1651

TABLE H (continued)

	N		
c	13	14	15
79	.0085	.0520	.1514
80	.0067	.0453	.1384
81	.0052	.0392	.1262
82	.0040	.0338	.1147
83	.0031	.0290	.1039
84	.0023	.0247	.0938
85	.0017	.0209	.0844
86	.0012	.0176	.0757
87	.0009	.0148	.0677
88	.0006	.0123	.0603
89	.0004	.0101	.0535
90	.0002	.0083	.0473
91	.0001	.0067	.0416
92		.0054	.0365
93		.0043	.0319
94		.0034	.0277
95		.0026	.0240
96		.0020	.0206
97		.0015	.0177
98		.0012	.0151
99		.0009	.0128
100		.0006	.0108
101		.0004	.0090
102		.0003	.0075
103		.0002	.0062
104		.0001	.0051
105		.0001	.0042
106			.0034
107			.0027
108			.0021
109			.0017
110			.0013
111			.0010
112			.0008
113			.0006
114			.0004
115			.0003
116			.0002
117			.0002
118			.0001
119			.0001
120			.0000+

TABLE I
Probabilities for Fourfold tables, Fisher exact test, $N \leq 15$*

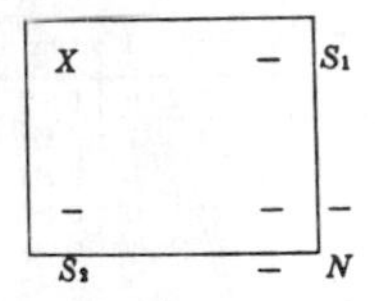

N is the total sample size, S_1 is the smallest marginal total, S_2 is the next smallest, and X is the frequency in the cell corresponding to the two smallest totals. For a given set of N, S_1 and S_2 possible values of X are $0, 1, 2, \ldots, S_1$. Underlined for each set is a value of X so that for this or smaller values $X/S_1 \leq (S_2 - X)/(N - S_1)$, while for larger values $X/S_1 > (S_2 - X)/(N - S_1)$. These cut points define the *same* and *opposite* directions from equality of the proportions in the two samples. The cumulative probability of a deviation as large or larger in the *same* direction from equality of proportions is in the column labeled "Obs," while the probability of a deviation as large or larger in the opposite direction from equality of proportions is in the column labeled "Other." The size of deviation here is measured by the absolute value of $X_1/S_1 - (S_2 - X)/(N - S_1)$.

These tables are extracted from more extensive tables prepared by Donald Goyette and M. Ray Mickey, Health Science Computing Facility, UCLA.

N	S_1	S_2	X	PROBABILITY Obs.	Other	Totals
2	1	1	0	0.500	0.500	1.000
			1	0.500	0.500	1.000
3	1	1	0	0.667	0.333	1.000
			1	0.333	0.000	0.333
4	1	1	0	0.750	0.250	1.000
			1	0.250	0.000	0.250
4	1	2	0	0.500	0.500	1.000
			1	0.500	0.500	1.000
4	2	2	0	0.167	0.167	0.333
			1	0.833	0.833	1.000
			2	0.167	0.167	0.333
5	1	1	0	0.800	0.200	1.000
			1	0.200	0.000	0.200
5	1	2	0	0.600	0.400	1.000
			1	0.400	0.000	0.400
5	2	2	0	0.300	0.100	0.400
			1	0.700	0.300	1.000
			2	0.100	0.000	0.100
6	1	1	0	0.833	0.167	1.000
			1	0.167	0.000	0.167
6	1	2	0	0.667	0.333	1.000
			1	0.333	0.000	0.333
6	1	3	0	0.500	0.500	1.000
			1	0.500	0.500	1.000
6	2	2	0	0.400	0.067	0.467
			1	0.600	0.400	1.000
			2	0.067	0.000	0.067
6	2	3	0	0.200	0.200	0.400
			1	0.800	0.800	1.000
			2	0.200	0.200	0.400
6	3	3	0	0.050	0.050	0.100
			1	0.500	0.500	1.000
			2	0.500	0.500	1.000
			3	0.050	0.050	0.100
7	1	1	0	0.857	0.143	1.000
			1	0.143	0.000	0.143
7	1	2	0	0.714	0.286	1.000
			1	0.286	0.000	0.286
7	1	3	0	0.571	0.429	1.000
			1	0.429	0.000	0.429

N	S_1	S_2	X	PROBABILITY Obs.	Other	Totals
7	2	2	0	0.476	0.048	0.524
			1	0.524	0.476	1.000
			2	0.048	0.000	0.048
7	2	3	0	0.286	0.143	0.429
			1	0.714	0.286	1.000
			2	0.143	0.000	0.143
7	3	3	0	0.114	0.029	0.143
			1	0.629	0.371	1.000
			2	0.371	0.114	0.486
			3	0.029	0.000	0.029
8	1	1	0	0.875	0.125	1.000
			1	0.125	0.000	0.125
8	1	2	0	0.750	0.250	1.000
			1	0.250	0.000	0.250
8	1	3	0	0.625	0.375	1.000
			1	0.375	0.000	0.375
8	1	4	0	0.500	0.500	1.000
			1	0.500	0.500	1.000
8	2	2	0	0.536	0.464	1.000
			1	0.464	0.536	1.000
			2	0.036	0.000	0.036
8	2	3	0	0.357	0.107	0.464
			1	0.643	0.357	1.000
			2	0.107	0.000	0.107
8	2	4	0	0.214	0.214	0.429
			1	0.786	0.786	1.000
			2	0.214	0.214	0.429
8	3	3	0	0.179	0.018	0.196
			1	0.714	0.286	1.000
			2	0.286	0.179	0.464
			3	0.018	0.000	0.018
8	3	4	0	0.071	0.071	0.143
			1	0.500	0.500	1.000
			2	0.500	0.500	1.000
			3	0.071	0.071	0.143
8	4	4	0	0.014	0.014	0.029
			1	0.243	0.243	0.486
			2	0.757	0.757	1.000
			3	0.243	0.243	0.486
			4	0.014	0.014	0.029

N	S_1	S_2	X	PROBABILITY Obs.	Other	Totals
9	1	1	0	0.889	0.111	1.000
			1	0.111	0.000	0.111
9	1	2	0	0.778	0.222	1.000
			1	0.222	0.000	0.222
9	1	3	0	0.667	0.333	1.000
			1	0.333	0.000	0.333
9	1	4	0	0.556	0.444	1.000
			1	0.444	0.000	0.444
9	2	2	0	0.583	0.417	1.000
			1	0.417	0.000	0.417
			2	0.028	0.000	0.028
9	2	3	0	0.417	0.083	0.500
			1	0.583	0.417	1.000
			2	0.083	0.000	0.083
9	2	4	0	0.278	0.167	0.444
			1	0.722	0.278	1.000
			2	0.167	0.000	0.167
9	3	3	0	0.238	0.226	0.464
			1	0.774	0.774	1.000
			2	0.226	0.238	0.464
			3	0.012	0.000	0.012
9	3	4	0	0.119	0.048	0.167
			1	0.595	0.450	1.000
			2	0.405	0.119	0.524
			3	0.048	0.000	0.048
9	4	4	0	0.040	0.008	0.048
			1	0.357	0.167	0.524
			2	0.643	0.357	1.000
			3	0.167	0.040	0.206
			4	0.008	0.000	0.008
10	1	1	0	0.900	0.100	1.000
			1	0.100	0.000	0.100
10	1	2	0	0.800	0.200	1.000
			1	0.200	0.000	0.200
10	1	3	0	0.700	0.300	1.000
			1	0.300	0.000	0.300
10	1	4	0	0.600	0.400	1.000
			1	0.400	0.000	0.400
10	1	5	0	0.500	0.500	1.000
			1	0.500	0.500	1.000

* Reproduced from table A-9e in Dixon, W. J., and Massey, F. J., Jr. (1983). *Introduction to a statistical analysis* (fourth edition). New York: McGraw-Hill, with the permission of the publisher. We are also grateful to Dr. M. R. Mickey and UCLA for permission to reproduce these tables.

TABLE I (continued)

N	S_1	S_2	X	PROBABILITY *Obs.*	*Other*	*Totals*
10	2	2	0	0.622	0.378	1.000
			1	0.378	0.000	0.378
			2	0.022	0.000	0.022
10	2	3	0	0.467	0.067	0.533
			1	0.533	0.467	1.000
			2	0.067	0.000	0.067
10	2	4	0	0.333	0.133	0.467
			1	0.667	0.333	1.000
			2	0.133	0.000	0.133
10	2	5	0	0.222	0.222	0.444
			1	0.778	0.778	1.000
			2	0.222	0.222	0.444
10	3	3	0	0.292	0.183	0.475
			1	0.708	0.292	1.000
			2	0.183	0.000	0.183
			3	0.008	0.000	0.008
10	3	4	0	0.167	0.033	0.200
			1	0.667	0.333	1.000
			2	0.333	0.167	0.500
			3	0.033	0.000	0.033
10	3	5	0	0.083	0.083	0.167
			1	0.500	0.500	1.000
			2	0.500	0.500	1.000
			3	0.083	0.083	0.167
10	4	4	0	0.071	0.005	0.076
			1	0.452	0.119	0.571
			2	0.548	0.452	1.000
			3	0.119	0.071	0.190
			4	0.005	0.000	0.005
10	4	5	0	0.024	0.024	0.048
			1	0.262	0.262	0.524
			2	0.738	0.738	1.000
			3	0.262	0.262	0.524
			4	0.024	0.024	0.048
10	5	5	0	0.004	0.004	0.008
			1	0.103	0.103	0.206
			2	0.500	0.500	1.000
			3	0.500	0.500	1.000
			4	0.103	0.103	0.206
			5	0.004	0.004	0.008
11	1	1	0	0.909	0.091	1.000
			1	0.091	0.000	0.091
11	1	2	0	0.818	0.182	1.000
			1	0.182	0.000	0.182
11	1	3	0	0.727	0.273	1.000
			1	0.273	0.000	0.273
11	1	4	0	0.636	0.364	1.000
			1	0.364	0.000	0.364
11	1	5	0	0.545	0.455	1.000
			1	0.455	0.000	0.455
11	2	2	0	0.655	0.345	1.000
			1	0.345	0.000	0.345
			2	0.018	0.000	0.018
11	2	3	0	0.509	0.055	0.564
			1	0.491	0.509	1.000
			2	0.055	0.000	0.055
11	2	4	0	0.382	0.109	0.491
			1	0.618	0.382	1.000
			2	0.109	0.000	0.109
11	2	5	0	0.273	0.182	0.455
			1	0.727	0.273	1.000
			2	0.182	0.000	0.182
11	3	3	0	0.339	0.152	0.491
			1	0.661	0.339	1.000
			2	0.152	0.000	0.152
			3	0.006	0.000	0.006

N	S_1	S_2	X	PROBABILITY *Obs.*	*Other*	*Totals*
11	3	4	0	0.212	0.024	0.236
			1	0.721	0.279	1.000
			2	0.279	0.212	0.491
			3	0.024	0.000	0.024
11	3	5	0	0.121	0.061	0.182
			1	0.576	0.424	1.000
			2	0.424	0.121	0.545
			3	0.061	0.000	0.061
11	4	4	0	0.106	0.088	0.194
			1	0.530	0.470	1.000
			2	0.470	0.106	0.576
			3	0.088	0.000	0.088
			4	0.003	0.000	0.003
11	4	5	0	0.045	0.015	0.061
			1	0.348	0.197	0.545
			2	0.652	0.348	1.000
			3	0.197	0.045	0.242
			4	0.015	0.000	0.015
11	5	5	0	0.013	0.002	0.015
			1	0.175	0.067	0.242
			2	0.608	0.392	1.000
			3	0.392	0.175	0.567
			4	0.067	0.013	0.080
			5	0.002	0.000	0.002
12	1	1	0	0.917	0.083	1.000
			1	0.083	0.000	0.083
12	1	2	0	0.833	0.167	1.000
			1	0.167	0.000	0.167
12	1	3	0	0.750	0.250	1.000
			1	0.250	0.000	0.250
12	1	4	0	0.667	0.333	1.000
			1	0.333	0.000	0.333
12	1	5	0	0.583	0.417	1.000
			1	0.417	0.000	0.471
12	1	6	0	0.500	0.500	1.000
			1	0.500	0.500	1.000
12	2	2	0	0.682	0.318	1.000
			1	0.318	0.000	0.318
			2	0.015	0.000	0.015
12	2	3	0	0.545	0.455	1.000
			1	0.455	0.545	1.000
			2	0.045	0.000	0.045
12	2	4	0	0.424	0.091	0.515
			1	0.576	0.424	1.000
			2	0.091	0.000	0.091
12	2	5	0	0.318	0.152	0.470
			1	0.682	0.318	1.000
			2	0.152	0.000	0.152
12	2	6	0	0.227	0.227	0.455
			1	0.773	0.773	1.000
			2	0.227	0.227	0.455
12	3	3	0	0.382	0.127	0.509
			1	0.618	0.382	1.000
			2	0.127	0.000	0.127
			3	0.005	0.000	0.005
12	3	4	0	0.255	0.236	0.491
			1	0.764	0.764	1.000
			2	0.236	0.255	0.491
			3	0.018	0.000	0.018
12	3	5	0	0.159	0.045	0.205
			1	0.636	0.364	1.000
			2	0.364	0.159	0.523
			3	0.045	0.000	0.045
12	3	6	0	0.091	0.091	0.182
			1	0.500	0.500	1.000
			2	0.500	0.500	1.000

N	S_1	S_2	X	PROBABILITY *Obs.*	*Other*	*Totals*
			3	0.091	0.091	0.182
12	4	4	0	0.141	0.067	0.208
			1	0.594	0.406	1.000
			2	0.406	0.141	0.547
			3	0.067	0.000	0.067
			4	0.002	0.000	0.002
12	4	5	0	0.071	0.010	0.081
			1	0.424	0.152	0.576
			2	0.576	0.424	1.000
			3	0.152	0.071	0.222
			4	0.010	0.000	0.010
12	4	6	0	0.030	0.030	0.061
			1	0.273	0.273	0.545
			2	0.727	0.727	1.000
			3	0.273	0.273	0.545
			4	0.030	0.030	0.061
12	5	5	0	0.027	0.001	0.028
			12	0.247	0.045	0.293
			2	0.689	0.311	1.000
			3	0.311	0.247	0.558
			4	0.045	0.027	0.072
			5	0.001	0.000	0.001
12	5	6	0	0.008	0.008	0.015
			1	0.121	0.121	0.242
			2	0.500	0.500	1.000
			3	0.500	0.500	1.000
			4	0.121	0.121	0.242
			5	0.008	0.008	0.015
12	6	6	0	0.001	0.001	0.002
			1	0.040	0.040	0.080
			2	0.284	0.284	0.567
			3	0.716	0.716	1.000
			4	0.284	0.284	0.567
			5	0.040	0.040	0.080
			6	0.001	0.001	0.002
13	1	1	0	0.923	0.077	1.000
			1	0.077	0.000	0.077
13	1	2	0	0.846	0.154	1.000
			1	0.154	0.000	0.154
13	1	3	0	0.769	0.231	1.000
			1	0.231	0.000	0.231
13	1	4	0	0.692	0.308	1.000
			1	0.308	0.000	0.308
13	1	5	0	0.615	0.385	1.000
			1	0.385	0.000	0.385
13	1	6	0	0.538	0.462	1.000
			1	0.462	0.000	0.462
13	2	2	0	0.705	0.295	1.000
			1	0.295	0.000	0.295
			2	0.013	0.000	0.013
13	2	3	0	0.577	0.423	1.000
			1	0.423	0.000	0.423
			2	0.038	0.000	0.038
13	2	4	0	0.462	0.077	0.538
			1	0.538	0.462	1.000
			2	0.077	0.000	0.077
13	2	5	0	0.359	0.128	0.487
			1	0.641	0.359	1.000
			2	0.128	0.000	0.128
13	2	6	0	0.269	0.192	0.462
			1	0.731	0.269	1.000
			2	0.192	0.000	0.192
13	3	3	0	0.420	0.108	0.528
			1	0.580	0.420	1.000
			2	0.108	0.000	0.108
			3	0.003	0.000	0.003

TABLE I (continued)

N	S_1	S_2	X	PROBABILITY Obs.	Other	Totals
13	3	4	0	0.294	0.203	0.497
			1	0.706	0.294	1.000
			2	0.203	0.000	0.203
			3	0.014	0.000	0.014
13	3	5	0	0.196	0.035	0.231
			1	0.685	0.315	1.000
			2	0.315	0.196	0.510
			3	0.035	0.000	0.035
13	3	6	0	0.122	0.070	0.192
			1	0.563	0.437	1.000
			2	0.437	0.122	0.559
			3	0.070	0.000	0.070
13	4	4	0	0.176	0.052	0.228
			1	0.646	0.354	1.000
			2	0.354	0.176	0.530
			3	0.052	0.000	0.052
			4	0.001	0.000	0.001
13	4	5	0	0.098	0.007	0.105
			1	0.490	0.119	0.608
			2	0.510	0.490	1.000
			3	0.119	0.098	0.217
			4	0.007	0.000	0.007
13	4	6	0	0.049	0.021	0.070
			1	0.343	0.217	0.559
			2	0.657	0.343	1.000
			3	0.217	0.049	0.266
			4	0.021	0.000	0.021
13	5	5	0	0.044	0.032	0.075
			1	0.315	0.249	0.565
			2	0.685	0.315	1.000
			3	0.249	0.044	0.293
			4	0.032	0.000	0.032
			5	0.001	0.000	0.001
13	5	6	0	0.016	0.005	0.021
			1	0.179	0.086	0.266
			2	0.587	0.413	1.000
			3	0.413	0.179	0.592
			4	0.086	0.016	0.103
			5	0.005	0.000	0.005
13	6	6	0	0.004	0.001	0.005
			1	0.078	0.025	0.103
			2	0.383	0.209	0.592
			3	0.617	0.383	1.000
			4	0.209	0.078	0.286
			5	0.025	0.004	0.029
			6	0.001	0.000	0.001
14	1	1	0	0.929	0.071	1.000
			1	0.071	0.000	0.071
14	1	2	0	0.857	0.143	1.000
			1	0.143	0.000	0.143
14	1	3	0	0.786	0.214	1.000
			1	0.214	0.000	0.214
14	1	4	0	0.714	0.286	1.000
			1	0.286	0.000	0.286
14	1	5	0	0.643	0.357	1.000
			1	0.357	0.000	0.357
14	1	6	0	0.571	0.429	1.000
			1	0.429	0.000	0.429
14	1	7	0	0.500	0.500	1.000
			1	0.500	0.500	1.000
14	2	2	0	0.725	0.275	1.000
			1	0.275	0.000	0.275
			2	0.011	0.000	0.011
14	2	3	0	0.604	0.396	1.000
			1	0.396	0.000	0.396
			2	0.033	0.000	0.033
14	2	4	0	0.495	0.066	0.560
			1	0.505	0.495	1.000
			2	0.066	0.000	0.066
14	2	5	0	0.396	0.110	0.505
			1	0.604	0.396	1.000
			2	0.110	0.000	0.110
14	2	6	0	0.308	0.165	0.473
			1	0.692	0.308	1.000
			2	0.165	0.000	0.165
14	2	7	0	0.231	0.231	0.462
			1	0.769	0.769	1.000
			1	0.231	0.231	0.462
14	3	3	0	0.453	0.093	0.547
			1	0.547	0.453	1.000
			2	0.093	0.000	0.093
			3	0.003	0.000	0.003
14	3	4	0	0.330	0.176	0.505
			1	0.670	0.330	1.000
			2	0.176	0.000	0.176
			3	0.011	0.000	0.011
14	3	5	0	0.231	0.027	0.258
			1	0.725	0.275	1.000
			2	0.275	0.231	0.505
			3	0.027	0.000	0.027
14	3	6	0	0.154	0.055	0.209
			1	0.615	0.385	1.000
			2	0.385	0.154	0.538
			3	0.055	0.000	0.055
14	3	7	0	0.096	0.096	0.192
			1	0.500	0.500	1.000
			2	0.500	0.500	1.000
			3	0.096	0.096	0.192
14	4	4	0	0.210	0.041	0.251
			1	0.689	0.311	1.000
			2	0.311	0.210	0.520
			3	0.041	0.000	0.041
			4	0.001	0.000	0.001
14	4	5	0	0.126	0.095	0.221
			1	0.545	0.455	1.000
			2	0.455	0.126	0.580
			3	0.095	0.000	0.095
			4	0.005	0.000	0.005
14	4	6	0	0.070	0.015	0.085
			1	0.406	0.175	0.580
			2	0.594	0.406	1.000
			3	0.175	0.070	0.245
			4	0.015	0.000	0.015
14	4	7	0	0.035	0.035	0.070
			1	0.280	0.280	0.559
			2	0.720	0.720	1.000
			3	0.280	0.280	0.559
			4	0.035	0.035	0.070
14	5	5	0	0.063	0.023	0.086
			1	0.378	0.203	0.580
			2	0.622	0.378	1.000
			3	0.203	0.063	0.266
			4	0.023	0.000	0.023
			5	0.000	0.000	0.000
14	5	6	0	0.028	0.003	0.031
			1	0.238	0.063	0.301
			2	0.657	0.343	1.000
			3	0.343	0.238	0.580
			4	0.063	0.028	0.091
			5	0.003	0.000	0.003
14	5	7	0	0.010	0.010	0.021
			1	0.133	0.133	0.266
			2	0.500	0.500	1.000
			3	0.500	0.500	1.000
			4	0.133	0.133	0.266
			5	0.010	0.010	0.021
14	6	6	0	0.009	0.000	0.010
			1	0.121	0.016	0.138
			2	0.471	0.156	0.627
			3	0.529	0.471	1.000
			4	0.156	0.121	0.277
			5	0.016	0.009	0.026
			6	0.000	0.000	0.000
14	6	7	0	0.002	0.002	0.005
			1	0.051	0.051	0.103
			2	0.296	0.296	0.592
			3	0.704	0.704	1.000
			4	0.296	0.296	0.592
			5	0.051	0.051	0.103
			6	0.002	0.002	0.005
14	7	7	0	0.000	0.000	0.001
			1	0.015	0.015	0.029
			2	0.143	0.143	0.286
			3	0.500	0.500	1.000
			4	0.500	0.500	1.000
			5	0.143	0.143	0.286
			6	0.015	0.015	0.029
			7	0.000	0.000	0.001
15	1	1	0	0.933	0.067	1.000
			1	0.067	0.000	0.067
15	1	2	0	0.867	0.133	1.000
			1	0.133	0.000	0.133
15	1	3	0	0.800	0.200	1.000
			1	0.200	0.000	0.200
15	1	4	0	0.733	0.267	1.000
			1	0.267	0.000	0.267
15	1	5	0	0.667	0.333	1.000
			1	0.333	0.000	0.333
15	1	6	0	0.600	0.400	1.000
			1	0.400	0.000	0.400
15	1	7	0	0.533	0.467	1.000
			1	0.467	0.000	0.467
15	2	2	0	0.743	0.257	1.000
			1	0.257	0.000	0.257
			2	0.010	0.000	0.010
15	2	3	0	0.629	0.371	1.000
			1	0.371	0.000	0.371
			2	0.029	0.000	0.029
15	2	4	0	0.524	0.057	0.581
			1	0.476	0.524	1.000
			2	0.057	0.000	0.057
15	2	5	0	0.429	0.095	0.524
			1	0.571	0.429	1.000
			2	0.095	0.000	0.095
15	2	6	0	0.343	0.143	0.486
			1	0.657	0.343	1.000
			2	0.143	0.000	0.143
15	2	7	0	0.267	0.200	0.467
			1	0.733	0.267	1.000
			2	0.200	0.000	0.200
15	3	3	0	0.484	0.081	0.565
			1	0.516	0.484	1.000
			2	0.081	0.000	0.081
			3	0.002	0.000	0.002
15	3	4	0	0.363	0.154	0.516
			1	0.637	0.363	1.000
			2	0.154	0.000	0.154
			3	0.009	0.000	0.009

TABLE I (continued)

N	S_1	S_2	X	PROBABILITY Obs.	Other	Totals
15	3	5	0	0.264	0.242	0.505
			1	0.758	0.758	1.000
			2	0.242	0.264	0.505
			3	0.022	0.000	0.022
15	3	6	0	0.185	0.044	0.229
			1	0.659	0.341	1.000
			2	0.341	0.185	0.525
			3	0.044	0.000	0.044
15	3	7	0	0.123	0.077	0.200
			1	0.554	0.446	1.000
			2	0.446	0.123	0.569
			3	0.077	0.000	0.077
15	4	4	0	0.242	0.033	0.275
			1	0.725	0.275	1.000
			2	0.275	0.242	0.516
			3	0.033	0.000	0.033
			4	0.001	0.000	0.001
15	4	5	0	0.154	0.077	0.231
			1	0.593	0.407	1.000
			2	0.407	0.154	0.560
			3	0.077	0.000	0.077
			4	0.004	0.000	0.004
15	4	6	0	0.092	0.011	0.103
			1	0.462	0.143	0.604

N	S_1	S_2	X	PROBABILITY Obs.	Other	Totals
			2	0.538	0.462	1.000
			3	0.143	0.092	0.235
			4	0.011	0.000	0.011
15	4	7	0	0.051	0.026	0.077
			1	0.338	0.231	0.569
			2	0.662	0.338	1.000
			3	0.231	0.051	0.282
			4	0.026	0.000	0.026
15	5	5	0	0.084	0.017	0.101
			1	0.434	0.167	0.600
			2	0.566	0.434	1.000
			3	0.167	0.084	0.251
			4	0.017	0.000	0.017
			5	0.000	0.000	0.000
15	5	6	0	0.042	0.047	0.089
			1	0.294	0.287	0.580
			2	0.713	0.713	1.000
			3	0.287	0.294	0.580
			4	0.047	0.042	0.089
			5	0.002	0.000	0.002
15	5	7	0	0.019	0.007	0.026
			1	0.182	0.100	0.282
			2	0.573	0.427	1.000
			3	0.427	0.182	0.608

N	S_1	S_2	X	PROBABILITY Obs.	Other	Totals
			4	0.100	0.019	0.119
			5	0.007	0.000	0.007
15	6	6	0	0.017	0.011	0.028
			1	0.168	0.119	0.287
			2	0.545	0.455	1.000
			3	0.455	0.168	0.622
			4	0.119	0.017	0.136
			5	0.011	0.000	0.011
			6	0.000	0.000	0.000
15	6	7	0	0.006	0.001	0.007
			1	0.084	0.035	0.119
			2	0.378	0.231	0.608
			3	0.622	0.378	1.000
			4	0.231	0.084	0.315
			5	0.035	0.006	0.041
			6	0.001	0.000	0.001
15	7	7	0	0.001	0.000	0.001
			1	0.032	0.009	0.041
			2	0.214	0.100	0.315
			3	0.595	0.405	1.000
			4	0.405	0.214	0.619
			5	0.100	0.032	0.132
			6	0.009	0.001	0.010
			7	0.000	0.000	0.000

TABLE J
Lower- and upper-tail probabilities for W_x, the Wilcoxon-Mann-Whitney rank-sum statistic*

Entries are $P[W_x \leq c_L]$ and $P[W_x \geq c_U]$. W_x is the rank-sum for the smaller group.

	m = 3																			
c_L	$n = 3$	c_U	$n = 4$	c_U	$n = 5$	c_U	$n = 6$	c_U	$n = 7$	c_U	$n = 8$	c_U	$n = 9$	c_U	$n = 10$	c_U	$n = 11$	c_U	$n = 12$	c_U
6	.0500	15	.0286	18	.0179	21	.0119	24	.0083	27	.0061	30	.0045	33	.0035	36	.0027	39	.0022	42
7	.1000	14	.0571	17	.0357	20	.0238	23	.0167	26	.0121	29	.0091	32	.0070	35	.0055	38	.0044	41
8	.2000	13	.1143	16	.0714	19	.0476	22	.0333	25	.0242	28	.0182	31	.0140	34	.0110	37	.0088	40
9	.3500	12	.2000	15	.1250	18	.0833	21	.0583	24	.0424	27	.0318	30	.0245	33	.0192	36	.0154	39
10	.5000	11	.3143	14	.1964	17	.1310	20	.0917	23	.0667	26	.0500	29	.0385	32	.0302	35	.0242	38
11	.6500	10	.4286	13	.2857	16	.1905	19	.1333	22	.0970	25	.0727	28	.0559	31	.0440	34	.0352	37
12	.8000	9	.5714	12	.3929	15	.2738	18	.1917	21	.1394	24	.1045	27	.0804	30	.0632	33	.0505	36
13	.9000	8	.6857	11	.5000	14	.3571	17	.2583	20	.1879	23	.1409	26	.1084	29	.0852	32	.0681	35
14	.9500	7	.8000	10	.6071	13	.4524	16	.3333	19	.2485	22	.1864	25	.1434	28	.1126	31	.0901	34
15	1.0000	6	.8857	9	.7143	12	.5476	15	.4167	18	.3152	21	.2409	24	.1853	27	.1456	30	.1165	33
16			.9429	8	.8036	11	.6429	14	.5000	17	.3879	20	.3000	23	.2343	26	.1841	29	.1473	32
17			.9714	7	.8750	10	.7262	13	.5833	16	.4606	19	.3636	22	.2867	25	.2280	28	.1824	31
18			1.0000	6	.9286	9	.8095	12	.6667	15	.5394	18	.4318	21	.3462	24	.2775	27	.2242	30
19					.9643	8	.8690	11	.7417	14	.6121	17	.5000	20	.4056	23	.3297	26	.2681	29
20					.9821	7	.9167	10	.8083	13	.6848	16	.5682	19	.4685	22	.3846	25	.3165	28
21					1.0000	6	.9524	9	.8667	12	.7515	15	.6364	18	.5315	21	.4423	24	.3670	27
22							.9762	8	.9083	11	.8121	14	.7000	17	.5944	20	.5000	23	.4198	26
23							.9881	7	.9417	10	.8606	13	.7591	16	.6538	19	.5577	22	.4725	25
24							1.0000	6	.9667	9	.9030	12	.8136	15	.7133	18	.6154	21	.5275	24

TABLE J (continued)

	m = 4																	
c_L	$n = 4$	c_U	$n = 5$	c_U	$n = 6$	c_U	$n = 7$	c_U	$n = 8$	c_U	$n = 9$	c_U	$n = 10$	c_U	$n = 11$	c_U	$n = 12$	c_U
10	.0143	26	.0079	30	.0048	34	.0030	38	.0020	42	.0014	46	.0010	50	.0007	54	.0005	58
11	.0286	25	.0159	29	.0095	33	.0061	37	.0040	41	.0028	45	.0020	49	.0015	53	.0011	57
12	.0571	24	.0317	28	.0190	32	.0121	36	.0081	40	.0056	44	.0040	48	.0029	52	.0022	56
13	.1000	23	.0556	27	.0333	31	.0212	35	.0141	39	.0098	43	.0070	47	.0051	51	.0038	55
14	.1714	22	.0952	26	.0571	30	.0364	34	.0242	38	.0168	42	.0120	46	.0088	50	.0066	54
15	.2429	21	.1429	25	.0857	29	.0545	33	.0364	37	.0252	41	.0180	45	.0132	49	.0099	53
16	.3429	20	.2063	24	.1286	28	.0818	32	.0545	36	.0378	40	.0270	44	.0198	48	.0148	52
17	.4429	19	.2778	23	.1762	27	.1152	31	.0768	35	.0531	39	.0380	43	.0278	47	.0209	51
18	.5571	18	.3651	22	.2381	26	.1576	30	.1071	34	.0741	38	.0529	42	.0388	46	.0291	50
19	.6571	17	.4524	21	.3048	25	.2061	29	.1414	33	.0993	37	.0709	41	.0520	45	.0390	49
20	.7571	16	.5476	20	.3810	24	.2636	28	.1838	32	.1301	36	.0939	40	.0689	44	.0516	48
21	.8286	15	.6349	19	.4571	23	.3242	27	.2303	31	.1650	35	.1199	39	.0886	43	.0665	47
22	.9000	14	.7222	18	.5429	22	.3939	26	.2848	30	.2070	34	.1518	38	.1128	42	.0852	46
23	.9429	13	.7937	17	.6190	21	.4636	25	.3414	29	.2517	33	.1868	37	.1399	41	.1060	45
24	.9714	12	.8571	16	.6952	20	.5364	24	.4040	28	.3021	32	.2268	36	.1714	40	.1308	44
25	.9857	11	.9048	15	.7619	19	.6061	23	.4667	27	.3552	31	.2697	35	.2059	39	.1582	43
26	1.0000	10	.9444	14	.8238	18	.6758	22	.5333	26	.4126	30	.3177	34	.2447	38	.1896	42
27			.9683	13	.8714	17	.7364	21	.5960	25	.4699	29	.3666	33	.2857	37	.2231	41
28			.9841	12	.9143	16	.7939	20	.6586	24	.5301	28	.4196	32	.3304	36	.2604	40
29			.9921	11	.9429	15	.8424	19	.7152	23	.5874	27	.4725	31	.3766	35	.2995	39
30			1.0000	10	.9667	14	.8848	18	.7697	22	.6448	26	.5275	30	.4256	34	.3418	38
31					.9810	13	.9182	17	.8162	21	.6979	25	.5804	29	.4747	33	.3852	37
32					.9905	12	.9455	16	.8586	20	.7483	24	.6334	28	.5253	32	.4308	36
33					.9952	11	.9636	15	.8929	19	.7930	23	.6823	27	.5744	31	.4764	35
34					1.0000	10	.9788	14	.9232	18	.8350	22	.7303	26	.6234	30	.5236	34

TABLE J (continued)

	$m = 5$											
c_L	$n = 5$	c_U	$n = 6$	c_U	$n = 7$	c_U	$n = 8$	c_U	$n = 9$	c_U	$n = 10$	c_U
15	.0040	40	.0022	45	.0013	50	.0008	55	.0005	60	.0003	65
16	.0079	39	.0043	44	.0025	49	.0016	54	.0010	59	.0007	64
17	.0159	38	.0087	43	.0051	48	.0031	53.	.0020	58	.0013	63
18	.0278	37	.0152	42	.0088	47	.0054	52	.0035	57	.0023	62
19	.0476	36	.0260	41	.0152	46	.0093	51	.0060	56	.0040	61
20	.0754	35	.0411	40	.0240	45	.0148	50	.0095	55	.0063	60
21	.1111	34	.0628	39	.0366	44	.0225	49	.0145	54	.0097	59
22	.1548	33	.0887	38	.0530	43	.0326	48	.0210	53	.0140	58
23	.2103	32	.1234	37	.0745	42	.0466	47	.0300	52	.0200	57
24	.2738	31	.1645	36	.1010	41	.0637	46	.0415	51	.0276	56
25	.3452	30	.2143	35	.1338	40	.0855	45	.0559	50	.0376	55
26	.4206	29	.2684	34	.1717	39	.1111	44	.0734	49	.0496	54
27	.5000	28	.3312	33	.2159	38	.1422	43	.0949	48	.0646	53
28	.5794	27	.3961	32	.2652	37	.1772	42	.1199	47	.0823	52
29	.6548	26	.4654	31	.3194	36	.2176	41	.1489	46	.1032	51
30	.7262	25	.5346	30	.3775	35	.2618	40	.1818	45	.1272	50
31	.7897	24	.6039	29	.4381	34	.3108	39	.2188	44	.1548	49
32	.8452	23	.6688	28	.5000	33	.3621	38	.2592	43	.1855	48
33	.8889	22	.7316	27	.5619	32	.4165	37	.3032	42	.2198	47
34	.9246	21	.7857	26	.6225	31	.4716	36	.3497	41	.2567	46
35	.9524	20	.8355	25	.6806	30	.5284	35	.3986	40	.2970	45
36	.9722	19	.8766	24	.7348	29	.5835	34	.4491	39	.3393	44
37	.9841	18	.9113	23	.7841	28	.6379	33	.5000	38	.3839	43
38	.9921	17	.9372	22	.8283	27	.6892	32	.5509	37	.4296	42
39	.9960	16	.9589	21	.8662	26	.7382	31	.6014	36	.4765	41
40	1.0000	15	.9740	20	.8990	25	.7824	30	.6503	35	.5235	40

TABLE J (continued)

	m = 6									
c_L	n = 6	c_U	n = 7	c_U	n = 8	c_U	n = 9	c_U	n = 10	c_U
21	.0011	57	.0006	63	.0003	69	.0002	75	.0001	81
22	.0022	56	.0012	62	.0007	68	.0004	74	.0002	80
23	.0043	55	.0023	61	.0013	67	.0008	73	.0005	79
24	.0076	54	.0041	60	.0023	66	.0014	72	.0009	78
25	.0130	53	.0070	59	.0040	65	.0024	71	.0015	77
26	.0206	52	.0111	58	.0063	64	.0038	70	.0024	76
27	.0325	51	.0175	57	.0100	63	.0060	69	.0037	75
28	.0465	50	.0256	56	.0147	62	.0088	68	.0055	74
29	.0660	49	.0367	55	.0213	61	.0128	67	.0080	73
30	.0898	48	.0507	54	.0296	60	.0180	66	.0112	72
31	.1201	47	.0688	53	.0406	59	.0248	65	.0156	71
32	.1548	46	.0903	52	.0539	58	.0332	64	.0210	70
33	.1970	45	.1171	51	.0709	57	.0440	63	.0280	69
34	.2424	44	.1474	50	.0906	56	.0567	62	.0363	68
35	.2944	43	.1830	49	.1142	55	.0723	61	.0467	67
36	.3496	42	.2226	48	.1412	54	.0905	60	.0589	66
37	.4091	41	.2669	47	.1725	53	.1119	59	.0736	65
38	.4686	40	.3141	46	.2068	52	.1361	58	.0903	64
39	.5314	39	.3654	45	.2454	51	.1638	57	.1099	63
40	.5909	38	.4178	44	.2864	50	.1942	56	.1317	62
41	.6504	37	.4726	43	.3310	49	.2280	55	.1566	61
42	.7056	36	.5274	42	.3773	48	.2643	54	.1838	60
43	.7576	35	.5822	41	.4259	47	.3035	53	.2139	59
44	.8030	34	.6346	40	.4749	46	.3445	52	.2461	58
45	.8452	33	.6859	39	.5251	45	.3878	51	.2811	57
46	.8799	32	.7331	38	.5741	44	.4320	50	.3177	56
47	.9102	31	.7774	37	.6227	43	.4773	49	.3564	55
48	.9340	30	.8170	36	.6690	42	.5227	48	.3962	54
49	.9535	29	.8526	35	.7136	41	.5680	47	.4374	53
50	.9675	28	.8829	34	.7546	40	.6122	46	.4789	52
51	.9794	27	.9097	33	.7932	39	.6555	45	.5211	51

TABLE J (continued)

			$m = 7$					
c_L	$n = 7$	c_U	$n = 8$	c_U	$n = 9$	c_U	$n = 10$	c_U
28	.0003	77	.0002	84	.0001	91	.0001	98
29	.0006	76	.0003	83	.0002	90	.0001	97
30	.0012	75	.0006	82	.0003	89	.0002	96
31	.0020	74	.0011	81	.0006	88	.0004	95
32	.0035	73	.0019	80	.0010	87	.0006	94
33	.0055	72	.0030	79	.0017	86	.0010	93
34	.0087	71	.0047	78	.0026	85	.0015	92
35	.0131	70	.0070	77	.0039	84	.0023	91
36	.0189	69	.0103	76	.0058	83	.0034	90
37	.0265	68	.0145	75	.0082	82	.0048	89
38	.0364	67	.0200	74	.0115	81	.0068	88
39	.0487	66	.0270	73	.0156	80	.0093	87
40	.0641	65	.0361	72	.0209	79	.0125	86
41	.0825	64	.0469	71	.0274	78	.0165	85
42	.1043	63	.0603	70	.0356	77	.0215	84
43	.1297	62	.0760	69	.0454	76	.0277	83
44	.1588	61	.0946	68	.0571	75	.0351	82
45	.1914	60	.1159	67	.0708	74	.0439	81
46	.2279	59	.1405	66	.0869	73	.0544	80
47	.2675	58	.1678	65	.1052	72	.0665	79
48	.3100	57	.1984	64	.1261	71	.0806	78
49	.3552	56	.2317	63	.1496	70	.0966	77
50	.4024	55	.2679	62	.1755	69	.1148	76
51	.4508	54	.3063	61	.2039	68	.1349	75
52	.5000	53	.3472	60	.2349	67	.1574	74
53	.5492	52	.3894	59	.2680	66	.1819	73
54	.5976	51	.4333	58	.3032	65	.2087	72
55	.6448	50	.4775	57	.3403	64	.2374	71
56	.6900	49	.5225	56	.3788	63	.2681	70
57	.7325	48	.5667	55	.4185	62	.3004	69
58	.7721	47	.6106	54	.4591	61	.3345	68
59	.8086	46	.6528	53	.5000	60	.3698	67
60	.8412	45	.6937	52	.5409	59	.4063	66
61	.8703	44	.7321	51	.5815	58	.4434	65
62	.8957	43	.7683	50	.6212	57	.4811	64
63	.9175	42	.8016	49	.6597	56	.5189	63

TABLE J (continued)

			$m = 8$			
c_L	$n = 8$	c_U	$n = 9$	c_U	$n = 10$	c_U
36	.0001	100	.0000	108	.0000	116
37	.0002	99	.0001	107	.0000	115
38	.0003	98	.0002	106	.0001	114
39	.0005	97	.0003	105	.0002	113
40	.0009	96	.0005	104	.0003	112
41	.0015	95	.0008	103	.0004	111
42	.0023	94	.0012	102	.0007	110
43	.0035	93	.0019	101	.0010	109
44	.0052	92	.0028	100	.0015	108
45	.0074	91	.0039	99	.0022	107
46	.0103	90	.0056	98	.0031	106
47	.0141	89	.0076	97	.0043	105
48	.0190	88	.0103	96	.0058	104
49	.0249	87	.0137	95	.0078	103
50	.0325	86	.0180	94	.0103	102
51	.0415	85	.0232	93	.0133	101
52	.0524	84	.0296	92	.0171	100
53	.0652	83	.0372	91	.0217	99
54	.0803	82	.0464	90	.0273	98
55	.0974	81	.0570	89	.0338	97
56	.1172	80	.0694	88	.0416	96
57	.1393	79	.0836	87	.0506	95
58	.1641	78	.0998	86	.0610	94
59	.1911	77	.1179	85	.0729	93
60	.2209	76	.1383	84	.0864	92
61	.2527	75	.1606	83	.1015	91
62	.2869	74	.1852	82	.1185	90
63	.3227	73	.2117	81	.1371	89
64	.3605	72	.2404	80	.1577	88
65	.3992	71	.2707	79	.1800	87
66	.4392	70	.3029	78	.2041	86
67	.4796	69	.3365	77	.2299	85
68	.5204	68	.3715	76	.2574	84
69	.5608	67	.4074	75	.2863	83
70	.6008	66	.4442	74	.3167	82
71	.6395	65	.4813	73	.3482	81
72	.6773	64	.5187	72	.3809	80
73	.7131	63	.5558	71	.4143	79
74	.7473	62	.5926	70	.4484	78
75	.7791	61	.6285	69	.4827	77
76	.8089	60	.6635	68	.5173	76

TABLE J (continued)

		$m = 9$							
c_L	$n = 9$	c_U	$n = 10$	c_U	c_L	$n = 9$ (cont.)		$n = 10$ (cont.)	c_U
45	.0000	126	.0000	135	68	.0680	103	.0394	112
46	.0000	125	.0000	134	69	.0807	102	.0474	111
47	.0001	124	.0000	133	70	.0951	101	.0564	110
48	.0001	123	.0001	132	71	.1112	100	.0667	109
49	.0002	122	.0001	131	72	.1290	99	.0782	108
50	.0004	121	.0002	130	73	.1487	98	.0912	107
51	.0006	120	.0003	129	74	.1701	97	.1055	106
52	.0009	119	.0005	128	75	.1933	96	.1214	105
53	.0014	118	.0007	127	76	.2181	95	.1388	104
54	.0020	117	.0011	126	77	.2447	94	.1577	103
55	.0028	116	.0015	125	78	.2729	93	.1781	102
56	.0039	115	.0021	124	79	.3024	92	.2001	101
57	.0053	114	.0028	123	80	.3332	91	.2235	100
58	.0071	113	.0038	122	81	.3652	90	.2483	99
59	.0094	112	.0051	121	82	.3981	89	.2745	98
60	.0122	111	.0066	120	83	.4317	88	.3019	97
61	.0157	110	.0086	119	84	.4657	87	.3304	96
62	.0200	109	.0110	118	85	.5000	86	.3598	95
63	.0252	108	.0140	117	86	.5343	85	.3901	94
64	.0313	107	.0175	116	87	.5683	84	.4211	93
65	.0385	106	.0217	115	88	.6019	83	.4524	92
66	.0470	105	.0267	114	89	.6348	82	.4841	91
67	.0567	104	.0326	113	90	.6668	81	.5159	90

TABLE J (continued)

$m = 10$					
c_L	$n = 10$	c_U	c_L	$n = 10$ (cont.)	c_U
55	.0000	155	81	.0376	129
56	.0000	154	82	.0446	128
57	.0000	153	83	.0526	127
58	.0000	152	84	.0615	126
59	.0001	151	85	.0716	125
60	.0001	150	86	.0827	124
61	.0002	149	87	.0952	123
62	.0002	148	88	.1088	122
63	.0004	147	89	.1237	121
64	.0005	146	90	.1399	120
65	.0008	145	91	.1575	119
66	.0010	144	92	.1763	118
67	.0014	143	93	.1965	117
68	.0019	142	94	.2179	116
69	.0026	141	95	.2406	115
70	.0034	140	96	.2644	114
71	.0045	139	97	.2894	113
72	.0057	138	98	.3153	112
73	.0073	137	99	.3421	111
74	.0093	136	100	.3697	110
75	.0116	135	101	.3980	109
76	.0144	134	102	.4267	108
77	.0177	133	103	.4559	107
78	.0216	132	104	.4853	106
79	.0262	131	105	.5147	105
80	.0315	130			

TABLE K
Critical values of $\grave{U}$ for the robust rank order test†

	n										
α	3	4	5	6	7	8	9	10	11	12	*m*
.10	**2.347**	**1.732**	**1.632**	**1.897**	**1.644**	**1.500**	**1.575**	**1.611**	**1.638**	**1.616**	
.05	∞*	3.273	2.324	2.912	2.605	2.777	2.353	2.553	2.369	2.449	
.025		**∞***	**4.195**	**5.116**	**6.037**	**4.082**	**3.566**	**3.651**	**3.503**	**3.406**	3
.01			∞*	∞*	∞*	6.957	7.876	8.795	5.831	5.000	
		1.586	**1.500**	**1.434**	**1.428**	**1.371**	**1.434**	**1.466**	**1.448**	**1.455**	
		2.502	2.160	2.247	2.104	2.162	2.057	2.000	2.067	2.096	
		4.483	**3.265**	**3.021**	**3.295**	**2.868**	**2.683**	**2.951**	**2.776**	**2.847**	4
		∞*	∞*	6.899	4.786	4.252	4.423	4.276	4.017	3.904	
			1.447	**1.362**	**1.308**	**1.378**	**1.361**	**1.361**	**1.340**	**1.369**	
			2.063	1.936	1.954	1.919	1.893	1.900	1.891	1.923	
			2.859	**2.622**	**2.465**	**2.556**	**2.536**	**2.496**	**2.497**	**2.479**	5
			7.187	3.913	4.246	3.730	3.388	3.443	3.435	3.444	
				1.335	**1.326**	**1.327**	**1.338**	**1.339**	**1.320**	**1.330**	
				1.860	1.816	1.796	1.845	1.829	1.833	1.835	
				2.502	**2.500**	**2.443**	**2.349**	**2.339**	**2.337**	**2.349**	6
				3.712	3.519	3.230	3.224	3.164	3.161	3.151	
					1.333	**1.310**	**1.320**	**1.313**	**1.302**	**1.318**	
					1.804	1.807	1.790	1.776	1.769	1.787	
					2.331	**2.263**	**2.287**	**2.248**	**2.240**	**2.239**	7
					3.195	3.088	2.967	3.002	2.979	2.929	
						1.295	**1.283**	**1.284**	**1.290**	**1.293**	
						1.766	1.765	1.756	1.746	1.759	
						2.251	**2.236**	**2.209**	**2.205**	**2.198**	8
						2.954	2.925	2.880	2.856	2.845	
							1.294	**1.304**	**1.288**	**1.299**	
							1.744	1.742	1.744	1.737	
							2.206	**2.181**	**2.172**	**2.172**	9
							2.857	2.802	2.798	2.770	
								1.295	**1.284**	**1.284**	
								1.723	1.726	1.720	
								2.161	**2.152**	**2.144**	10
								2.770	2.733	2.718	
									1.289	**1.290**	
									1.716	1.708	
									2.138	**2.127**	11
									2.705	2.683	
										1.283	
										1.708	
										2.117	12
										2.661	

Tabled values in successive rows are for α = .10, .05, .025, .01 for various values of *m* and *n*.

Note: *m* is the smaller sample size and *n* is the large sample size. Value in the table is the one-tailed critical point with level closest to the traditional values.

* The highest value of $\grave{U}$ is used, in which V_x or V_y is 0, or $\grave{U}$ is undefined.

† Adapted from Fligner, M. A. & Policello, G. E., II (1981). Robust tank procedures for the Behrens-Fisher problem. *Journal of the American Statistical Association*, **76**, 162–168. With the permission of authors and publisher.

TABLE L_I
Kolmogorov-Smirnov two-sample test*

Critical values for one-tailed rejection region $mnD_{m,n} \geqslant c$. The upper, middle, and lower numbers are $c_{.10}$, $c_{.05}$, and $c_{.01}$ for each (m, n) entry.

n	m: 3	4	5	6	7	8	9	10	11	12	13	14	15	16	17	18	19	20	21	22	23	24	25
3	9	10	11	15	15	16	21	19	22	24	25	26	30	30	32	36	36	37	42	40	43	45	46
	9	10	13	15	16	19	21	22	25	27	28	31	33	34	35	39	40	41	45	46	47	51	52
	**	**	**	**	19	22	27	28	31	33	34	37	42	43	43	48	49	52	54	55	58	63	64
4	10	16	13	16	18	24	21	24	26	32	29	32	34	40	37	40	41	48	45	48	49	56	53
	10	16	16	18	21	24	25	28	29	36	33	38	38	44	44	46	49	52	52	56	57	60	61
	**	**	17	22	25	32	29	34	37	40	41	46	46	52	53	56	57	64	64	66	69	76	73
5	11	13	20	19	21	23	26	30	30	32	35	37	45	41	44	46	47	55	51	54	56	58	65
	13	16	20	21	24	26	28	35	35	36	40	42	50	46	49	51	56	60	60	62	65	67	75
	**	17	25	26	29	33	36	40	41	46	48	51	60	56	61	63	67	75	75	76	81	82	90
6	15	16	19	24	24	26	30	32	33	42	37	42	45	48	49	54	54	56	60	62	63	72	67
	15	18	21	30	25	30	33	36	38	48	43	48	51	54	56	66	61	66	69	70	73	78	78
	**	22	26	36	31	38	42	44	49	54	54	60	63	66	68	78	77	80	84	88	91	96	96
7	15	18	21	24	35	28	32	34	38	40	44	49	48	51	54	56	59	61	70	68	70	72	74
	16	21	24	25	35	34	36	40	43	45	50	56	56	58	61	64	68	72	77	77	79	83	85
	19	25	29	31	42	42	46	50	53	57	59	70	70	71	75	81	85	87	98	97	99	103	106
8	16	24	23	26	28	40	33	40	41	48	47	50	52	64	57	62	64	72	71	74	76	88	81
	19	24	26	30	34	40	40	44	48	52	53	58	60	72	65	72	73	80	81	84	89	96	95
	22	32	33	38	42	48	49	56	59	64	66	72	75	88	81	88	91	100	100	106	107	120	118
9	21	21	26	30	32	33	45	43	45	51	51	54	60	61	65	72	70	73	78	79	82	87	88
	21	25	28	33	36	40	54	46	51	57	57	63	69	68	74	81	80	83	90	91	94	99	101
	27	29	36	42	46	49	63	61	62	69	73	77	84	86	92	99	99	103	111	111	117	123	124
10	19	24	30	32	34	40	43	50	48	52	55	60	65	66	69	72	74	90	80	86	88	92	100
	22	28	35	36	40	44	46	60	57	60	62	68	75	76	77	82	85	100	91	98	101	106	110
	28	34	40	44	50	56	61	70	69	74	78	84	90	94	97	104	104	120	118	120	125	130	140
11	22	26	30	33	38	41	45	48	66	54	59	63	66	69	72	76	79	84	85	99	95	98	100
	25	29	35	38	43	48	51	57	66	64	67	72	76	80	83	87	92	95	101	110	108	111	116
	31	37	41	49	53	59	62	69	88	77	85	89	95	100	104	108	114	117	124	143	132	138	143
12	24	32	32	42	40	48	51	52	54	72	61	68	72	76	77	84	85	92	93	98	100	108	106
	27	36	36	48	45	52	57	60	64	72	71	78	84	88	89	96	98	104	108	110	113	132	120
	33	40	46	54	57	64	69	74	77	96	92	94	102	108	111	120	121	128	132	138	138	156	153
13	25	29	35	37	44	47	51	55	59	61	78	72	75	79	81	87	89	95	97	100	105	109	111
	28	33	40	43	50	53	57	62	67	71	91	78	86	90	94	98	102	108	112	117	120	124	131
	34	41	48	54	59	66	73	78	85	92	104	102	106	112	118	121	127	135	138	143	150	154	160
14	26	32	37	42	49	50	54	60	63	68	72	84	80	84	87	92	94	100	112	108	110	116	119
	31	38	42	48	56	58	63	68	72	78	78	98	92	96	99	104	108	114	126	124	127	132	136
	37	46	51	60	70	72	77	84	89	94	102	112	111	120	124	130	135	142	154	152	157	164	169

TABLE L_I (continued)

Critical values for one-tailed rejection region $mnD_{m,n} \geqslant c$. The upper, middle, and lower numbers are $c_{.10}$, $c_{.05}$, and $c_{.01}$ for each (m, n) entry.

n	m = 3	4	5	6	7	8	9	10	11	12	13	14	15	16	17	18	19	20	21	22	23	24	25
15	**30**	**34**	**45**	**45**	**48**	**52**	**60**	**65**	**66**	**72**	**75**	**80**	**90**	**87**	**91**	**99**	**100**	**110**	**111**	**111**	**117**	**123**	**130**
	33	38	50	51	56	60	69	75	75	84	86	92	105	101	105	111	113	125	126	130	134	141	145
	42	*46*	*60*	*63*	*70*	*75*	*84*	*90*	*95*	*102*	*106*	*111*	*135*	*120*	*130*	*138*	*142*	*150*	*156*	*160*	*165*	*174*	*180*
16	**30**	**40**	**41**	**48**	**51**	**64**	**61**	**66**	**69**	**76**	**79**	**84**	**87**	**112**	**94**	**100**	**104**	**112**	**114**	**118**	**122**	**136**	**130**
	34	44	46	54	58	72	68	76	80	88	90	96	101	112	109	116	120	128	130	136	140	152	148
	43	*52*	*56*	*66*	*71*	*88*	*86*	*94*	*100*	*108*	*112*	*120*	*120*	*144*	*139*	*142*	*149*	*156*	*162*	*168*	*174*	*184*	*185*
17	**32**	**37**	**44**	**49**	**54**	**57**	**65**	**69**	**72**	**77**	**81**	**87**	**91**	**94**	**119**	**102**	**108**	**113**	**118**	**122**	**128**	**132**	**137**
	35	44	49	56	61	65	74	77	83	89	94	99	105	109	136	118	125	130	135	141	146	150	156
	43	*53*	*61*	*68*	*75*	*81*	*92*	*97*	*104*	*111*	*118*	*124*	*130*	*139*	*153*	*150*	*157*	*162*	*168*	*175*	*181*	*187*	*192*
18	**36**	**40**	**46**	**54**	**56**	**62**	**72**	**72**	**76**	**84**	**87**	**92**	**99**	**100**	**102**	**126**	**116**	**120**	**126**	**128**	**133**	**144**	**142**
	39	46	51	66	64	72	81	82	87	96	98	104	111	116	118	144	127	136	144	148	151	162	161
	48	*56*	*63*	*78*	*81*	*88*	*99*	*104*	*108*	*120*	*121*	*130*	*138*	*142*	*150*	*180*	*160*	*170*	*177*	*184*	*189*	*198*	*201*
19	**36**	**41**	**47**	**54**	**59**	**64**	**70**	**74**	**79**	**85**	**89**	**94**	**100**	**104**	**108**	**116**	**133**	**125**	**128**	**132**	**137**	**142**	**148**
	40	49	56	61	68	73	80	85	92	98	102	108	113	120	125	127	152	144	147	151	159	162	168
	49	*57*	*67*	*77*	*85*	*91*	*99*	*104*	*114*	*121*	*127*	*135*	*142*	*149*	*157*	*160*	*190*	*171*	*183*	*189*	*197*	*204*	*211*
20	**37**	**48**	**55**	**56**	**61**	**72**	**73**	**90**	**84**	**92**	**95**	**100**	**110**	**112**	**113**	**120**	**125**	**140**	**134**	**138**	**143**	**152**	**155**
	41	52	60	66	72	80	83	100	95	104	108	114	125	128	130	136	144	150	154	160	163	172	180
	52	*64*	*75*	*80*	*87*	*100*	*103*	*120*	*117*	*128*	*135*	*142*	*156*	*156*	*162*	*170*	*171*	*200*	*193*	*196*	*203*	*212*	*220*
21	**42**	**45**	**51**	**60**	**70**	**71**	**78**	**80**	**85**	**93**	**97**	**112**	**111**	**114**	**118**	**126**	**128**	**134**	**147**	**142**	**147**	**156**	**158**
	45	52	60	69	77	81	90	91	101	108	112	126	126	130	135	144	147	154	168	163	170	177	182
	54	*64*	*75*	*84*	*98*	*100*	*111*	*118*	*124*	*132*	*138*	*154*	*156*	*162*	*168*	*177*	*183*	*193*	*210*	*205*	*212*	*222*	*225*
22	**40**	**48**	**54**	**62**	**68**	**74**	**79**	**86**	**99**	**98**	**100**	**108**	**111**	**118**	**122**	**128**	**132**	**138**	**142**	**176**	**151**	**158**	**163**
	46	56	62	70	77	84	91	98	110	110	117	124	130	136	141	148	151	150	163	198	173	182	188
	55	*66*	*76*	*88*	*97*	*106*	*111*	*120*	*143*	*138*	*143*	*152*	*160*	*168*	*175*	*184*	*189*	*196*	*205*	*242*	*217*	*228*	*234*
23	**43**	**49**	**56**	**63**	**70**	**76**	**82**	**88**	**95**	**100**	**105**	**110**	**117**	**122**	**128**	**133**	**137**	**143**	**147**	**151**	**184**	**160**	**169**
	47	57	65	73	79	89	94	101	108	113	120	127	134	140	146	151	159	163	170	173	207	183	194
	58	*69*	*81*	*91*	*99*	*107*	*117*	*125*	*132*	*138*	*150*	*157*	*165*	*174*	*181*	*189*	*197*	*203*	*212*	*217*	*253*	*228*	*242*
24	**45**	**56**	**58**	**72**	**72**	**88**	**87**	**92**	**98**	**108**	**109**	**116**	**123**	**136**	**132**	**144**	**142**	**152**	**156**	**158**	**160**	**192**	**178**
	51	60	67	78	83	96	99	106	111	132	124	132	141	152	150	162	162	172	177	182	183	216	204
	63	*76*	*82*	*96*	*103*	*120*	*123*	*130*	*138*	*156*	*154*	*164*	*174*	*184*	*187*	*198*	*204*	*212*	*222*	*228*	*228*	*264*	*254*
25	**46**	**53**	**65**	**67**	**74**	**81**	**88**	**100**	**100**	**106**	**111**	**119**	**130**	**130**	**137**	**142**	**148**	**155**	**158**	**163**	**169**	**178**	**200**
	52	61	75	78	85	95	101	110	116	120	131	136	145	148	156	161	168	180	182	188	194	204	225
	64	*73*	*90*	*96*	*106*	*118*	*124*	*140*	*143*	*153*	*160*	*169*	*180*	*185*	*192*	*201*	*211*	*220*	*225*	*234*	*242*	*254*	*275*

* Adapted from Gail, M. H., and Green, S. B. (1976). Critical values for the one-sided two-sample Kolmogorov-Smirnov statistic. *Journal of the American Statistical Association*, *71*, 757–760, with the permission of the authors and publisher.

** Statistic cannot achieve this significance level.

TABLE L_{II}
Kolmogorov-Smirnov two-sample test*

Critical values for two-tailed rejection region $mnD_{m,n} \geqslant c$. The upper, middle, and lower numbers are $c_{.10}$, $c_{.05}$, and $c_{.01}$ for each (m, n) entry.

	m																								
n	1	2	3	4	5	6	7	8	9	10	11	12	13	14	15	16	17	18	19	20	21	22	23	24	25
1																			19	20	21	22	23	24	25
2					10	12	14	16 16	18 18	18 20	20 22	22 24	24 26	24 26	26 28	28 30	30 32	32 34	32 36 38	34 38 40	36 38 42	38 40 44	38 42 46	40 44 48	42 46 50
3			9	12	15 15	15 18	18 21	21 21	21 24 27	24 27 30	27 30 33	27 30 36	30 33 39	33 36 42	33 36 42	36 39 45	36 42 48	39 45 51	42 45 54	42 48 57	45 51 57	48 51 60	48 54 63	51 57 66	54 60 69
4			12	16 16	16 20	18 20 24	21 24 28	24 28 32	27 28 36	28 30 36	29 33 40	36 36 44	35 39 48	38 42 48	40 44 52	44 48 56	44 48 60	46 50 60	49 53 64	52 60 68	52 59 72	56 62 72	57 64 76	60 68 80	63 68 84
5		10	15 15	16 20	20 25 25	24 24 30	25 28 35	27 30 35	30 35 40	35 40 45	35 39 45	36 43 50	40 45 52	42 46 56	50 55 60	48 54 64	50 55 68	52 60 70	56 61 71	60 65 80	60 69 80	63 70 83	65 72 87	67 76 90	75 80 95
6		12	15 18	18 20 24	24 24 30	30 30 36	28 30 36	30 34 40	33 39 45	36 40 48	38 43 54	48 48 60	46 52 60	48 54 64	51 57 69	54 60 72	56 62 73	66 72 84	64 70 83	66 72 88	69 75 90	70 78 92	73 80 97	78 90 102	78 88 107
7		14	18 21	21 24 28	25 28 35	28 30 36	35 42 42	34 40 48	36 42 49	40 46 53	44 48 59	46 53 60	50 56 65	56 63 77	56 62 75	59 64 77	61 68 84	65 72 87	69 76 91	72 79 93	77 91 105	77 84 103	80 89 108	84 92 112	86 97 115
8		16 16	21 21	24 28 32	27 30 35	30 34 40	34 40 48	40 48 56	40 46 55	44 48 60	48 53 64	52 60 68	54 62 72	58 64 76	60 67 81	72 80 88	68 77 88	72 80 94	74 82 98	80 88 104	81 89 107	84 94 112	89 98 115	96 104 128	95 104 125
9		18 18	21 24 27	27 28 36	30 35 40	33 39 45	36 42 49	40 46 55	54 54 63	50 53 63	52 59 70	57 63 75	59 65 78	63 70 84	69 75 90	69 78 94	74 82 99	81 90 108	80 89 107	84 93 111	90 99 117	91 101 122	94 106 126	99 111 132	101 114 135
10		18 20	24 27 30	28 30 36	35 40 45	36 40 48	40 46 53	44 48 60	50 53 63	60 70 80	57 60 77	60 66 80	64 70 84	68 74 90	75 80 100	76 84 100	79 89 106	82 92 108	85 94 113	100 110 130	95 105 126	98 108 130	101 114 137	106 118 140	110 125 150
11		20 22	27 30 33	29 33 40	35 39 45	38 43 54	44 48 59	48 53 64	52 59 70	57 60 77	66 77 88	64 72 86	67 75 91	73 82 96	76 84 102	80 89 106	85 93 110	88 97 118	92 102 122	96 107 127	101 112 134	110 121 143	108 119 142	111 124 150	117 129 154
12		22 24	27 30 36	36 36 44	36 43 50	48 48 60	46 53 60	52 60 68	57 63 75	60 66 80	64 72 86	72 84 96	71 81 95	78 86 104	84 93 108	88 96 116	90 100 119	96 108 126	99 108 130	104 116 140	108 120 141	110 124 148	113 125 149	132 144 168	120 138 165
13		24 26	30 33 39	35 39 48	40 45 52	46 52 60	50 56 65	54 62 72	59 65 78	64 70 84	67 75 91	71 81 95	91 91 117	78 89 104	87 96 115	91 101 121	96 105 127	99 110 131	104 114 138	108 120 143	113 126 150	117 130 156	120 135 161	125 140 166	131 145 172

TABLE L_{II} (continued)

Critical values for two-tailed rejection region $mnD_{m,n} \geqslant c$. The upper, middle, and lower numbers are $c_{.10}$, $c_{.05}$, and $c_{.01}$ for each (m, n) entry.

	m																								
n	1	2	3	4	5	6	7	8	9	10	11	12	13	14	15	16	17	18	19	20	21	22	23	24	25
14		24	33	38	42	48	56	58	63	68	73	78	78	98	92	96	100	104	110	114	126	124	127	132	136
		26	36	42	46	54	63	64	70	74	82	86	89	112	98	106	111	116	121	126	140	138	142	146	150
			42	48	56	64	77	76	84	90	96	104	104	126	123	126	134	140	148	152	161	164	170	176	182
15		26	33	40	50	51	56	60	69	75	76	84	87	92	105	101	105	111	114	125	126	130	134	141	145
		28	36	44	55	57	62	67	75	80	84	93	96	98	120	114	116	123	127	135	138	144	149	156	160
			42	52	60	69	75	81	90	100	102	108	115	123	135	133	142	147	152	160	168	173	179	186	195
16		28	36	44	48	54	59	72	69	76	80	88	91	96	101	112	109	116	120	128	130	136	141	152	149
		30	39	48	54	60	64	80	78	84	89	96	101	106	114	128	124	128	133	140	145	150	157	168	167
			45	56	64	72	77	88	94	100	106	116	121	126	133	160	143	154	160	168	173	180	187	200	199
17		30	36	44	50	56	61	68	74	79	85	90	96	100	105	109	136	118	126	132	136	142	146	151	156
		32	42	48	55	62	68	77	82	89	93	100	105	111	116	124	136	133	141	146	151	157	163	168	173
			48	60	68	73	84	88	99	106	110	119	127	134	142	143	170	164	166	175	180	187	196	203	207
18		32	39	46	52	66	65	72	81	82	88	96	99	104	111	116	118	144	133	136	144	148	152	162	162
		34	45	50	60	72	72	80	90	92	97	108	110	116	123	128	133	162	142	152	159	164	170	180	180
			51	60	70	84	87	94	108	108	118	126	131	140	147	154	164	180	176	182	189	196	204	216	216
19	19	32	42	49	56	64	69	74	80	85	92	99	104	110	114	120	126	133	152	144	147	152	159	164	168
		36	45	53	61	70	76	82	89	94	102	108	114	121	127	133	141	142	171	160	163	169	177	183	187
		38	54	64	71	83	91	98	107	113	122	130	138	148	152	160	166	176	190	187	199	204	209	218	224
20	20	34	42	52	60	66	72	80	84	100	96	104	108	114	125	128	132	136	144	160	154	160	164	172	180
		38	48	60	65	72	79	88	93	110	107	116	120	126	135	140	146	152	160	180	173	176	184	192	200
		40	57	68	80	88	93	104	111	139	127	140	143	152	160	168	175	182	187	220	199	212	219	228	235
21	21	36	45	52	60	69	77	81	90	95	101	108	113	126	126	130	136	144	147	154	168	163	171	177	182
		38	51	59	69	75	91	89	99	105	112	120	126	140	138	145	151	159	163	173	189	183	189	198	202
		42	57	72	80	90	105	107	117	126	134	141	150	161	168	173	180	189	199	199	231	223	227	237	244
22	22	38	48	56	63	70	77	84	91	98	110	110	117	124	130	136	142	148	152	160	163	198	173	182	189
		40	51	62	70	78	84	94	101	108	121	124	130	138	144	150	157	164	169	176	183	198	194	204	209
		44	60	72	83	92	103	112	122	130	143	148	156	164	173	180	187	196	204	212	223	242	237	242	250
23	23	38	48	57	65	73	80	89	94	101	108	113	120	127	134	141	146	152	159	164	171	173	207	183	195
		42	54	64	72	80	89	98	106	114	119	125	135	142	149	157	163	170	177	184	189	194	230	205	216
		46	63	76	87	97	108	115	126	137	142	149	161	170	179	187	196	204	209	219	227	237	253	249	262
24	24	40	51	60	67	78	84	96	99	106	111	132	125	132	141	152	151	162	164	172	177	182	183	216	204
		44	57	68	76	90	92	104	111	118	124	144	140	146	156	168	168	180	183	192	198	204	205	240	225
		48	66	80	90	102	112	128	132	140	150	168	166	176	186	200	203	216	218	228	237	242	249	288	262
25	25	42	54	63	75	78	86	95	101	110	117	120	131	136	145	149	156	162	168	180	182	189	195	204	225
		46	60	68	80	88	97	104	114	125	129	138	145	150	160	167	173	180	187	200	202	209	216	225	250
		50	69	84	95	107	115	125	135	150	154	165	172	182	195	199	207	216	224	235	244	250	262	262	300

* Adapted from table 55 in Pearson, E. S., and Hartley, H. O. (1972). *Biometrika tables for statisticians, vol. 2.* Cambridge, Cambridge University Press, with the kind permission of the *Biometrika* trustees.

TABLE L_{III}
Critical values of $D_{m,n}$ for Kolmogorov-Smirnov two-sample test (Large samples, two-tailed)*

Level of significance	Value of $D_{m,n}$ so large as to call for rejection of H_0 at the indicated level of significance, where $D_{m,n} = \text{maximum } \lvert S_m(X) - S_n(X) \rvert$
.10	$1.22\sqrt{\frac{m+n}{mn}}$
.05	$1.36\sqrt{\frac{m+n}{mn}}$
.025	$1.48\sqrt{\frac{m+n}{mn}}$
.01	$1.63\sqrt{\frac{m+n}{mn}}$
.005	$1.73\sqrt{\frac{m+n}{mn}}$
.001	$1.95\sqrt{\frac{m+n}{mn}}$

* Adapted from Smirnov, N. (1948). Tables for estimating the goodness of fit of empirical distributions. *Annals of Mathematical Statistics*, **19**, 280–281, with the kind permission of the publisher.

TABLE M

Critical values for the Friedman two-way analysis of variance by ranks statistic, F_r*

k	N	$\alpha \leq .10$	$\alpha \leq .05$	$\alpha \leq .01$
3	3	6.00	6.00	—
	4	6.00	6.50	8.00
	5	5.20	6.40	8.40
	6	5.33	7.00	9.00
	7	5.43	7.14	8.86
	8	5.25	6.25	9.00
	9	5.56	6.22	8.67
	10	5.00	6.20	9.60
	11	4.91	6.54	8.91
	12	5.17	6.17	8.67
	13	4.77	6.00	9.39
	∞	4.61	5.99	9.21
4	2	6.00	6.00	—
	3	6.60	7.40	8.60
	4	6.30	7.80	9.60
	5	6.36	7.80	9.96
	6	6.40	7.60	10.00
	7	6.26	7.80	10.37
	8	6.30	7.50	10.35
	∞	6.25	7.82	11.34
5	3	7.47	8.53	10.13
	4	7.60	8.80	11.00
	5	7.68	8.96	11.52
	∞	7.78	9.49	13.28

* Some entries adapted and reproduced by permission of the publishers Charles Griffin & Co. Ltd., 16 Pembridge Road, London W11 3HL, from appendix table 5 of Kendall, M. G. (1970). *Rank correlation methods* (fourth edition). Other entries adapted from table A.15 of Hollander, M., and Wolfe, D. A. (1973). *Nonparametric statistics.* New York: J. Wiley. Reproduced by permission of the authors and publisher.

TABLE N
Critical values for Page's L statistic*

	k = 3			k = 4			k = 5			k = 6		
	α			α			α			α		
N	.05	.01	.001	.05	.01	.001	.05	.01	.001	.05	.01	.001
2	28			58	60		103	106	109	166	173	178
3	41	42		84	87	89	150	155	160	244	252	260
4	54	55	56	111	114	117	197	204	210	321	331	341
5	66	68	70	137	141	145	244	251	259	397	409	420
6	79	81	83	163	167	172	291	299	307	474	486	499
7	91	93	96	189	193	198	338	346	355	550	563	577
8	104	106	109	214	220	225	384	393	403	625	640	655
9	116	119	121	240	246	252	431	441	451	701	717	733
10	128	131	134	266	272	278	477	487	499	777	793	811
11	141	144	147	292	298	305	523	534	546	852	869	888
12	153	156	160	317	324	331	570	581	593	928	946	965
13	165	169	172									
14	178	181	185									
15	190	194	197									
16	202	206	210									
17	215	218	223									
18	227	231	235									
19	239	243	248									
20	251	256	260									

* Tabled values are L_a, $P[L \geq L_a] = \alpha$

TABLE N (continued)

N	$k = 7$			$k = 8$			$k = 9$			$k = 10$		
		α			α			α			α	
	.05	.01	.001	.05	.01	.001	.05	.01	.001	.05	.01	.001
2	252	261	269	362	376	388	500	520	544	670	696	726
3	370	382	394	532	549	567	736	761	790	987	1019	1056
4	487	501	516	701	722	743	971	999	1032	1301	1339	1382
5	603	620	637	869	893	917	1204	1236	1273	1614	1656	1704
6	719	737	757	1037	1063	1090	1436	1472	1512	1927	1972	2025
7	835	855	876	1204	1232	1262	1668	1706	1750	2238	2288	2344
8	950	972	994	1371	1401	1433	1900	1940	1987	2549	2602	2662
9	1065	1088	1113	1537	1569	1603	2131	2174	2223	2859	2915	2980
10	1180	1205	1230	1703	1736	1773	2361	2407	2459	3169	3228	3296
11	1295	1321	1348	1868	1905	1943	2592	2639	2694	3478	3541	3612
12	1410	1437	1465	2035	2072	2112	2822	2872	2929	3788	3852	3927

* Adapted from Page, E. B. (1963). Ordered hypotheses for multiple treatments: a significance test for linear ranks. *Journal of the Americaan Statistical Association*, **58**, 216–230 with the permission of the author and publisher.

TABLE O
Critical values for the Kruskal-Wallis one-way analysis of variance by ranks statistic, *KW*

Sample sizes			α				
n_1	n_2	n_3	.10	.05	.01	.005	.001
2	2	2	4.25				
3	2	1	4.29				
3	2	2	4.71	4.71			
3	3	1	4.57	5.14			
3	3	2	4.56	5.36			
3	3	3	4.62	5.60	7.20	7.20	
4	2	1	4.50				
4	2	2	4.46	5.33			
4	3	1	4.06	5.21			
4	3	2	4.51	5.44	6.44	7.00	
4	3	3	4.71	5.73	6.75	7.32	8.02
4	4	1	4.17	4.97	6.67		
4	4	2	4.55	5.45	7.04	7.28	
4	4	3	4.55	5.60	7.14	7.59	8.32
4	4	4	4.65	5.69	7.66	8.00	8.65
5	2	1	4.20	5.00			
5	2	2	4.36	5.16	6.53		
5	3	1	4.02	4.96			
5	3	2	4.65	5.25	6.82	7.18	
5	3	3	4.53	5.65	7.08	7.51	8.24
5	4	1	3.99	4.99	6.95	7.36	
5	4	2	4.54	5.27	7.12	7.57	8.11
5	4	3	4.55	5.63	7.44	7.91	8.50
5	4	4	4.62	5.62	7.76	8.14	9.00
5	5	1	4.11	5.13	7.31	7.75	
5	5	2	4.62	5.34	7.27	8.13	8.68
5	5	3	4.54	5.71	7.54	8.24	9.06
5	5	4	4.53	5.64	7.77	8.37	9.32
5	5	5	4.56	5.78	7.98	8.72	9.68
Large samples			4.61	5.99	9.21	10.60	13.82

Note: The absence of an entry in the extreme tails indicates that the distribution may not take on the necessary extremes values.

Adapted from Table F in Kraft, C. H., and van Eeden, C., (1968). *A nonparametric introduction to statistics.* New York: Macmillan, with the permission of the publisher.

TABLE P
Critical values for the Jonckheere statistic J

Entries are $P(J \geq$ tabled value] for $k = 3$ and $n_i \leq 8$ and equal n's ($2 \leq n \leq 6$) for $k = 4, 5, 6, 7, 8$.

Sample Sizes	α .10	.05	.01	.005
2 2 2	10	11	12	--
2 2 3	13	14	15	16
2 2 4	16	17	19	20
2 2 5	18	20	22	23
2 2 6	21	23	25	27
2 2 7	24	26	29	30
2 2 8	27	29	32	33
2 3 3	16	18	19	20
2 3 4	20	21	23	25
2 3 5	23	25	27	29
2 3 6	26	28	31	33
2 3 7	30	32	35	37
2 3 8	33	35	39	41
2 4 4	24	25	28	29
2 4 5	27	29	33	34
2 4 6	31	34	37	39
2 4 7	35	38	42	44
2 4 8	39	42	46	49
2 5 5	32	34	38	40
2 5 6	36	39	43	45
2 5 7	41	44	48	51
2 5 8	45	48	53	56
2 6 6	42	44	49	51
2 6 7	47	50	55	57
2 6 8	52	55	61	64
2 7 7	52	56	61	64
2 7 8	58	62	68	71
2 8 8	64	68	75	78
3 3 3	20	22	24	25
3 3 4	24	26	29	30

Note: Tabled critical values have been chosen to achieve *rounded* significance levels, e.g., a value of J with a probability $\leq .0149$ is the tabled entry for the $\alpha = .01$ significance level.

TABLE P (continued)

Sample Sizes	α .10	.05	.01	.005
3 3 5	28	30	33	35
3 3 6	32	34	38	40
3 3 7	36	38	42	44
3 3 8	40	42	47	49
3 4 4	29	31	34	36
3 4 5	33	35	39	41
3 4 6	38	40	44	46
3 4 7	42	45	49	52
3 4 8	47	50	55	57
3 5 5	38	41	45	47
3 5 6	43	46	51	53
3 5 7	48	51	57	59
3 5 8	53	57	63	65
3 6 6	49	52	57	60
3 6 7	54	58	64	67
3 6 8	60	64	70	73
3 7 7	61	64	71	74
3 7 8	67	71	78	81
3 8 8	74	78	86	89
4 4 4	34	36	40	42
4 4 5	39	41	45	48
4 4 6	44	47	51	54
4 4 7	49	52	57	60
4 4 8	54	57	63	66
4 5 5	44	47	52	55
4 5 6	50	53	58	61
4 5 7	56	59	65	68
4 5 8	61	65	71	75
4 6 6	56	60	66	69
4 6 7	62	66	73	76
4 6 8	68	73	80	83
4 7 7	69	73	81	84
4 7 8	76	80	88	92
4 8 8	83	88	97	100

TABLE P (continued)

Sample Sizes	α .10	.05	.01	.005
5 5 5	50	54	59	62
5 5 6	57	60	66	69
5 5 7	63	67	73	76
5 5 8	69	73	80	84
5 6 6	63	67	74	77
5 6 7	70	74	82	85
5 6 8	77	81	89	93
5 7 7	77	82	90	94
5 7 8	85	89	98	102
5 8 8	92	98	107	111
6 6 6	71	75	82	86
6 6 7	78	82	91	94
6 6 8	85	90	99	103
6 7 7	86	91	100	103
6 7 8	94	99	109	113
6 8 8	102	108	118	122
7 7 7	94	99	109	113
7 7 8	102	108	119	123
7 8 8	111	117	129	133
8 8 8	121	127	139	144
2 2 2 2	18	19	21	22
2 2 2 2 2	28	30	33	34
2 2 2 2 2 2	40	43	46	49
3 3 3 3	37	39	43	45
3 3 3 3 3	58	62	68	70
3 3 3 3 3 3	85	89	97	101
4 4 4 4	63	66	72	76
4 4 4 4 4	100	105	115	119
4 4 4 4 4 4	146	153	166	171
5 5 5 5	95	100	109	113
5 5 5 5 5	152	159	173	178
5 5 5 5 5 5	223	233	251	258
6 6 6 6	134	140	153	158
6 6 6 6 6	215	225	243	250
6 6 6 6 6 6	316	329	353	362

Adapted from Odeh, R. E. (1971). On Jonckheere's k-sample test against ordered alternatives. *Technometrics*, **13**, 912–918, with the permission of the author and publisher, and from Jonckheere, A. R. (1954). A distribution-free k-sample test against ordered alternatives. *Biometrika*, **41**, 133–145, with the permission of the *Biometrika* trustees.

TABLE Q
Critical values of r_s, the Spearman rank-order correlation coefficient

	α	.25	.10	.05	.025	.01	.005	.0025	.001	.0005 (one-tailed)
N	α	.50	.20	.10	.05	.02	.01	.005	.002	.001 (two-tailed)
4		.600	1.000	1.000						
5		.500	.800	.900	1.000	1.000				
6		.371	.657	.829	.886	.943	1.000	1.000		
7		.321	.571	.714	.786	.893	.929	.964	1.000	1.000
8		.310	.524	.643	.738	.833	.881	.905	.952	.976
9		.267	.483	.600	.700	.783	.833	.867	.917	.933
10		.248	.455	.564	.648	.745	.794	.830	.879	.903
11		.236	.427	.536	.618	.709	.755	.800	.845	.873
12		.224	.406	.503	.587	.671	.727	.776	.825	.860
13		.209	.385	.484	.560	.648	.703	.747	.802	.835
14		.200	.367	.464	.538	.622	.675	.723	.776	.811
15		.189	.354	.443	.521	.604	.654	.700	.754	.786
16		.182	.341	.429	.503	.582	.635	.679	.732	.765
17		.176	.328	.414	.485	.566	.615	.662	.713	.748
18		.170	.317	.401	.472	.550	.600	.643	.695	.728
19		.165	.309	.391	.460	.535	.584	.628	.677	.712
20		.161	.299	.380	.447	.520	.570	.612	.662	.696
21		.156	.292	.370	.435	.508	.556	.599	.648	.681
22		.152	.284	.361	.425	.496	.544	.586	.634	.667
23		.148	.278	.353	.415	.486	.532	.573	.622	.654
24		.144	.271	.344	.406	.476	.521	.562	.610	.642
25		.142	.265	.337	.398	.466	.511	.551	.598	.630

TABLE Q (continued)

N	α .25 / α .50	.10 / .20	.05 / .10	.025 / .05	.01 / .02	.005 / .01	.0025 / .005	.001 / .002	.0005 (one-tailed) / .001 (two-tailed)
26	.138	.259	.331	.390	.457	.501	.541	.587	.619
27	.136	.255	.324	.382	.448	.491	.531	.577	.608
28	.133	.250	.317	.375	.440	.483	.522	.567	.598
29	.130	.245	.312	.368	.433	.475	.513	.558	.589
30	.128	.240	.306	.362	.425	.467	.504	.549	.580
31	.126	.236	.301	.356	.418	.459	.496	.541	.571
32	.124	.232	.296	.350	.412	.452	.489	.533	.563
33	.121	.229	.291	.345	.405	.446	.482	.525	.554
34	.120	.225	.287	.340	.399	.439	.475	.517	.547
35	.118	.222	.283	.335	.394	.433	.468	.510	.539
36	.116	.219	.279	.330	.388	.427	.462	.504	.533
37	.114	.216	.275	.325	.383	.421	.456	.497	.526
38	.113	.212	.271	.321	.378	.415	.450	.491	.519
39	.111	.210	.267	.317	.373	.410	.444	.485	.513
40	.110	.207	.264	.313	.368	.405	.439	.479	.507
41	.108	.204	.261	.309	.364	.400	.433	.473	.501
42	.107	.202	.257	.305	.359	.395	.428	.468	.495
43	.105	.199	.254	.301	.355	.391	.423	.463	.490
44	.104	.197	.251	.298	.351	.386	.419	.458	.484
45	.103	.194	.248	.294	.347	.382	.414	.453	.479
46	.102	.192	.246	.291	.343	.378	.410	.448	.474
47	.101	.190	.243	.288	.340	.374	.405	.443	.469
48	.100	.188	.240	.285	.336	.370	.401	.439	.465
49	.098	.186	.238	.282	.333	.366	.397	.434	.460
50	.097	.184	.235	.279	.329	.363	.393	.430	.456

Source: Zar, J. H. (1972). Significance testing of the Spearman rank correlation coefficient. *Journal of the American Statistical Association*, **67**, 578–580. Adapted with the permission of author and publisher.

TABLE R_I

Upper-tail probabilities for T, the Kendall rank-order correlation coefficient ($N \leq 10$)*

Entries are $p = P[T \geq \text{tabled value}]$.

N	T	p	N	T	p	N	T	p	N	T	p
4	.000	.625	7	.048	.500	9	.000	.540	10	.022	.500
	.333	.375		.143	.386		.056	.460		.067	.431
	.667	.167		.238	.281		.111	.381		.111	.364
	1.000	.042		.333	.191		.167	.306		.156	.300
				.429	.119		.222	.238		.200	.242
5	.000	.592		.524	.068		.278	.179		.244	.190
	.200	.408		.619	.035		.333	.130		.289	.146
	.400	.242		.714	.015		.389	.090		.333	.108
	.600	.117		.810	.005		.444	.060		.378	.078
	.800	.042		.905	.001		.500	.038		.422	.054
	1.000	.008		1.000	.000		.556	.022		.467	.036
							.611	.012		.511	.023
6	.067	.500	8	.000	.548		.667	.006		.556	.014
	.200	.360		.071	.452		.722	.003		.600	.008
	.333	.235		.143	.360		.778	.001		.644	.005
	.467	.136		.214	.274		.833	.000		.689	.002
	.600	.068		.286	.199		.889	.000		.733	.001
	.733	.028		.357	.138		.944	.000		.778	.000
	.867	.008		.429	.089		1.000	.000		.822	.000
	1.000	.001		.500	.054					.867	.000
				.571	.031					.911	.000
				.643	.016					.956	.000
				.714	.007					1.000	.000
				.786	.003						
				.857	.001						
				.929	.000						
				1.000	.000						

* Adapted and reproduced by permission of the publishers Charles Griffin & Co. Ltd., 16 Pembridge Road, London W11 3HL, from Appendix Table 5 of Kendall, M. G. (1970). *Rank correlation methods* (fourth edition).

TABLE R_{II}
Critical values for *T*, the Kendall rank-order correlation coefficient*

Entries are values of T such that $P[T \geq \text{tabled value}] \leq \alpha$.

N	α	.100	.050	.025	.010	.005 (one-tailed)
	α	.200	.100	.050	.020	.010 (two-tailed)
11		.345	.418	.491	.564	.600
12		.303	.394	.455	.545	.576
13		.308	.359	.436	.513	.564
14		.275	.363	.407	.473	.516
15		.276	.333	.390	.467	.505
16		.250	.317	.383	.433	.483
17		.250	.309	.368	.426	.471
18		.242	.294	.346	.412	.451
19		.228	.287	.333	.392	.439
20		.221	.274	.326	.379	.421
21		.210	.267	.314	.371	.410
22		.195	.253	.295	.344	.378
23		.202	.257	.296	.352	.391
24		.196	.246	.290	.341	.377
25		.193	.240	.287	.333	.367
26		.188	.237	.280	.329	.360
27		.179	.231	.271	.322	.356
28		.180	.228	.265	.312	.344
29		.172	.222	.261	.310	.340
30		.172	.218	.255	.301	.333

* Adapted and reproduced by permission of the publishers Charles Griffin & Co. Ltd., 16 Pembridge Road, London W11 3HL, from Appendix Table 5 of Kendall, M. G. (1970). *Rank correlation methods* (fourth edition).

TABLE S
Critical values for $T_{xy.z}$, the Kendall partial rank-order correlation coefficient*

	α							
N	.25	.20	.10	.05	.025	.01	.005	.001
3	.500	1.000						
4	.447	.500	.707	.707	1.000			
5	.333	.408	.534	.667	.802	.816	1.000	
6	.277	.327	.472	.600	.667	.764	.866	1.000
7	.233	.282	.421	.527	.617	.712	.761	.901
8	.206	.254	.382	.484	.565	.648	.713	.807
9	.187	.230	.347	.443	.515	.602	.660	.757
10	.170	.215	.325	.413	.480	.562	.614	.718
11	.162	.202	.305	.387	.453	.530	.581	.677
12	.153	.190	.288	.465	.430	.505	.548	.643
13	.145	.180	.273	.347	.410	.481	.527	.616
14	.137	.172	.260	.331	.391	.458	.503	.590
15	.133	.166	.251	.319	.377	.442	.485	.570
16	.125	.157	.240	.305	.361	.423	.466	.549
17	.121	.151	.231	.294	.348	.410	.450	.532
18	.117	.147	.222	.284	.336	.395	.434	.514
19	.114	.141	.215	.275	.326	.382	.421	.498
20	.111	.139	.210	.268	.318	.374	.412	.488
25	.098	.122	.185	.236	.279	.329	.363	.430
30	.088	.110	.167	.213	.253	.298	.329	.390
35	.081	.101	.153	.196	.232	.274	.303	.361
40	.075	.094	.142	.182	.216	.255	.282	.335
45	.071	.088	.133	.171	.203	.240	.265	.316
50	.067	.083	.126	.161	.192	.225	.250	.298
60	.060	.075	.114	.147	.174	.206	.227	.270
70	.056	.070	.106	.135	.160	.190	.210	.251
80	.052	.065	.098	.126	.150	.178	.197	.235
90	.049	.061	.092	.119	.141	.167	.185	.221

* Adapted from Maghsoodloo, S., (1975). Estimates of the quantiles of Kendall's partial rank correlation coefficient. *Journal of Statistical Computing and Simulation*, **4**, 155–164, and Maghsoodloo, S. & Pallos, L. L., (1981). Asymptotic behavior of Kendall's partial rank correlation coefficient and additional quantile estimates. *Journal of Statistical Computing and Simulation*, **13**, 41–48, with the kind permission of author and publisher.

TABLE T

Critical values for the Kendall coefficient of concordance W*

N = 3

k	α .05	.01
8	.376	.522
9	.333	.469
10	.300	.425
12	.250	.359
14	.214	.311
15	.200	.291
16	.187	.274
18	.166	.245
20	.150	.221

	N = 4		N = 5		N = 6		N = 7	
k	α .05	.01	.05	.01	.05	.01	.05	.01
3	—	—	.716	.840	.660	.780	.624	.737
4	.619	.768	.552	.683	.512	.629	.484	.592
5	.501	.644	.449	.571	.417	.524	.395	.491
6	.421	.553	.378	.489	.351	.448	.333	.419
8	.318	.429	.287	.379	.267	.347	.253	.324
10	.256	.351	.231	.309	.215	.282	.204	.263
15	.171	.240	.155	.211	.145	.193	.137	.179
20	.129	.182	.117	.160	.109	.146	.103	.136

Note: For $N = 3$ and $k < 8$, no value of W has upper tail probability of occurrence less than .05.

* Adapted and reproduced by permission of the publishers Charles Griffin & Co. Ltd., 16 Pembridge Road, London W11 3HL, from Appendix Table 5 of Kendall, M. G. (1970). *Rank correlation methods* (fourth edition).

TABLE U

Upper-tail probabilities of *u*, the Kendall coefficient of agreement when data are based upon paired comparisons

k = 3

N	S	u	p
2	1	-.333	1.0000
	3	1.000	.2500
3	5	.111	.5781
	7	.556	.1563
	9	1.000	.0156
4	10	.111	.4661
	12	.333	.1694
	14	.556	.0376
	16	.778	.0046
	18	1.000	.0002
5	16	.067	.4744
	18	.200	.2241
	20	.333	.0781
	22	.467	.0197
	24	.600	.0035
	26	.733	.0004
6	23	.022	.5387
	25	.111	.3135
	27	.200	.1484
	29	.289	.0566
	31	.378	.0173
	33	.467	.0042
	35	.556	.0008
	37	.644	.0001
7	33	.048	.4334
	35	.111	.2564
	37	.175	.1299
	39	.238	.0561
	41	.302	.0206
	43	.365	.0064
	45	.429	.0017
	47	.492	.0004
	49	.556	.0001

k = 3 (cont)

N	S	u	p
8	42	0.000	.5721
	44	.048	.4003
	46	.095	.2499
	48	.143	.1385
	50	.190	.0679
	52	.238	.0294
	54	.286	.0112
	56	.333	.0038
	58	.381	.0011
	60	.429	.0003
	62	.476	.0001

k = 4

N	S	u	p
2	2	-.333	1.0000
	3	0.000	.6250
	6	1.000	.1250
3	9	0.000	.4551
	10	.111	.3301
	11	.222	.2773
	12	.333	.1367
	14	.556	.0430
	15	.667	.0254
	18	1.000	.0020
4	18	0.000	.5242
	19	.056	.4097
	20	.111	.2779
	21	.167	.1853
	22	.222	.1372
	23	.278	.0877
	24	.333	.0438
	25	.389	.0271
	26	.444	.0188
	27	.500	.0079
	28	.556	.0030
	29	.611	.0025
	30	.667	.0011
	32	.778	.0002
	33	.833	.0001

k = 4 (cont)			
N	S	u	p
5	30	0.000	.5137
	31	.033	.4126
	32	.067	.3266
	33	.100	.2491
	34	.133	.1795
	35	.167	.1271
	36	.200	.0903
	37	.233	.0604
	38	.267	.0376
	39	.300	.0242
	40	.333	.0156
	41	.367	.0088
	42	.400	.0048
	43	.433	.0030
	44	.467	.0017
	45	.500	.0007
	46	.533	.0004
	47	.567	.0002
	48	.600	.0001
6	45	0.000	.5134
	46	.022	.4310
	47	.044	.3532
	48	.067	.2837
	49	.089	.2231
	50	.111	.1708
	51	.133	.1277
	52	.156	.0939
	53	.178	.0676
	54	.200	.0472
	55	.222	.0324
	56	.244	.0219
	57	.267	.0145
	58	.289	.0092
	59	.311	.0058
	60	.333	.0037
	61	.356	.0022
	62	.378	.0013
	63	.400	.0008
	64	.422	.0004
	65	.444	.0002
	66	.467	.0001
	67	.489	.0001

k = 4 (cont)			
N	S	u	p
7	63	0.000	.5111
	64	.016	.4413
	65	.032	.3746
	66	.048	.3124
	67	.063	.2562
	68	.079	.2066
	69	.095	.1637
	70	.111	.1275
	71	.127	.0977
	72	.143	.0736
	73	.159	.0545
	74	.175	.0397
	75	.190	.0285
	76	.206	.0201
	77	.222	.0139
	78	.238	.0095
	79	.254	.0064
	80	.270	.0042
	81	.286	.0028
	82	.302	.0018
	83	.317	.0011
	84	.333	.0007
	85	.349	.0004
	86	.365	.0003
	87	.381	.0002
	88	.397	.0001
	89	.413	.0001
8	84	0.000	.5098
	85	.012	.4490
	86	.024	.3903
	87	.036	.3348
	88	.048	.2833
	89	.060	.2366
	90	.071	.1949
	91	.083	.1585
	92	.095	.1271
	93	.107	.1006
	94	.119	.0786
	95	.131	.0606
	96	.143	.0461

TABLE U (continued)

k = 4 (cont)

N	S	u	p
8	97	.155	.0346
	98	.167	.0257
	99	.179	.0188
	100	.190	.0136
	101	.202	.0097
	102	.214	.0068
	103	.226	.0048
	104	.238	.0033
	105	.250	.0022
	106	.262	.0015
	107	.274	.0010
	108	.286	.0007
	109	.298	.0004
	110	.310	.0003
	111	.321	.0002
	112	.333	.0001
	113	.345	.0001

k = 5

N	S	u	p
2	4	-.200	1.0000
	6	.200	.3750
	10	1.000	.0620
3	16	.067	.3896
	18	.200	.2065
	20	.333	.1028
	22	.467	.0295
	24	.600	.0112
	26	.733	.0039
	30	1.000	.0002
4	30	0.000	.5381
	32	.067	.3533
	34	.133	.2080
	36	.200	.1074
	38	.267	.0528
	40	.333	.0238
	42	.400	.0093
	44	.467	.0036
	[illegible]	.533	.0012
	[illegible]	.600	.0004
	[illegible]	.667	.0001

k = 5 (cont)

N	S	u	p
5	52	.040	.3838
	54	.080	.2544
	56	.120	.1579
	58	.160	.0918
	60	.200	.0500
	62	.240	.0257
	64	.280	.0124
	66	.320	.0057
	68	.360	.0025
	70	.400	.0010
	72	.440	.0004
	74	.480	.0001
6	76	.013	.4663
	78	.040	.3453
	80	.067	.2428
	82	.093	.1623
	84	.120	.1034
	86	.147	.0628
	88	.173	.0364
	90	.200	.0202
	92	.227	.0108
	94	.253	.0055
	96	.280	.0027
	98	.307	.0013
	100	.333	.0006
	102	.360	.0002
	104	.387	.0001
7	106	.010	.4718
	108	.029	.3674
	110	.048	.2750
	112	.067	.1980
	114	.086	.1372
	116	.105	.0916
	118	.124	.0589
	120	.143	.0366
	122	.162	.0220
	124	.181	.0128
	126	.200	.0072
	128	.219	.0039
	130	.238	.0021

k = 5 (cont)

N	S	u	p
7	132	.257	.0011
	134	.276	.0005
	136	.295	.0003
	138	.314	.0001
	140	.333	.0001
8	140	0.000	.5233
	142	.014	.4291
	144	.029	.3411
	146	.043	.2629
	148	.057	.1965
	150	.071	.1425
	152	.086	.1003
	154	.100	.0686
	156	.114	.0456
	158	.129	.0294
	160	.143	.0185
	162	.157	.0113
	164	.171	.0068
	166	.186	.0039
	168	.200	.0022
	170	.214	.0012
	172	.229	.0007
	174	.243	.0003
	176	.257	.0002
	178	.271	.0001

k = 6

N	S	u	p
2	6	-.200	1.0000
	7	-.067	.6875
	10	.333	.2188
	15	1.000	.0312
3	23	.022	.4682
	24	.067	.3034
	26	.156	.1798
	27	.200	.1469
	28	.244	.0883
	29	.289	.0608
	30	.333	.0402

k = 6 (cont)

N	S	u	p
3	31	.378	.0336
	32	.422	.0226
	35	.556	.0062
	36	.600	.0029
	37	.644	.0020
	40	.778	.0006
4	45	0.000	.4656
	46	.022	.4094
	47	.044	.3374
	48	.067	.2569
	49	.089	.2086
	50	.111	.1746
	51	.133	.1332
	52	.156	.0970
	53	.178	.0725
	54	.200	.0566
	55	.222	.0433
	56	.244	.0289
	57	.267	.0198
	58	.289	.0160
	59	.311	.0114
	60	.333	.0072
	61	.356	.0049
	62	.378	.0034
	63	.400	.0025
	64	.422	.0016
	65	.444	.0008
	66	.467	.0007
	67	.489	.0005
	68	.511	.0003
	69	.533	.0002
	70	.556	.0001
	71	.578	.0001
5	75	0.000	.4841
	76	.013	.4258
	77	.027	.3665
	78	.040	.3085
	79	.053	.2600
	80	.067	.2190
	81	.080	.1800

TABLE U (continued)

N	S	u	p
k = 6 (cont)			
5	82	.093	.1452
	83	.107	.1173
	84	.120	.0949
	85	.133	.0753
	86	.147	.0583
	87	.160	.0452
	88	.173	.0355
	89	.187	.0272
	90	.200	.0202
	91	.213	.0151
	92	.227	.0115
	93	.240	.0085
	94	.253	.0062
	95	.267	.0044
	96	.280	.0033
	97	.293	.0024
	98	.307	.0017
	99	.320	.0011
	100	.333	.0008
	101	.347	.0006
	102	.360	.0004
	103	.373	.0003
	104	.387	.0002
	105	.400	.0001
	106	.413	.0001
	107	.427	.0001
6	113	.004	.4640
	114	.013	.4126
	115	.022	.3637
	116	.031	.3186
	117	.040	.2768
	118	.049	.2380
	119	.058	.2030
	120	.067	.1723
	121	.076	.1451
	122	.084	.1209
	123	.093	.1000
	124	.102	.0824
	125	.111	.0674
	[illegible]	.120	.0546
	[illegible]	.129	.0439

N	S	u	p
k = 6 (cont)			
6	128	.138	.0352
	129	.147	.0280
	130	.156	.0221
	131	.164	.0173
	132	.173	.0135
	133	.182	.0105
	134	.191	.0081
	135	.200	.0062
	136	.209	.0047
	137	.218	.0036
	138	.227	.0027
	139	.236	.0020
	140	.244	.0015
	141	.253	.0011
	142	.262	.0008
	143	.271	.0006
	144	.280	.0004
	145	.289	.0003
	146	.298	.0002
	147	.307	.0002
	148	.316	.0001
	149	.324	.0001
	150	.333	.0001
7	158	.003	.4694
	159	.010	.4258
	160	.016	.3838
	161	.022	.3436
	162	.029	.3057
	163	.035	.2703
	164	.041	.2375
	165	.048	.2074
	166	.054	.1800
	167	.060	.1553
	168	.067	.1332
	169	.073	.1136
	170	.079	.0963
	171	.086	.0812
	172	.092	.0680
	173	.098	.0567
	174	.105	.0470
	175	.111	.0388

k = 6 (cont)			
N	S	u	p
7	176	.117	.0318
	177	.124	.0260
	178	.130	.0211
	179	.137	.0170
	180	.143	.0137
	181	.149	.0110
	182	.156	.0087
	183	.162	.0069
	184	.168	.0054
	185	.175	.0043
	186	.181	.0033
	187	.187	.0026
	188	.194	.0020
	189	.200	.0015
	190	.206	.0012
	191	.213	.0009
	192	.219	.0007
	193	.225	.0005
	194	.232	.0004
	195	.238	.0003
	196	.244	.0002
	197	.251	.0002
	198	.257	.0001
	199	.263	.0001
	200	.270	.0001
8	210	0.000	.4930
	211	.005	.4545
	212	.010	.4169
	213	.014	.3805
	214	.019	.3455
	215	.024	.3122
	216	.029	.2807
	217	.033	.2511
	218	.038	.2235
	219	.043	.1980
	220	.048	.1745
	221	.052	.1531
	222	.057	.1337
	223	.062	.1162
	224	.067	.1005
	225	.071	.0866

k = 6 (cont)			
N	S	u	p
8	226	.076	.0742
	227	.081	.0633
	228	.086	.0538
	229	.090	.0455
	230	.095	.0383
	231	.100	.0321
	232	.105	.0268
	233	.110	.0223
	234	.114	.0185
	235	.119	.0152
	236	.124	.0125
	237	.129	.0102
	238	.133	.0083
	239	.138	.0068
	240	.143	.0055
	241	.148	.0044
	242	.152	.0035
	243	.157	.0028
	244	.162	.0022
	245	.167	.0018
	246	.171	.0014
	247	.176	.0011
	248	.181	.0009
	249	.186	.0007
	250	.190	.0005
	251	.195	.0004
	252	.200	.0003
	253	.205	.0002
	254	.210	.0002
	255	.214	.0001
	256	.219	.0001
	257	.224	.0001
	258	.229	.0001

Note: Values are tabled only for probabilities $c \geq .0001$ (rounded). Thus, the upper tail probabilities for larger values of u have probabilities $< .00005$.

TABLE V

Upper-tail probabilities of T_C, the correlation of k rankings with a criterion ranking*

$k = 2$			$k = 3$		
N	T_c	p	N	T_c	p
2	0.000	.750	2	.333	.500
	1.000	.250		1.000	.125
3	0.000	.639	3	.111	.500
	.333	.361		.333	.278
	.667	.139		.556	.116
	1.000	.028		.778	.033
				1.000	.005
4	0.000	.592	4	0.000	.576
	.167	.408		.111	.424
	.333	.241		.222	.282
	.500	.118		.333	.167
	.667	.045		.444	.086
	.833	.012		.556	.038
	1.000	.002		.667	.014
				.778	.004
				.889	.001
				1.000	.000+
5	0.000	.567	5	0.000	.556
	.100	.433		.067	.445
	.200	.306		.113	.338
	.300	.198		.200	.243
	.400	.116		.267	.164
	.500	.060		.333	.103
	.600	.027		.400	.060
	.700	.010		.467	.032
	.800	.003		.533	.016
	.900	.001		.600	.007
	1.000	.000+		.667	.003
				.733	.001
				.800	.000+

* Adapted from Stilson, D. W., and Campbell, V. N. (1962). A note on calculating tau and average tau and on the sampling distribution of average tau with a criterion ranking. *Journal of the American Statistical Association*, **57**, 567–571, with the permission of author and publisher.

TABLE W
Factorials

N	$N!$
0	1
1	1
2	2
3	6
4	24
5	120
6	720
7	5040
8	40320
9	362880
10	3628800
11	39916800
12	479001600
13	6227020800
14	87178291200
15	1307674368000
16	20922789888000
17	355687428096000
18	6402373705728000
19	121645100408832000
20	2432902008176640000

TABLE X
Binomial coefficients

N	$\binom{N}{0}$	$\binom{N}{1}$	$\binom{N}{2}$	$\binom{N}{3}$	$\binom{N}{4}$	$\binom{N}{5}$	$\binom{N}{6}$	$\binom{N}{7}$	$\binom{N}{8}$	$\binom{N}{9}$	$\binom{N}{10}$
0	1										
1	1	1									
2	1	2	1								
3	1	3	3	1							
4	1	4	6	4	1						
5	1	5	10	10	5	1					
6	1	6	15	20	15	6	1				
7	1	7	21	35	35	21	7	1			
8	1	8	28	56	70	56	28	8	1		
9	1	9	36	84	126	126	84	36	9	1	
10	1	10	45	120	210	252	210	120	45	10	1
11	1	11	55	165	330	462	462	330	165	55	11
12	1	12	66	220	495	792	924	792	495	220	66
13	1	13	78	286	715	1287	1716	1716	1287	715	286
14	1	14	91	364	1001	2002	3003	3432	3003	2002	1001
15	1	15	105	455	1365	3003	5005	6435	6435	5005	3003
16	1	16	120	560	1820	4368	8008	11440	12870	11440	8008
17	1	17	136	680	2380	6188	12376	19448	24310	24310	19448
18	1	18	153	816	3060	8568	18564	31824	43758	48620	43758
19	1	19	171	969	3876	11628	27132	50388	75582	92378	92378
20	1	20	190	1140	4845	15504	38760	77520	125970	167960	184756

APPENDIX II PROGRAMS

1. Single-sample case: Test for symmetry
2. One-sample, two measures: Permutation test for paired replicates
3. Two independent samples: Permutation test for two independent samples
4. k independent samples: Chi-square test for $r \times k$ contingency tables with partitioning
5. k independent samples: Jonckheere test for ordered alternatives

PROGRAM 1

Single-Sample Case: Test for Symmetry

```
100 REM Test for Section 4.4
110 REM Randles, R. H., Fligner, M. A., Policello, G. E., and Wolfe, D. A.,
120 REM An Asymptotically Distribution-Free Test for Symmetry Versus Asymmetry,
130 REM Journal of the American Statistical Association, 1980, 75, 168-172.
140 REM Coded by N. J. Castellan, Jr., Copyright 1982.
150 PRINT"An Asymptotically Distribution-Free Test for Symmetry Versus Asymmetry"
160 INPUT "How many observations (N)"; N
170 DIM X(N),T1(N),T2(N,N)
180 REM -- read data
190 PRINT "Enter the data values one at a time."
200 FOR I=1 TO N : INPUT X(I) : NEXT I
210 REM -- begin computations
220 REM -- this program assumes that all variables and arrays
230 REM -- are initialized to zero's
240 FOR I=1 TO N-2
250     FOR J=I+1 TO N-1
260         FOR K=J+1 TO N
270             AVE = (X(I)+X(J)+X(K))/3
280             MIN=X(I) : MED=X(J) : MAX=X(K)
290             IF MIN>MED THEN SWAP MIN,MED
300             IF MED>MAX THEN SWAP MED,MAX
310             IF MIN>MED THEN SWAP MIN,MED
320             IF AVE>MED THEN RL=1 ELSE IF AVE<MED THEN RL=-1 ELSE RL=0
330             T = T+RL
340             T1(I)=T1(I)+RL
350             T1(J)=T1(J)+RL
360             T1(K)=T1(K)+RL
370             T2(I,J)=T2(I,J)+RL
380             T2(I,K)=T2(I,K)+RL
390             T2(J,K)=T2(J,K)+RL
400         NEXT K
410     NEXT J
420 NEXT I
430 B1=T1(N)^2 : B2=0
440 FOR I=1 TO N-1
450     B1=B1+T1(I)^2
460     FOR J=I+1 TO N
470         B2=B2+T2(I,J)^2
480     NEXT J
490 NEXT I
500 PRINT "N =";N;", Sum B2(i) =";B1;", Sum B2(ij) =";B2
510 VAR = B1*(N-3)*(N-4)/((N-1)*(N-2)) + B2*(N-3)/(N-4) + N*(N-1)*(N-2)/6
520 VAR = VAR - (1 - (N-3)*(N-4)*(N-5)/(N*(N-1)*(N-2)))*T^2
530 PRINT "T =";T;", Var(T) =";VAR;", z = T/sqr(var(T)) =";T/SQR(VAR)
540 END
```

PROGRAM 2

One-Sample, Two Measures: Permutation Test for Paired Replicates

```
' THE PERMUTATION TEST FOR PAIRED REPLICATES, Section 5.4
' Coded in QuickBASIC.  Copyright 1987 N. John Castellan, Jr.
' Algorithm will work if number of pairs of data (N) < 15
' Note: This limit is not checked by the program.
' For larger sample sizes remove the DEFINT statement.
' (Removing DEFINT allows larger samples sizes at the expense of
' increased execution time.)
' This version of the program has not been optimized to minimize
' the number of iterations.  (This was done to make program more readable.)
' Integrated package version is optimized and handles large N.
DEFINT I,N,W,U ' Remove this statement if N>14.
UPPERTAIL=0 : NPERM=0: CRIT=0
INPUT "What is the sample size":N
DIM D(N,2),INDEX(N)
PRINT "Input the data, pair by pair (two entries separated by a comma):"
' The following data are from example in Section 5.4
DATA 82,63, 69,42, 73,74, 43,37, 58,51, 56,43, 76,80, 85,82
FOR I=1 TO N
    ' After debugging, insert a ' before the following READ statement and
    ' delete the ' from the next line so data may be entered from keyboard.
    READ D1,D2:D(I,1)=D1-D2:D(I,2)=D2-D1
    ' INPUT D1,D2 : D(I,1)=D1-D2 : D(I,2)=D2-D1
    CRIT=CRIT+D(I,1)
    INDEX(I)=1
NEXT I
LOOP1:
      SUM=0
      FOR I=1 TO N
          SUM=SUM+D(I,INDEX(I))
      NEXT I
      NPERM=NPERM+1
      IF SUM>=CRIT THEN UPPERTAIL=UPPERTAIL+1
      I=N
      WHILE I>0
            IF INDEX(I)=1 THEN INDEX(I)=2 : GOTO LOOP1
            INDEX(I)=1 ' Reset index
            I=I-1
      WEND
' Calculations done, print summary
PRINT "PERMUTATION TEST FOR PAIRED REPLICATES"
PRINT USING "Observed sum of differences = #####.##";CRIT
PRINT USING "Number of sums >= observed sum: ##### out of ##### sums.";UPPERTAIL
,NPERM
PRINT USING "Upper Tail Probability = #.####";UPPERTAIL/NPERM
END
```

Copyright Microsoft Corporation, 1982, 1983, 1984, 1985, 1986, 1987. All rights reserved.

Sample Output for Program 2

The following data are from Example 5.4, page 97.

```
What is the sample size? 8
Input the data, pair by pair (two entries separated by a comma):
? 82,63
? 69,42
? 73,74
? 43,37
? 58,51
? 56,43
? 76,80
? 85,82

PERMUTATION TEST FOR PAIRED REPLICATES

Observed sum of differences =     70.00

Number of sums >= observed sum:      6 out of    256 sums.

Upper Tail Probability = 0.0234


Normal termination. Press any key.
```

PROGRAM 3

Two Independent Samples: Permutation Test for Two Independent Samples

```
' PERMUTATION TEST FOR TWO INDEPENDENT SAMPLES. Section 6.7
' Coded in QuickBASIC.  Copyright 1987 N. J. Castellan, Jr.
' Algorithm will work if number of permutations is less than 32768
' Limits:  M + N < 18
'          or (M=7, N<12), (M=6, N<14), (M=5, N<18), (M=4, N<28), (M=3, N<57)
' Note: These limits are not checked by program.
' Program will run significantly faster if the smaller group is entered first.
' This version of the program has not been optimized to minimize
' the number of iterations.  (This was done to make program more readable.)
' Integrated package version is optimized and handles large M and N.
DEFINT I,M,N,U
INPUT "What are the samples sizes":M,N
MN=M+N
DIM X(MN), INDEX(MN)
PRINT "Input the data for Group 1. (One datum at a time.)"
FOR I=1 TO M : INPUT X(I) : NEXT I
PRINT "Input the data for Group 2. (One datum at a time.)"
FOR I=1 TO N : INPUT X(M+I) : NEXT I
' Get totals and set indexes
FOR I=1 TO MN
    SUM = SUM + X(I)
    IF I=M THEN CRIT1=SUM
    INDEX(I)=I
NEXT I
NPERM=1 : UPPERTAIL=1 ' NPERM = # permutations, UPPERTAIL = # in uppertail
LOOP1:
      I=M
      LOOP2:
            IF INDEX(I)=MN THEN I=I-1 : IF I=0 GOTO WRAPUP ELSE GOTO LOOP2
            INDEX(I)=INDEX(I)+1
            IF I<M THEN ' get next element of permutation
                   I=I+1
                   INDEX(I)=INDEX(I-1)
                   GOTO LOOP2
               ELSE ' Evaluate current sum
                   NPERM=NPERM+1
                   SUM1=0
                   FOR I=1 TO M
                       SUM1=SUM1+X(INDEX(I))
                   NEXT I
                   IF SUM1 >= CRIT1 THEN UPPERTAIL=UPPERTAIL+1
                   GOTO LOOP1
            END IF
WRAPUP: ' Computation is done, print results
PRINT "                PERMUTATION TEST"
PRINT "      Group:       1         2"
PRINT USING "Sample Size:  ###        ###":M,N
PRINT USING "Sample Sums: #####.##  #####.##":CRIT1,SUM-CRIT1
PRINT USING "Number of Sums >= Group 1 Sum: ##### out of ##### sums.";UPPERTAIL,
NPERM
PRINT USING "Upper Tail Probability = #.####";UPPERTAIL/NPERM
END
```

Copyright Microsoft Corporation, 1982, 1983, 1984, 1985, 1986, 1987. All rights reserved.

Sample Output for Program 3

The following data are from Sec. 6.7.2, page 151.

```
What are the samples sizes? 5,4
Input the data for Group 1. (One datum at a time.)
? 22
? 19
? 16
? 29
? 24
Input the data for Group 2. (One datum at a time.)
? 11
? 12
? 20
? 0
                       PERMUTATION TEST
         Group:          1           2
Sample Size:             5           4
Sample Sums:        110.00       43.00
Number of Sums >= Group 1 Sum:       3 out of    126 sums.
Upper Tail Probability = 0.0238




Normal termination.  Press any key.
```

PROGRAM 4

k Independent Samples: Chi-Square Test for *r* × *k* Contingency Tables with Partitioning

```
100 REM Test for Section 8.1
110 REM Coded by N. J. Castellan, Jr., Copyright 1984, 1985.
120 PRINT "Routine to calculate chi-square and partitioned chi-square"
130 PRINT "for general r by k contingency table."
140 PRINT : PRINT"    You must enter the size of the contingency table,"
150 PRINT "    followed by the cell frequencies." : PRINT
160 INPUT "How many rows":R
170 INPUT "How many columns":K
180 DIM X(R,K), ROW(R), COL(K), E(R,K)
190 REM Read Data -- READ X(I,J) at line 240 may be changed to INPUT X(I,J)
200 REM                 Remove the REM at the beginning of line 250
210 PRINT : PRINT"Now enter the data, cell by cell."
220 FOR I=1 TO R
230     FOR J=1 TO K
240     READ X(I,J)
250     REM PRINT "Enter the data for cell":I:",":J; : INPUT X(I,J)
260     NEXT J
270 NEXT I
280 REM Calculate marginal frequencies
290 FOR I=1 TO R
300     FOR J=1 TO K
310          ROW(I)=ROW(I)+X(I,J)
320          COL(J)=COL(J)+X(I,J)
330          N=N+X(I,J)
340     NEXT J
350 NEXT I
360 REM Find expected values and calculate chi-square (X2)
370 FOR I=1 TO R
380     FOR J=1 TO K
390          E(I,J)=ROW(I)*COL(J)/N
400          X2=X2+(X(I,J)^2)/E(I,J)
410     NEXT J
420 NEXT I
430 X2=X2-N
440 PRINT : PRINT "Chi-square =":X2:" with ":(R-1)*(K-1):" degrees of freedom."
450 REM Begin partitioning procedure
460 PRINT : PRINT"Partition  cell(i,j)   Chi-Square"
470 FOR J=2 TO K
480     UR=X(1,J) : UL=0 : LL=0 : LR=0
490     FOR JJ=1 TO J-1 : UL=UL+X(1,JJ) : NEXT JJ
500     SR=0 : SC=SC+COL(J-1)
510     FOR I=2 TO R
520          UL=UL+LL
530          UR=UR+LR
540          LL=0 : FOR JJ=1 TO J-1 : LL=LL+X(I,JJ) : NEXT JJ
550          LR=X(I,J)
560          SR=SR+ROW(I-1)
570          XT=N*(COL(J)*(ROW(I)*UL - SR*LL) - SC*(ROW(I)*UR - LR*SR))^2
580          XT=XT/(COL(J)*ROW(I)*SC*(SC+COL(J))*SR*(SR+ROW(I)))
590          T=(R-1)*(J-2)+I-1
600          PRINT USING "  ###          ##:##       ###.###";T,I,J,XT
610     NEXT I
620 NEXT J
     P : '-------------------------------------------------------------
        Data from Sample Problem of Section 8.1
         = 4 Groups, r = 3 levels or rows
        3,8,10,3, 20,23,27,18, 11,12,12,21
```

Sample Output for Program 4

The following data are from Examples 8.1a and 8.1b, pages 192 and 197.

```
Routine to calculate chi-square and partitioned chi-square
for general r by k contingency table.

    You must enter the size of the contingency table,
    followed by the cell frequencies.

How many rows?  3
How many columns?  4


Chi-square = 12.778 with 6 degrees of freedom.

Partition  cell(i,j)  Chi-Square
    1         2: 2        1.620
    2         3: 2        0.085
    3         2: 3        0.415
    4         3: 3        0.055
    5         2: 4        1.840
    6         3: 4        8.762
```

PROGRAM 5

k Independent Samples: Jonckheere Test for Ordered Alternatives

```
100 REM Test for Section 8.4
110 REM Coded by N. J. Castellan, Jr., Copyright 1982.
120 PRINT "Routine to Calculate the Jonckheere Test for Ordered Alternatives"
130 INPUT "How many groups";K
140 DIM N(K), U(K,K)
150 REM Read Group sizes and Calculate terms for Mean and Variance
160 REM -- This program assumes that all variables and arrays
170 REM -- are initialized to zero's
180 FOR I = 1 TO K
190     PRINT "How many observations in group ";I; : INPUT N(I)
200     N1 = N1 + N(I)
210     N2 = N2 + N(I)^2
220     N3 = N3 + N(I)^3
230 NEXT I
240 REM Read Data -- READ X(IJ) may be changed to INPUT X(IJ)
250 DIM X(N1)
260 FOR I = 1 TO K
270     FOR J = 1 TO N(I)
280             IJ=IJ+1
290             READ X(IJ)
300     NEXT J
310 NEXT I
320 REM Calculate Mean and Variance
330 MEAN = (N1^2 - N2)/4
340 VARIANCE = ((N1^2)*(2*N1 + 3) - (2*N3 + 3*N2))/72
350 REM Calculate Mann-Whitney U-counts
360 ILOW-0 : IHIGH=0
370 FOR I = 1 TO K-1
380     ILOW = IHIGH + 1
390     IHIGH = ILOW + N(I) - !
400     FOR IX = ILOW TO IHIGH
410         JHIGH = IHIGH
420         FOR J = I+1 TO K
430             JLOW = JHIGH + 1
440             JHIGH = JLOW + N(J) - 1
450             FOR JX = JLOW TO JHIGH
460                 IF X(IX) < X(JX) THEN U(I,J) = U(I,J) + 1
470                 IF X(IX) = X(JX) THEN U(I,J) = U(I,J) + .5
480             NEXT JX
490         NEXT J
500     NEXT IX
510 NEXT I
520 PRINT "Group          Group        U(i,j)"
530 FOR I=1 TO K-1
540     FOR J=I+1 TO K
550         PRINT I,J,U(I,J)
560         JS = JS + U(I,J)
570     NEXT J
580 NEXT I
590 PRINT : PRINT "Jonckheere Statistic: J = ";JS
600 PRINT : PRINT "Mean = "; MEAN; ", Variance = "; VARIANCE
610 PRINT "Standard Normal Approximation: J* = "; (JS - MEAN)/SQR(VARIANCE)
620 STOP : '-------------------------------------------------------------
630 REM Data from Sample Problem of Section 8.4
640 REM k = 4 Groups, n(1)=12, n(2)=9, n(3)=8, n(4)=6
650 DATA  8.82, 11.27, 15.78, 17.39, 24.99, 39.05, 47.54, 48.85
660 DATA 71.66, 72.77, 90.38, 103.13
670 DATA 13.53, 28.42, 48.11, 48.64, 51.40, 59.91, 67.98, 79.13, 103.05
680 DATA 19.23, 67.83, 73.68, 75.22, 77.71, 83.67, 86.83, 93.25
690 DATA 73.51, 85.25, 85.82, 88.88, 90.33, 118.11
700 END
```

Sample Output for Program 5

The following data are from Example 8.4, page 218.

```
How many observations in group 1 ? 12
How many observations in group 2 ? 9
How many observations in group 3 ? 8
How many observations in group 4 ? 6

Group          Group          U(i,j)
 1               2              66
 1               3              73
 1               4              62
 2               3              52
 2               4              48
 3               4              36

Jonckheere Statistic: J =  337

Mean =  255 , Variance =  1140
Standard Normal Approximation: J* =  3.31715
```

AUTHOR INDEX

EXAMPLE AUTHOR INDEX

SUBJECT INDEX

Nonparametric Statistical Tests

Level of measurement	One-sample case (Chap. 4)	Two-sample case: Related or matched samples (Chap. 5)	Two-sample case: Independent samples (Chap. 6)
Nominal or categorical	Binomial test (4.1) Chi-square goodness-of-fit test (4.2)	McNemar change test (5.1)	Fisher exact test for 2 × 2 tables (6.1) Chi-square test for $r \times 2$ tables (6.2)
Ordinal or ordered	Kolmogorov-Smirnov one-sample test, $D_{m,n}$ (4.3) One-sample runs test (4.4) Change-point test (4.5)	Sign test (5.2) Wilcoxon signed ranks test, T^+ (5.3)	Median test (6.3) Wilcoxon-Mann-Whitne test, W_x (6.4) Robust rank-order test, $\grave{U}$(6.5) Komogorov-Smirnov two-sample test, $D_{m,}$ (6.6) Siegel-Tukey test for scale differences (6.8
Interval		Permutation test for paired replicates (5.4)	Permutation test for two independent samples (6.7) Moses rank-like test for scale differences (6.9)

Note: Each column lists, cumulatively downward, the tests applicable for the given level of measurement. For example, in the case of k related samples, when the variables are ordered, both the Friedman two-way analysis of variance and the Cochran Q test are

k-sample case		Measures of association (Chap. 9)
Related samples (Chap. 7)	**Independent samples (Chap. 8)**	
Cochran Q test (7.1)	Chi-square test for $r \times k$ tables (8.1)	Cramer coefficient, C (9.1) Phi coefficient, r_ϕ (9.2) The kappa coefficient of agreement, K (9.8) Asymmetrical association, the lambda statistic, L_B (9.10)
Friedman two-way analysis of variance by ranks, F_r (7.2) Page test for ordered alternatives, L (7.3)	Extension of the median test (8.2) Kruskal-Wallis one-way analysis of variance, KW (8.3) Jonckheere test for ordered alternatives J (8.4)	Spearman rank-order correlation coefficient, r_s (9.3) Kendall rank-order correlation coefficient, T (9.4) Kendall partial rank-order correlation coefficient, $T_{xy.z}$ (9.5) Kendall coefficient of concordance, W (9.6) Kendall coefficient of agreement, u (9.7) Correlation between k judges and a criterion, T_C (9.7.4) Gamma statistic, G (9.9) Somer's index of asymmetric association, d_{BA} (9.11)

applicable. However, see text for a discussion of appropriateness of a particular test to a given type of data. The numbers in parentheses refer to chapter sections.